# HERITAGE:

## AN ILLUSTRATED HISTORY OF WESTERN CULTURE

Blind adherence to tradition will bind and stultify where
unbiased examination will bring
a liberal understanding which can stabilize and inspire.

# HERITAGE:

## AN ILLUSTRATED HISTORY OF WESTERN CULTURE

*Written and Illustrated by*

·ALLISON TRAVIS BROWN·

COWARD-McCANN, Inc. NEW YORK

This book

is dedicated

to my late father

who inspired it

and

to my mother

who made it possible

 Published simultaneously in the Dominion of Canada by Longmans, Green & Company, Toronto.

Library of Congress Catalog Card Number: 56-11518

MANUFACTURED IN THE UNITED STATES OF AMERICA

# · PREFACE ·

Asked about the most important ingredient for life in the twentieth century, an unthinking person would answer "money," a more thoughtful one would substitute "education." Unfortunately, they have become synonymous. In twelve years of teaching at a large eastern university, I found the most persistent query of the new students and their parents to be: "What is the starting salary in your field?"

In theory we know that education should not be presented to the young solely as a means of making money. Why do we not instill in them a higher aspiration for personal improvement? We would do well to consider Plato's definition for the aim of education, which is: "To develop in the body and in the soul all the beauty and all the perfection of which they are capable." And, we would do well to quote Harold Taylor, who states, "We need to say that education is as big as life, that education is the most exciting, the most controversial, the most rewarding and the most fulfilling combination of philosophy, action and spiritual endeavor that there is on earth."

This book was written because as a teacher I was not able to find a textbook that contained exactly what I wanted to teach in precisely the way I wished to teach it.

My assignment was to present, in one semester, the six thousand years of man's recorded artistic achievements. I found the crowded schedule complicated by the fact that although I was teaching on the college level, my students (most of them freshmen) had been exposed to only the most fragmentary snatches of history. It therefore became necessary to supply historical background for the sake of continuity.

While this book is intended primarily to introduce the aesthetic aspects of our culture, it is written with the hope that, in addition to the enjoyment to be found in the beauty of the arts, and the benefit to be gained in understanding their development, a deeper appreciation will be felt for both the tangible and the intangible endowments of Western civilization.

It must be kept in mind that the material of a work of this size must be compressed and abbreviated. It can only deal with the most obvious and general characteristics.

A brief summary is given of the essential elements that distinguish one period from another. The written text and the illustrations support each other. The architecture is analyzed, that each street and every building may have more meaning. The furniture and accessories are classified that they may be sympathetically combined. The painting and sculpture are catalogued to facilitate interpretation. Other information is listed chronologically for orientation and correlation.

A. T. B.

*All men by nature desire to know.*
*Aristotle (384-322 B.C.)*

By searching, men gradually find out what is better for them.
Xenophanes of Elea (570-480 B.C.)

AND YE SHALL KNOW THE TRUTH, AND THE TRUTH SHALL MAKE YOU FREE.
THE GOSPEL of JOHN

Every man takes the limits of his own field of vision for the limits of the world.
Arthur Schopenhauer (1788-1860)

*'Tis education forms the human mind, just as the twig is bent the tree's inclined.*
*Alexander Pope (1688-1748)*

There is nothing more frightful than ignorance in action.
Johann Wolfgang von Goethe (1749-1832)

*I do not propose a variety and stock of knowledge but a variety and freedom of thinking an increase of the powers and activity of the mind not an enlargement of its possessions.*
*John Locke (1633-1704)*

GREAT MEN ARE THEY WHO SEE THAT SPIRITUAL IS STRONGER THAN ANY MATERIAL FORCE; THAT THOUGHTS RULE THE WORLD.
RALPH WALDO EMERSON (1803-1882)

Man consists of body, mind and imagination.
His body is faulty,
his mind is untrustworthy,
but his imagination has made him remarkable.
John Masefield (1874- )

*...education is a matter of inspiration. It is a personal experience and it occurs between living minds.*
*Agnes de Mille*

"EASTLAKE" ORGAN 1876.

# ·TABLE OF CONTENTS·

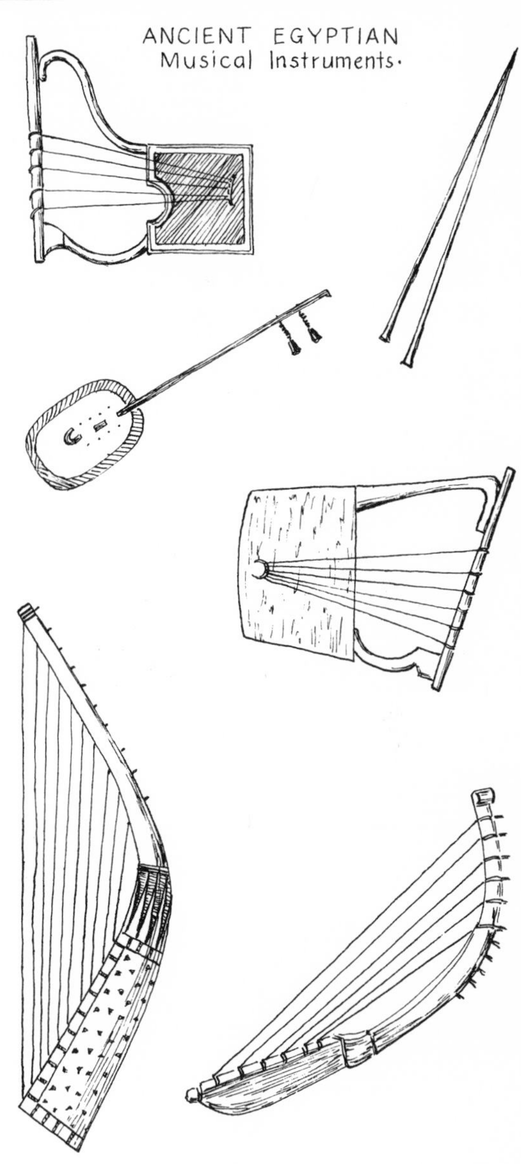
ANCIENT EGYPTIAN
Musical Instruments·

## • INTRODUCTION •



## • THE ANCIENT CULTURES •
## 4000 BC—476 AD



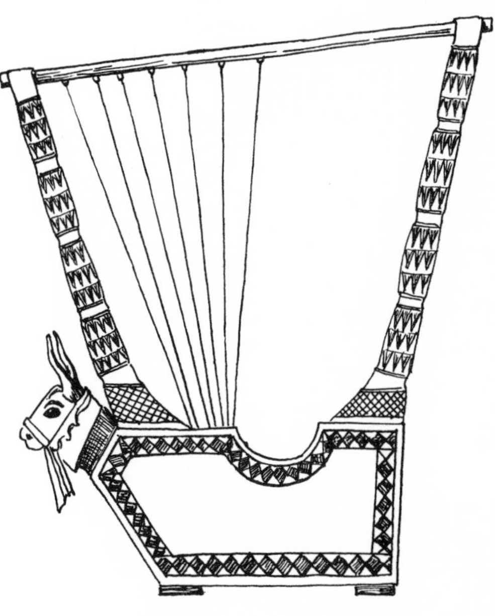
MESOPOTAMIAN HARP·

## • THE MIDDLE AGES •
## 1 AD—1500

# · TABLE OF CONTENTS ·

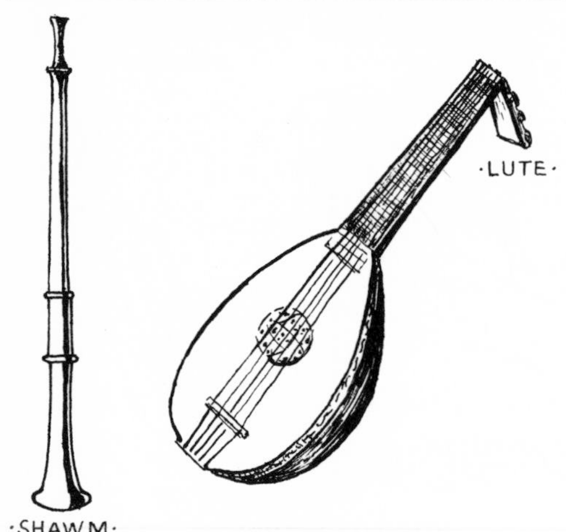
·LUTE·
·SHAWM·

· DULCIMER ·



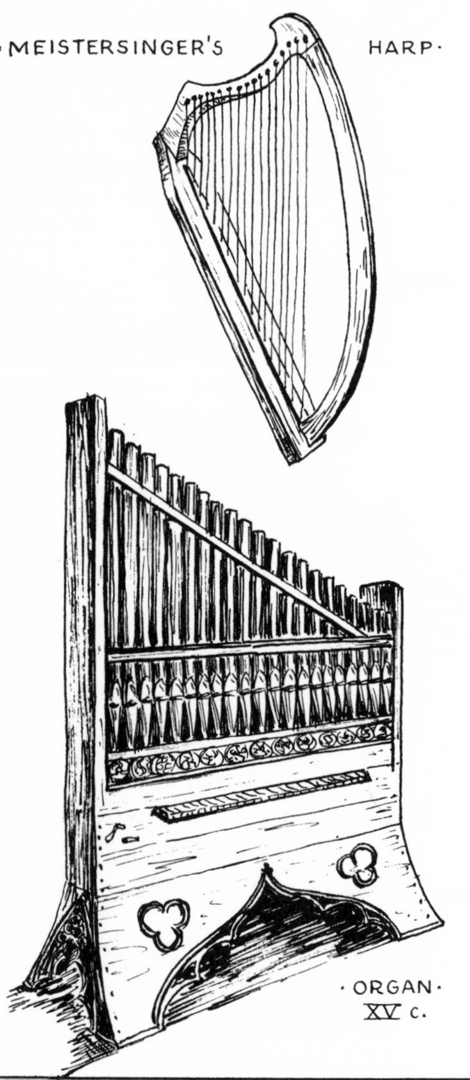
·MEISTERSINGER'S HARP·
· ORGAN ·
XV c.

# ·TABLE OF CONTENTS·



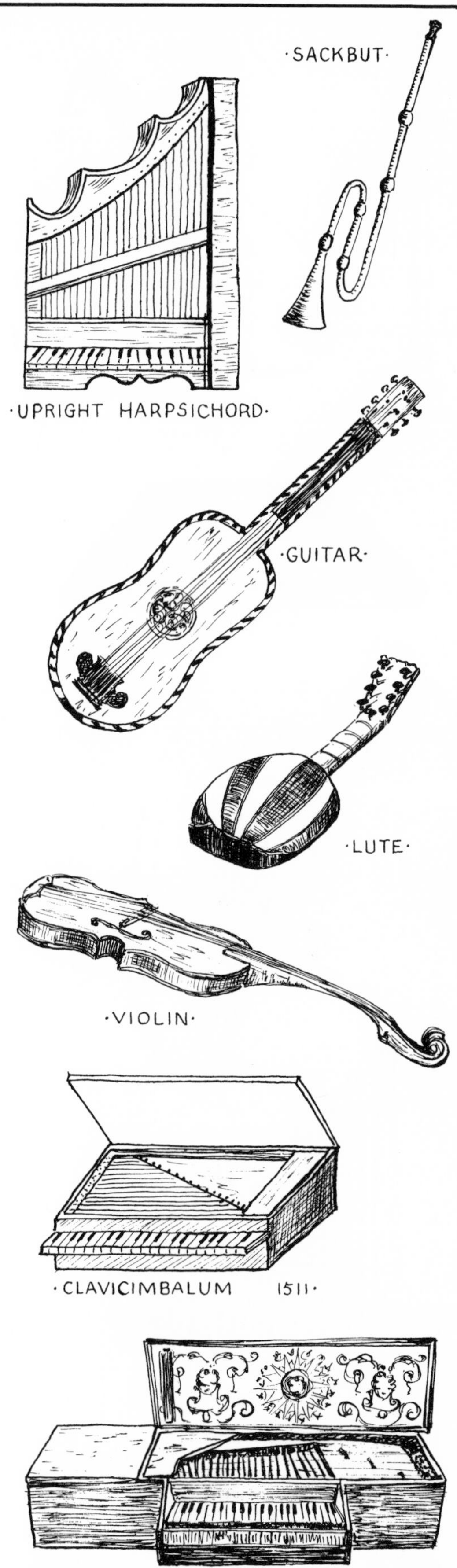

·SACKBUT·
·UPRIGHT HARPSICHORD·
·GUITAR·
·LUTE·
·VIOLIN·
·CLAVICIMBALUM 1511·
·MANICORDO 1689·

MUSIC
LITERATURE
MINOR ARTS
SCULPTURE
ARCHITECTURE
PAINTING
FURNITURE

# INTRODUCTION

*I disapprove of what you say
but I will defend to the death
your right to say it.*

*Voltaire (1694-1778)*

# ·INTRODUCTION·

The past is our heritage. The centuries which make up the history of the Western world are peopled with men whose ideas and actions have long outlived them. These are the result of their perceptive comprehension of the demands made by the ever-changing pattern of society.

Western culture is the evolution of their intellectual concepts as disseminated through the arts of painting, sculpture, architecture, literature and music.

The Greek sculptor, the Greek and Roman philosopher, the medieval stonecutter, the Italian painter, the German printer, the Spanish mystic, the English playwright, the French and English pamphleteer, architect and craftsman, the nineteenth-century novelist and musician, and the present-day designer and script-writer, are the apostles of Western civilization.

One reason for the successful development and growth of Western culture is that it has been influenced by men from every nation and that the responsibility for promoting it has been shared by artists of every kind.

We are grateful to the artists who have beautified our world externally, but we are deeply indebted to those who have recorded events and explained ideals. An artist's value lies not so much in his ability to handle his tools as in his capacity to communicate ideas. As an artisan he is important; as a chronographer he is valuable, but as an interpreter he is indispensable. It is when an artist takes a subject which we know, need, think about, or feel, and returns it to us magically transformed in terms of his medium, that he delights us most.

That man's course through history has been like that of a mountain climber is most clearly demonstrated in the arts. The struggle of the ascent, the glory of attainment at the peak, and the inevitable anticlimax of the descent can be recognized time and again in the fluctuating rhythm and the recurrent pattern of his artistic output.

In his climb from the plains of an animal existence to the heights of human achievement, man reveals himself through the arts. His good and his evil, his strength and his weakness, his wisdom and his folly, his success and his failure, are documented in the cultural attainments of the different stages of his development. His intellectual aspirations, his spiritual needs, and his emotional urges are voiced in the balance of architecture, the force of sculpture, the release of painting, the magic of music and the power of the printed word. These are the humanities —the products of man's human nature—the qualities which distinguish him from all other living things.

MAN is forever striving toward a GOAL.
Once obtained his interest fades.
He is always formulating CHANGE.

° ° °

The THREE STAGES of artistic development throughout this book are numbered ①, ② and ③

① The PRIMITIVE experimental beginnings.

Pottery Bowl

° ° °

② The HIGH - the purest expression of a selected style, medium or technique.

Porcelain Urn

° ° °

③ The DECLINE - the overconfidence following the disciplined reserve of the HIGH.

Porcelain Vase

° ° °

The assessment we place on the products of the different phases is the outcome of education.
Popular taste is acceptance conditioned by the level of established society.

# ·The RANGE of WESTERN CIVILIZATION·

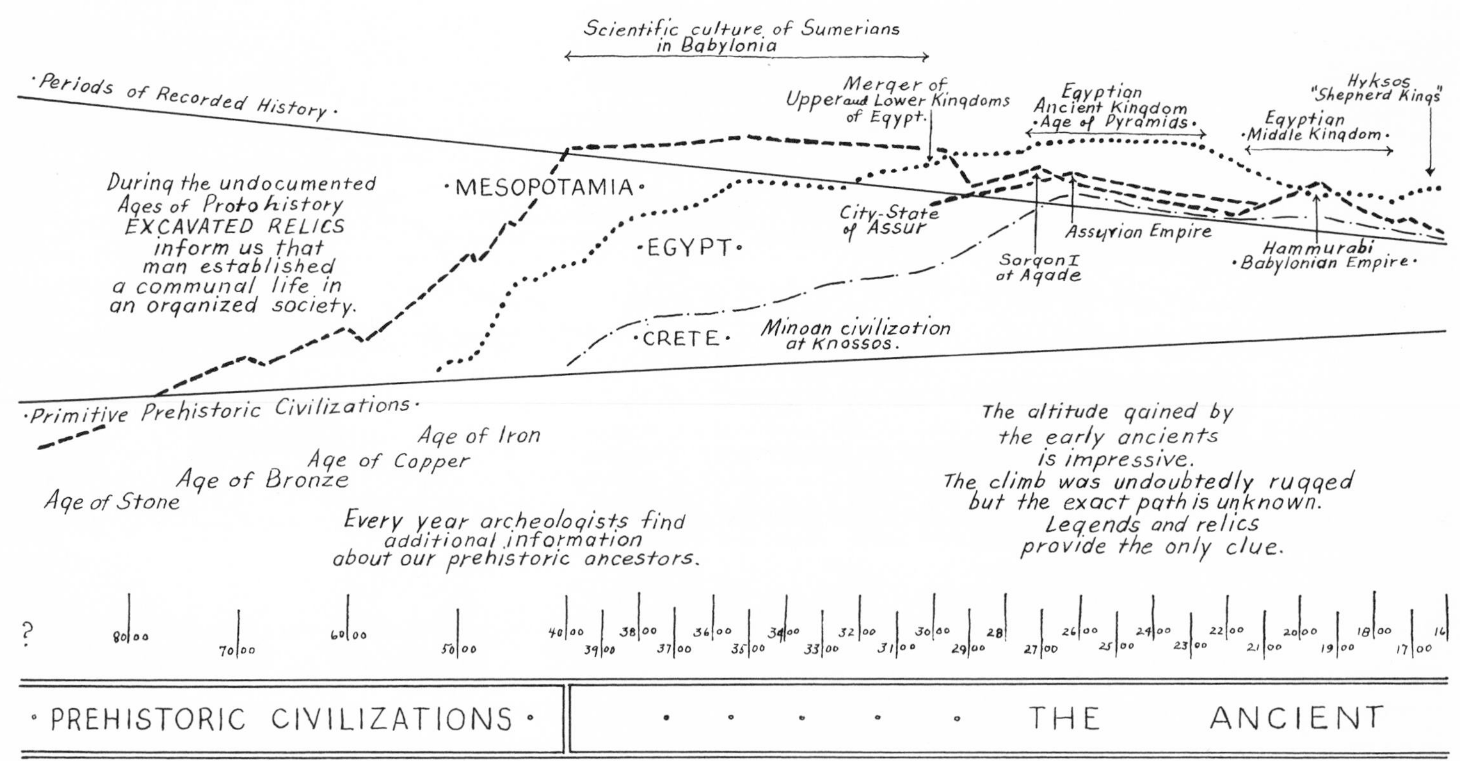
Scientific culture of Sumerians in Babylonia
·Periods of Recorded History·
Merger of Upper and Lower Kingdoms of Egypt
Egyptian Ancient Kingdom
·Age of Pyramids·
Hyksos "Shepherd Kings"
Egyptian ·Middle Kingdom·
During the undocumented Ages of Proto history EXCAVATED RELICS inform us that man established a communal life in an organized society.
·MESOPOTAMIA·
·EGYPT·
City-State of Assur
Assyrian Empire
Sargon I of Agade
Hammurabi
·Babylonian Empire·
·CRETE·
Minoan civilization at Knossos.
·Primitive Prehistoric Civilizations·
Age of Iron
Age of Copper
Age of Bronze
Age of Stone
Every year archeologists find additional information about our prehistoric ancestors.
The altitude gained by the early ancients is impressive. The climb was undoubtedly rugged but the exact path is unknown. Legends and relics provide the only clue.
? 8000 7000 6000 5000 4000 3900 3800 3700 3600 3500 3400 3300 3200 3100 3000 2900 28 2700 2600 2500 2400 2300 2200 2100 2000 1900 1800 1700 16
· PREHISTORIC CIVILIZATIONS ·
THE ANCIENT

## THE CHART

As the social, artistic, political and economic phases of any civilization occur at different times, it is difficult to judge at what exact moment a civilization reaches its greatest height. This chart is an attempt to show the comparative strength of the different peoples—their relationship to one another and to the world today.

This graph seems justified for the way in which certain interesting facts are immediately evident, although other equally important factors do not even appear.

First, it comes as something of a shock that the modern world, of which we are so proud, is such a short and unimposing range on the mountainous expanse of over 5,000 years of recorded history.

Secondly, it is discouraging to find that modern man has climbed only a short way beyond the level of his ancient ancestors, and that this progress was accomplished only by building upon the ideas inherited from them.

## THE ANCIENT WORLD

Although on similar levels, the undulating line of the controlled, inbred culture of the Egyptians forms a contrast with the separate ages of different racial dominations in Mesopotamia. It is amazing that both reached the stage of highest development early in their history and never again attained it. It is not surprising that two such closely matched countries should have fought more than once for supremacy. After being conquered by the Persians and Greeks they ceased to be contributing factors in the cultural pattern when they became part of the Roman Empire in 30 B. C.

Directly influenced by the cultures at Crete (Minoan) and Mycenae, Greece soared to the most dazzling pinnacle of all. Although conquered, she strengthened Rome through the latter's period of greatest triumph, emerging in the form of Byzantine culture, as the only permanent bridge across the crevasse which separates the ancient world from the modern.

# ·The RANGE of WESTERN CIVILIZATION·

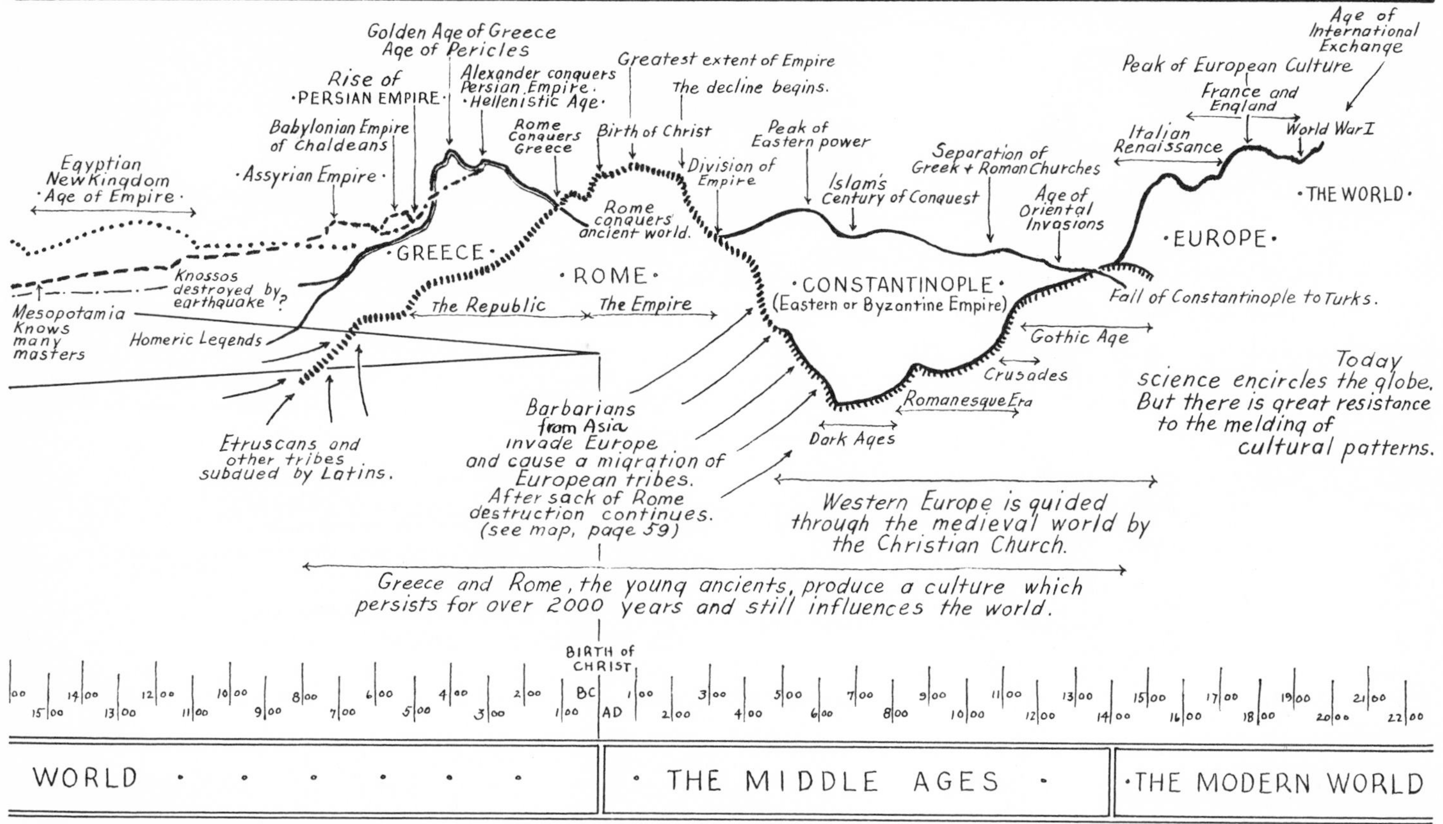

Egyptian New Kingdom ·Age of Empire·
Mesopotamia Knows many masters
Knossos destroyed by earthquake?
Homeric Legends
·Assyrian Empire·
Babylonian Empire of Chaldeans
Rise of ·PERSIAN EMPIRE·
Golden Age of Greece Age of Pericles
Alexander conquers Persian Empire. ·Hellenistic Age·
Rome Conquers Greece
·GREECE·
Etruscans and other tribes subdued by Latins.
·ROME·
The Republic
The Empire
Birth of Christ
Greatest extent of Empire
The decline begins.
Division of Empire
Rome conquers ancient world.
Barbarians from Asia invade Europe and cause a migration of European tribes. After sack of Rome destruction continues. (see map, page 59)
Peak of Eastern power
Islam's Century of Conquest
·CONSTANTINOPLE· (Eastern or Byzantine Empire)
Separation of Greek + Roman Churches
Age of Oriental Invasions
Dark Ages
Romanesque Era
Crusades
Gothic Age
Western Europe is guided through the medieval world by the Christian Church.
Fall of Constantinople to Turks.
Italian Renaissance
·EUROPE·
Peak of European Culture
France and England
World War I
Age of International Exchange
·THE WORLD·
Today science encircles the globe. But there is great resistance to the melding of cultural patterns.
Greece and Rome, the young ancients, produce a culture which persists for over 2000 years and still influences the world.
BIRTH of CHRIST
1500 1400 1300 1200 1100 1000 900 800 700 600 500 400 300 200 100 BC AD 100 200 300 400 500 600 700 800 900 1000 1100 1200 1300 1400 1500 1600 1700 1800 1900 2000 2100 2200
WORLD · · · · · ·
· THE MIDDLE AGES ·
·THE MODERN WORLD


### THE MIDDLE AGES

While the medieval Church was responsible for the rise of European civilization from the barbarian level, the rigid rule it imposed on the people accounts for the lack of progress evidenced in many fields— science in particular. This is indicated by the low level of medieval society. What the chart fails to show is that the same strong power inspired one of the greatest and most sincere artistic ages in the history of man.

### THE EUROPEAN WORLD

Renaissance Italy struggled out of the valley of medievalism and gained her summit in the fifteenth century, leaving France and England to climb gradually to loftier heights in the eighteenth.

In the nineteenth century the industries born of science turned England into an empire on which the sun never set. In 1914 the nationalistic imperialism of Germany caused the fall of the continent. The badly shaken Old World was saved from a fatal plunge by the strength of the New in World War I.

### THE WORLD TODAY

Since 1918 the United States, endowed with its European heritage and its rich natural resources, has become a leader in world affairs. Today the U. S. S. R., an even younger nation with equal resources but with a totally different philosophy, has declared itself a rival power. All over the globe, countries are finding themselves in the position of having to choose between the directions offered by the conflicting ideologies.

If we are successful in persuading the undecided that ours is the better way, when one all-encompassing cultural pattern evolves it may be based upon the most worthy ideal of Western culture: freedom from the suppression of the rights of the individual by either Church or State.

# ·OUTLINE of WESTERN CULTURE·

• VENUS •
Goddess of Love and Beauty

Ancient Greek Sculpture

100,000 B. C. —THE PREHISTORIC AGES—4,000 B. C.

100,000—Man discovers his ability to use—10,000 B. C.
the world of nature.

10,000 B. C. —Age of Protohistory—4,000 B. C.
Man learns the advantages of organized society.

4,000 B. C. —THE ANCIENT CLASSIC CULTURES—476 A. D.

The invention of writing.
The foundations of modern civilization.

MESOPOTAMIAN EGYPTIAN GREEK ROMAN

Philosophers recognize the dignity of man.

• EVE and the SERPENT •
medieval stone carving from a Romanesque capital.

1 A. D. —THE MIDDLE AGES—1500

The centuries dominated by the dictates of the growing Christian Church.

EARLY CHRISTIAN
A small group spreads the teachings of Jesus of Nazareth.

ROMAN CHRISTIAN
Organization of the Christian Church.

BYZANTINE
The development of Christian theology continues in the Eastern Empire after the fall of Rome. Constantinople saves Europe from Oriental invaders.

600—THE DARK AGES—800
Conversion of Europe's pagan barbarians to Christianity.

The Ages of Faith
Man becomes a servant of the Church.

ROMANESQUE GOTHIC

The growing strength of the nations threatens the position of the Church.

# · OUTLINE of WESTERN CULTURE ·

## 1400 — THE RENAISSANCE MOVEMENT — 1700

Man the individual is born of a revival of ancient classic ideals.

| Italy | France | England |
|---|---|---|
| 1400–1650 | 1525–1700 | 1550–1700 |

1400 — The Fifteenth Century — 1500
New style of architecture and painting flourishes in Italy.
Printing invented in Germany.

1500 — The Sixteenth Century — 1600
The acme of Italian production in art and architecture.
Religious revolt and reform starts in Germany.
Age of Exploration.

1600 — The Seventeenth Century — 1700
Spain and the Counter Reformation vainly try to re-establish the temporal power of the Church.
The state becomes all-powerful.
Age of Scientific Awakening. Age of Colonization.

## 1700 — THE EIGHTEENTH CENTURY — 1800

Age of Intellectual Activity.
The peak of European culture under the leadership of France.
England's American Colonies revolt.
Demands for political freedom destroy absolute monarchy in France.

## 1800 — THE NINETEENTH CENTURY — 1900

England revolutionizes entire world.
Every phase of culture effected by scientific invention.
Ascendency of the intellectual arts.

## 1900 — THE TWENTIETH CENTURY — 2000

Age of Scientific Achievement.
International experimentation and individual expression in the arts.
Western culture exposed to world-wide influences and responsibilities.

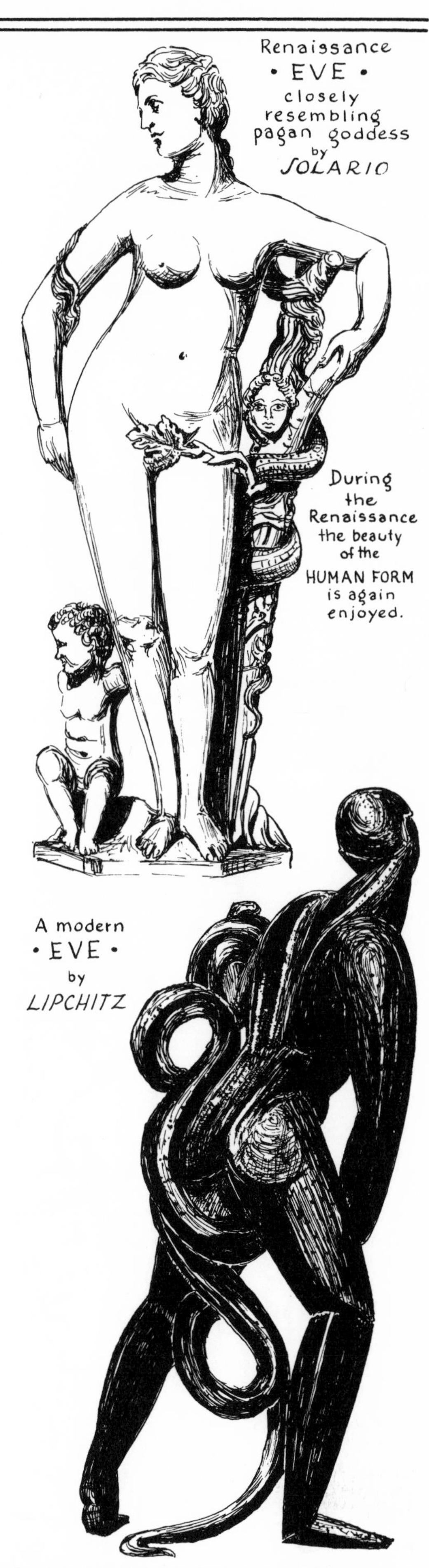
Renaissance
• EVE •
closely resembling pagan goddess
by
SOLARIO
During the Renaissance the beauty of the HUMAN FORM is again enjoyed.
A modern
• EVE •
by
LIPCHITZ

# · The ELEMENTS of DESIGN ·

NATURE
lays the ground rules for
· DESIGN ·

These examples, in addition to showing the THREE BASIC TYPES of BALANCE, are also illustrations of other important aspects of design.

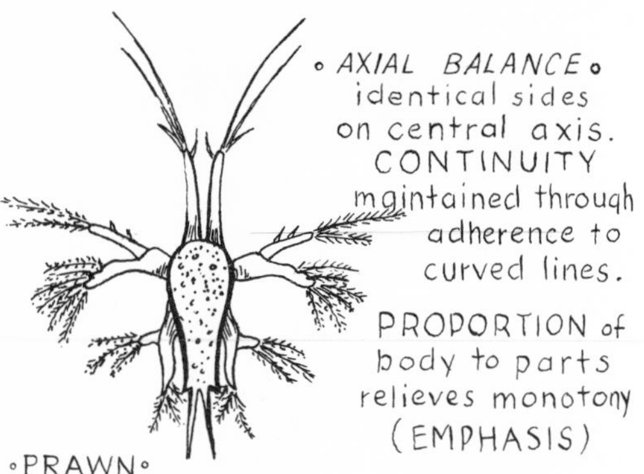

· AXIAL BALANCE ·
identical sides
on central axis.
CONTINUITY
maintained through
adherence to
curved lines.
PROPORTION of
body to parts
relieves monotony
(EMPHASIS)
·PRAWN·


· RADIAL BALANCE ·
symmetrical composition springs from central point. The RHYTHM of the recurrent shapes gives CONTINUITY.

· SNOWFLAKE ·

· OCCULT BALANCE ·
achieved not by formula but by sensitive judgment. This type of OPTICAL BALANCE may be strengthened through the use of COLOR and TEXTURE.

·AMOEBA·

In groups of growing organisms NATURE tends to compensate for uneven placement and often produces BALANCED DESIGN.

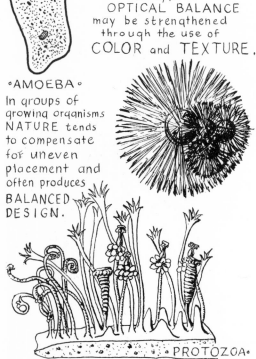

· PROTOZOA ·

There are, loosely speaking, two kinds of art—visual and intellectual. Drawing, painting, sculpture (three-dimensional design) and printing are visual, while literature and music are intellectual. The visual and intellectual arts are blended on stage and screen. The visual arts are emphasized in this book, but it is well to remember that the relationship between all the arts is very close because they are founded on the same motivations and outlined on the same principles.

Beauty is an aesthetic phase of art. But as a different style of beauty is selected by each passing age, beauty is an inconstant and undefinable ideal—not a fundamental objective. Art is based not upon beauty but upon the organization of ideas and the application of techniques according to the recognized principles of design.

Unlike the concept of beauty, there is nothing elusive about design. It is timeless and definable. It constitutes the basic standard for art in every medium and in all periods. Its elements have been singled out after repeated analytical observations of the creations of both man and nature. While terminology on the subject may differ, the fundamentals remain the same.

In the visual arts design is organization of space. It may be two dimensional like a drawing or painting, or three dimensional like a sculpture or building. Its principles are employed in the placement or grouping of two or more objects as well as in the fashioning of each individual piece.

Many contemporary masterpieces are conceived and enjoyed entirely through knowledge and appreciation of design for itself alone.

The success of any composition depends upon the handling of its component parts. This involves the application of three principles—balance, continuity and emphasis.

Balance supplies stability through the distribution and proportion of the parts.

Continuity is obtained through a consistency of treatment which brings the separate features into harmony.

Emphasis relieves monotony through dominance and subordination of selected areas.

Together these elements produce unified design. Whether a work is stylized, realistic or abstract, aesthetic or functional, these rules apply.

Man must arrange his selections
with great care
to obtain
BALANCE
and UNITY.
· FORMAL BALANCE ·
· INFORMAL BALANCE ·

# ·The CLASSIFICATION of ARTISTS·

The urge to create is the inexhaustible compulsion of all artists. But the desire to create does not in itself produce a masterpiece. Examination of the works of different periods reveals that every artist functions with greatest acumen when challenged by a specific directive. The most outstanding work is brought forth by disciplined talent. The ivory tower is neither as stimulating nor as prolific as the workshop, because it is divorced from reality.

Quality depends first upon the artist's capacity to grasp his subject and then upon his ability to carry it out. Painters and sculptors are classified accordingly.

The primitive through enthusiasm for the theme attempts to present an idea in spite of obvious deficiencies in skill or training. A current vogue for primitive painting has caused many artists to affect distortion. This is unfortunate, because a primitive is charming not because the draftsmanship is crude, but because the spontaneous naïveté of the presentation is convincing.

The master (unless through circumstance he is a primitive) understands the fundamental principles of color and design, and perfects the intricacies of technique. His skill is automatic and his mind is free. His style is uninhibited and sincere. Even the most hackneyed subject comes to life under his sensitive perception and originality.

A mannerist produces a beautiful object by adhering to the rules of design and by perfecting an accepted style. He is an able craftsman whose hand will bear inspection, but whose concern with surface effect makes his work cold and impersonal. However, his lack of introspective interest in the subject is not detected by every viewer.

A copyist through discipline or lack of imagination is satisfied to imitate rather than invent. He is a capable technician who is able to reproduce the finest work. His value lies in duplicating, restoring, or amplifying someone else's designs or ideas.

An artist is described as decadent when preoccupation with the exhibition of technical prowess interferes with his interpretation of the theme.

Until an artist proves that he has the ability to translate an idea into a style of his own, he makes no major contribution to his field.

Great ART is born of HUMAN NEEDS and INTERESTS

It is organized according to
the ELEMENTS of DESIGN
and presented through
the sensitivity, creative ability and dexterity of individual artists.

The CONTINUITY
between form and decoration
EMPHASIZES the roundness of the vase.

The LACK of CONTINUITY
between top and base
results in poor design.

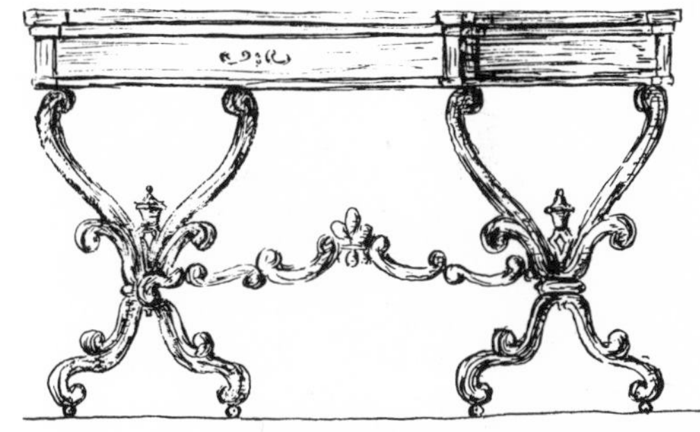

EMPHASIS
through dominance and subordination
relieves unified design of monotony.

The Pitti Palace, Florence,
presents a tiresome facade to the Piazza
because the design lacks a focal point.

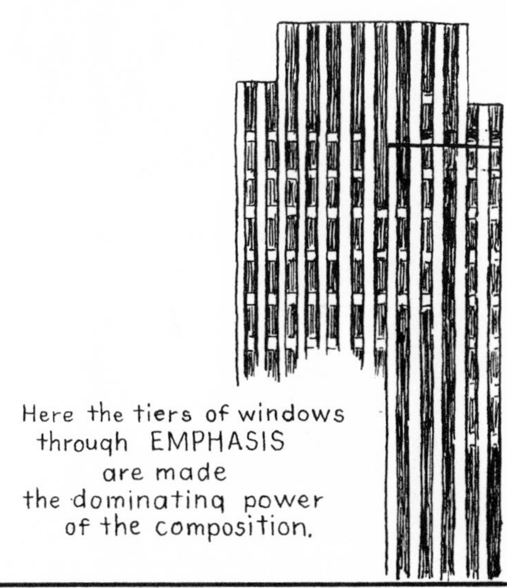

Here the tiers of windows
through EMPHASIS
are made
the dominating power
of the composition.

# ·INDIVIDUAL SELECTION·

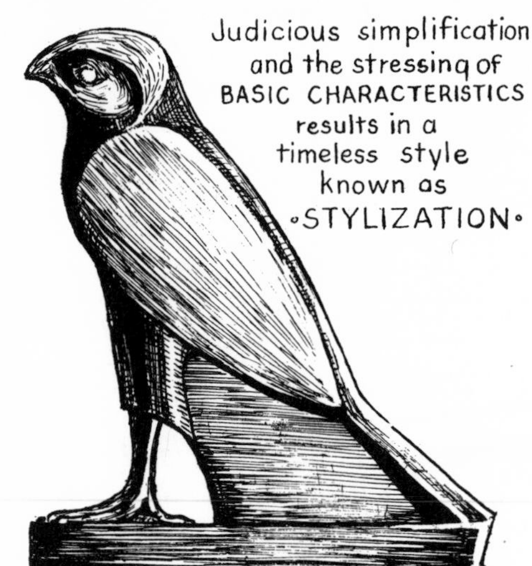

Judicious simplification and the stressing of BASIC CHARACTERISTICS results in a timeless style known as ·STYLIZATION·

*·HORUS· God and Legendary King of Egypt Black Granite Sculpture*

The selection of a work of art in the last analysis is one of personal preference. Critics are called upon to give their opinions. Through intellectual analysis they usually can agree upon a list of the most gifted artists, but they seldom make the same choice of greatest paintings. This is very natural.

Let us suppose an artist has made an eloquent presentation. There is no misunderstanding the subject. It is not difficult to recognize the accepted standards of good design. The proficiency of technique speaks for itself.

While these qualities give pleasure, it is not for these alone that pictures are chosen. There is a less easily defined, more variable basis for personal selection.

Each person takes what the artist has to give and weighs it in terms of his own imagination, experience, training and taste. A person of broad scope, because he has more to put into his examination of the work, will get more out of it than will a child or an adult with limited interests.

Thus every viewer makes his own evaluation, and even the professional critic is not strong enough to exclude from his appraisal certain influences of a major or trivial nature, which exist in his conscious or subconscious mind. These are sentimental attractions or repulsions which cause any individual to accept or reject a particular piece. It is unlikely that any two people ever judge an object by exactly the same standards.

*Bronze Eagle Hellenistic Greek*

·REALISM· for centuries has been the goal of many artists. It is only one of several approaches to a subject.

·SYMBOLISM· is as old as man himself.

Magic and religion, always in close association in primitive society, are often supported by rituals composed of symbols.

However, when the KEY is lost the SYMBOL becomes MEANINGLESS.

Psychologists hold that we are influenced by ancient symbols still cherished in our subconscious minds.

Modern artists attempt to express ideas and emotions through symbolism which often is not sufficiently clear for general comprehension.

Two views of ·*BIRD in SPACE*· a metal ·ABSTRACTION· by *Constantin Brancusi*

It conveys the grace of a bird in elemental forms bearing no actual resemblance to nature.

The UNKNOWN SYMBOLISM of the African Cave Paintings below is now believed to be an expression of the same culture which produced the excellent drawings in the prehistoric caves of Europe. (see page 24)

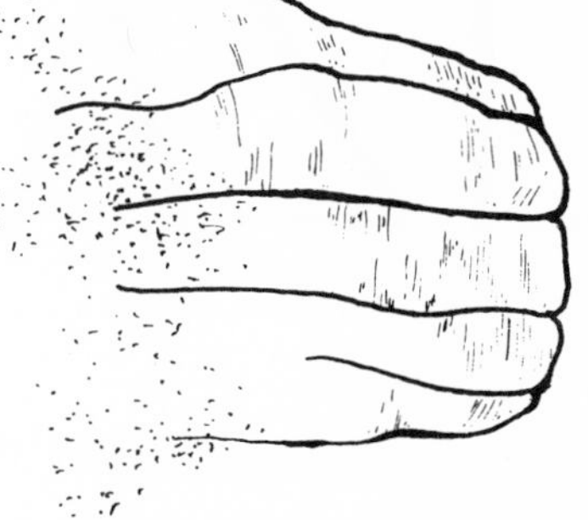

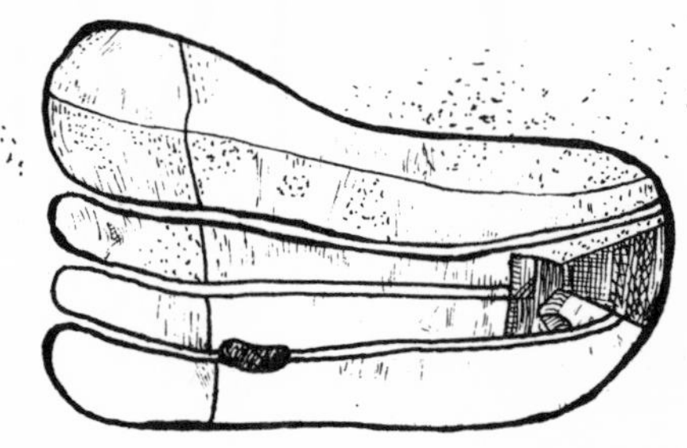

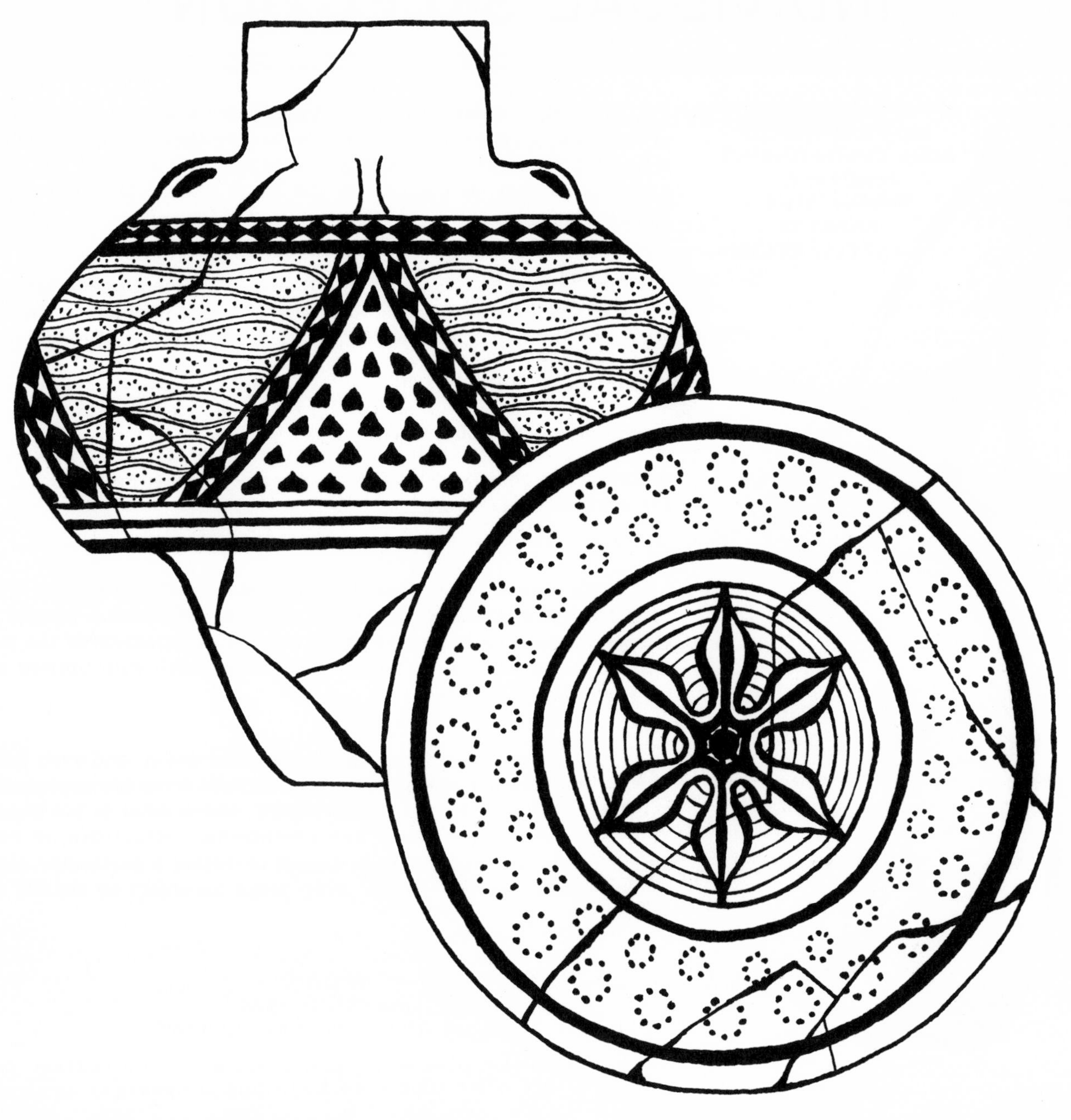

# PREHISTORIC CIVILIZATIONS

## 2,000,000,000—ESTIMATED GEOLOGIC ERAS—2,000,000 B.C. of the EARTH

The earth appears in the universe.
The planet experiences turbulent physical changes.
Evidence of primordial life dates back over
a billion years.
Many forms of life of increasing variety
and complexity evolve from
changing natural conditions.

Age of Mammals begins 60,000,000 years ago.

## 2,000,000—ESTIMATED PREHISTORIC AGES of MAN—4,000 B.C.

2,000,000 years ago
Animals and plants of modern types appear.

1,000,000—100,000
Man conforms to world of nature.

100,000—Ages of Stone and Copper—30,000
Man proves superior intellect by discovering
use of natural forces such as fire.

30,000—Age of Bronze—10,000
Man learns to live in the society of
his fellow men.

10,000 B.C. —Age of Protohistory—4,000 B.C.
Man organizes and regulates
community life.

# ·PREHISTORIC CIVILIZATIONS·

**Every time an archeologist puts a spade into the ground the popular conception of the prehistoric cave man is pushed back several thousand years as evidences of civilizations of earlier and earlier dates are exposed. That man forsook "the state of nature for his natural state—organized society" many thousands of years ago becomes more evident with each find. Cave men are now thought to have lived 20,000 to 50,000 years ago—while civilization in Mesopotamia, the oldest now on record, goes back about ten thousand years. Archeologists are at work the world over, and at any moment newly discovered relics may tell us of other more ancient peoples.**

Fear of unknown motivates RELIGIOUS RITUAL including ANIMAL or HUMAN SACRIFICES to appease gods representing the FORCES OF NATURE

DOLMAN-altar? MONOLITHS

Carefully placed natural boulders undoubtedly have religious significance.

**Man is considered to be in a prehistoric state until he is able to record his story in written form. But art is a form of communication older than writing. Through an inherent sense of beauty and a natural ability to express himself in some artistic form, prehistoric man left behind a part of himself as he enhanced his crude weapons, tools, utensils, and uncomfortable dwellings, first with geometric, then with naturalistic, designs and symbols.**

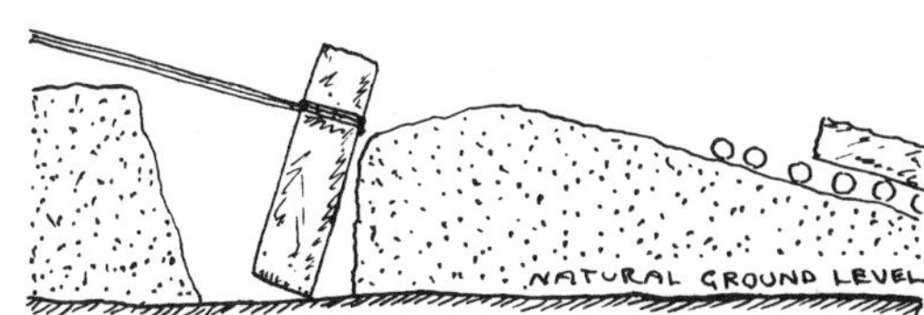
NATURAL GROUND LEVEL

METHOD of PLACING MONOLITHS

1. Earth ramps constructed.
2. Tools:- Logs - Rope - Lever.
3. Stone pulled up ramp.
4. Stone dropped into well and pulled into upright position.
5. Ramps removed.

**The custom of filling graves with utilitarian and ornamental objects for an after-life was shared by many primitive peoples. Careful study of these objects has enabled us to reconstruct the daily life of our prehistoric ancestors in all parts of the world.**

STONEHENGE notable example of monolith construction.

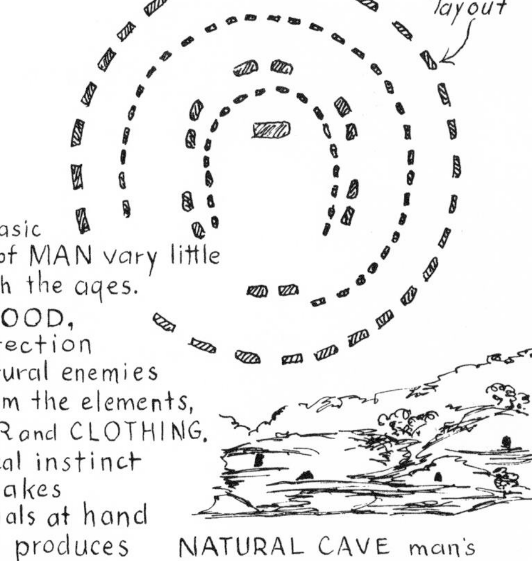
plan of layout

**First hunters, shepherds, farmers, and then townsmen, prehistoric men entered into a long period of protohistory. This is a stage in which men did not yet know how to write but when in other respects their lives and mores were very similar to those in the first centuries of documented history. This we can tell by the objects both artistic and utilitarian which have been found on the sites of their buried cities.**

TYPOGRAPHY, CLIMATE and RELIGION prime influential factors in architectural form.

Basic NEEDS of MAN vary little through the ages. FOOD, Protection from natural enemies and from the elements, SHELTER and CLOTHING. Practical instinct takes materials at hand and produces FUNCTIONAL SOLUTIONS.

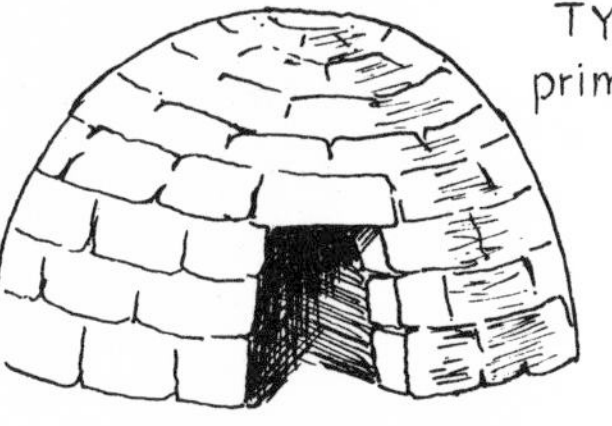

ESKIMO IGLOO excellent example of building with limited native material. Not unlike PREHISTORIC BEEHIVE HUTS of stone (Scotland).

TROPICAL HUT of leaves and branches.

TENT of bark or skins.

NATURAL CAVE man's first home in many regions.

PRIMITIVE APARTMENT Long house of American Indians.

Swiss LAKE HUTS.

TROPICAL TREE PLATFORMS.

# · PREHISTORIC CIVILIZATIONS ·

NECESSITY
produces UTILITARIAN OBJECTS.
ESTHETIC INSTINCT
produces pleasing DECORATION.

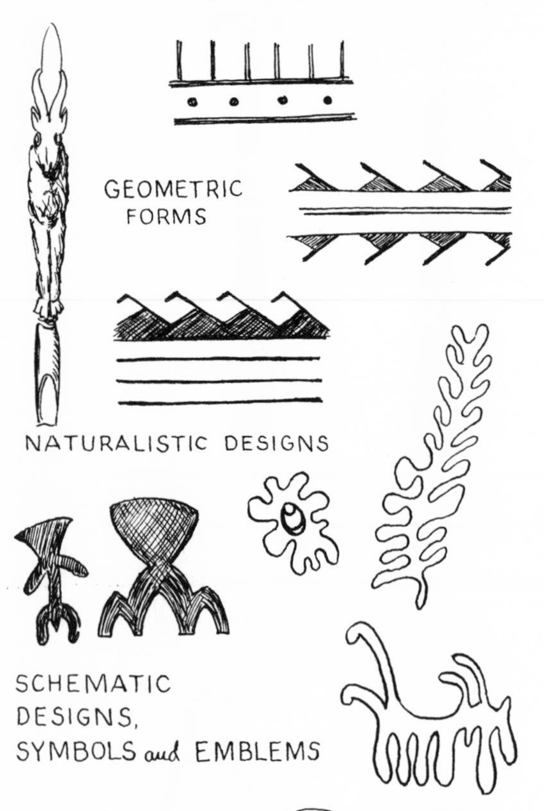

GEOMETRIC FORMS
NATURALISTIC DESIGNS
SCHEMATIC DESIGNS, SYMBOLS and EMBLEMS


**Cuneiform impressions on clay tablets and hieroglyphic writings on walls and papyrus were deciphered in the nineteenth century and have given us a detailed history of the peoples of ancient Mesopotamia and Egypt from c. 4000 B.C.**

**But the people before that were born into a naked world and, having none to teach them, learned to make nature serve their human needs.**

**The achievements of these people seem incomprehensible to subsequent generations who have encountered great difficulty in further advancement. These were the men who built the foundation of the Western world by creating it through their own intellect. It is tragic that they were able to move from the primitive cave to the organized city before they were prepared to acquaint their descendants with an account of their methods or the story of their experiences.**

**It is interesting to note that while an extremely high form of civilization existed on the eastern shores of the Mediterranean as early as 4,000 B.C., western and northern Europe were in a prehistoric state.**

**Only several hundred years after he himself had progressed beyond a primitive existence, European man had the opportunity of meeting prehistoric savages when he came face to face with the American Indian. Even today in certain shrinking areas of Africa, South America, Australia, etc., there are tribes living a crude existence similar to that which our forebears experienced perhaps 20,000 years ago.**

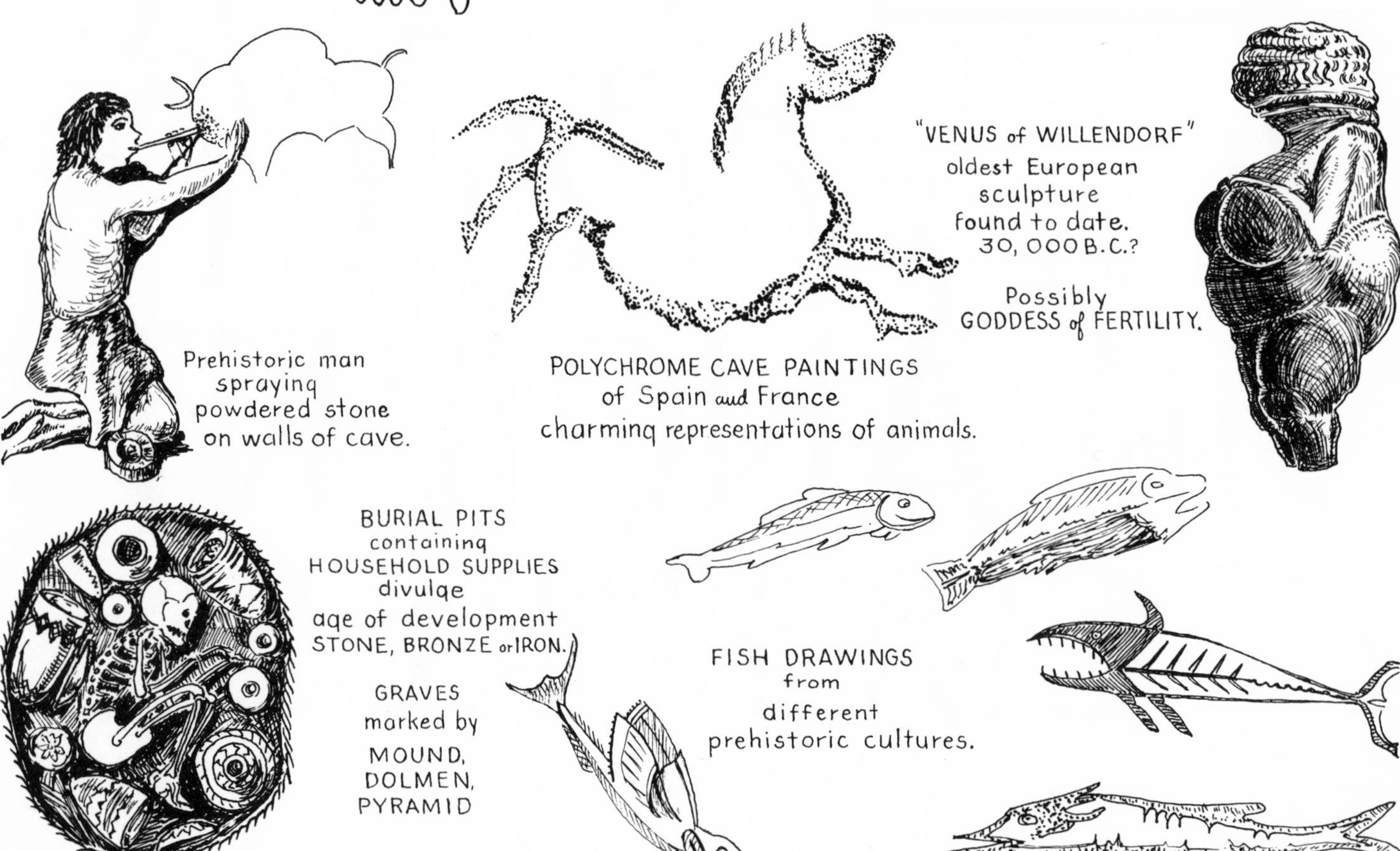

Prehistoric man spraying powdered stone on walls of cave.
POLYCHROME CAVE PAINTINGS of Spain and France charming representations of animals.
"VENUS of WILLENDORF" oldest European sculpture found to date. 30,000 B.C.?
Possibly GODDESS of FERTILITY.
BURIAL PITS containing HOUSEHOLD SUPPLIES divulge age of development STONE, BRONZE or IRON.
GRAVES marked by MOUND, DOLMEN, PYRAMID
FISH DRAWINGS from different prehistoric cultures.

# THE ANCIENT CULTURES

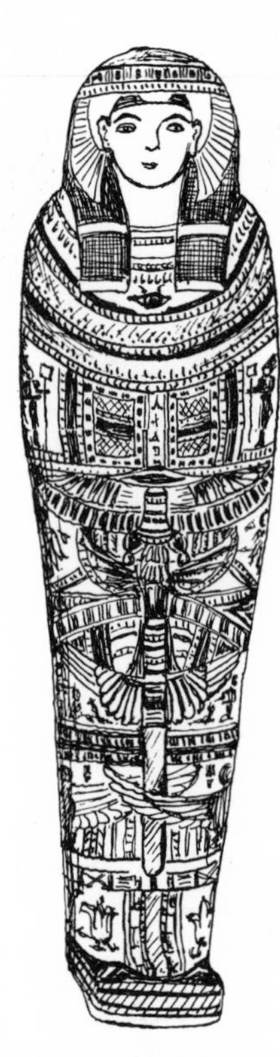

·EGYPTIAN MUMMY CASE·

# ·4000 B.C. THE ANCIENT CULTURES 476 A.D.·

The invention of writing.
Age of Iron.

The foundations of modern Western civilization
were laid in these countries.
Great refinements achieved in the art of living.

MESOPOTAMIAN bas-relief.
Captives paying tribute.

4,000 B. C.—MESOPOTAMIA—30 B. C.

Desirable fertile lands often change hands.
Eclectic culture evolved by many peoples
over a period of several thousand years.

EGYPTIAN sandstone window.

3,200 B. C.—EGYPT—30 B. C.

An inbred culture is controlled in a land
which enjoys natural geographical protection
from invaders.

Comic painting from GREEK vase.

1,000 B. C.—GREECE—124 B. C.

Hellenic civilization is built upon
the pre-Hellenic Helladic (Mycenae) and Minoan (Crete)
cultures.
Aesthetics and ethics are stressed.
Philosophers recognize the dignity of man.

750 B. C.—ROME—476 A. D.

An ambitious people conquer first
Italy and then the Western world.

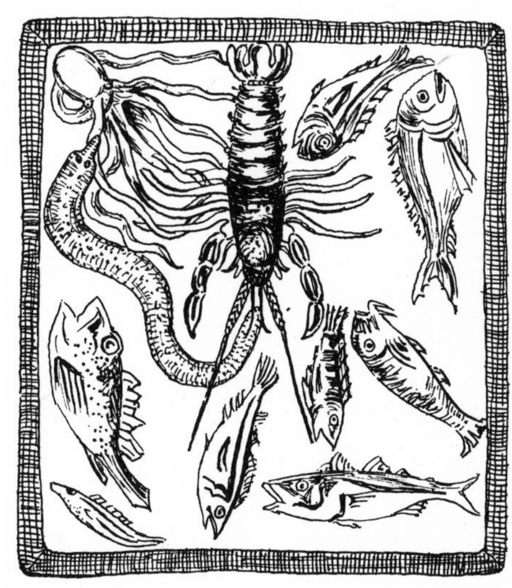

ROMAN mosaic.

Greek, Roman and Greco-Roman cultures dominate
the West for almost half the years
of the recorded history of mankind.
(See Byzantine culture)

# · MESOPOTAMIAN CULTURE ·

Goat of gold. MINOR DEITY perhaps household shrine.

GOLD OBJECTS from the ROYAL GRAVES at UR (See map, p.38)

Nothing has changed more in the last hundred and fifty years than our concepts of ancient history.

During the nineteenth century, archeology which started as a hopeful digging operation developed into a science and revealed to an enthusiastic world the remains of the civilizations described in the Old Testament and other ancient records. Among them the cities of the Land between the Rivers appeared. Here nomadic tribesmen were able to establish grazing areas for their flocks, and stationary settlements soon set up cultural patterns. This desirable valley fell into the power of a succession of invaders. The strongest and most influential civilizations were those which spread from the cities of Babylon and Assur.

The Babylonians worshiped the sun, moon and stars, and through their mathematical instinct worked out the science of astronomy and the superstitions of astrology. They originated the divisions of months, weeks, days, hours, minutes and seconds that we follow, and devised the sundial and a water clock. They are also responsible for a system of weights and measures, and the first code of laws.

The aggressive and warlike Assyrians carried their empire and Babylonian culture beyond the natural river boundaries.

CLAY TABLET and CLAY ENVELOPE inscribed in cuneiform 4,000 years ago. All writing is done on stone or clay.

Charming, imaginative PERSONAL SEAL cut on STONE by SCRIBE. Impression on wet clay serves as SIGNATURE

Constantly under attack from the Egyptians, Persians, Greeks and Romans, Mesopotamia was in turn a part of their ancient empires. During the Middle Ages it was dominated first by Arabs, then by Turks. Today it is part of the modern country of Iraq.

Other ancient peoples who made worthy contributions to the modern world were:

The Lydians—who replaced barter with coinage.

The Phoenicians—the Missionaries of Civilization who carried their alphabet and Eastern culture to all shores of the Mediterranean.

The Hebrews—whose monotheism and religious writings were the foundation of Christian literature.

ARTISTIC EXPRESSIONS prove valuable source for information concerning CUSTOMS, COSTUMES and FURNITURE.

HAMMURABI'S "An eye for an eye, a tooth for a tooth" is oldest recorded CODE of LAWS

GAMING BOARD

# · MESOPOTAMIAN ARCHITECTURE ·

Scarcity of wood, lack of stone result in invention of KILN-DRIED BRICK for building.

ARCH, VAULT and DOME CONSTRUCTION developes.

ENAMEL in bright colors used to DECORATE and GLAZE BRICK and TILE used on Walls and Floors.

DRAGON RELIEF from ISHTAR GATE

Time has destroyed the buildings but BRICK FOUNDATIONS and SECTIONS of WALLS reveal the layout of HUGE TEMPLES and PALACES with many SMALL ROOMS and LARGE OUTDOOR COURTYARDS. ROOFTOP TERRACES (Hanging Gardens of Babylon) are fertilized by water pumped from Euphrates. THICK WALLS and SMALL WINDOWS keep out heat of sun.

ISHTAR GATE BABYLON 6th c.

Perspective drawing is unknown but depth is suggested by overlapping figures.

Note: Method of showing three horses on chariot.

The LION HUNT once conducted for protection becomes a controlled SPORT by releasing CAGED LIONS.

NEBUCHADNEZZAR'S BABYLON as described by the historian HERODOTUS is enjoyed by the CHALDEANS until the Persian conquest in 539 B.C.

Natural sand-colored brick. Vermilion paint. White plaster finish.

THREE SHRINES are reconstructed from ruins found in mound on site of ancient NINEVEH

A MINOR DEITY stylized muscles in arms and legs indicate KNOWLEDGE of ANATOMY

A double-ramped Chaldean TEMPLE SEVEN levels honor PLANETS. OBSERVATORY on top. These ZIGGURATS resembled towers on the flat plains. The Biblical Tower of Babel was undoubtedly one.

A pair of FIVE-LEGGED MINOR DEITIES guard entrances to Assyrian palaces. Four legs are seen on side elevation two on front.

# ·EGYPTIAN CULTURE·

Because the pyramids and sphinxes had been exposed to the eyes of man for as long as he could remember, he supposed that Egypt was the oldest country in the world. Archeological findings have proved that, although Egypt is even older than assumed, it is probably not the oldest of the ancient cultures.

Beginning with the discovery of the Rosetta Stone in 1799, the study of Egyptology has continued with increasing reward. The most exciting of all finds, to date, was the discovery in 1922 of the untouched tomb of Tut-Ankh-Amen. Then modern man had his first opportunity to see the fabulous, much-talked-of golden wealth of antiquity.

We know that about 2,500 B. C., when the pyramids were built, Egypt reached the zenith of her greatness. In the years which followed she failed to advance the genius which had enabled her to originate the solar calendar (365 days), the decimal system, geometry, algebra, and agricultural methods which earned her the title of Granary of the Ancient World.

While she had many gods and minor deities, her belief in a divine mother and child, and in the judgment of the immortal soul by a Supreme Being, strongly influenced the Hebrews, who in turn influenced Christian teachings.

Like all the ancient civilizations, her economy was supported by a large slave population. Her society was set up on a class system headed by the Pharaoh, ruler and minor deity. Next came the priests, who were the guardians of religion, morals and learnings. Then the nobles, government officials, professional soldiers, merchants, artisans, and peasants. The classes were not established through heredity alone. Intelligence, ambition or graft enabled a man to improve his station.

Her civilization is an example of an inbred culture seldom affected by foreign influences. Her stylized art was so controlled that any deviation from the established formulae met with ostracism. The Greek and Roman occupations broke the individualistic style and since then nothing has replaced it.

Egypt was conquered first by the Moslem Arabs and then by the Turks in the medieval era. In 1798 Napoleon tried to add her to the French African colonies. England's Nelson intercepted. After that Britain took an active interest in the administration of the country. In 1954 Egypt expelled her pro-British sovereign and faced the world without the "protection" of a foreign army for the first time in a thousand years.

The ROSETTA STONE named after the Napoleonic soldier who found it (1798) gave the KEY to HIEROGLYPHIC picture writing.
INSCRIPTION WRITTEN in HIEROGLYPHIC, DEMOTIC (Simplified hieroglyphics) and GREEK.

FORMULA for PAINTING and BAS-RELIEF
HEAD in PROFILE • EYE and SHOULDERS face FRONT.
BODY from waist down in PROFILE.

IMPORTANT PEOPLE, large scale; SLAVES, small.
WOMEN have PALE complexion.
MEN, BROWN skin.

LITTLE or NO ATTEMPT at REALISM.
All art forms highly STYLIZED.
No perspective.
ART rigidly controlled by PRIESTS.
All surfaces—
walls, ceilings, column shafts—
covered with designs.

EGYPTIAN DEAD
EVISCERATED, EMBALMED and BOUND.
MUMMY CASES show facial likeness.
VISCERA placed in 4 JARS guarded by 4 Sons of HORUS.
HUMAN-HEADED BIRD symbolizes SOUL

PAPER made from PAPYRUS is pieced together in LONG ROLLED BOOKS.
Every grave is supplied with BOOK of the DEAD giving instructions for the After-Life.

# ·EGYPTIAN ARCHITECTURE·

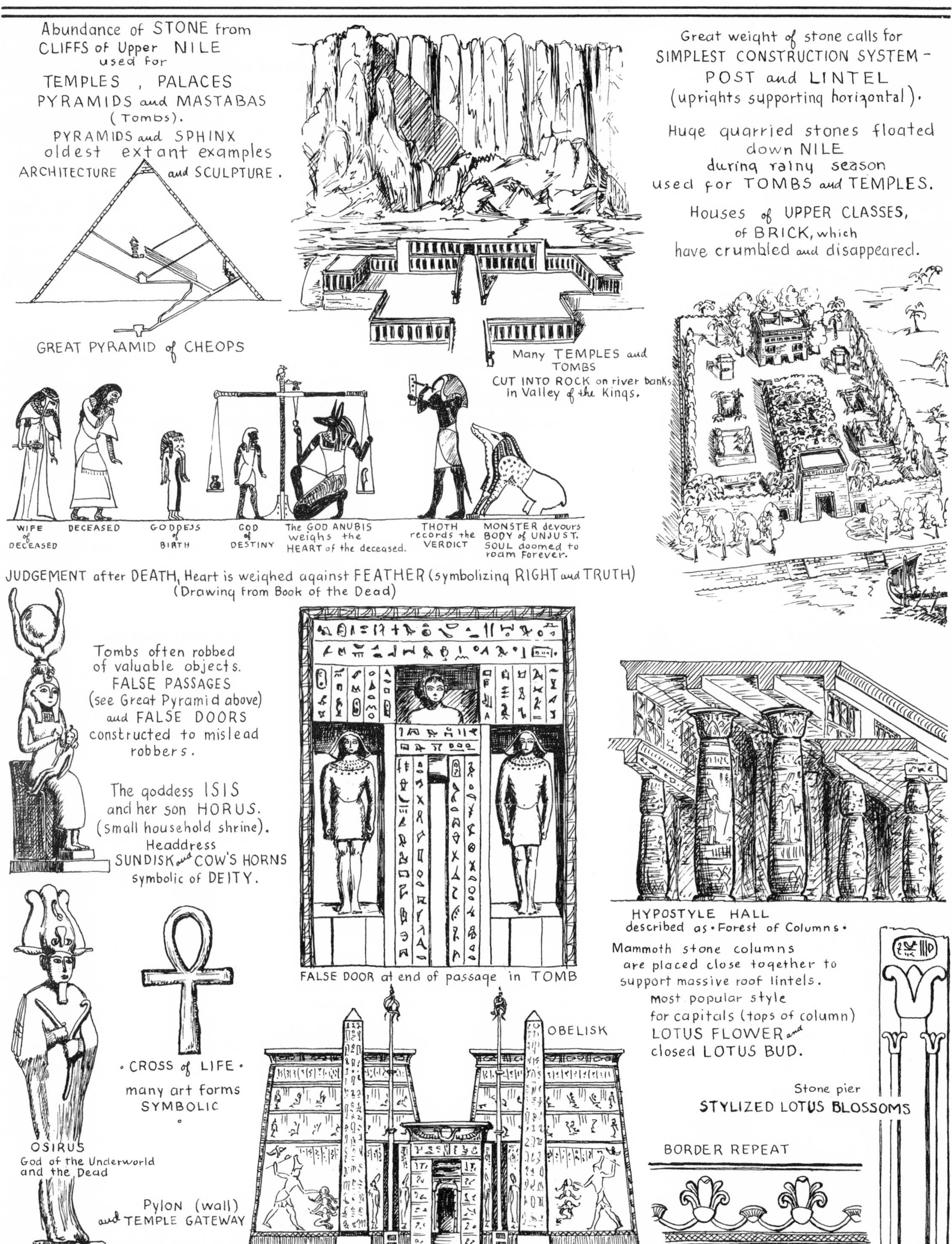

Abundance of STONE from CLIFFS of Upper NILE used for TEMPLES, PALACES PYRAMIDS and MASTABAS (Tombs).
PYRAMIDS and SPHINX oldest extant examples ARCHITECTURE and SCULPTURE.
GREAT PYRAMID of CHEOPS
Many TEMPLES and TOMBS CUT INTO ROCK on river banks in Valley of the Kings.
Great weight of stone calls for SIMPLEST CONSTRUCTION SYSTEM – POST and LINTEL (uprights supporting horizontal).
Huge quarried stones floated down NILE during rainy season used for TOMBS and TEMPLES.
Houses of UPPER CLASSES, of BRICK, which have crumbled and disappeared.
WIFE of DECEASED
DECEASED
GODDESS of BIRTH
GOD of DESTINY
The GOD ANUBIS weighs the HEART of the deceased.
THOTH records the VERDICT
MONSTER devours BODY of UNJUST. SOUL doomed to roam Forever.
JUDGEMENT after DEATH, Heart is weighed against FEATHER (symbolizing RIGHT and TRUTH)
(Drawing from Book of the Dead)
Tombs often robbed of valuable objects. FALSE PASSAGES (see Great Pyramid above) and FALSE DOORS constructed to mislead robbers.
The goddess ISIS and her son HORUS. (small household shrine). Headdress SUNDISK and COW'S HORNS symbolic of DEITY.
FALSE DOOR at end of passage in TOMB
HYPOSTYLE HALL described as ·Forest of Columns·
Mammoth stone columns are placed close together to support massive roof lintels.
Most popular style for capitals (tops of column) LOTUS FLOWER and closed LOTUS BUD.
· CROSS of LIFE ·
many art forms SYMBOLIC
OSIRUS
God of the Underworld and the Dead
OBELISK
Pylon (wall) and TEMPLE GATEWAY
Stone pier
STYLIZED LOTUS BLOSSOMS
BORDER REPEAT

# ·The SCIENCE of ASTRONOMY·

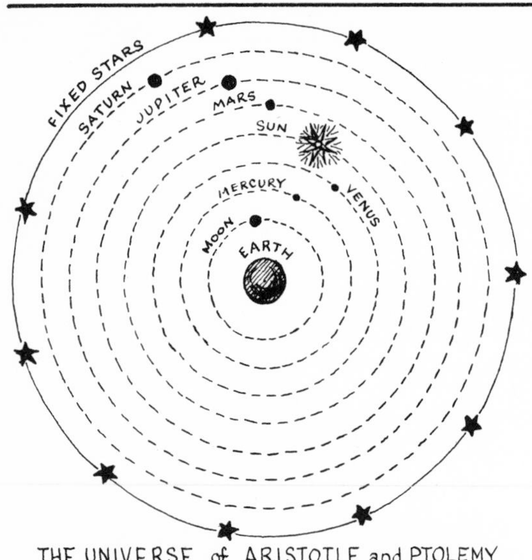
FIXED STARS
SATURN
JUPITER
MARS
SUN
MERCURY
VENUS
MOON
EARTH

THE UNIVERSE of ARISTOTLE and PTOLEMY and the EARLY and MEDIEVAL CHRISTIAN CHURCH.

The Mesopotamians and Egyptians were masters of mathematics and it is not surprising that their architecture was so well conceived. They also excelled in sculpture, bas-relief, painting and crafts. The Mesopotamians made the mathematical structure of the universe a science many centuries ago. Their recognition of the planets was accepted by the other ancients and passed on to us. As the originators of astronomy their culture was the basis for later discoveries in the field.

An awareness of the heavenly bodies has played a part in every religion. Therefore, there is religious as well as scientific significance to each new development.

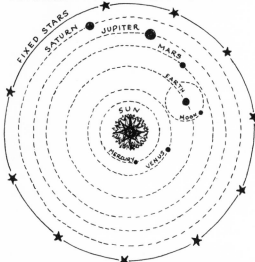

THE UNIVERSE according to COPERNICUS 16th c.

PYTHAGORAS (B. C. 6th c. Greek)
Declared earth was round.

PTOLEMY (B. C. 2nd c. Greco-Egyptian) Systematized universe with earth as center. Christian doctrine was built around this theory.

COPERNICUS (16th c. Polish)
Solar system—earth revolving around sun. Denied but finally accepted by Church authorities.

GALILEO (17th c. Italian)
Advanced Copernican theory and discovered rotation of the earth. (Imprisoned for heresy.)

KEPLER (17th c. German)
Ellipse of the planets.

NEWTON (18th c. English)
Gravitation of the earth.

EINSTEIN (20th c. U. S. A.)
Theory of relativity.
Infinite universe?

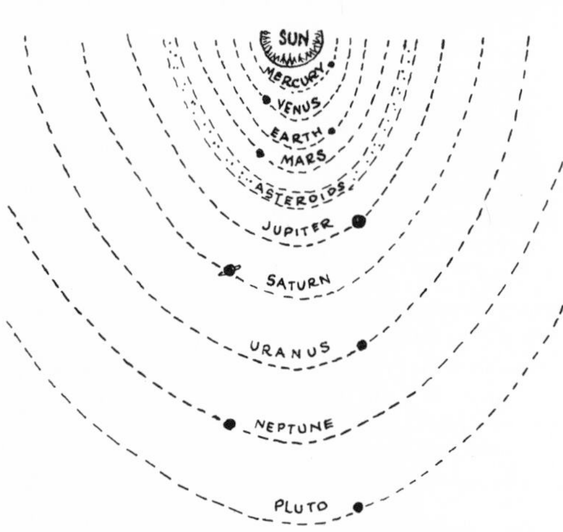
SUN
MERCURY
VENUS
EARTH
MARS
ASTEROIDS
JUPITER
SATURN
URANUS
NEPTUNE
PLUTO

What was once considered the UNIVERSE is now the SOLAR SYSTEM.

Additional planets have been discovered revolving around the sun, including some 1500 tiny planets or ASTEROIDS

It is now believed that the universe is composed of MANY SIMILAR SOLAR SYSTEMS, all of which are moving through what may be INFINITE SPACE.

This type of chair adapted during 19th c. CLASSIC REVIVAL

EGYPTIAN
Tombs equipped for LIFE - AFTER - DEATH yield complete PICTURE of DAILY LIFE.

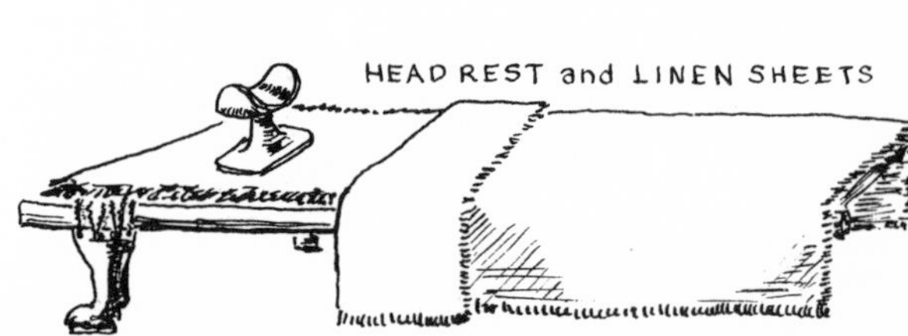

HEAD REST and LINEN SHEETS

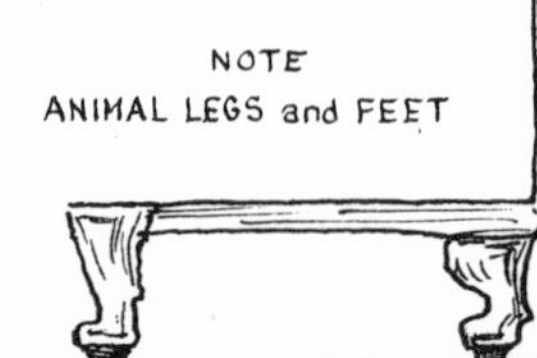

NOTE ANIMAL LEGS and FEET

# ·MESOPOTAMIAN : EGYPTIAN CHRONOLOGY·

## MESOPOTAMIA

8000 B. C.—Earliest relics now known

4000—Sumerians in Babylonia Semitics at Kish

3000—First contemporary records

2750—Sargon at Agade

2400—Sumerians at Ur. Aryan migrations

2225—First Babylonian Empire (Semitic)

2090—Code of Hammurabi

2075—1700—Kassites, Hittites, Mitanni conquests of upper Euphrates

1600—Assyrian Empire: Assur, capital

1400–1360—Diplomatic relations established with Egypt

1200—Migrations of Northern peoples

1045—Hebrew kingdom under Saul

945—Disruption of Jews
910—Rise of Assyria: Nineveh, capital

625—Chaldean Empire: Babylon, capital Nebuchadnezzar
610—Fall of Assyria to Persians

## EGYPT

4000—Pre-dynastic period (copper in use)

3200—First Dynasty combines Lower and Upper Kingdoms: Memphis, capital "Age of Pyramids"

Invasion of Asiatics

2500—Middle Kingdom: Thebes, capital "Age of Nobles" (bronze in use)

1800—Hyksos conquest "Shepherd Kings" (use of war chariot)

1600—New Kingdom "Age of Empire" Queen Hatshepsut

1450—Moses leads Israelites
1358—Tut-Ankh-Amen
1321—Rameses I
Conquests in Syria

1280—(iron in use)
1250—Rameses II
1100—End of New Kingdom
21st–26th dynasties
Weakness and discord

670—Egypt dependency of Assyria

540–486—Persian Empire of Cyrus and Cambyses, Darius and Xerxes

330—Persian Empire conquered by Alexander the Great
(Hellenistic Age of Greek Culture)
The Ptolemies
Cleopatra

30 B. C.—Ancient world overpowered by Roman Empire

PHARAOH wearing the CROWNS of both UPPER and LOWER EGYPT

GUDEA of LAGASH Sumerian PRIEST-KING of early Babylonian Empire.

CLEOPATRA Queen of Egypt had romantic attachments with both JULIUS CAESAR and MARK ANTONY

EGYPTIAN SPHINX
Symbol of royal power.
Head is portrait of ruling pharaoh

# ·MAPS of the ANCIENT EMPIRES·

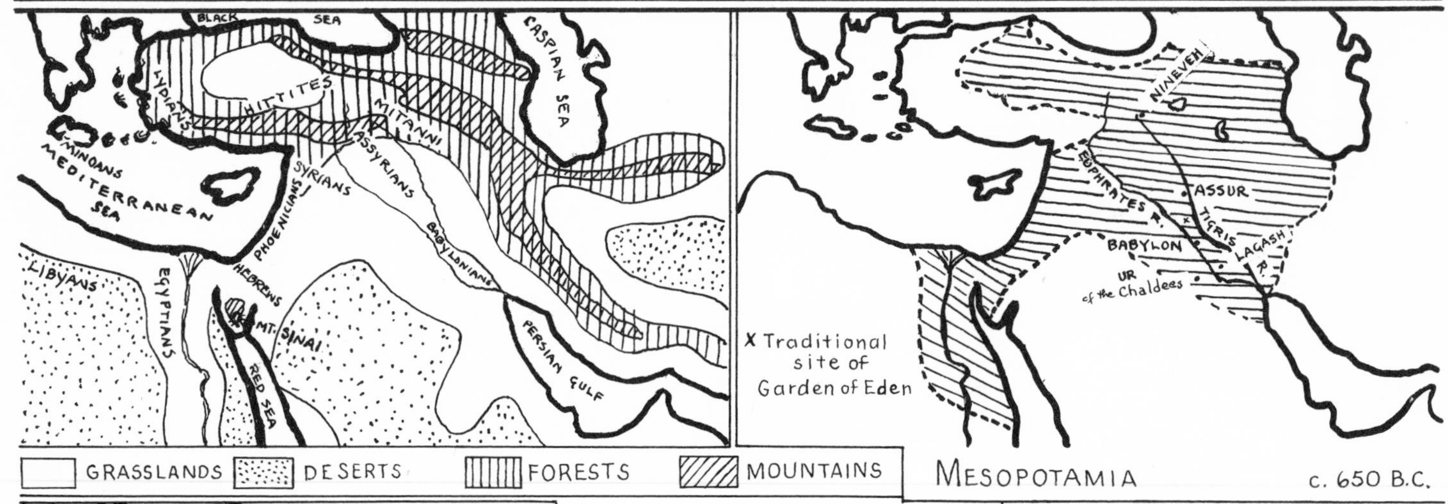
BLACK SEA
CASPIAN SEA
HITTITES
LYDIANS
MINOANS
MEDITERRANEAN SEA
MITANNI
ASSYRIANS
SYRIANS
PHOENICIANS
HEBREWS
BABYLONIANS
LIBYANS
EGYPTIANS
MT. SINAI
RED SEA
PERSIAN GULF
GRASSLANDS
DESERTS
FORESTS
MOUNTAINS
NINEVEH
EUPHRATES R.
ASSUR
TIGRIS R.
BABYLON
LAGASH R.
UR of the Chaldees
X Traditional site of Garden of Eden

MESOPOTAMIA c. 650 B.C.

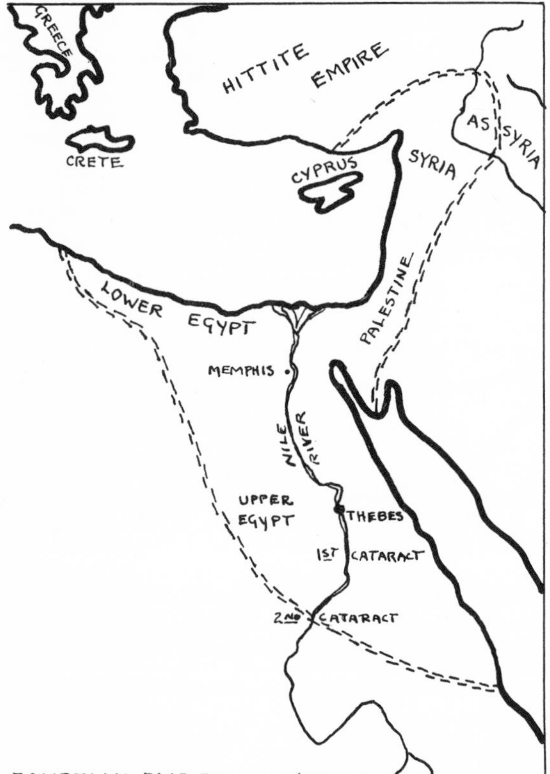
GREECE
HITTITE EMPIRE
CRETE
CYPRUS
SYRIA
ASSYRIA
LOWER EGYPT
PALESTINE
MEMPHIS
NILE RIVER
UPPER EGYPT
THEBES
1ST CATARACT
2ND CATARACT

EGYPTIAN EMPIRE c. 1400 B.C.

FERTILE CRESCENT swinging from the Red Sea to the Persian Gulf is CRADLE of WESTERN CIVILIZATION. Desert has now encroached and covered most of it.

In the flat lands MOUNDS called Tells or Tepes have yielded BURIED CITIES of ancient civilizations.

The Chaldean city of UR was unburied in the middle of the 19th Century. The Royal Graves with their RICH APPOINTMENTS tell a story of MASS BURIAL and HUMAN SACRIFICE.

BABYLONIANS, GREEKS and HEBREWS all have legends concerning A GREAT FLOOD

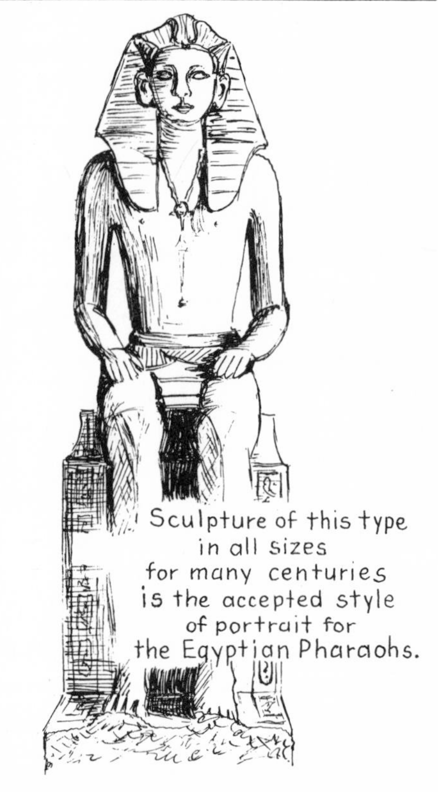

Sculpture of this type in all sizes for many centuries is the accepted style of portrait for the Egyptian Pharaohs.

KING DARIUS of PERSIA

Effects many reforms. Establishes postal system, unifies coinage.

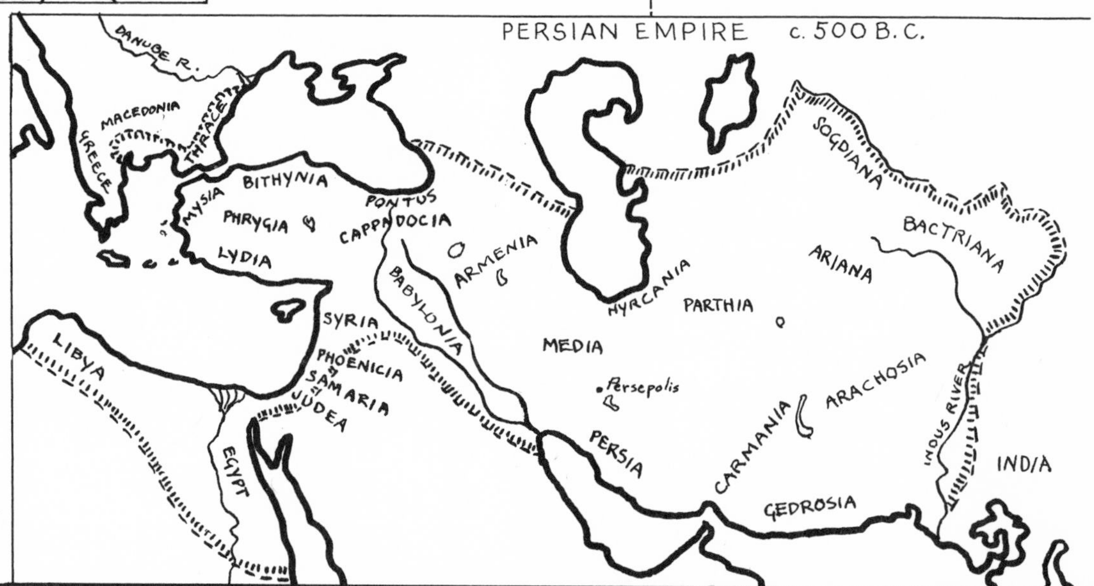
DANUBE R.
MACEDONIA
THRACE
GREECE
BITHYNIA
MYSIA
PHRYGIA
LYDIA
PONTUS
CAPPADOCIA
ARMENIA
BABYLONIA
SYRIA
PHOENICIA
SAMARIA
JUDEA
LIBYA
EGYPT
HYRCANIA
PARTHIA
MEDIA
Persepolis
PERSIA
CARMANIA
ARACHOSIA
ARIANA
BACTRIANA
SOGDIANA
INDUS RIVER
INDIA
GEDROSIA

PERSIAN EMPIRE c. 500 B.C.

# ·MAPS of the ANCIENT EMPIRES·

DORIANS from the mountainous north and IONIANS from Asia Minor and the islands (founders of Athens) conquered and absorbed the early ACHAEANS and AEGEANS and with the AEOLIANS evolved the the CLASSIC GREEK or ATTIC culture.

As colonists and traders the Greeks spread thier civilization to SICILY and ITALY and other Mediterranean shores.

The HELLENISTIC EMPIRE of Alexander carries Greek culture as far east as the Indus River in INDIA.

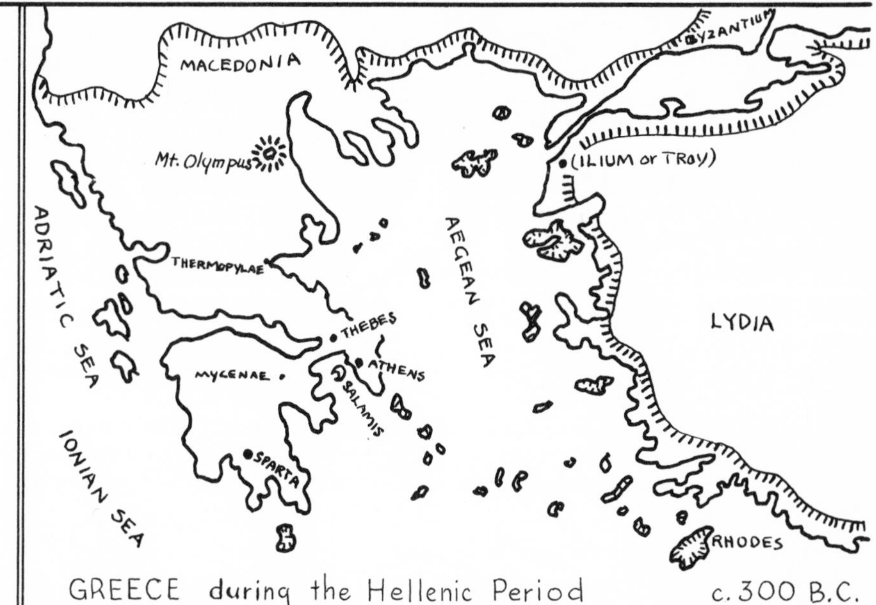
MACEDONIA
BYZANTIUM
Mt. Olympus
(ILIUM or TROY)
ADRIATIC SEA
THERMOPYLAE
AEGEAN SEA
THEBES
LYDIA
MYCENAE
ATHENS
SALAMIS
IONIAN SEA
SPARTA
RHODES

GREECE during the Hellenic Period c. 300 B.C.

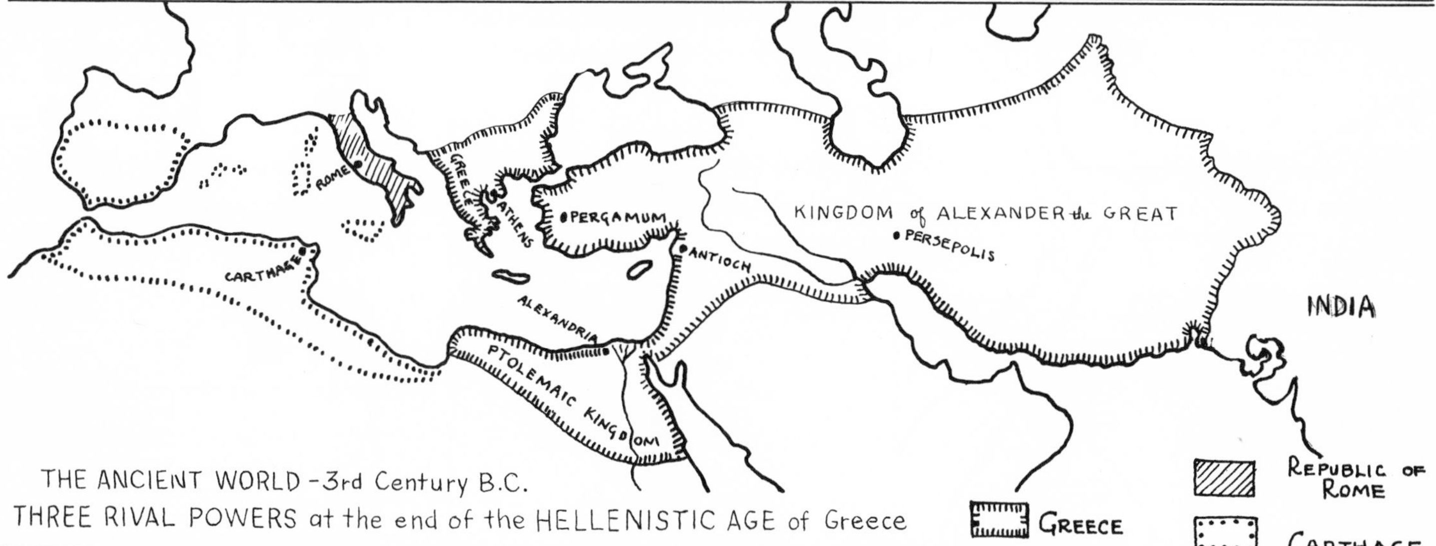
ROME
GREECE
ATHENS
PERGAMUM
KINGDOM of ALEXANDER the GREAT
PERSEPOLIS
CARTHAGE
ANTIOCH
INDIA
ALEXANDRIA
PTOLEMAIC KINGDOM
REPUBLIC OF ROME
GREECE
CARTHAGE

THE ANCIENT WORLD - 3rd Century B.C.
THREE RIVAL POWERS at the end of the HELLENISTIC AGE of Greece

ALEXANDER the GREAT, *Son of Philip of Macedonia,* is tutored by ARISTOTLE and educated by his father to CONQUER the WORLD.

After seizing the eastern Persian Empire and while planning to turn west he dies of fever at 32 years of age.

The young, belligerent and ambitious REPUBLIC of ROME attacks and conquers CARTHAGE and GREECE and proceeds to pick up pieces of the *Hellenistic Empire.*

Through skillful organization Rome becomes the STRONGEST and most ENDURING of the ancient empires.

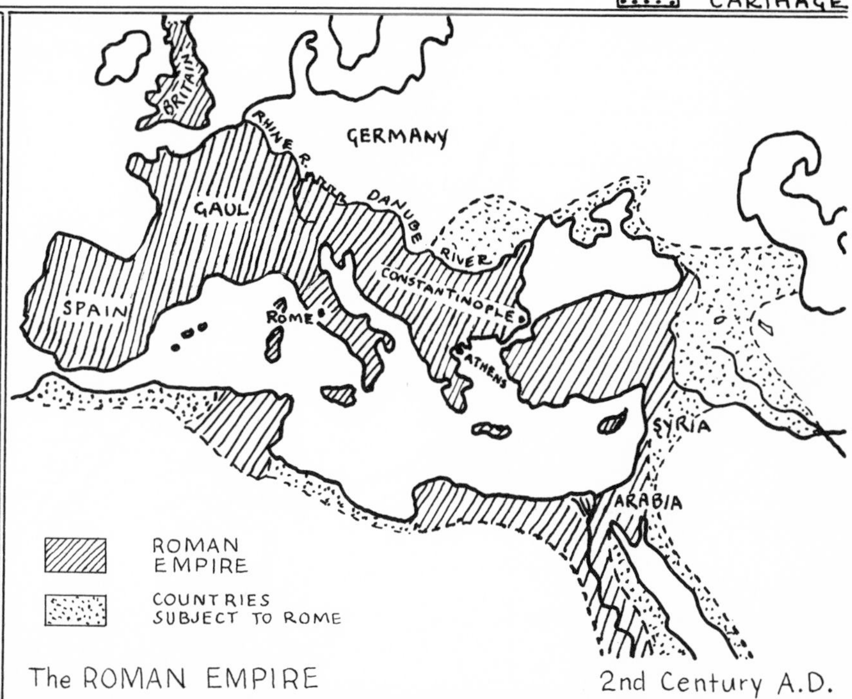
BRITAIN
RHINE R.
GERMANY
GAUL
DANUBE RIVER
SPAIN
CONSTANTINOPLE
ROME
ATHENS
SYRIA
ARABIA
ROMAN EMPIRE
COUNTRIES SUBJECT TO ROME

The ROMAN EMPIRE 2nd Century A.D.

# · GREEK CULTURE ·

*Every race creates an explanatory myth to account for the* CREATION *of the* UNIVERSE *and for the presence of* MAN.

*A simplification of the Greek version appears below.*

° ° °

The ROMANS adopt the GREEK RELIGION.

During the Renaissance GREEK and ROMAN MYTHOLOGY is indelibly stamped on the ARTS of the western world.

———— ° ————

In the beginning there was CHAOS, composed of void, mass and darkness.

Next came MOTHER EARTH, EREBUS the darkness beneath, and NIGHT.

The starry HEAVEN proceeded from EARTH.

Then came LOVE, which made all things male and FEMALE and provided an instinctive affinity one for the other.

From the union of HEAVEN (Uranus) and EARTH (Gaea) were born the

| TITANS | HECATONCHIRES | CYCLOPS |
|---|---|---|
| Personifications of the violent FORCES of nature PROGENITORS of the GODS. | Three 100-handed monsters who were banished by their father to TARTARUS, an abyss below. (waves of the sea) | Three one-eyed GIANTS representing Rolling Thunder, Lightning Flash, Thunder Bolt. |

GAEA persuaded her son, the Titan CRONUS, to kill the tyrannical URANUS.

For incalculable years CRONUS and his sister-queen RHEA ruled the world.

They were the parents of the GODS: PLUTO, NEPTUNE, JUPITER, VESTA, CERES, JUNO.

The Gods successfully battled the TITANS and the GIANTS and divided the world between themselves.

To PRO-ME'THEUS and EPI-ME'THEUS, sons of the Titan IAPETUS, was given the task of making MAN and ANIMALS

PROMETHEUS fashioned MAN in the IMAGE of the GODS

PANDORA the first woman was a gift of the Gods It was she who opened the FORBIDDEN BOX and released DISEASES of BODY and MIND. Only HOPE remained inside.

GODS and MORTALS consorted in the Age of Demigods and Heroes until MAN became so arrogant that the Gods arranged a FLOOD to destroy the race.

Ducalion, son of Prometheus, and Pyrra, daughter of Epimetheus were spared.

Their son HELLEN was the ancestor of the HELLENES or the GREEK people.

Founded on the civilizations of Crete and Mycenae, and strengthened by contact with Mesopotamia and Egypt, Hellenic (Greek) culture with its keen sense of aesthetics surpassed all other cultures of the ancient world in art, architecture, drama, literature, and history. It outstripped them in the sciences of philosophy, politics, mathematics, physics and medicine. The Romans adopted it; it was kept alive in Constantinople for a thousand years; its philosophy and literature enjoyed a new life in the Renaissance movement of the fifteenth century; its fashions in dress, furniture and architecture, a revival in the early nineteenth. Modern science is based on Greek inquiry, and the vocabulary of the scientific world is made up of Greek terms. No civilization of any age has given so much to the world.

A civilization made up of city-states, its great weakness was the lack of a central government. The two greatest cities, Athens and Sparta, were built on such different concepts that even compromise could not bring them together. Years of warfare between them weakened the entire country. Although successful in defeating the Persians, the combined states were not able to withstand Alexander the Great. As part of his empire, Greek culture affected and was affected by other countries. The result was a decadent Hellenistic civilization which lasted until the whole known world was knocked down before the ruthless armies of Rome.

*Uranus (Heaven) and Gaea (Earth) were the parents of the thirteen Titans. The children of the Titans were the gods, demigods and heroes.

The Titans Cronus and Rhea (the Latin *Saturn and Cybele) were rulers of Heaven and Earth and the parents of:

| GREEK | GODS AND GODDESSES | | ROMAN |
|---|---|---|---|
| Zeus | God of Heaven — Father of Gods and Men | | *Jupiter (Jove) |
| Poseidon | God of the Sea | | *Neptune |
| Hades | God of the Underworld | | *Pluto |
| Demeter | Goddess of the Earth (Agriculture) | | Ceres |
| Hestia | Goddess of the Home (Virgin goddess) | | Vesta |
| Hera | Goddess of Marriage (Sister-wife of Jove) | | Juno |
| Athena | Goddess of Wisdom and War (Sprang from brain of Jove. Eternal virgin) | | Minerva |
| Ares | God of War | Children of Jove and Juno | *Mars |
| Hephaestus | God of Fire | | Vulcan |
| Hebe | Cupbearer of the Gods | | Hebe |
| Phoebus | God of Music (Later, Sun) | Twin children of Jove and Latona | Apollo |
| Artemis | Goddess of Chase (Later, Moon. Perpetual maiden) | | Diana |
| Aphrodite | Goddess of Love and Beauty (Daughter of Jove and Dione) (According to one myth she rose from the sea.) | | *Venus |
| Eros | God of Love (Son of Venus and Vulcan) | | Cupid |
| Hermes | Messenger of the Gods (Son of Jove and Maia) | | *Mercury |
| Dionysus | God of Wine (Son of Jove and Semele) | | Bacchus |
| Persephone | Goddess of Spring (Daughter of Jove and Ceres. Wife of Pluto) | | Proserpina |
| Nike | Goddess of Victory | | Victoria |

*As planets they shine nightly in our sky.

# ·ROMAN CULTURE·

When Rome took over the world, she extracted and absorbed the best from each of the vanquished peoples. She enslaved Greek scholars, and forced Greek artists to produce for her. The delicacy and refinement of Greek taste was soon affected by the ostentation and extravagance of the Roman state, and the two merged into a Greco-Roman style which served the Empire for its duration.

For many years the world has speculated as to how great Rome might have grown along artistic lines had she developed a style of her own. As it is, except for her strong portrait sculptures she deserves little credit.

Where she used ingenuity and originality she came forth triumphant. The many new types of structures which she originated to serve her active civic and military life show her unsurpassed skill in engineering. These functional inventions include her roads, aqueducts, public baths, triumphal arches, commemorative columns, basilicas, theatres, amphi-theatres, circuses, forums and arenas, many of which still stand today.

Her strength is also to be admired in the management of her many conquered subjects. The government and laws by which she ruled are the forms which have been followed by every successful administrative power since her day. The Latin language lived through the destruction of her Empire to become the mother of the modern Romance tongues.

The GIANTS and Three Avenging FURIES leap from the blood of the slain URANUS.
NEMESIS, the daughter of NIGHT, is also an avenging deity.
She represents the RIGHTEOUS ANGER of the GODS

THE'MIS Goddess of JUSTICE, a Titaness, daughter of URANUS, sits beside JOVE on his throne.
Their children: the HOURS, the goddesses who regulate the seasons, and the Three FATES who spin the thread of HUMAN DESTINY.
A likeness of the blindfolded Roman goddess JUSTITIA appears in our modern courts of law.

An eloquent COMPARISON of GREEK and ROMAN ART
The GREEKS are aesthetic ORIGINATORS.
The ROMANS are unimaginative and often heavy-handed COPYISTS.
The Greek CARYATID from the porch of the ERECTHEION displays a casual grace which disassociates her from the heavy responsibility of supporting a stone roof.
The Roman "copy" appears so strong and so capable that were she to step aside there is no doubt but that the roof would fall.

The NINE MUSES daughters of JOVE and the Titaness Mne mus'y ne preside over song and prompt memory.
CAL-LI'-O-PE - epic poetry
EU-TER'-PE - lyric poetry
POL-Y-HYM'NI A - sacred poetry
ER'A-TO - love poetry
TERP-SICH'O-RE - Choral dance and Song
THA-LI'A - Comedy MEL-POM'E-NE - Tragedy
CLIO - History U-RA'NI-A - Astronomy

TERPSICHORE

The THREE GRACES, daughters of JOVE and Euryhome, who was the daughter of the Titan Oceanus, are goddesses who preside over all social pleasures and accomplishments (19th c. group)

# · GREEK ARCHITECTURE ·

To simple POST and LINTEL ARCHITECTURE the Greeks add a PITCHED ROOF.

Before Roman conquest VAULTING and DOMES were not used.

GREEK ARCHITECTURE noted for BALANCE and SYMMETRY.

TEMPLES of NATIVE MARBLES most important buildings.

INNATE AESTHETIC SENSE guides ARTISTIC OUTPUT and in ARCHITECTURE many refinements are developed to offset OPTICAL ILLUSIONS.

Nothing remains of DOMESTIC ARCHITECTURE which has an open plan copied by the Romans.

• • •

WOMEN have no position outside the home. Are not given • RIGHT of CITIZENSHIP •

appearance WITHOUT CORRECTIONS (A)

BUILDING which appears like this - - if built without CORRECTIONS would look like (A). CORRECTIONS at (B) make building appear as above.

actual CORRECTIONS (B)

COLUMNS

UNTAPERED POSTS appear wider at top

POSTS tapered from bottom too abrupt.

Corrected by ENTASIS (See below left)

DORIC TEMPLE

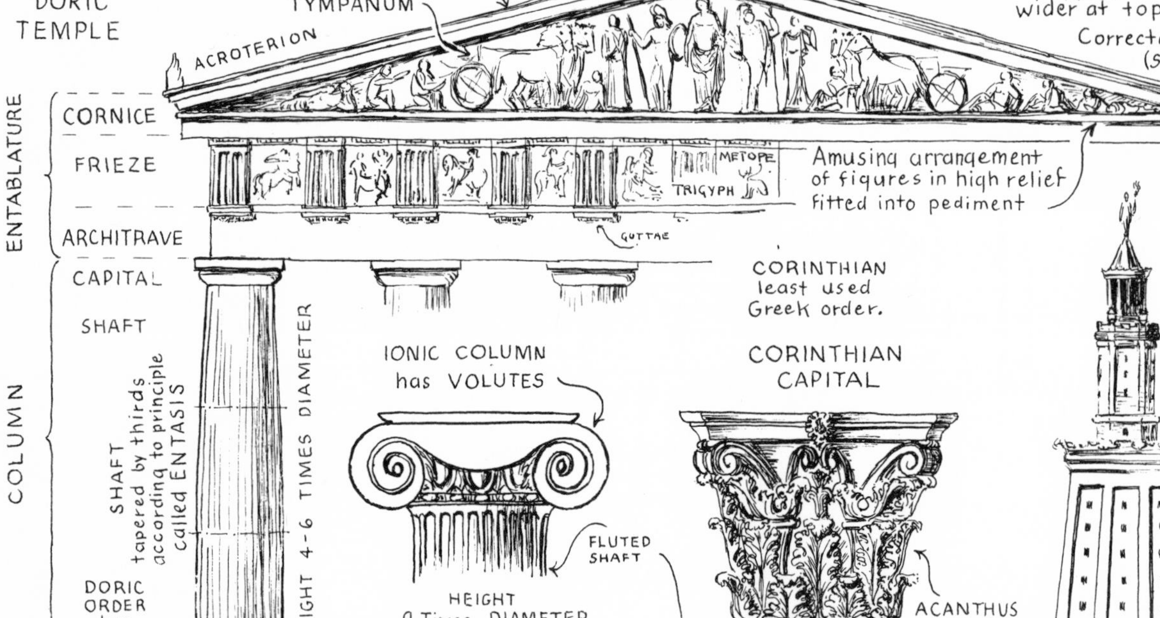

PEDIMENT
TYMPANUM
ACROTERION
ENTABLATURE
CORNICE
FRIEZE
ARCHITRAVE
METOPE
TRIGYPH
GUTTAE
COLUMN
CAPITAL
SHAFT
SHAFT tapered by thirds according to principle called ENTASIS
HEIGHT 4-6 TIMES DIAMETER
DORIC ORDER has no base.
STYLOBATE
IONIC COLUMN has VOLUTES
FLUTED SHAFT
HEIGHT 9 Times DIAMETER
CORINTHIAN least used Greek order.
CORINTHIAN CAPITAL
ACANTHUS LEAVES
HEIGHT 10 Times DIAMETER


Amusing arrangement of figures in high relief fitted into pediment

The Greeks evolved THREE CLASSIC ORDERS

DORIC
IONIC
and CORINTHIAN

An order consists of COLUMN and ENTABLATURE and is easily identified by the CAPITAL of the COLUMN

Sculptured base unusual feature

Possible reconstruction of the LIGHTHOUSE at ALEXANDRIA 30 stories high. Built c.300 B.C. Destroyed in 1326 A.D. Influenced by ASIATIC DESIGNS, it served as **model** for CHRISTIAN CHURCH SPIRES.

ALEXANDRIA outstanding city of HELLENISTIC CIVILIZATION

• The SEVEN WONDERS of the ANCIENT WORLD • HANGING GARDENS of BABYLON • TEMPLES of ARTEMIS at EPHESUS • COLOSUS of RHODES (100 ft. Statue of Apollo) • PYRAMIDS of EGYPT • PHIDIAS' STATUE of ZEUS • LIGHTHOUSE at ALEXANDRIA • TOMB of MAUSOLUS at HELICARNASSUS •

# · ROMAN ARCHITECTURE ·

ROMAN VARIATIONS
of the
CLASSIC ORDERS.
HIGHER COLUMNS,
SHAFTS
FLUTED and UNFLUTED.

CLEAR CONTOURS
of MOLDINGS
often buried
beneath
ELABORATE ORNAMENT

(see page 46 for
moldings and ornament.)

TUSCAN
CAPITAL

Derived from
DORIC
which they also use.

IONIC
CAPITAL
lacks
GRACEFUL SWAG
between volutes

COMPOSITE
CAPITAL

ROMAN
DESIGN

The CORINTHIAN and COMPOSITE ORDERS Roman favorites

*An essential difference between Greek and Roman motivation:*
*The Greeks seek aesthetic perfection,*
*the Romans, to impress the people they conquer.*

As the ROMANS were imitators
and copied
GREEK ARCHITECTURE
it is sometimes difficult
to distinguish
the GREEK from the ROMAN.
However,
the ROMAN Empire,
which encompasses
many different
TERRAINS,
uses a
VARIETY of BUILDING MATERIAL
including
· CONCRETE ·

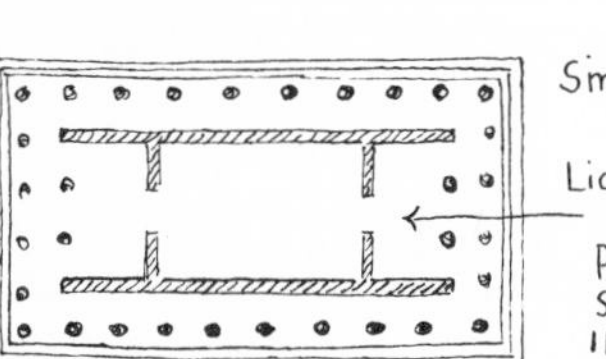

Plan
Small Greek Temple
NO WINDOWS
Lighted through doorway

Placed in
SACRED
INCLOSURE

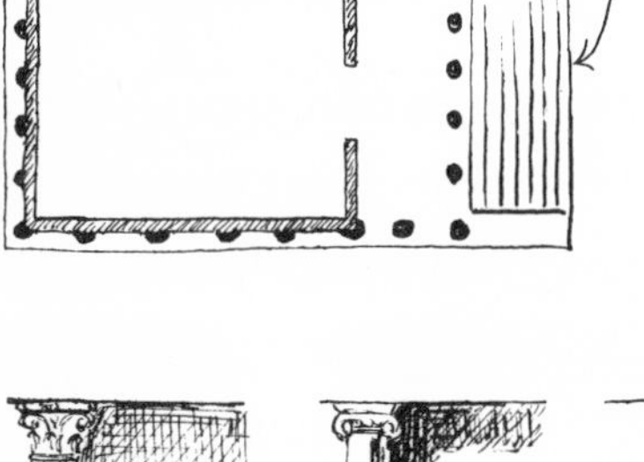

*engaged columns*

ROMAN TEMPLE
*only one approach*

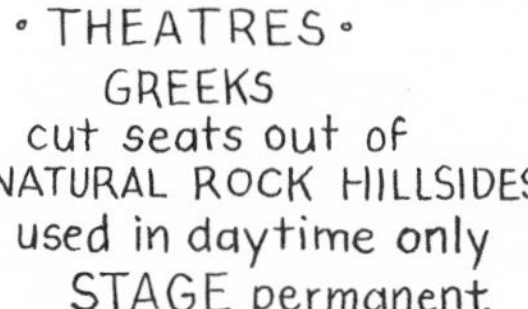

· PLAN ·

Restoration of Roman Temple with PERIBOLUS
*In addition to the POST and LINTEL*
*the ARCH, VAULT and DOME were used.*

COMMEMORATIVE
COLUMN

· COLUMN ·
· PILASTER ·
· ENGAGED COLUMN ·

FLOOR PLANS and ELEVATIONS

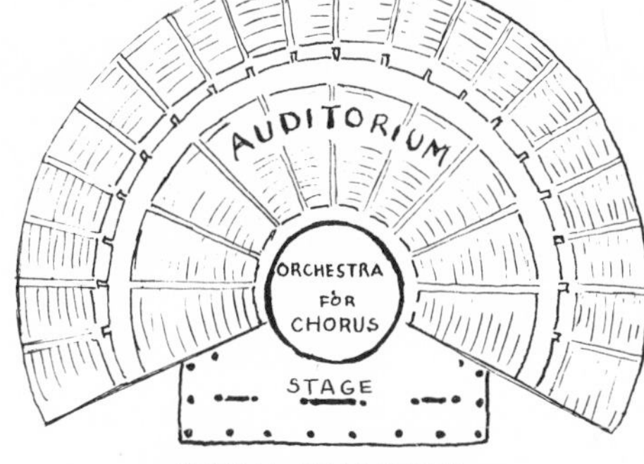

AUDITORIUM
ORCHESTRA
FOR
CHORUS
STAGE

GREEK THEATRE
and
Greek STADION
are precursors of
Roman amphitheatre and circus.

· THEATRES ·
GREEKS
cut seats out of
NATURAL ROCK HILLSIDES.
used in daytime only
STAGE permanent.

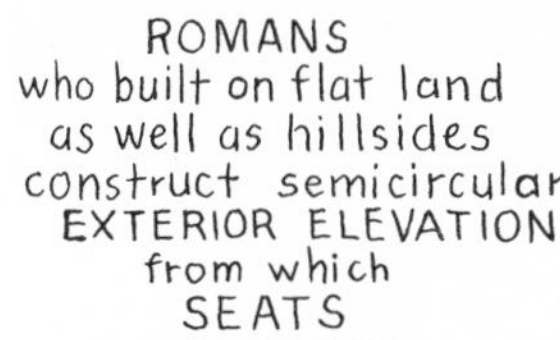

ROMANS
who built on flat land
as well as hillsides
construct semicircular
EXTERIOR ELEVATION
from which
SEATS
are swung
ORCHESTRA
reserved for dignitaries
STAGE
larger and enclosed

Vaulted TRIUMPHAL ARCH

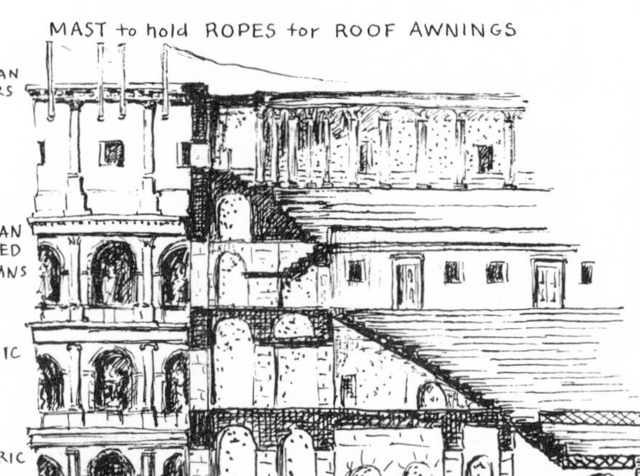

MAST to hold ROPES for ROOF AWNINGS
CORINTHIAN
PILASTERS
CORINTHIAN
ENGAGED
COLUMNS
IONIC
DORIC

EXTERIOR CROSS SECTION INTERIOR

Two types of coffers (boxes)
used for CEILING DECORATION

The COLOSSEUM at ROME is used
for entertainment and is
flooded to stage mock sea battles.

# · GREEK and ROMAN CHRONOLOGY ·

PERICLES of GREECE'S GOLDEN AGE

ALEXANDER THE GREAT founder of GREECE'S HELLENISTIC AGE

| GREECE | ROME |
|---|---|
| PRE-HELLENIC AGE 1000–500 B.C. | |
| c. 1000 Homeric legends<br>Lycurgus at Sparta<br>First Olympiad | c. 800 B.C. Carthage founded |
| 600–510 Age of Tyrants | 753 Rome founded (legend) |
| | Twelve Kings |
| HELLENIC AGE 550–360 | 510 ROMAN REPUBLIC |
| Persian Wars<br>Golden Age of Pericles | Twelve Tablets of Roman Law |
| Peloponnesian Wars<br>Rivalry of City-States<br>461–404 Athenian Empire<br>404–370 Spartan Supremacy<br>371–360 Theban Supremacy | Intermittent Wars with Etruscans, Samnites, etc. |
| HELLENISTIC AGE 360–280 | 275 Roman Supremacy in Italy |
| Philip of Macedonia<br>Alexander the Great<br>330 Conquest of Persian Empire | Punic Wars<br>Hannibal—Scipio |
| c. 300 Alexandrian library founded<br>(burned by Moslems 7th c.) | Corinth and Carthage destroyed 146 |
| 124 ROMAN CONQUEST of Greek Empire | 133–127 Revolt and Civil War<br>Overthrow of Republic |
| Greek artists produce for Rome | 60 First Triumvirate: Caesar, Pompey, Crassus |
| | Gallic Wars |
| Results in Greco-Roman School of Art | Conquest of Britain |
| | Mediterranean conquests |
| | 30 ROMAN EMPIRE |
| | Octavius Augustus Caesar |

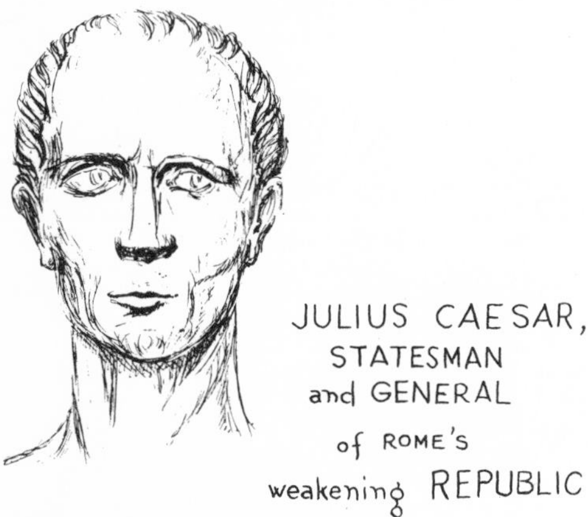

JULIUS CAESAR, STATESMAN and GENERAL of ROME'S weakening REPUBLIC

BIRTH OF CHRIST

64 A.D. Nero—Burning of Rome

98–117 Trajan—Greatest extent of Empire

211–330 Decline of Empire

365 Division of Empire—Dual empire
West—Rome East—Constantinople

Barbarian invasions in West

476 Fall of Western Rome to Odoacer

OCTAVIUS CAESAR ROME'S first EMPEROR

# · GREEK and ROMAN CULTURE ·

HERODOTUS
SOPHOCLES
EURIPIDES
AESCHYLUS
ARISTOPHANES
PLATO
EUCLID
SOCRATES

## GREEK SCULPTURE

| Pre-Hellenic Age (Archaic) | Hellenic Age (Classic) | Hellenistic Age (Decadent) |
|---|---|---|
| Primitives | Phidias Myron Polycletus | Scopas Lysippus Praxiteles |

## ARCHITECTURE

| Hellenic | Greco-Roman | Roman |
|---|---|---|
| Ictinus | Apollodorus | Vitruvius |

## PAINTING

The Greeks mastered perspective in the fourth century B. C. There are no extant examples, but existing Roman works are probably very close in style. The painting on Greek vases exemplifies charming and graceful stylization.

## MUSIC

The art of the Muses—allied to poetry, drama and athletic games. Singing was accompanied by flute and lyre. Imperial Rome introduced the hydraulic organ.

## POETRY and DRAMA

| Pre-Hellenic | Hellenic | Hellenistic | Roman (B. C.) |
|---|---|---|---|
| Homer<br>Sappho<br>Aesop | Pindar Sophocles<br>Euripides Aeschylus<br>Aristophanes | Meander | Terence Virgil<br>Lucretius Horace<br>Ovid |

## HISTORY

| Hellenic | Roman (B. C.) | Roman (A. D.) |
|---|---|---|
| Herodotus<br>Thucydides<br>Hippocrates<br>Xenophon | Cato, the Censor<br>Cicero Caesar<br>Sallust | Livy<br>Plutarch Tacitus |

## PHILOSOPHY

| Hellenic | Hellenistic | Roman |
|---|---|---|
| The Sophists<br>Socrates<br>Plato<br>Aristotle | Zeno (stoic)<br>Epicurus<br>Diogenes (cynic) | Lucretius<br>Seneca<br>Epictetus (Gk. stoic)<br>Marcus Aurelius<br>Boethius |

## THE SCIENCES

| | | |
|---|---|---|
| Thales of Miletus | Pythagoras | Archimedes |
| Euclid | Eratosthenes | Galen |

# ·ANCIENT SCULPTURE·

EGYPTIAN c. 1500 B.C.

The fashioning of nonfunctional objects for aesthetic enjoyment has long been one answer to man's urge to create. For centuries men modeled clay, or carved wood, stone, marble, bone and ivory, or hammered metal, in order to make pleasing forms. These methods produced only one of a kind, but the process of mold-casting for duplication was apparently an early discovery.

It remained for the Greeks and the Romans to refine the art of casting metal. Their bronze statues are unrivaled in delicacy of detail and it is believed that they used the "lost-wax" process later employed during the Renaissance.

SCULPTURE in the ROUND is more NATURALISTIC than BAS-RELIEF and PAINTING

•

QUEEN NEFERTITI

A carefully modeled clay core is covered with an even skin of wax. This is encased in closely fitting soft clay. The mass is spiked together and baked. The layer of wax between the two clay molds runs off, leaving a space into which the molten bronze is poured. The outer spoil-mold is chiseled away and the core is taken out in pieces through a convenient aperture (perhaps in the sole of a foot). The bronze figure is then polished.

The bronze works of classic times for the most part have disintegrated. The sculptures which remain are those executed in marble. In them we can appreciate the genius of the sculptor and recognize the emphasis which was placed upon the physical beauty of both sexes. The Greek preference for idealized types rather than individual characterizations gives their figures superhuman strength and dignity as well as beauty.

EGYPTIAN ART is dominated by HELLENISTIC GREECE and finally swallowed by the overwhelming ROMAN EMPIRE.

① ARCHAIC GREEK

"APOLLO" c. 600 B.C.

PREHISTORIC GREEK c. 8th c. B.C.

• • • •

The THREE PHASES of GREEK SCULPTURE

① ARCHAIC - The primitive attempt at NATURALISM.

② CLASSIC - The impersonal portrayal of PHYSICAL BEAUTY
Portraits are uncommon.

③ HELLENISTIC - Dramatic, unpleasant and emotional subjects fascinate the artist and challenge his abilities.

The renowned Greek profile.

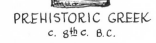

② CLASSIC STYLE
MYRON'S DISCOBOLUS - There are several Roman copies of this work.

③ HELLENISTIC PERIOD
The story of LAOCOÖN and his two sons is a favorite of the times. Below - one son is about to escape.

# · ANCIENT SCULPTURE ·

From lowly primitive conceptions to the perfection of naturalistic expression, followed by preoccupation with physical and emotional exaggerations, Greek sculpture exhibits unmistakable evidence of the inescapable undulating path of human endeavor.

Greek artists were motivated by a profound respect for mankind. Medieval sculptors, inspired by spiritual love and fear, showed tremendous originality in their work. The sculpture of the two ages reveals the different philosophies with exceptional clarity.

Renaissance enthusiasm over the rediscovery of classic beauty turned goldsmiths, silversmiths, architects and painters into proficient masters of the art of modeling and stonecutting.

But lack of new ideals soon turned creative sculpture into the impersonal reproduction of classic forms. Since the eighteenth century the actual cutting of the stone too often has been left to assistants and mechanical methods. The resulting pieces have had a dull lifelessness and little meaning.

Experimentation with abstract form has done much to shake the sculptor from his apathy. The decoration of churches in a twentieth-century style has given him an opportunity to retell the Christian story with vigor and uncompromising sincerity.

A new chemical poured-stone simplifies the problems of production, and lowers the cost to about a tenth of what it was before the Second World War. This puts excellent reproductions of primitive, traditional and modern work on the consumers' market, and sculpture is being used most effectively with unpretentious domestic architecture both indoors and out.

Head of the 45 foot CULT STATUE of the goddess • *PALLAS ATHENE* •
IVORY - face and arms.
GOLD - headdress and garments.

° ° °

*The primitive Greeks believe their deities really exist.*
*But later, philosophers use them to represent* PHYSICAL and MORAL TRUTHS.

· *VENUS* ·
Pagan goddess of LOVE and BEAUTY.

· *VIRGIN of the ANNUNCIATION* ·
*(polychrome wood carving)*

*Medieval Christianity seeks SPIRITUALITY through personifications of* INNOCENCE and PURITY.

It is difficult to realize that most ANCIENT STATUARY was REALISTICALLY TINTED.

° ° °

This BRONZE equestrian statue of the pagan philosopher-emperor *MARCUS AURELIUS* inspired many heroic statues during the Renaissance.

The THREE STAGES of GREEK SCULPTURE

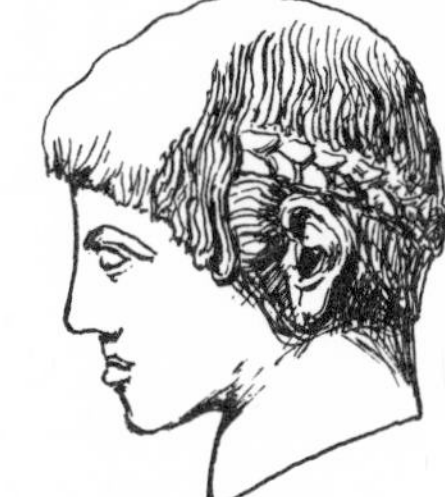

① *ARCHAIC*

② *CLASSIC*

③ *HELLENISTIC*

Portrait of the *triumvir POMPEY.*

The ROMAN sculptor produces *CANDID IMPRESSIONS* of outstanding citizens.

# · CERAMICS ·

Almost all PREHISTORIC CIVILIZATIONS have developed and used well-shaped DECORATED POTTERY utensils (unglazed)

Mudpies left by prehistoric children to dry in the sun may have been the beginning of both brick and pottery. Primitive men all over the world have taught themselves to fashion useful and decorative objects from the clay at their feet. It is an art which has no geographical boundaries, and it is almost as old as man himself.

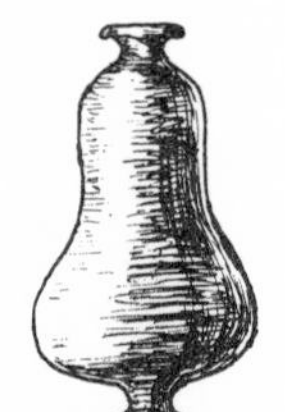

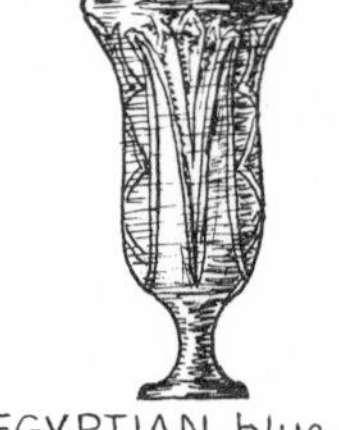

ASSYRIAN Pottery · EGYPTIAN blue glaze

The potter's wheel for shaping bowls and vases, and the kiln for drying them at high temperatures, are inventions of very early days. Glazing for added color, finish and durability is not a modern refinement —it seems to date back at least to 2000 B. C. Before a Greek vogue for metal vessels about two centuries before Christ, all household needs were served by pottery or glass receptacles. Actually metal cooking utensils are comparatively new and they have by no means replaced pottery in many remote areas.

Kylix

RED glossy ground, BLACK figures, also POLYCHROME decoration.

GREEK VASES vary in shape and size according to use.

Six-gallon WINE JAR

The most important feature of a ceramic object is its form or shape —the most intriguing is its decoration. That may be excised or incised, outlined in slip (liquid clay), pigment or crayon, or supplied by a colored glaze. Glazes are made from minerals and mineral oxides and are not easy to control. Most pieces are given an initial firing, then painted and fired again with a transparent glaze. It is possible to decorate over a final glaze, but as such decoration tends to wear off the practice is usually restricted to gilding, which otherwise vanishes in the heat.

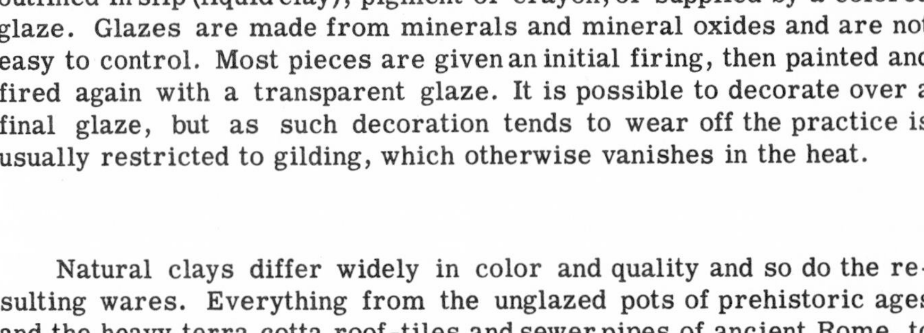

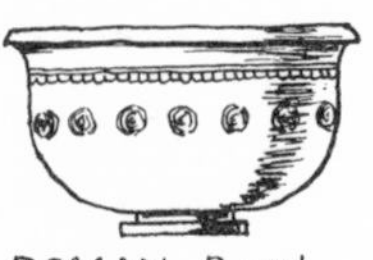

ROMAN Bowl

Little is known about European ceramics between the fall of Rome and the CRUSADES 4th to 13th centuries.

Natural clays differ widely in color and quality and so do the resulting wares. Everything from the unglazed pots of prehistoric ages and the heavy terra cotta roof-tiles and sewer pipes of ancient Rome, to the delicate white translucent porcelains of the Orient, result from the same fundamental process of baking moist clay substances.

PERSIAN Ware -13th c. · 15th c. FAÏENCE

By the end of the fifteenth century Europe was endeavoring to reproduce Chinese porcelains. The first successful venture took place at Meissen, Germany, about 1710. Not long after that factories in other countries found satisfactory formulae.

Ceramic sculpture has always been entertaining and often beautiful. Piece-molds make possible its reproduction at relatively low cost.

The machine age has facilitated the production of ceramics in large quantity, but has not amended the basic process in any way. The art makes an interesting and not too expensive hobby for the patient amateur.

CHINESE Sang de Boeuf PORCELAIN

MEISSEN TUREEN

During the eighteenth century EUROPEAN PORCELAIN reflects the elaborate fashions set by the COURT OF FRANCE.

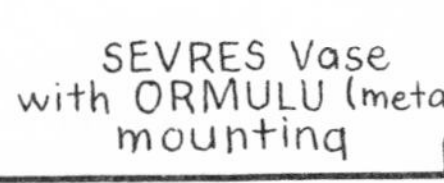

DRESDEN figure

SEVRES Vase with ORMULU (metal) mounting

one of a pair of VICTORIAN VASES

INFORMAL DESIGNS

Twentieth-century SHAPES are simple. TEXTURES and GLAZES of unusual interest.

# ·GLASS·

The origin of glass-making is unknown. Glass vessels have been excavated on Mesopotamian and Egyptian sites which date back to the days of protohistory. But these specimens though crudely shaped show an advancement of technique which would indicate that the process was even then a familiar one. As the necessary ingredients are common in most parts of the world, its invention could have taken place almost anywhere.

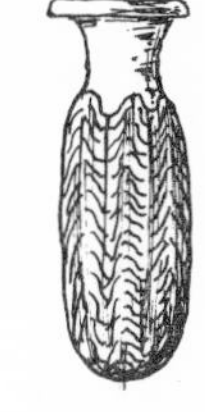

BLOWN GLASS BOTTLES
5th - 2nd century B.C.

All the ancient civilizations used blown glass for table service and toilet articles. Chunks of colored glass were imbedded in mosaic decorations, and sometimes set in jewelry. Small pieces of sheet glass were fixed within frames of alabaster, bronze or wood to form ornamental windows.

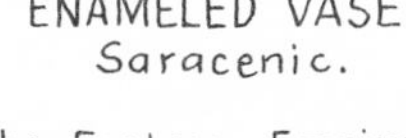
ENAMELED VASE →
Saracenic.

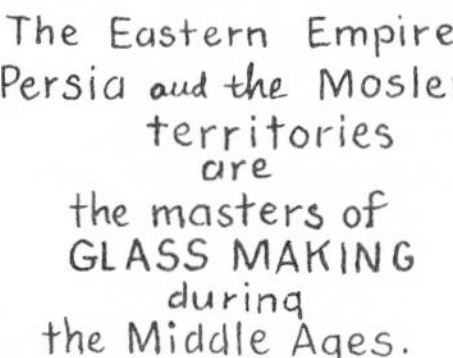

The Eastern Empire Persia and the Moslem territories are the masters of GLASS MAKING during the Middle Ages.

Glass is made by melting sand (silica) with a selected alkali such as sodium. Imperfections in the raw materials will cloud or tint the finished product. Colors can be varied and controlled by the addition of different metallic oxides. This was common practice during the Middle Ages. Colorless glass was sometimes achieved but it remained for the Renaissance in Germany to perfect the crystal clarity admired for formal tableware and necessary to the manufacture of lenses.

The REPUBLIC of VENICE was the first Western manufacturer of glass.
VENETIAN GLASS is colorful, fanciful but sometimes POORLY DESIGNED and IMPRACTICAL because of delicate, projecting parts.

The transparent, translucent and opaque qualities of the material, and its fluidity at high temperatures, enable it to be handled a number of ways, thus creating a variety of effects which serve many different purposes. It can be blown into hollow objects. It can be poured and pressed into a mold to carry out either hollow or solid designs. Rolling produces the sheet (plate) glass used for windows and since the late seventeenth century for mirrors. Pulling or drawing will produce ordinary window panes or the threads which are used in today's fireproof fabrics. Powdered glass is reheated to form enamel. Transparent glass of different thicknesses is joined, molded or ground to serve optical needs.

Great variety in post-Renaissance European glassware.
MOTTLED
ETCHED
CUT CRYSTAL

AMERICAN PRESSED (Molded) GLASS.

The production of glass has been implemented by mechanical methods. Regularity has been assured, output has been increased, and new treatment has extended its usability.

Florid shapes, jewel-toned Bohemian glass, iridescent TIFFANY glass and sparkling CUT GLASS characterize the 19th century.

Glass has always been popular for architectural decoration and in the twentieth century it has been given structural importance in large plate-glass windows and supporting walls. Fiber-glass products have many uses—a major one is for roofing. Clearly the use of glass is of great contemporary importance.

SWEDEN holds the leadership in modern designs. They vary from DELICATE to HEAVY. ENGRAVED glass their SPECIALTY.

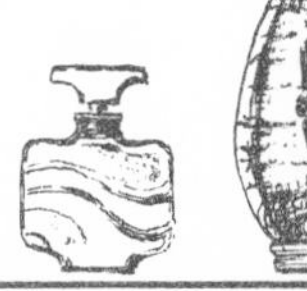

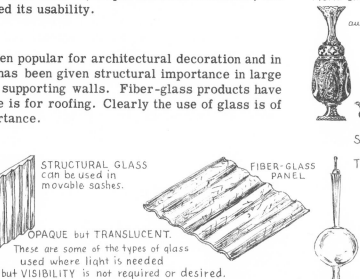

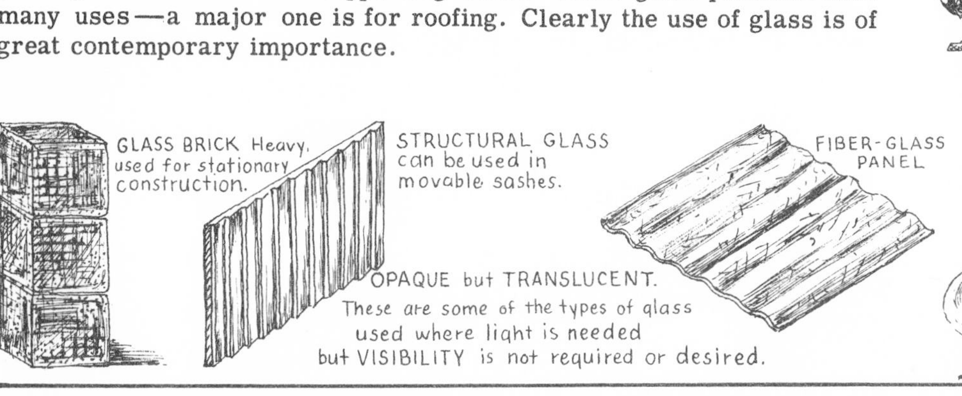
GLASS BRICK Heavy, used for stationary construction.
STRUCTURAL GLASS can be used in movable sashes.
FIBER-GLASS PANEL
OPAQUE but TRANSLUCENT.
These are some of the types of glass used where light is needed but VISIBILITY is not required or desired.

# · ORNAMENT and MOLDINGS ·

A MOLDING is an ornament shaped to produce interesting variations of LIGHT and SHADE. It is usually composed of a SERIES or COMBINATION of the following MEMBERS and is to be found on buildings, furniture and objects.

The ORNAMENT sketched below was originated by the ancients and has since been used in VARIATION by CRAFTSMEN of ALL PERIODS. The MOLDINGS are chiefly of Greek origin and have been adapted by DESIGNERS through the AGES.

The ORNAMENTAL DESIGNS are to be found in MOSAIC, CARVING and PAINTING. In variation they have been used on WALLS, FLOORS and CEILINGS; FURNITURE, SILVER, CHINA, FABRIC and JEWELRY.

I · OVOLO ·

This is half an egg in shape. To get full effect of contour it should be used ABOVE EYE LEVEL

A supporting member.

II · CYMA RECTA ·

The S curve. one of the most USEFUL moldings in architecture.

A crowning member.

III · CYMA REVERSA ·

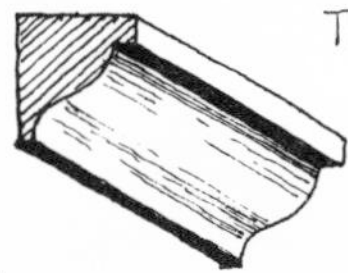

The reverse curve. Makes a bold and decided ACCENT

A supporting member.

IV · TORUS ·

A half-circle in form.

Intended to BIND and STRENGTHEN other members.

V · BEAD or ASTRAGAL ·

A small Torus.

A binding member.

VI · FILLET ·

RAISED.
SUNKEN.


A plain surface used to separate.

VII · SCOTIA ·

In general used BELOW EYE LEVEL.

Used to SEPARATE, CONTRAST and STRENGTHEN.

VIII · CAVETTO ·

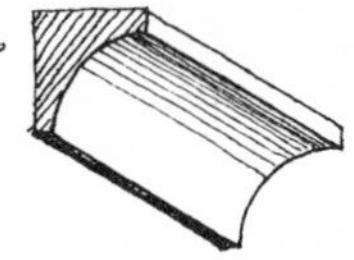

chiefly a CROWNING member like the cyma recta.

IX · CORONA ·

A BAND or FACIA forming a PROTECTIVE PROJECTION. Also ACCENTS and SEPARATES

NOTE: Square members are seldom DECORATED.

X · THUMB · (not classic)

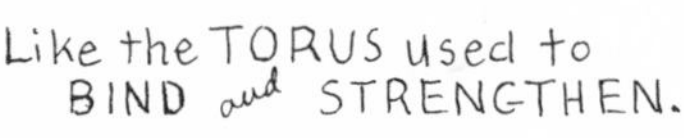

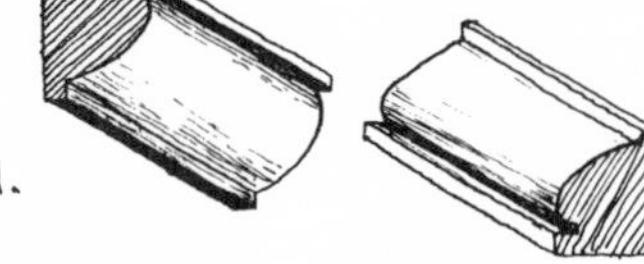

Like the TORUS used to BIND and STRENGTHEN.

XI · BEAK · (not classic). →

A crowning member.

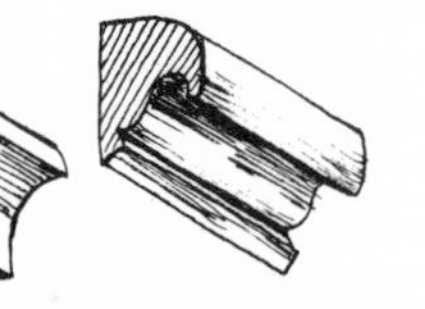

XII BIRD'S BEAK (Greek)

For accent and separation Casts a deep shadow.

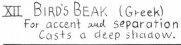

An assembled · CORNICE with MODILLIONS ·

MODILLION — SOFFIT — FACIA

FACIA – A broad fillet, band or face.

SOFFIT – Underside of square molding.

CORBEL – A projecting stone or timber which supports a superincumbent weight

CONSOLE or MODILLION – An ornamental Corbel more for effect than function.

WATCH FOR THESE DESIGNS

A · SCROLL or WAVE ·

B · TWIST or GUILLOCHE ·

C · FRET or GREEK KEY ·

D · ANTHEMION or ANTEFIX ·

E · LEAF BORDER ·

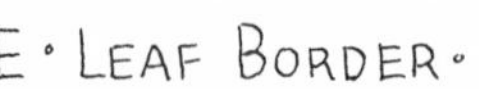

F · EGG and DART · and TONGUE

G · LEAF and TONGUE ·

H · RINCEAU or Meander ·

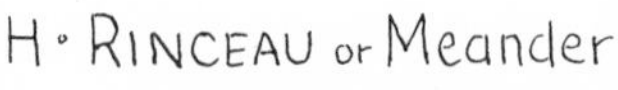

I · BAY LEAF GARLAND ·

J · ACANTHUS LEAF ·

KEY.

L · PATERA

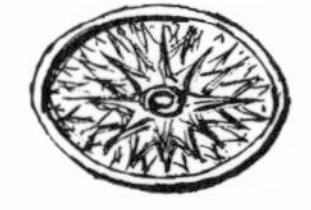

M · BUCRAMIUM

N · IMBRICATIONS

K · SWAG

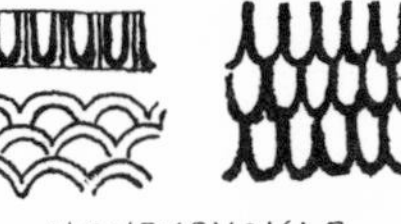

· BEAD or REEL ·

· HONEYSUCKLE or BUD ·

· LOTUS, PAPYRUS, PALMETTO (Egyptian) ·

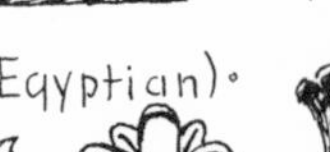

· FLUTING ·

used on COLUMNS, PILASTERS, FACIAE, APRONS on furniture.

· REEDING ·

Vertical reeds used on architecture and furniture.

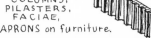

# · ANCIENT PAINTING ·

Drawings and paintings have given us valuable information about the lives and customs of our prehistoric ancestors and their immediate descendants. Whether on weapons, pottery, papyrus, walls, or floors, and regardless of aesthetic worth, paintings have made major contributions to our reconstruction of the past.

Painting began as the addition of color to outline and form. The most ancient sculptures were tinted. The paints were powders or liquids of mineral (stone), vegetable and animal origin. To these natural pigments, modern chemistry has added many others and the artist of today is benefited by a dazzling range of color.

The major paintings of ancient times were the wall decorations. Enameled tiles and mosaics were often used, and in Egypt encaustic (wax) designs were added to smoothly finished walls. But the most ambitious murals were those in the fresco medium. The Romans credit the Greeks with the discovery of this technique, but there remain only Roman examples for us to admire. The Roman architect Vitruvius gives an exact account of the procedure.

Over rough-plaster walls a carefully prepared layer of smooth lime-plaster is added. The design is then worked onto the fresh (a fresco) plaster with pigment dissolved in distilled water. Chemical reaction fuses paint and plaster into a hard, lustered surface. This protects the finished composition from fading and deterioration.

Fresco painting is of necessity a rapid process, as it must be completed before the plaster base dries. This forces a simple, uncomplicated application which is most pleasing in its directness.

The art was revived with great success during the Italian Renaissance. The disadvantage of working on wet unfinished walls was largely overcome in the nineteenth century by expedient changes in the technique. While inferior in finish and permanence, the convenience of the variations on dry plaster has led to their adoption and today the original method is not often practiced.

ROMAN WALL PANELS – *painted to look like sculpture (grisaille).*
*Romans learn to draw in perspective from the Greeks.*
Extant Roman paintings probably copies of Greek style.

Colorful
EGYPTIAN WALL PAINTING
scarab-headed
SOLAR GOD

PAINTING follows same formula as BAS-RELIEF

many SYMBOLIC forms used.

PAINTING was not the MAJOR ART of any of the ancient cultures.

Portrait in GRECO-EGYPTIAN style.

STYLIZED PORTRAITURE taken from DEATH MASKS is practiced by Egyptians on MUMMY CASES. REALISTIC PORTRAITURE as introduced by the Greeks is adapted by the Egyptians and Romans and used in the FRESCO medium.

*Skillful, stylized paintings on GREEK VASES.*
Red figures on black ground. Black figures on red ground.

# · DOMESTIC FURNISHINGS ·

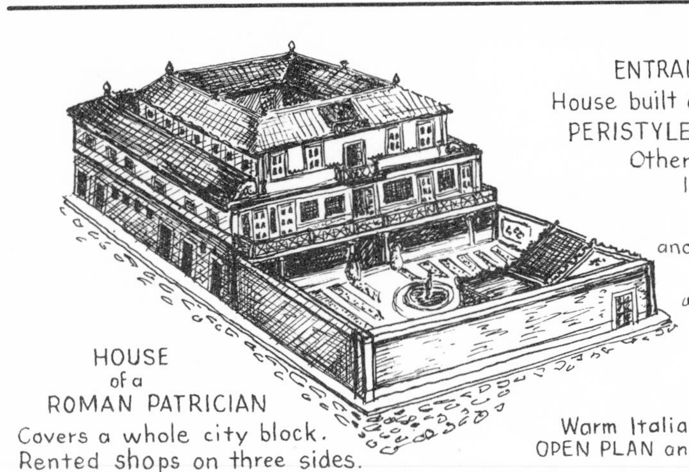

HOUSE
of a
ROMAN PATRICIAN
Covers a whole city block.
Rented shops on three sides.

ENTRANCE through garden.
House built around open court called
PERISTYLE with pool (Impluvium).
Other rooms open off this
INTERIOR GARDEN.
•
ATRIUM
another unroofed area
contains ALTARS
and ANCESTRAL STATUES.
•
SMALL BEDROOMS
called
CUBICULA

Warm Italian climate permits
OPEN PLAN and small windows.

TRICLINIUM or DINING ROOM
FRESCOES in perspective make
small room appear larger.
COUCHES for NINE
the accepted number for a banquet.

° WALLS painted in FRESCO. FLOORS laid in MOSAIC °

Excavations
of the Roman suburb of
POMPEII
show us
the COMFORTS and LUXURIES
with which
wealthy Romans
surround themselves.

Dr. Schliemann's excavations at TROY (1871) uncover many small objects.

19th C. Designers copied this

WOODEN CHAIR

GOLD JEWELRY from TROY

MARBLE TABLE
This type of support is
adapted to wood carving
during the Renaissance.

GOLD
ORNAMENTS
(TROJAN)

MARBLE SEAT with
SPHINX

SILVER
BOWL

In addition
to HEATING EQUIPMENT
of this type
HOT WATER
running through
LEAD PIPES
under STONE FLOORS
is used.

· BRAZIER ·

· TOILET ARTICLES ·

IVORY and GOLD HAIR PINS

PIN BOX

COMB

CARVED IVORY BOX

HAND MIRROR of POLISHED METAL

BED and TABLE from a mural

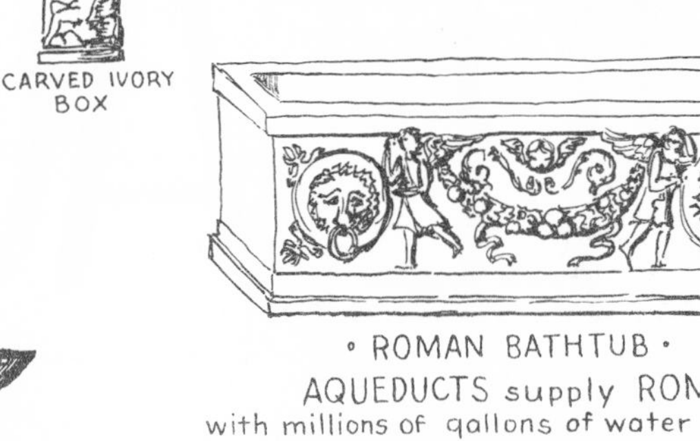

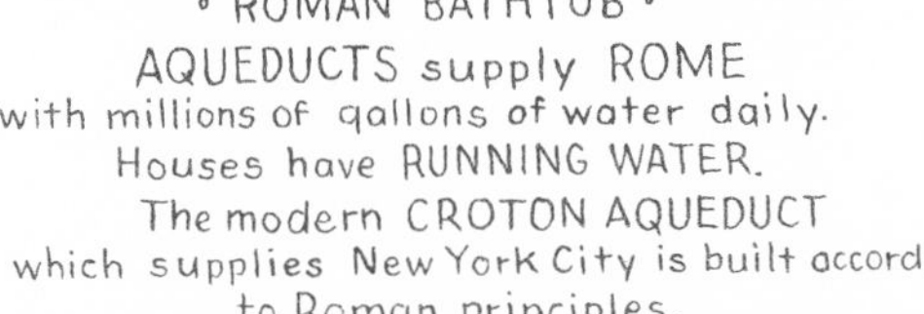

· ROMAN BATHTUB ·

AQUEDUCTS supply ROME
with millions of gallons of water daily.
Houses have RUNNING WATER.
The modern CROTON AQUEDUCT
which supplies New York City is built according
to Roman principles.

Portable LIBRARY of papyrus SCROLLS
INKWELL for red ink made from cinnabar.
REED PEN

Metal TABULAE
with WAXED SURFACE
and
IRON STYLUS for
writing.

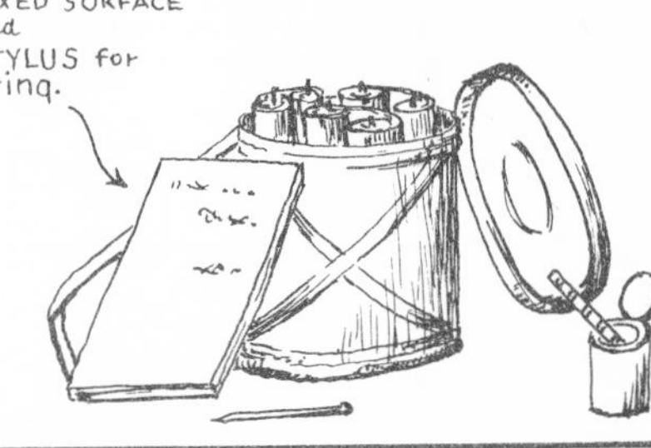

· BRONZE LAMP ·

# THE MIDDLE-AGES

## 1 A. D.—THE MIDDLE AGES—1500

The Middle Ages is the universal description of the years between the death of the ancient world and the birth of the modern. Because the Christian Church became the dominating influence and control in all affairs—spiritual, temporal, social, artistic and scientific—in this book it dates from the Birth of Christ to the end of the Gothic Age: an overlapping of several hundred years in the beginning; one hundred, at the close.

The term medieval, however, refers to the years between 600–1400, and includes the products of the Dark Ages, and the Romanesque and Gothic periods.

1 A. D—EARLY CHRISTIAN PERIOD—323
A small group spreads the
teachings of Jesus of Nazareth.

323—Roman Christian—476
The organization of the Christian Church.

365—BYZANTINE CULTURE—1454
The development of Christian
theology continues in
Eastern Empire after the fall of Rome.
Constantinople saves Europe from Oriental invaders.

600—THE DARK AGES—800
Conversion of Europe's pagan barbarians
to Christianity.

800—The Ages of Faith—1500

800—THE ROMANESQUE PERIOD—1150
Man becomes servant of the Church.

1150—THE GOTHIC AGE—1500
The growing strength of the nations
threatens the position of the Church.

# ·EARLY CHRISTIAN CHRONOLOGY·

## 1 A.D.—THE EARLY CHRISTIAN ERA—476

1 A.D.—Early Christian—323
(A small group spreads the teaching of Jesus of Nazareth.)

1 A.D. Traditional beginning of Christian Era.*
29 Crucifixion of Jesus.
70 Jerusalem destroyed by Emperor Titus.
79 Pompeii and Herculaneum destroyed by eruption of Mt. Vesuvius.
313 Toleration of Christianity proclaimed in Edict of Milan.
323 Constantine legalizes Christianity.

325—Roman Christian—476
(Organization of the Christian Church.)
325 Council of Nicaea defines orthodox Christian doctrine.

379 Emperor Theodosius declares Christianity official religion of Roman Empire.

403–540 Ravenna political center in Italy.
410 Rome sacked by Alaric the Visigoth.
452 Attila the Hun invades Italy;
Pope Leo the Great persuades him to spare Rome.
476 Rome and the Western Empire fall to the Teutonic Odoacer.
End of the Dual Roman Empire.

The EMPEROR CONSTANTINE I protector of Christianity was baptized on his deathbed. (337 A.D.)

The EMPEROR JULIAN (361-363) called the APOSTATE because of his declared paganism was an intelligent and moral man whose influence might have destroyed Christian gains had he lived longer.

## 476—ITALY FROM FALL OF EMPIRE TO THE PRESENT—1955

(Rome and all Italy become pawn of barbarian invaders.)

476–493 Rome ruled by Odoacer.
493–526 Ostrogothic Kingdom of Theodoric.
541–552 Totila battles the Eastern Empire for supremacy in Italy.
552–568 Eastern Empire sets up weak rule in Italy.
568—Lombard Kingdom established.
800—Central and northern Italy proclaimed part of Holy Roman Empire.
827–878 Saracen conquest of Sicily.
847 Saracen fleet destroyed by storm off Rome. Italy saved.
End of Saracen conquests in West.
1070—Norman Kingdom established in Southern Italy and Sicily.

Italy constantly divided into duchies and states (map page 120) until 1870, when united kingdom is formed under Victor Emmanuel II.
1922–45 Monarch puppet under dictatorship of Mussolini
1946 Italy votes for a Republic.

THEODOSIUS Emperor of the East (379-94) Made Christianity triumph.

*Historical findings have convinced modern Biblical scholars that Jesus was born no later than 4 B.C.

# ·1 A.D. - The EARLY CHRISTIAN Era - 476·

The Christian era according to tradition began in 1 A.D. with the birth of Jesus in Bethlehem. Actually, His boyhood passed unnoticed. Even the short period of His dynamic ministry fostered only local interest within the vast Roman Empire. Had He not been crucified as a minor political agitator, His words might never have become a major influence. The posthumous power of the philosophy of Jesus of Nazareth was built up by the enthusiasm of His disciples.

After the death of Jesus His followers tried to convince their fellow Jews that the resolute carpenter was the Messiah promised by the great Hebrew prophets who would return to usher them into the long-awaited Messianic Kingdom. The proselytes went forth to spread His teachings by word of mouth. As the promised kingdom automatically was to bring this world to an end, the early Christians made no preparations for an extended life on earth. They did not consider forsaking Judaism for the establishment of either sect or church. Many years were to pass before Christianity was outlined or documented.

The converted Paul of Tarsus offered a new interpretation of the Kingdom of God by asserting it was to be, not a supernatural and exclusive Jewish state, but a peaceful earthly kingdom attainable through the teachings of Jesus and through faith. This opened the religion to all mankind.

There were many converts. Christianity had much to offer the oppressed members of a society built on slavery. Its message of love, peace and charity and its promise of eternal salvation appealed to people whose life and religion had given them no hope and little spiritual satisfaction.

WALL DECORATION
from catacombs.

CHRIST the GOOD SHEPHERD
is most popular
*Early Christian representation.*

Also CHRIST, the LAMB of GOD.

The lamb of pagan sacrificial ritual
becomes
the symbol of
CHRIST the REDEEMER
of humanity through sacrifice.

· THE GOOD SHEPHERD ·

The
ROMAN
SCULPTOR
now expresses
CHRISTIAN
themes.

The GOOD SHEPHERD
and his flock of
Christians
(See Symbolism page 86)

The mosaic
technique
is still practiced
and
is to be found
in
churches
and
public buildings.

· A MOSAIC PICTURE ·
An ancient form of pictorial art

DESIGN is carried out in
SMALL TILES and PIECES of GLASS.
Technique used to DECORATE
FLOORS, WALLS and CEILINGS.

Later MOSAICS often have GOLD-LEAF
background.
( For detail see page 56)

Crude carving
of
the GOOD SHEPHERD
in VINTAGE SCENE
from
Christian
SARCOPHAGUS

# ·I A.D. - The EARLY CHRISTIAN Era - 476·

The Romans were tolerant of the overlapping polytheistic beliefs of the people they conquered. They merely insisted that the Roman deities—the reigning emperor in particular—be added to the miscellaneous array of gods. The Christians, who tried to escape attention by carrying on their religious pursuits in the secrecy of underground catacombs, managed to make themselves conspicuous by their refusal to worship the emperor and serve in the army. But this affront to authority was overlooked as long as all went well with the Empire. When things did not go smoothly and a political scapegoat was needed, it was usually the Christians who were singled out. Beginning under Nero, a series of ten long bloody persecutions was staged (67–303) to appease the hardened Roman masses.

In 313 an edict for toleration was drawn up at Milan. Ten years later Constantine legalized Christianity. While the pagans were still strong politically, the future of avowed Christians promised to be less troubled.

But all the difficulties which the new religion encountered were not caused by her enemies. Conflicting theories of faithful Christians created schisms which threatened its survival. In 325 a council met at Nicaea to discuss the heresies and define orthodox Christian belief. The doctrine of the Trinity was agreed upon and a creed drawn up. The Church was now unified and organized for a decisive stand against the yet unbroken patrician pagan forces. Its wealth and power increased as the political state weakened. When the government of the Western Empire finally fled from the barbarians (476) the Church stayed behind and by sending out missionaries, quietly laid the groundwork for retaking the lost territories.

Only the CATACOMBS as they tunnel under Rome attest to the very early Christian era.

A typical floor plan of a BASILICA CHURCH, the earliest form of Christian architecture.

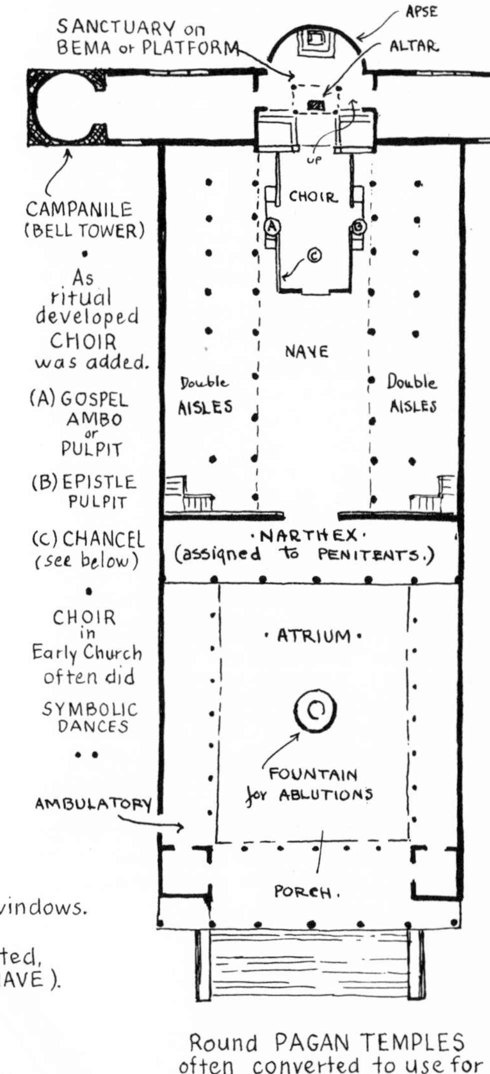
SANCTUARY on BEMA or PLATFORM
APSE
ALTAR
UP
CAMPANILE (BELL TOWER)
CHOIR
As ritual developed CHOIR was added.
NAVE
Double AISLES
Double AISLES
(A) GOSPEL AMBO or PULPIT
(B) EPISTLE PULPIT
(C) CHANCEL (see below)
·NARTHEX· (assigned to PENITENTS.)
CHOIR in Early Church often did SYMBOLIC DANCES
·ATRIUM·
FOUNTAIN for ABLUTIONS
AMBULATORY
PORCH.

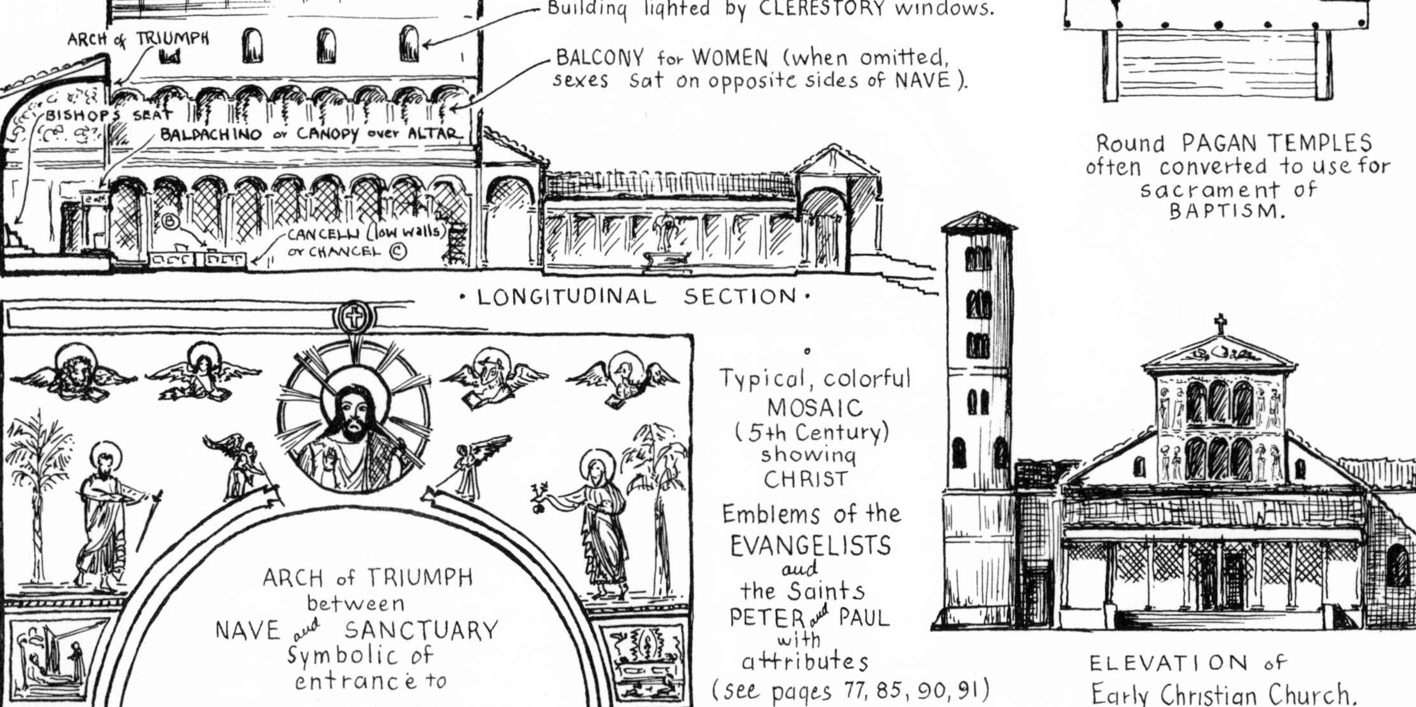
Building lighted by CLERESTORY windows.
ARCH of TRIUMPH
BALCONY for WOMEN (when omitted, sexes sat on opposite sides of NAVE).
BISHOPS SEAT
BALDACHINO or CANOPY over ALTAR
CANCELLI (low walls) or CHANCEL ©
·LONGITUDINAL SECTION·
ARCH of TRIUMPH between NAVE and SANCTUARY Symbolic of entrance to ·LIFE ETERNAL·
Typical, colorful MOSAIC (5th Century) showing CHRIST
Emblems of the EVANGELISTS and the Saints PETER and PAUL with attributes
(see pages 77, 85, 90, 91)
Round PAGAN TEMPLES often converted to use for sacrament of BAPTISM.
ELEVATION of Early Christian Church.

# · CHRISTIAN WRITINGS ·

The Prophet MOSES
by
the 20th c. MESTROVIC
(See page 185)

The moral laws of the TEN COMMANDMENTS are observed by both Jews and Christians

The first two centuries of the Christian era are known as the Apostolic Age and the New Testament is the major work of the period. This, combined with the sacred writings of the Hebrews called by Christians the Old Testament, comprises the Bible (Gr. books, library). The Old Testament for centuries, the New for decades, was passed along by oral rendition. Recording the Judaic texts took from c. 900 to 300 B.C.; the New Testament from c. 50 to 150 A.D. Until 1450 (invention of printing) the Bible was preserved by hand copies of copies of copies.

The Holy Bible has long been regarded by orthodox Christians as the revealed word of God—which, however, is subject to interpretation. The Catholic Church holds that it alone is capable of rendering the true significance. It bases its doctrine on the Bible and other documentary sources. Protestants put greater emphasis on the Holy Scriptures.

The widely used Biblical text of the middle ages was the fourth-century Latin Vulgate translation by Jerome. Translated into modern languages, this is still the accepted Catholic form. The most popular Protestant Bible in English is the seventeenth-century King James Version in the original or the recent revised edition.

11th c. Romanesque CHRIST

ARAMAIC is the native tongue of JESUS, the NEW TESTAMENT which records His Life and Teachings is written in GREEK

The Christian translations of the Old Testament are arranged in three parts: the historic-history and laws (Genesis—Esther), the poetic (Job—Song of Songs) and the prophetic (Isaiah—Malachi). The Old Testament Apocrypha (see below) is a small section of Jewish manuscripts of doubtful authorship which were not written in Hebrew. These books are included in the Vulgate but if contained in Protestant translations are presented separately.

The earliest books of the New Testament were not intended for posterity. They were letters inscribed by the apostle Paul to be read aloud when he himself was unable to appear. They were written approximately twenty years after the crucifixion.

Gothic Sculpture

The Jewish Saul of Tarsus became the Christian convert PAUL, Apostle of the Gentiles. Although not one of the original twelve disciples the Apostle Paul through his speeches and epistles is historically the most influential of all.

The New Testament opens with the gospels of the four evangelists and is composed of a selection made by early churchmen from a vast number of epistles and documents. Those books which were not included were suppressed as being of doubtful origin, spurious authority or because they presented false or contradictory information. These works are known as apocryphal (Gr., hidden, spurious) writings and are studied and analyzed by scholars of history and ancient languages as well as by theological students.

Some writings of the Judaic and early Christian cultures, whether or not they appear in the Bible, fall into a category termed apocalyptic (Gr., uncover). These are unfulfilled prophecies or accounts of visions and revelations describing the rewards and comforts of a future age which is to offset the disappointments and persecutions of this one. There are many such passages in the Bible. The promise of the kingdom of the Messiah is one example from the Old Testament. The famous apocalypse of the New Testament is the Book of Revelations.

# ·CHRISTIAN WRITINGS·

Only thirty per cent of the world's population is guided by Christianity. But the Bible has been translated into every language and outsells every other book ever written.

ST. JEROME

Theological writings did not come to an end with the Apostolic Age. Between the second and fifth centuries there were many men who helped to fashion church doctrine.

The Church fathers, of course, head the list. The early bishops come next, then such laymen as Justin Martyr, Origen, Tertullian and others. St. Athanasius and St. Augustine both reconciled Platonism with Christianity—while many years later Thomas Aquinas worked Aristotelian philosophy into Christian thought.

PLATO

ST. AUGUSTINE

A valuable form of theological reasoning is the method called apologetics (Gr., defense)—a systematic statement of belief in the supernatural revelation, divine redemption and other premises on which orthodox Christianity is based. From the second to sixth centuries these works were aimed chiefly at pagans, Jews, and Arian Christians. Tatian, Bishop Cyril of Jerusalem and Cyril of Alexandria were active apologists.

Bishop Eusebius of Caesarea, Africanus (both 3rd c.), the Frankish Gregory of Tour (6th c.) and the English Bede (7th c.) are numbered as ecclesiastical historians—who wrote about Christianity and effected many conversions.

VENERABLE BEDE

Theologians of the Middle Ages avidly examined all early writings seeking proof or precedent for establishing doctrinal claims. The accusation has been made that they were not above falsifying such documents. Whether intentional or not, it is factual that many decisions were based on false information. The case of the Pseudo-Dionysius (see Attributes) is one of foremost interest to the field of art.

ARISTOTLE

THOMAS AQUINAS

Christian theology had been based on the Egyptian Ptolemaic system of the universe. When Galileo (1564–1642) with his telescope upheld the Copernican theory that the sun does not revolve around the earth, but the earth around the sun, the Church proclaimed it a heresy. The new theory contradicted not only the early views of the Church but also principles propounded by Aristotle. As Thomas Aquinas (1225–1274) had blended Aristotelian and Christian philosophies to the satisfaction of the Church, to accept the system was to admit error on two counts.

This and later scientific discoveries caused both Catholic and Protestant theologians great consternation, and brought back the form of written apology which had fallen into disuse during the years when free discussion was banned. Philosophers as well as churchmen have spent years in trying to reconcile science and reason with religion. The nineteenth-century Darwin with his theories of evolution and origin of the species presented them with the task of greatest magnitude.

KING JAMES I of ENGLAND
in the 17th century
sponsors
the first authorized translation
of the Bible
in the English language.

# ·365 - BYZANTINE CULTURE - 1454·

Black Sea
Golden Horn
Bosporus
Fortified city of Constantinople
Sea of Marmara
Dardanelles
·CONSTANTINOPLE·
Now Turkish city of ISTANBUL.
GOLD and ENAMEL PENDANT
JEWELRY
has charm
but often lacks
refinement.


NECKLACE of
GOLD, PEARLS and QUARTZ

In the fourth century the Emperor Constantine moved the capital of the Roman Empire to the ancient Greek colony at Byzantium, and renamed the city Constantinople. In 365 the Empire was divided into two parts, with Constantinople becoming the center of the eastern half. After the fall of Rome it stood for a thousand years.

During the reign of the pious Theodosius (379–395) it became almost as dangerous not to be a Christian as it once had been to be one. To avoid persecution or the confiscation of their property, pagans clamored for the rite of baptism. The Church was still collecting its literature, devising its rituals, selecting its holidays, clarifying its beliefs, and working out a system of education through art. The multifarious converts contributed ideas from their assorted backgrounds.

The Greco-Roman culture of Constantinople was very naturally affected by the Asiatic races across the Bosphorus. From the end of Justinian's reign until the era of the crusades (6th to 12th centuries) there was little intercourse with the West. "Founded on Roman traditions, modified by Greek taste and tinctured by oriental influences" the art of the Byzantine Empire shed the severity of its classic birth.

Suddenly Islam, a religion newer than Christianity, sprang up in the East. The followers of the prophet Mohammad in a hundred years (632–732) nearly succeeded in conquering the world. The east Asiatic and African shores of the Mediterranean were taken by the Moslems.

The ignorant and unprepared peoples of the disorganized European continent would have been next had it not been for the Christian forces at Constantinople. The Eastern Empire gave the West its chance to rise again by holding back the Saracen hordes. When the Moslems did break through they were defeated not far from Paris (731). They were driven behind the Pyrenees, from which the Spanish were not able to evict them until 1492. The rest of Europe was saved from their domination but deprived of their advanced culture.

After ICONOCLAST Period
NATURAL FORMS
continue to dominate
ART.
The EAGLE is
often used
but is not symbolic.
Design of woven
·SILK DAMASK·

The SCULPTURED
HUMAN FORM
is
prohibited
but human figure appears
in STYLIZED
PAINTING, MOSAICS
and BAS-RELIEFS of stone, ivory, wood and metal.

PRINTED NAMES
make
ATTRIBUTES
unnecessary.
IVORY CARVING

Detail of
MOSAIC work.

# ·365 - BYZANTINE CULTURE - 1454·

Mohammadan influence combined with the Judaic aversion to graven images was undoubtedly responsible for the iconoclastic controversy which rocked the Church for over a hundred years. The Emperor Leo III (717–741) ordered the destruction of all "idols"—paintings, sculptures and relics. Although officially the division of the church into Roman Catholic and Greek Orthodox did not take place until 1054, sculptures of the human form were banned in the Eastern church after the eighth century. The sculptor thereafter specialized in geometric and naturalistic designs. Manuals of acceptable rules for painting were issued. Thus began a traditional conventionalized style which through the ensuing centuries is noticeably static. It forms an interesting contrast to the ever-changing art of the West.

The suppression of sculpture and the control of painting brought about cultivation of other techniques. The artist was able to use his ingenuity in designing and executing mosaics, coins, gold and enamel jewelry and ivory carvings. Magnificent textiles woven of Chinese silk and Egyptian cotton were sold in great quantity. Reproductions of them are to be found on today's market.

The crusades introduced Europeans to the superior culture of the East. Many crusaders died on the long journey but those who survived benefited themselves and raised the standards of the Western world by what they saw and took home.

Thus the Byzantine Empire served the West, which not only attacked her during the fourth crusade but failed to come to her aid when the gradually weakened and diminished boundaries at last surrendered to the Turks in 1453.

Byzantine culture is perpetuated in the rituals of the Greek Orthodox Church.

The •ICON• a devotional picture, takes the place of sculptured images in the GREEK CHURCH.

Figure painted on wood.
Face and neck revealed through cutout in REPOUSSÉ (pressed) GOLD COVER.

Right hand of IVORY holds BAROQUE pearl flower.

GOLD FRAME encrusted with CABOCHON GEMS and ENAMELED MEDALLIONS.

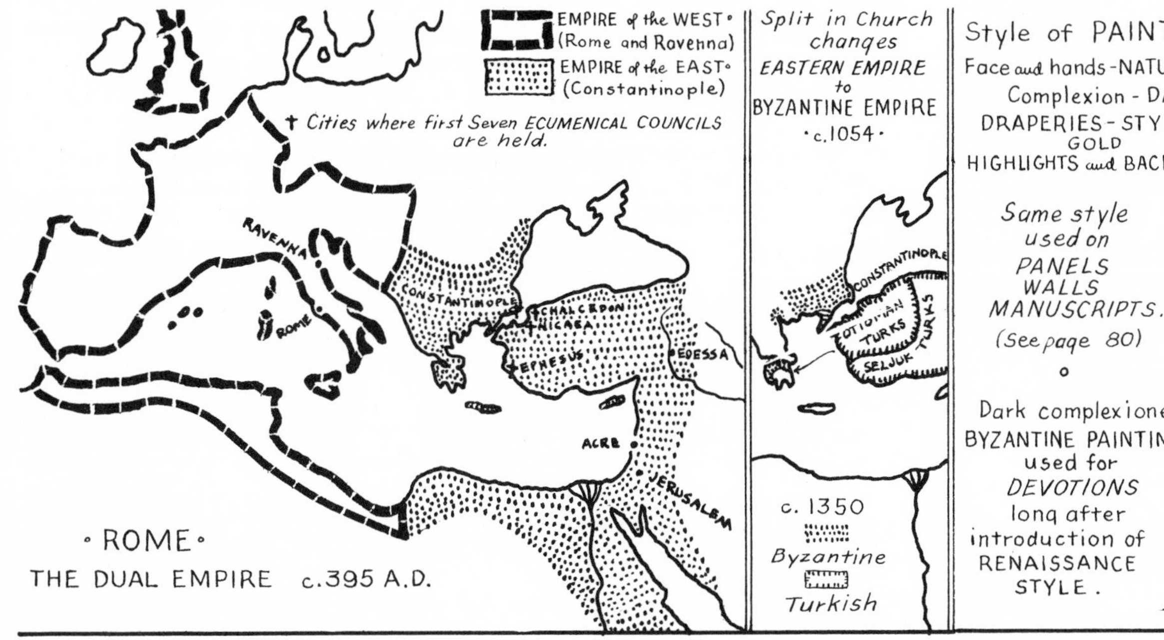
EMPIRE of the WEST• (Rome and Ravenna)
EMPIRE of the EAST• (Constantinople)
† Cities where first Seven ECUMENICAL COUNCILS are held.
RAVENNA
ROME
CONSTANTINOPLE
CHALCEDON
NICAEA
EPHESUS
EDESSA
ACRE
JERUSALEM
Split in Church changes EASTERN EMPIRE to BYZANTINE EMPIRE •c.1054•
CONSTANTINOPLE
OTTOMAN TURKS
SELJUK TURKS
c. 1350
Byzantine
Turkish

• ROME •
THE DUAL EMPIRE c.395 A.D.

Style of PAINTING.
Face and hands - NATURALISTIC.
Complexion - DARK
DRAPERIES - STYLIZED
GOLD HIGHLIGHTS and BACKGROUND
Same style used on PANELS WALLS MANUSCRIPTS.
(See page 80)
Dark complexioned BYZANTINE PAINTINGS used for DEVOTIONS long after introduction of RENAISSANCE STYLE.

# · BYZANTINE CHRONOLOGY ·

BYZANTINE ARCHITECTURE
is dominated by at least
one DOME over SQUARE AREA with
radiating half-domes and arches.

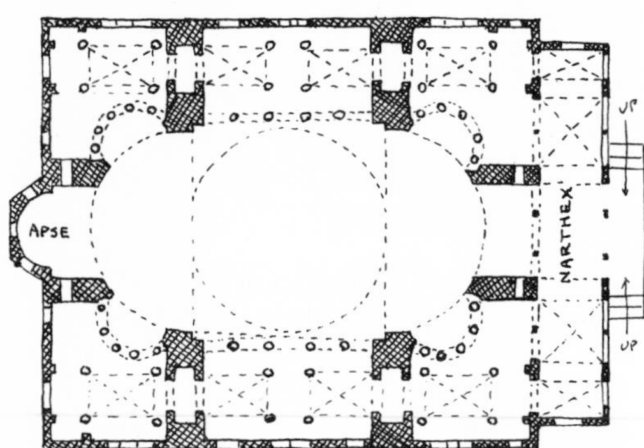

APSE
NARTHEX
UP
UP


FLOOR PLAN - Suggestive of Greek Cross in Square.
Central dome and radiating half-domes make
LARGE OPEN CENTRAL AREA.

INTERIORS: Brilliant MOSAICS
cover all surfaces,
making molding unnecessary.

EXTERIORS: Give disjointed appearance.
Colorful brick construction
much more crude than marble interiors.
(See page 82).

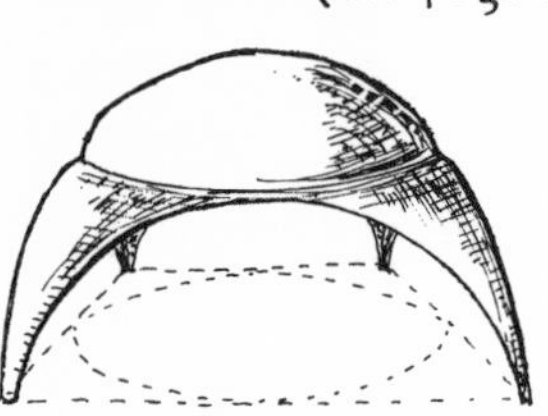

Spherical triangles called
PENDENTIVES
form transition between
SQUARE floor space
and DOMED roof.

DOME
often set on
DRUM
Windows in drum
light space below.

ROOFS of TILE

NATURALISTIC
and GEOMETRIC
DESIGNS
in PIERCED CARVING

BYZANTINE CAPITALS

CUSHION CAPITAL

BRASS COLLAR
on marble shaft
strengthens column.

CLASSIC ENTABLATURE
is discarded in favor of
SERIES of ARCHES.

CUSHION CAPITALS
appear to
ELONGATE ARCH.

BYZANTINE ARCHITECTURE
is to be found in
ITALY
at RAVENNA and VENICE
as well as in
GREECE and ASIA MINOR,
the BALKAN Countries
and RUSSIA.

(The Eastern Empire is forsaken by the West and menaced by the Orient.)

326 Dedication of Constantinople at ancient Byzantium.

337 Division of the Roman Empire between
three sons of Constantine.
365 DUAL EMPIRE (East and West) inaugurated.

476 Recognition of Odoacer as ruler of Italy.

527–565 Reign of Emperor Justinian.
Height of power of Eastern Empire.
In East, Persians are defeated.
In West, Italy is lost to Ostrogoths.

632–732 ALL CHRISTENDOM endangered by ISLAM.
570 Mohammad the prophet born.
622 The Hegira, his flight from Mecca.
Birth of the religion called Islam.
Followers called Moslems; during middle ages, Saracens.
Term Mohammadan today considered incorrect.

586 Arianism (refusal to place Christ on plane with God)
finally abandoned.
European barbarians united in orthodox Christian belief
in Trinity.

717–1054 ICONOCLASTIC CONTROVERSY separates East and West.
787 Fourth Ecumenical Council at Nicaea defines
veneration of images.
In art the Crucified Christ replaces the Good Shepherd.

866 Actual severance of Greek and Latin churches—
1054 official separation;
Eastern Empire thereafter called
GREEK or BYZANTINE EMPIRE.
1070 The East loses last Italian foothold.
1071 Asia Minor lost to Seljuk Turks.

1096–1291 THE CRUSADING ERA.
1204 Sack and occupation of Constantinople
by Latins of the Fourth Crusade.

1206–1294 AGE OF ORIENTAL IMPERIALISM threatens Europe.
1206–27 Jenghiz Khan, Mongol and Tatar emperor.
1241 Eastern European Continent invaded.
1260–94 Kublai Khan. Hulagu, brother.
Heir of Khan converted to Islam.
1369–1405 Timur of Tamerlane, King of Samarkand,
ruthless Moslem conqueror of central Asia and Asia Minor.
Constantinople is spared when hordes turn east to attack China.

1454 Constantinople captured by Seljuk (Moslems) Turks.
END of GREEK EMPIRE.

After 375 years of Turkish rule Greece wins her independence
in 1829.

# ·600- THE DARK AGES -800·

Roman legions were withdrawn from their northern and western outposts by the crumbling empire. A great wave of invasions followed as Roman frontiers were pushed back by barbaric tribes migrating from the fierce Asiatic Huns. Rome itself succumbed in 476. The process of stamping out Roman culture did not take place overnight, but in several generations descendants of the citizens of the once powerful and progressive Roman Empire had stepped backward to join their crude and primitive conquerors in a much lower form of civilization.

The Dark Ages seems a most expressive term for the years which followed the fall from the brilliant heights of Rome to the black depths of barbarism. The times were tumultuous with struggles for supremacy, and the seething population had little need or inspiration for the creation of beautiful objects.

Gregory the Great (590–604), Bishop of Rome, was acknowledged as Pope—the spiritual head of western Christendom and temporal ruler of Rome. During the unsettled Dark Ages, the Christian Church was the only steadfast power in Europe. Churchmen were sent to the northern provinces, where they won the confidence and respect of the people.

To the monastic system and to such individual missionaries as Isidore, Bishop of Seville; Augustine, Archbishop of Canterbury; Boniface, Apostle of Germany and later Pope; and Cyril, Apostle of the Slavs, goes the credit for spreading Christian doctrine during this period. By the beginning of the feudal age Western Europe was completely won over to Christianity.

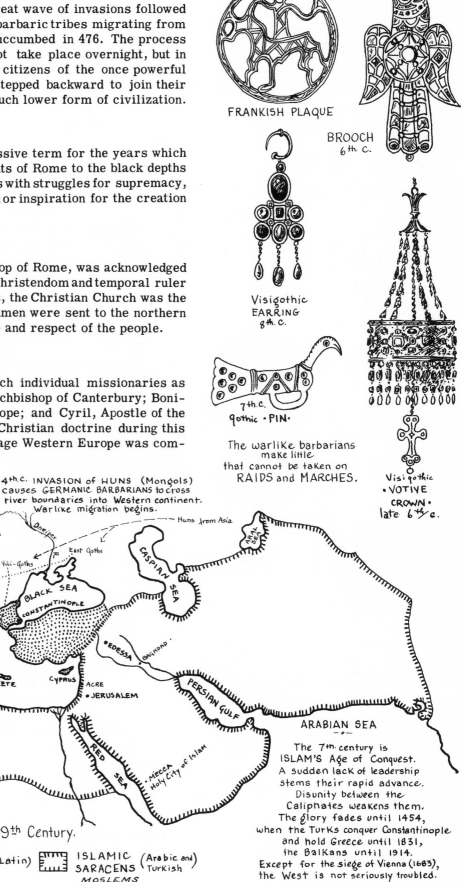

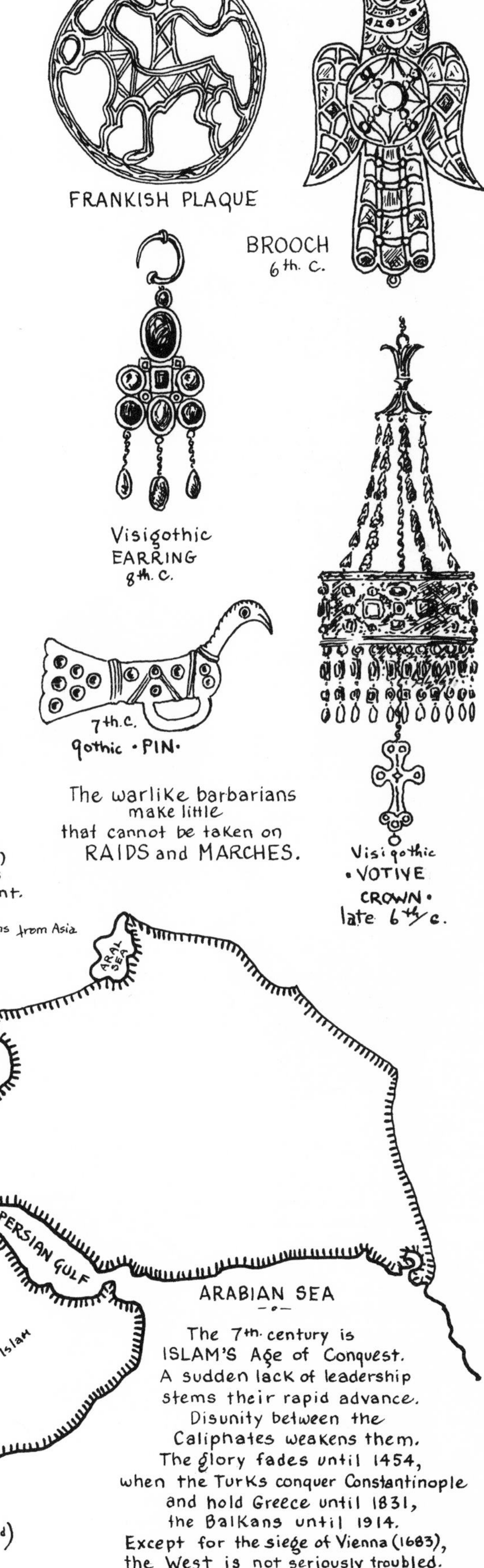
FRANKISH PLAQUE
BROOCH
6th. C.
Visigothic
EARRING
8th. C.
7th. C.
gothic · PIN ·
The warlike barbarians
make little
that cannot be taken on
RAIDS and MARCHES.
Visigothic
· VOTIVE
CROWN ·
late 6th c.

4th. C. INVASION of HUNS (Mongols)
causes GERMANIC BARBARIANS to cross
river boundaries into Western continent.
Warlike migration begins.
Jutes
Saxons
Angles
Vandals
Lombards
Burgundians
Franks
AIX-LA-CHAPELLE
TOURS
Rhine R.
Dneiper R.
Huns from Asia
East Goths
West or Visi-goths
Danube R.
BLACK SEA
CONSTANTINOPLE
CASPIAN SEA
ARAL SEA
SARDINIA
SICILY
CRETE
CYPRUS
ACRE
· JERUSALEM
· EDESSA
BAGHDAD
PERSIAN GULF
RED SEA
MECCA
Holy City of Islam
ARABIAN SEA
The 7th. century is
ISLAM'S Age of Conquest.
A sudden lack of leadership
stems their rapid advance.
Disunity between the
Caliphates weakens them.
The glory fades until 1454,
when the Turks conquer Constantinople
and hold Greece until 1831,
the Balkans until 1914.
Except for the siege of Vienna (1683),
the West is not seriously troubled.
THREE POWERS at the beginning of the 9th Century.
EASTERN EMPIRE (Greek)
HOLY ROMAN EMPIRE (Latin)
CHRISTIANS
ISLAMIC SARACENS (Arabic and Turkish)
MOSLEMS

# ·800-THE ROMANESQUE PERIOD-1150·

All the countries of Western Europe provide diversified and ingenious examples of the style.
FRANCE.
• PIECRUST ARCH •
(English Norman)
• BARREL VAULT •
Weight and thrust borne by sidewalls
Fear of weakening walls with apertures leads to use of decorative BLIND OPENINGS, especially on EXTERIORS.
• STONE MEDALLION •
• CROSS VAULT •
Weight and thrust is distributed and supported by FOUR MASSIVE PIERS.
CATHEDRAL, BAPTISTRY and CAMPANILE (Belltower) dominate ITALIAN towns
CROSS SECTION of CLUSTERED NAVE PIER
CROSS VAULTING and PIERS:
ENGLAND.
CROSS VAULTING on typical FLOOR PLAN of church with TRANSEPT.
ITALY.
GUILLOCHE
• STORIED CAPITALS •
Most interesting examples.
Sculptured PANEL above door is called TYMPANUM
GERMANY.
NOTE: ROUND ARCHES and BLIND OPENINGS.
• ROMANESQUE COLUMN •
Proportion of CAPITAL and SHAFT follows no set formula.
TYPICAL STRUCTURES:
Above, note CLASSICAL leaf and VOLUTES
Large Abbey Churches
Cloisters
Crypts of GOTHIC Cathedrals
A few Secular buildings.
In a series of columns - each capital and shaft is apt to be a DIFFERENT DESIGN.
Elaborate recessed doorway with VARIEGATED COLUMNS.

When Charlemagne died (814) his vast empire was divided and the continent was again in turmoil. Some degree of order was brought about by feudalism, a complicated system which supplied a way of life and served as a substitute for government for about five hundred years. The colorful institutions of chivalry and knighthood were developments of the system. By 1300 the feudal age had passed because the conditions which fostered it no longer existed.

During the Romanesque period all phases of culture were developed and sustained by the monastic orders. In remote sections of the continent, the Latin language was kept alive only in secluded monasteries. Cut off from Rome physically, the monasteries did not share in the growing power and wealth of the Roman Church, but humbly continued to teach and comfort the harassed peoples. Gratitude was shown by the erection of churches in the Romanesque style.

So called because it was supposed to copy ancient Roman architecture, this product of the Middle Ages in no way actually resembled the well-designed, carefully executed work of the skilled Roman architect and sculptor. It did start where Roman Christian architecture left off, and a transept was added to the basilica form, making the building the shape of the Christian cross. But the workmanship was unmistakably that of untutored hands.

The style developed in all European countries. The variety of the stone in different vicinities and the unequal local talents account for the many regional differences. However, they are all easily identified as belonging to the period by the general crudeness, and by one or more of the points listed below.

Characteristics:

1. Unfailing use of ROUND ARCH.
2. LOW STONE ROOF — Barrel or Cross vault.
3. SMALL WINDOWS in thick stone walls.
4. Series of BLIND OPENINGS on exteriors.
5. Three or more TOWERS (seven in Germany).
6. Alternate bands of black and white stone (Italy).
7. Exteriors (except for regional exceptions) profusely decorated with RELIEF and SCULPTURE.
8. Interiors — large wall surfaces decorated with MOSAICS or FRESCOES.
9. HEAVY CAPITALS — stylized or storied.
10. DECORATED SHAFTS.

In England the style is called Norman because it was introduced by William the Conqueror, who sailed from Normandy in 1066.

When barbarians settle in permanent locations, strongest leaders are proclaimed KING. (Title later becomes hereditary.)

NEED of PROTECTION from rival kingdoms produces FEUDAL SYSTEM.
LAND is apportioned in FIEFS to VASSALS in return for FEALTY and HOMAGE, (Loyalty and service).

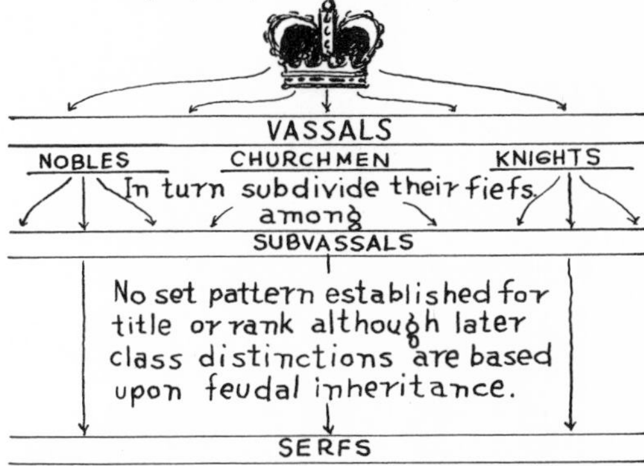
VASSALS
NOBLES
CHURCHMEN
KNIGHTS
In turn subdivide their fiefs among
SUBVASSALS
No set pattern established for title or rank although later class distinctions are based upon feudal inheritance.
SERFS

Like slaves, these men are considered the property of FEUDAL LORDS.

Even FREEMEN and TOWNSPEOPLE are largely dependent upon feudal lords as large areas including entire villages are part of feudal estates.

*In England Henry VIII by distributing church lands establishes an hereditary landed nobility which thrives as long as the country remains agricultural. (16th-19th C.)*

*In France Louis XIV (17th C.) calls the nobles away from their lands to serve him at court. This weakens rural France and contributes to the causes of the Revolution. (1787)*

A KNIGHT doing HOMAGE to his LIEGE LORD

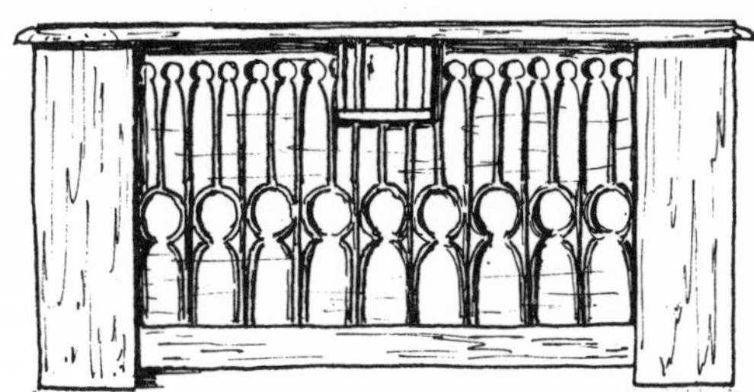

• OAK CHEST •

This piece of furniture serves as CLOSET, BUREAU, CRIB, TABLE and BENCH in sparsely furnished castles.

# · ROMANESQUE CHRONOLOGY ·

ST. PETER gives equal blessing to POPE LEO III and the newly crowned EMPEROR CHARLEMAGNE 9th. c. MOSAIC) (note square halos)

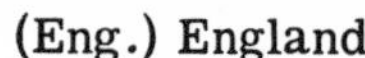

(Eng.) England (Fr.) France (It.) Italy

### LITERATURE

Beowulf
(Eng. 8th c.)

Anglo-Saxon Chronicle
(9th–12th c.)

Chanson de Roland
(Fr. 11th c.?)

Abelard
(Fr. 12th c.)

### MUSIC

Church music
Development of choral chants

Music and literature blended in songs sung by troubadours and meistersingers to lute accompaniment

11th c. Franconian period of Church music

### HISTORY

800–14 Charlemagne
Holy Roman Empire

Carolingians, Holy Roman Emperors
800–986

Leif Ericsson 1000

Church split into Roman Catholic and Greek Orthodox
1054

William the Conqueror in England—1066

Beginning of crusading era
1096–1270

### PAINTING and SCULPTURE

Religious art by anonymous artists.
Sculpture more important than painting.

Frescoes—Mosaics—Altarpieces.

Gold and semiprecious stones.
The reputed CROWN of CHARLEMAGNE
Now in Vienna

Jewel of ALFRED the GREAT of England
"Alfred had me made".

Toward the end of the DARK AGES fortified castles are built by the warlords on high inaccessible land for purposes of defense.

Horse-borne soldiers of WILLIAM the NORMAN cross the channel to conquer England.

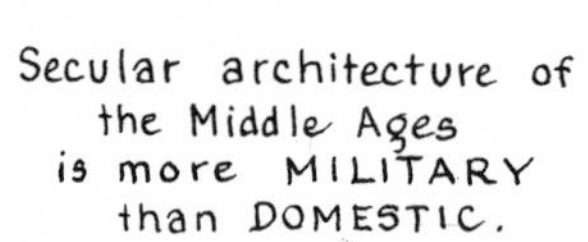

Secular architecture of the Middle Ages is more MILITARY than DOMESTIC.
The home of the most powerful noble lacks the comforts enjoyed by a middle-class citizen of ancient Rome.

SWORD of the period

Entire ROMANESQUE VILLAGES are walled for protection against RIVAL powers.

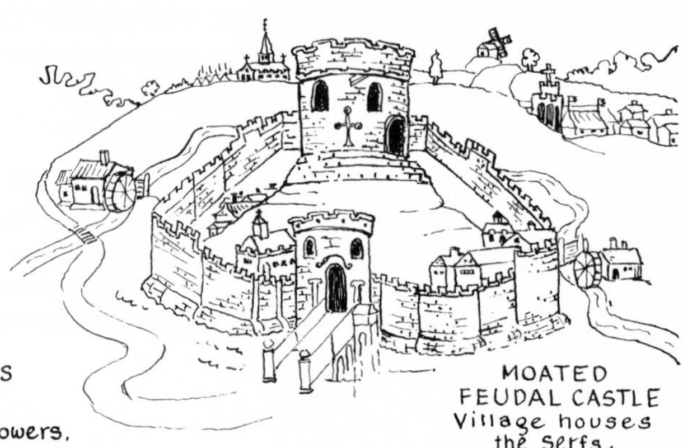

MOATED FEUDAL CASTLE
Village houses the Serfs.

# ·1096-The CRUSADING Era-1270·

Although Jerusalem had been in the hands of Moslem Arabs since 637, Christian penitents had been free to make their holy pilgrimages. But it fell to the unfriendly Seljuk Turks who were not tolerant of the religious practices of the "unclean" Christians. The Eastern Empire voiced concern over the strength and ruthlessness of these new enemies. In 1085 Pope Urban II called a council at Clermont, France, and inspired the first crusade.

Church of the HOLY SEPULCHRE in Jerusalem was first erected by Constantine on reputed site of the TOMB of CHRIST. The present structure was rebuilt by crusaders during the 11th c.

The idea behind the venture was the rescue of the Holy Land. An open path to heaven and glory in the after-life were promised to all who would participate. In addition to this reward, many individuals had more personal reasons for going. It offered an escape from the famine and pestilence at home, and the prospect of riches and the love of adventure were additional lures. The Church too had its motives. It was anxious to have under its jurisdiction not only the colonies lost to the Moslems, but also the territory newly organized under the Greek Orthodox Church. It dreamed of being again the undivided Church of all Christendom.

Of the eight excursions which resulted, the first (1096–1099) was the most effective. A Christian kingdom was set up at Jerusalem, where the rest of the regained principalities were to pay allegiance to the "Protector of the Holy Sepulchre."

CRUSADERS
On their way to the Holy Land.

The second crusade (1147–1149) was organized by St. Bernard of Clairvaux, Louis VII of France (accompanied by his wife Eleanor of Aquitaine) and Conrad III of Germany because the Latin Kingdom of Jerusalem was threatened by the fall of neighboring Edessa. Poor management made this expedition a miserable failure and it never reached Jerusalem.

In 1187 the famous Saladin recaptured Jerusalem. The romantic third crusade (1189–1192) which attempted to retake the city was headed by Philip Augustus of France, Richard Coeur-de-Lion of England (son of Eleanor of Aquitaine by her second husband, Henry Plantagenet) and Emperor Frederick Barbarossa of Germany. Barbarossa was killed; Philip quarreled with Richard and withdrew. Richard was left to negotiate with the Moslem leader, who granted Christians permission to travel unmolested to and from the sacred shrines.

SALADIN
Sultan of Egypt and Syria, antagonist of crusaders, wearing the green turban of the Prophet and a large-patterned robe signifying high rank. The HALO is the Oriental symbol of POWER.

The infamous fourth crusade (1201–1204) was started by Pope Innocent III and financed by the greedy merchants of the Republic of Venice. The attack was focused on the Christian city of Constantinople, and the victorious Latin forces ruled there for fifty years. Instead of uniting the Greek and Latin Christians as intended, it made their separation irrevocable.

# ·1096 - The CRUSADING Era - 1270·

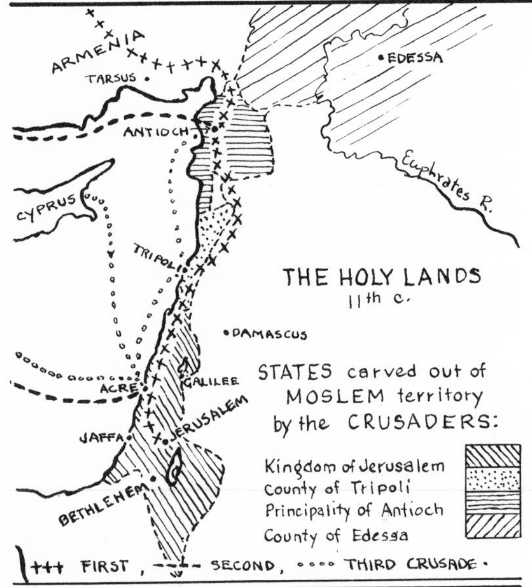

ARMENIA
TARSUS
EDESSA
ANTIOCH
Euphrates R.
CYPRUS
TRIPOLI
THE HOLY LANDS
11th c.
DAMASCUS
GALILEE
ACRE
JAFFA
JERUSALEM
BETHLEHEM
STATES carved out of MOSLEM territory by the CRUSADERS:
Kingdom of Jerusalem
County of Tripoli
Principality of Antioch
County of Edessa
+++ FIRST, - - - SECOND, oooo THIRD CRUSADE.


The Children's Crusade (1212) was a heartbreaking folly. Frederick II (1228–1229) managed by treaty to regain Jerusalem, but it was soon retaken by the Turks, who held it until World War I (1918). The French King Louis IX fought against the Mohammedans in Egypt (1248) and again in Tunis (1270) where he died.

In 1291 the Turkish conquest of Acre, Syria, brought an end to all Latin holdings in the east and to the crusading era.

The main objective of the crusades was never permanently accomplished, and the lack of cooperation between Eastern and Western Christians compared unfavorably with the leadership of sagacious opponents such as Saladin.

However, the gains were considerable. The wealth of plunder, spices, fruits, textiles, fashions, powder, mirrors, and Persian prayer beads (which developed into the rosary) were tangible assets of the two hundred years of action.

The crusades helped to bring an end to the feudal system by giving the bound serf a chance to break his allegiance to his local master in order to serve a holy cause. The cities which grew along the pilgrims' routes were places of refuge which offered paid employment.

Within these towns occupational organizations known as guilds developed. These were the forerunners of the modern labor unions. They regulated hours, wages and quality of the wares. Entertainment, sick benefits and pensions were provided in return for membership fees. The system of apprenticeship took the place of training schools in preparing men to be masters of their chosen trade.

But most important was the contact with the Greek and Moslem cultures. This valuable experience served as a form of liberal education in warfare, commerce, finance, geography, agriculture, politics, literature and freedom of thought. Because of this experience European Gothic man was advanced far beyond his Romanesque father.

12th c
ROMANESQUE CAPITAL
portraying
HENRY II of England (Plantagenet)
and ELEANOR of Aquitaine.

TRIPTYCH
(3-part altarpiece)
designed around piece of TRUE CROSS.
Fragments of the Cross were valued purchases of the Crusaders.

A bloody fight,
from
GERMAN
MANUSCRIPT
c. 1200

# ·THE MEDIEVAL MINOR ARTS·

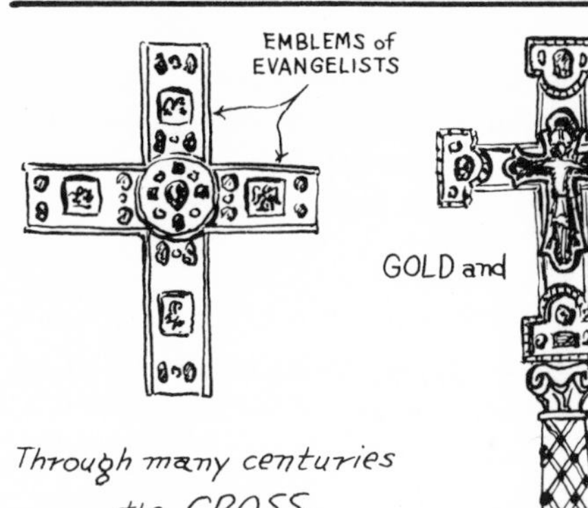
EMBLEMS of EVANGELISTS

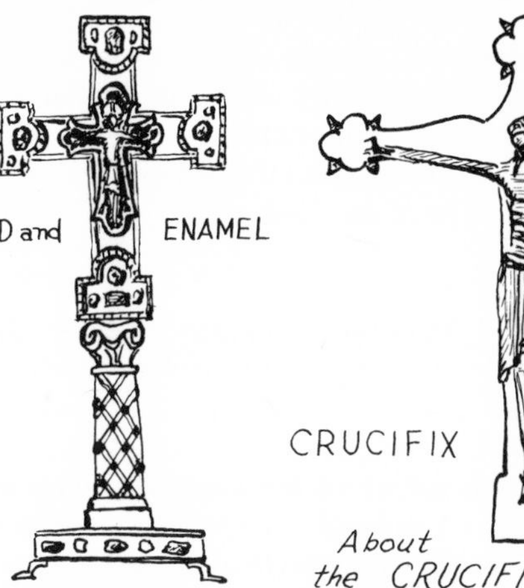
GOLD and ENAMEL

Through many centuries the CROSS has been used as the symbol of CHRISTIANITY.

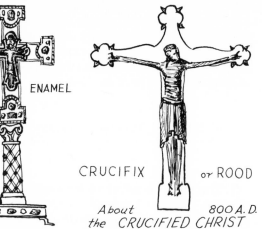

CRUCIFIX or ROOD

About 800 A.D. the CRUCIFIED CHRIST becomes a devotional image.

ARM RELIQUARY

SCENES from SCRIPTURES

Consecrated, portable ALTAR of gold and enamel.

GOLD and SILVER – polished and uncut SEMIPRECIOUS STONES and ENAMEL are combined to make beautiful and valuable objects for religious ritual.

Houses of POWERFUL and WEALTHY have nothing to compare with CHURCH POSSESSIONS.

·CROZIER·

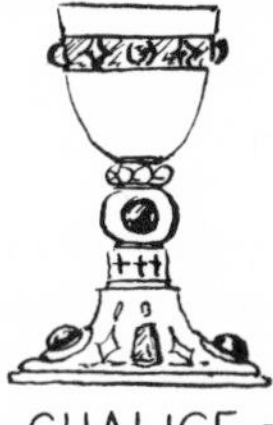

·CHALICE·

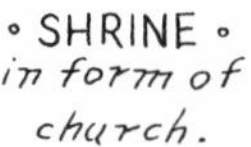

·PATEN· For distribution of WAFFERS in COMMUNION SERVICE.

Relics of SAINTS and HOLY PERSONAGES encased in jeweled shrines.

·SHRINE· in form of church.

SIX-WINGED SERAPHS

EMBLEMS of EVANGELISTS

Carved Ivory ·DIPTYCH· (Two-part altarpiece)

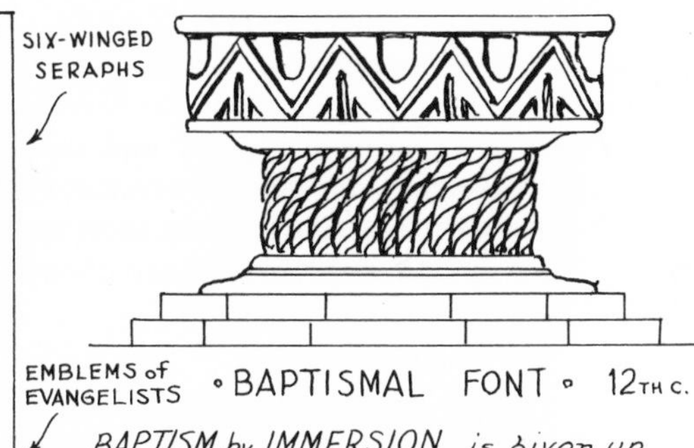

·BAPTISMAL FONT· 12TH C.

BAPTISM by IMMERSION is given up in northern countries.

INFUSION (pouring water on head) becomes accepted form.

ASPERSION (sprinkling) later rite.

·BOOK COVER· of CARVED IVORY and GOLD set with PRECIOUS STONES.

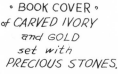

No BOOK COVER considered too valuable for RELIGIOUS WORKS.

HAND LETTERING and ILLUMINATIONS add to beauty and interest.

·BASINET HELMET· over chain mail 14TH C.

Inlaid metal SURFACE DECORATION on plate armor. 16TH C.

·COAT of ARMS· Necessary identification on shield in combat.

12TH-17TH C. ·HERALDRY·

·BISHOP'S MITRE· Embroidered in gold and colors. (Late Gothic)

Cast metal ·MONSTRANCE· for CONSECRATED HOST (Wafers)

# ·1150 - THE GOTHIC AGE - 1500·

Gothic architecture
VERTICAL
with
HIGH ROOFS.
Large
STAINED GLASS
windows
impressive in
interiors.
FLOOR PLANS
simple
with
TRANSEPT.
No permanent seating
permits
religious processions.
WEST FRONT
Note round
ROSE WINDOWS
SIDE ELEVATION
TRANSEPT

The mendicant monks in France were responsible for bringing freedom of spirit to the oppressed serfs, through preachings of brotherhood and equality. This contributed to the breaking up of the feudal system, to the growth of cities, and to the stabilization of individual countries.

Through ignorance, superstition and lack of medical knowledge, whole communities were destroyed by epidemics of the plague. However, the survivors were comforted by their faith, and combined their spiritual convictions with their artistic talents to decorate church buildings and illustrate Christian teachings. To insure their eternal salvation, people eagerly contributed time, skill and money to the erection of cathedrals. Great civic pride was taken in the construction and design. A desire to outshine neighboring towns led to a healthy and productive rivalry. Inspired primarily by religious fervor, the architecture was a strong, honest style now known as "Gothic."

As the ribbed vault helped the piers support the weight of the heavy stone roof, the side walls, freed from much of their burden, could be broken by larger openings. This, plus the use of the pointed arch, led to huge windows, less wall space and higher roofs. In time wall space diminished to such an extent that buttresses had to be added to the outside of the building to withstand the thrust of the roof. This obvious physical weakness was masterfully conquered through a system of balanced thrusts and it was developed into an aesthetically dynamic style.

Originating on French soil, the style spread to other countries. While the greatest examples of Gothic architecture are the cathedrals, interesting buildings were designed for civic and domestic purposes. The many-walled towns and fortified castles of the Middle Ages are seldom either Romanesque or Gothic in style and are simply classified as medieval military architecture.

After FRANCE, ENGLAND produces the most impressive Gothic architecture.

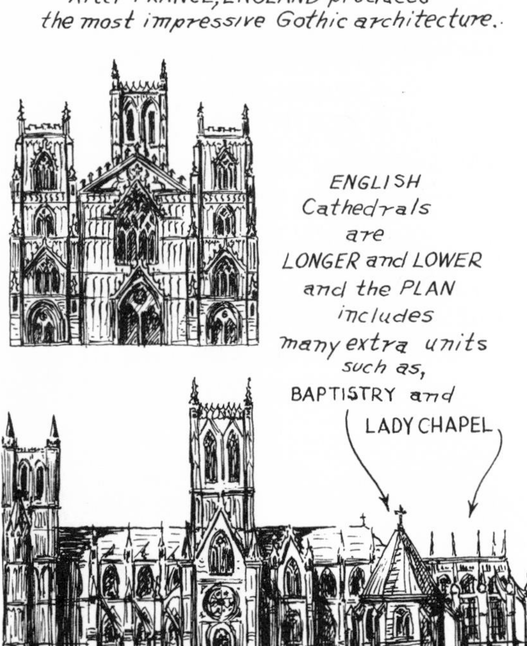
ENGLISH
Cathedrals
are
LONGER and LOWER
and the PLAN
includes
many extra units
such as,
BAPTISTRY and
LADY CHAPEL
SIDE ELEVATION

On interior trim GEOMETRIC PATTERNS replaced by FOLIAGE and NATURAL FORMS.

CAPITAL from Cluster-Columned PIER.

SPIRE of PIERCED STONE

GERMANY

In Italy
SECULAR Gothic
buildings
are more pleasing than
ecclesiastical, for which
ROMANESQUE style
continues in popularity,
with GOTHIC DETAIL.

ITALY never fully embraces GOTHIC architecture. Warm climate creates no need for large windows.

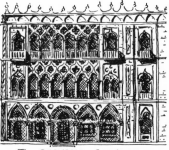

The REPUBLIC of VENICE produces charming GOTHIC PALAZZOS.

The CATHEDRAL of MILAN, considered best ITALIAN example, was designed by GERMAN architects and is TRANSITIONAL (Gothic-Renaissance).

# · GOTHIC ARCHITECTURE ·

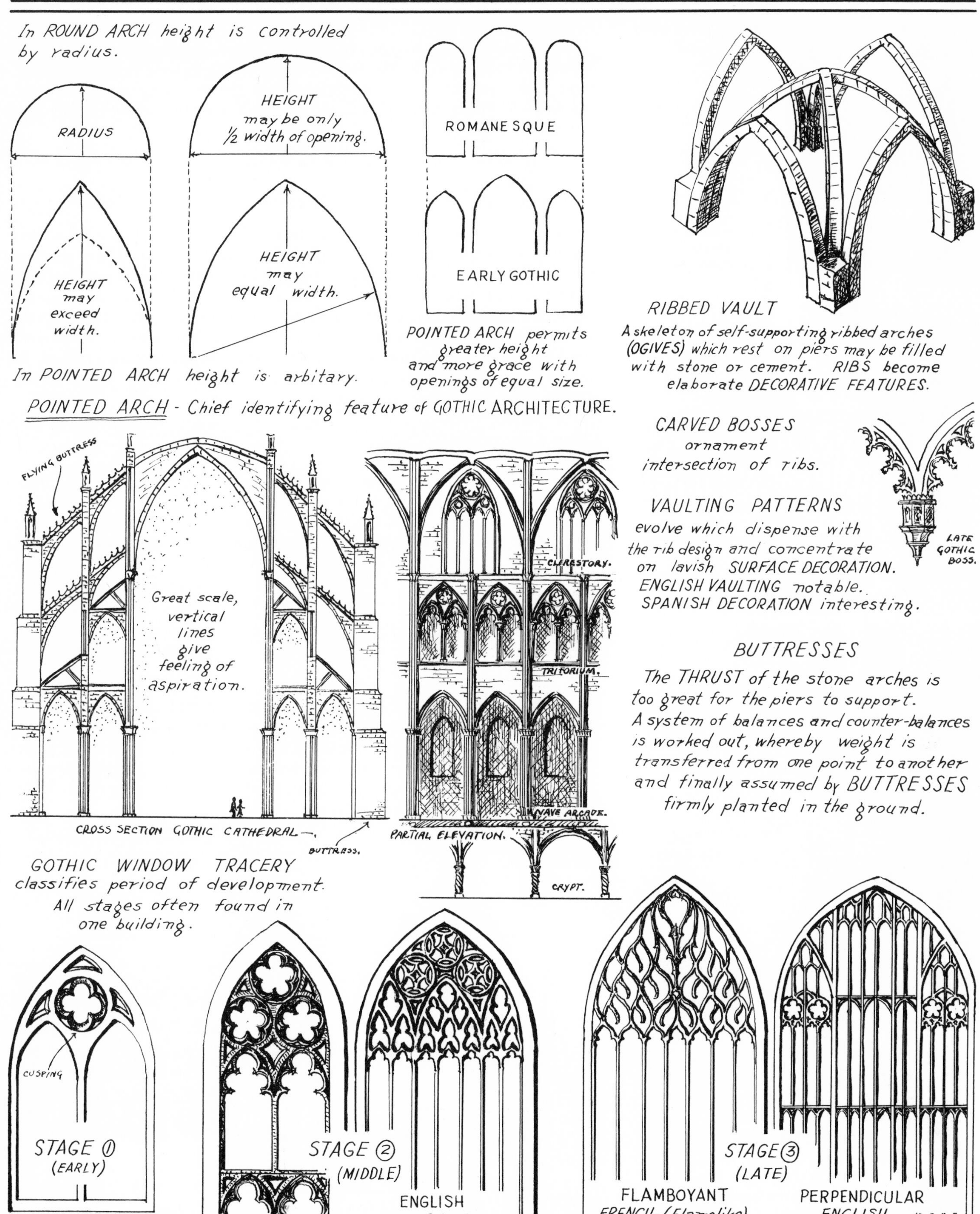

In ROUND ARCH height is controlled by radius.
RADIUS
HEIGHT may be only ½ width of opening.
HEIGHT may exceed width.
HEIGHT may equal width.
In POINTED ARCH height is arbitary.
ROMANESQUE
EARLY GOTHIC
POINTED ARCH permits greater height and more grace with openings of equal size.
RIBBED VAULT
A skeleton of self-supporting ribbed arches (OGIVES) which rest on piers may be filled with stone or cement. RIBS become elaborate DECORATIVE FEATURES.
POINTED ARCH - Chief identifying feature of GOTHIC ARCHITECTURE.
CARVED BOSSES ornament intersection of ribs.
LATE GOTHIC BOSS.
VAULTING PATTERNS evolve which dispense with the rib design and concentrate on lavish SURFACE DECORATION. ENGLISH VAULTING notable. SPANISH DECORATION interesting.
FLYING BUTTRESS
Great scale, vertical lines give feeling of aspiration.
CLERESTORY.
TRIFORIUM.
NAVE ARCADE.
CROSS SECTION GOTHIC CATHEDRAL.
BUTTRESS.
PARTIAL ELEVATION.
CRYPT.
BUTTRESSES
The THRUST of the stone arches is too great for the piers to support. A system of balances and counter-balances is worked out, whereby weight is transferred from one point to another and finally assumed by BUTTRESSES firmly planted in the ground.
GOTHIC WINDOW TRACERY classifies period of development. All stages often found in one building.
CUSPING
STAGE ① (EARLY)
STAGE ② (MIDDLE)
STAGE ③ (LATE)
FRENCH LANCE-SHAPED
EARLY ENGLISH
FRENCH RADIATING
Very tall, graceful.
ENGLISH DECORATED
Considered best ENGLISH period.
FLAMBOYANT
FRENCH-(Flamelike)
Spontaneous.
PERPENDICULAR
ENGLISH
Mechanical.

# · 13th and 14th CENTURY CULTURE ·

The meeting of ST. DOMINIC and ST. FRANCIS (in black and white) (in brown) founders of the mendicant (begging) orders which bear their names.

DANTE in his Divine Comedy gives the orthodox Christian conception of LIFE after DEATH.

GEOFFREY CHAUCER in describing the age in which he lived also reveals a timeless understanding of HUMAN CHARACTER.

(Eng.) England (Fr.) France (It.) Italy

## LITERATURE

Scholars study and write in Latin

## SCULPTURE AND PAINTING

Anonymous works

Sculpture and Stained Glass

Manuscripts
Altarpieces
Tapestries

### 13th century

| LITERATURE | SCULPTURE AND PAINTING |
|---|---|
| Thomas Aquinas (It.) | (painters) |
| | Cimabue (It.) |
| Roger Bacon (Eng., Science) | Duccio (It.) |
| | Giotto (It.) |

### 14th century

| LITERATURE | SCULPTURE AND PAINTING |
|---|---|
| St. Francis of Assisi (It.) | Simone Martini (It.) |
| Writings in vernacular languages. | Gaddi (It.) |
| Dante (It.) | Pucelle (Fr., illuminator) |
| Petrarch (It.) | |
| John Wycliffe (Eng., Bible) | |
| Chaucer (Eng.) | |

## HISTORY

Capets on French throne 987–1322

French house of Valois 1328–1574

Magna Carta 1215

Genghis Khan uses gunpowder

Marco Polo visits China—1271

Papal Supremacy 1198–1305

Crusades 1096–1270

100-Year-War between France and England 1350–1450
Plantagenets on English throne.

Popes at Avignon 1305–1377

Great Schism 1377–1417

Restoration of papal power at Rome 1417

## MUSIC

Beginning of contrapuntal composition. Rounds, catches, madrigals, villanelles, chanson, virelays—social music.

SIR GALAHAD sets forth on the QUEST of the GRAIL

Although the story of the cup used at the LAST SUPPER is a medieval favorite, the subject is seldom represented in art except in ILLUMINATED MANUSCRIPTS.

The legend is featured by TENNYSON and the PRE-RAPHAELITES during the 19th c. GOTHIC REVIVAL.

SOCIAL PRACTICES are depicted in MANUSCRIPTS.

The sport of HAWKING is popular.

After dinner the Great Hall is cleared for DANCING.

# 15th CENTURY CULTURE

## HISTORICAL EVENTS

Early Renaissance in Italy (page 104)

Gothic Age continues in other countries

John Huss burned as heretic 1415

Battle of Agincourt, 1415

Jeanne d'Arc 1429–1431

Fall of Constantinople, 1454

War of Roses in England Lancaster-York 1455–1485

Ferdinand and Isabella in Spain 1479–1509

Discovery of America, 1492

Beginning of Age of Exploration

Savonarola burned as heretic 1498

Spanish Inquisition begins

## LITERATURE

### England

Thomas Malory
William Caxton

### France

François Villon

### Germany

Erasmus
Gutenberg Bible

### Italy

Savonarola
Pico della Mirandola

## PAINTING

### The Netherlands

The van Eycks introduce oil pigment.
Weyden Memling Bouts

### France

Fouquet

### Franco-Flemish School

The Limburg Brothers

### Germany

Printing—Johannes Gutenberg
Engraving—Schongauer
Painting—Hans Holbein the Elder

### Italy

The Early Renaissance
(See page 102)

## MUSIC

The Netherlands perfects the five- six-part madrigal.

The GREAT HALL of of an early Gothic castle.
FIRE on open hearth without chimney. Smoke escapes through hole in roof.
FLARES provide light at night.
TAPESTRIES and WAINSCOT PANELING for warmth and pleasing decoration.
WALLS and FLOOR of STONE
CEILING—wooden BEAMS.
FURNITURE is still scarce.
Only heads of house provided with CHAIR. Others sit on BENCH, STOOL or CHEST.

British Coronation CHAIR – built in 1300 contains the STONE of SCONE on which early Scottish Kings were crowned.

OPEN FIRE acquires a FLUE.
All food prepared in cookhouse on spits and in copper kettles.

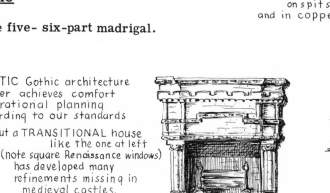

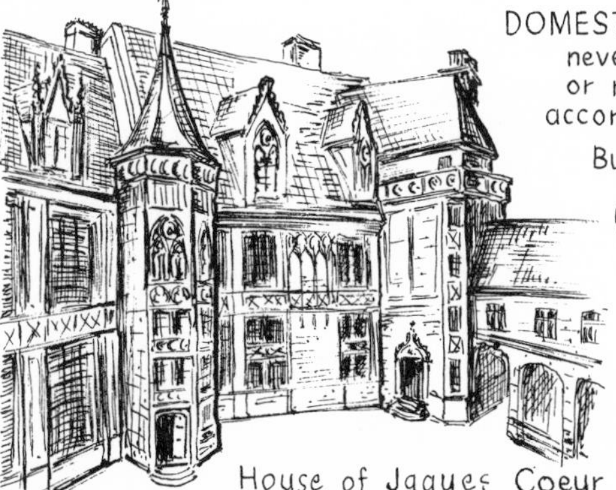

House of Jaques Coeur

DOMESTIC Gothic architecture never achieves comfort or rational planning according to our standards
But a TRANSITIONAL house like the one at left (note square Renaissance windows) has developed many refinements missing in medieval castles.
"The Moneyman" (Thomas Costain)

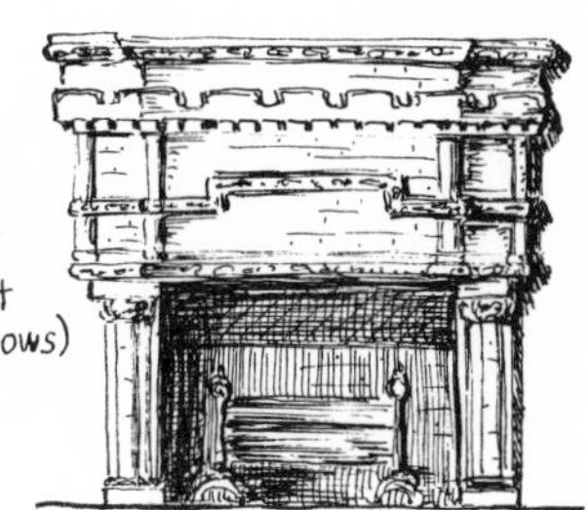

STONE FIREPLACE
High-ceilinged rooms have floor-to-ceiling FIREPLACES with openings 6 to 7 feet high.

# · MEDIEVAL SCULPTURE ·

① ROMANESQUE
*Figures conform to vertical lines of columns.*

② Middle GOTHIC
*Freestanding figure under canopy.*

③ *Flamboyant* GOTHIC *wood carving with minute detail.*

Never has sculpture played so important a part as it did in medieval religious architecture. There it fuses with the building in aesthetic and spiritual harmony.

In examining the iconography on a Romanesque or Gothic cathedral it must be remembered that each individual carving—and there are often thousands—is a selected symbol or character. These works are the schools and libraries through which the Bible stories and religious doctrines were presented to an unlettered population. Here there is no dull mechanical repetition but active purpose in every stroke of the chisel.

The early sculpture is not unlike archaic Greek work. The adherence to the vertical, and the fear of extending parts, give the figures a rigid but not uncharming conformity to the lines of the architecture of which they are a part.

As naturalism develops, the figures are freed from their background, appearing first in protective niches; then with casual grace under architectural canopies. During this middle period the sculptor is at his best—producing beauty combined with inspired characterization.

Bas-relief is used to advantage on flat surfaces and has the same characteristics as the sculpture.

The most elaborate carvings are to be found on wooden screens, choir stalls, pulpits, altars, etc. Stone was not considered too hard for this intricate work, but most of the cathedral buildings were completed by the time Gothic sculpture reached its final stage and the need was for interior trim. For indoor use there are also interesting large figures carved in wood and painted in naturalistic polychrome.

The amount of skillful detail in these late pieces is fascinating. But the figures had become the product of the knife rather than of inspired faith. The power of the earlier subtle, conscientious interpretations is lost. One marvels at the hand which created, but forgets to read its message.

The funeral statuary on the stone caskets should not be overlooked. It started with a stylized reclining figure symbolizing the sleep of the just. Personal realism was brought in by the use of death masks in the fourteenth century. The fifteenth-century expressions of agony and suffering are reminiscent of Hellenistic portrayals.

This is a fitting place to mention that the Crucifixion, which when first introduced showed a serene Christ in triumph over death, during the fifteenth century for the first time presents Him in torment. This is true of representations in any medium.

# · SEPULCHRAL SCULPTURE ·

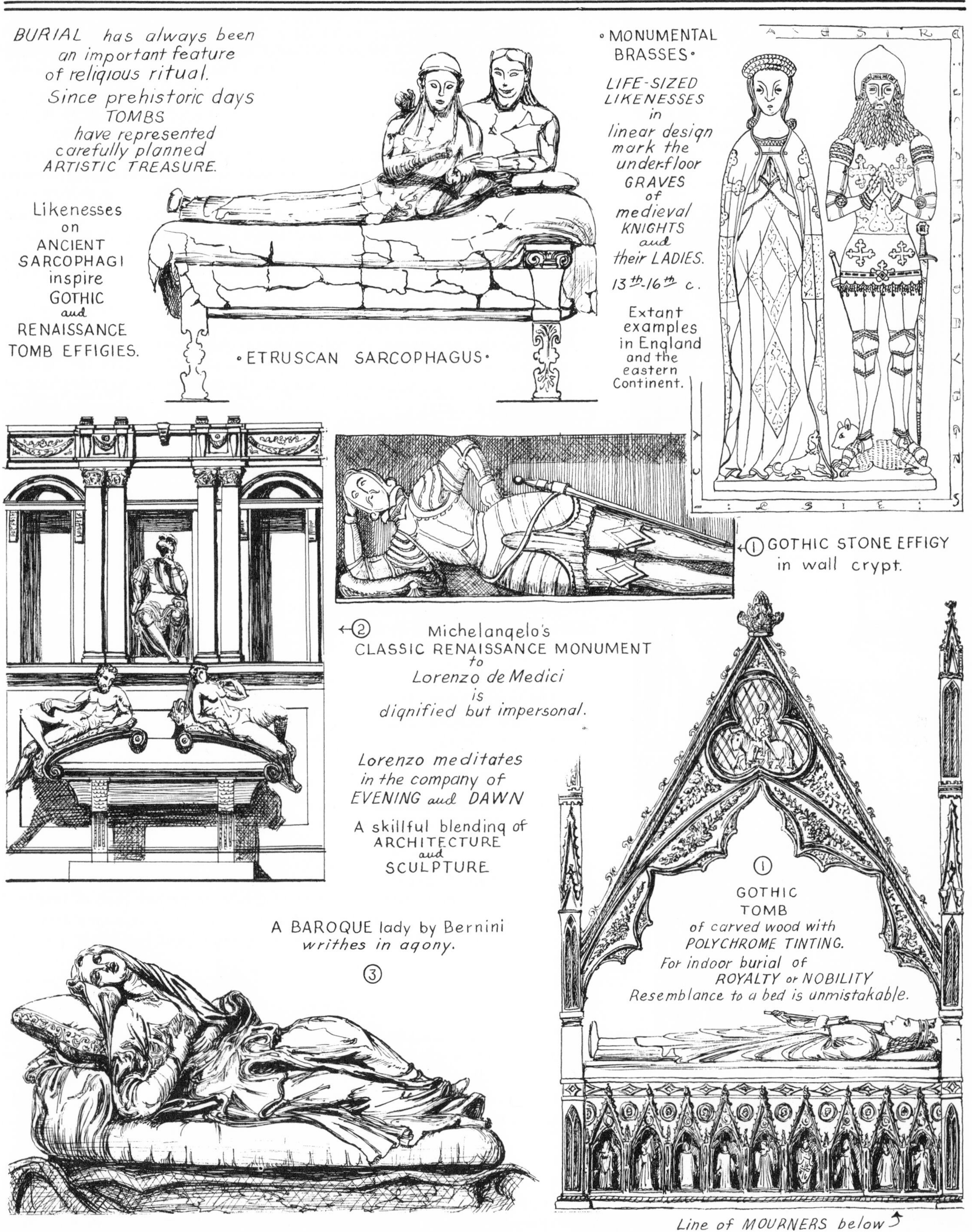
BURIAL has always been an important feature of religious ritual.
Since prehistoric days TOMBS have represented carefully planned ARTISTIC TREASURE.
Likenesses on ANCIENT SARCOPHAGI inspire GOTHIC and RENAISSANCE TOMB EFFIGIES.
· ETRUSCAN SARCOPHAGUS ·
· MONUMENTAL BRASSES ·
LIFE-SIZED LIKENESSES in linear design mark the under-floor GRAVES of medieval KNIGHTS and their LADIES.
13th-16th c.
Extant examples in England and the eastern Continent.
← ① GOTHIC STONE EFFIGY in wall crypt.
← ② Michelangelo's CLASSIC RENAISSANCE MONUMENT to Lorenzo de Medici is dignified but impersonal.
Lorenzo meditates in the company of EVENING and DAWN
A skillful blending of ARCHITECTURE and SCULPTURE
A BAROQUE lady by Bernini writhes in agony.
③
①
GOTHIC TOMB of carved wood with POLYCHROME TINTING.
For indoor burial of ROYALTY or NOBILITY
Resemblance to a bed is unmistakable.
Line of MOURNERS below ↑
① GOTHIC – Experimental ② RENAISSANCE – Naturalistic ③ BAROQUE – Emotional and exaggerated.

# · STAINED GLASS ·

13th c. Geometric Design. LEAD joinings are worked into overall design of TRANSLUCENT MOSAIC.

Early Leading STRENGTHENS design. Note: HAIR, EYE and HAND LEAD OUTLINE. Enameled details fused to glass suggest dark leadwork.

Stained glass windows were first used toward the end of the tenth century—probably in northern France, perhaps in the Low Countries. Although no examples from that date are extant, it is evident from the windows which survive from the following decades that the early stage of experimentation was over. With the development of the Gothic style, the colorful mosaics were transferred from the shrinking walls to the large window areas in the form of colored glass. The tinted glass with enameled detail was held in place by lead, which was advantageously worked into the design. These translucent mosaics warmed the gray stone interiors and showed practical and honest use of the brilliant new medium.

Stained glass windows are more alive than painting because the play of changing light behind the transparent, opaque and translucent glass gives a wealth and range of color not to be obtained by paint. To deaden the colors as was done during the Renaissance, when glass became an imitation of the prevailing style of painting, was a desecration of the art.

The biblical and legendary scenes worked into the church windows of the thirteenth century are less stylized than earlier ones and the leading is more artistically handled. But the colors are less glowing, with mauve taking the place of the beautiful sapphire-blue background. Toward the middle of the century there was a fad for grisaille (suggestion of sculpture), and the luminescent gray glass was introduced in other designs.

The use of stained glass spread from churches to private houses and public buildings, and in increased production the quality of color, design and workmanship suffered. Striving for the subtlety of an easel painting ruined the art in the sixteenth century, leaving it virtually forgotten until the Gothic Revival of the nineteenth.

Then the clumsy attempts of workmen appeared in the over-doors, bathroom windows, skylights, of the Historic Period Revival. Today we find them in many of our conventionalized period churches. The milky marbleization and the thin pastel colors have little in common with the fiery lights of the Middle Ages.

It is exciting to note that since World War II colored glass has been used in twentieth-century architecture. With the same basic need that gave the medium its start in the past, and the chemical color processes now available, it is possible that the lost art of yesterday may become a recognized skill of today.

Middle Gothic ARCHITECTURAL CANOPY and BORDER

Individual LIGHTS, themselves complete, form UNIFIED COMPOSITION within sectioned window. COLORS: Limited but Brilliant.

Renaissance Design within Gothic Tracery. 15th c. Beginning of an unfortunate DISREGARD for:
(a) The Architectural Framework
(b) The Construction Outlines of the Leading, and the
(c) Brilliance of Transparency.
Colors lightened and dulled as PAINTING supplies detail and interest.

END of GLAZIER'S ART and CRAFT.

(See page 169 for recent work)

Late 16th c. Renaissance stained glass windows are little more than NATURALISTIC PAINTINGS on glass, encumbered by leading.

Designed by the painter and executed by a mechanic, skillful planning and handling of medium becomes a LOST ART.

# · ILLUMINATED MANUSCRIPTS ·

Although sculpture was the important voice of medieval Europe, there are delightful and colorful painted presentations to be found in frescoes, illuminated manuscripts, altarpieces and retables of both the Romanesque and Gothic periods.

At first the work was done in monasteries but gradually the demand was too great to be handled by the monks, and other men were trained. Mosaics and paintings were reserved for important religious subjects, while frivolous society was served by lively drawings, woodcuts and tapestries. But always the medieval artist remained anonymous.

Illuminated manuscripts belong exclusively to the Middle Ages. They apparently originated at the time the rolled classic scroll was abandoned in favor of the flat page, and were Byzantine in origin. These hand-lettered, beautifully illustrated pages in brilliant color with gold detail set a fashion which was carried out in larger paintings on wood. The clear bright colors of egg tempera combined with gold leaf give a desirable unreality to the mysticism of religious story-telling, and the paintings shine with resplendent glory.

An independent element seems to have sprung up in the north when, toward the end of the seventh century, Ireland made an important contribution with her Book of Kells. This is an example of mechanical decoration at its greatest perfection, carried out to give the effect of sparkling enamel—without the use of gold.

Western European manuscripts combine the two styles. The work was done on vellum or parchment (treated animal skin), and was produced by almost assembly-line procedure. A scribe was responsible for the letters of the text; an illuminator, for the capitals and border decorations; and a miniaturist supplied the exquisitely detailed illustrations. But only one copy could be made, and books were rare and almost without price.

By the middle of the sixteenth century printing had revised the entire method of bookmaking. The manuscripts were a great artistic loss but had to be sacrificed to the practicality of the new process.

B - INITIAL
Whole page is given to free-hand drawing of almost mechanical PRECISION and DETAIL to introduce The PSALMS of DAVID.
"BEATUS VIR" - Blessed is the man.
Medallions illustrate episodes from life of DAVID.

ILLUMINATED MANUSCRIPTS present a continuous record of PAINTING for over 1000 years. Each period style is represented. MINIATURES inspire designs for other types of painting and for tapestries.

*CHRIST ENTHRONED in capital letter V* (primitive 10th c.)

16th c. MINIATURES are intricate renderings in CLASSIC RENAISSANCE STYLE.

• • • • •

omine
auguas
me: ne

GOSPELS, PSALTERS, MISSALS and BOOKS of HOURS (Selected quotations to be read on canonical hours) are popular.

• • • •

Volumes become jewel-like PICTURE BOOKS with Latin text held to a minimum.

• • • •

*DAVID and BATHSHEBA*

For other MINATURES see pages 68, 71, 80, 85, 112, 113, 127.

# ·TAPESTRIES·

The BATTLE of HASTINGS, 1066, *from the Bayeux Tapestry.* *Actually embroidery on linen NOT WOVEN. The strip-231 feet long-was ordered in 1083 to commemorate the NORMAN CONQUEST of ENGLAND.*

Wall hangings were not unknown in ancient times, but during the Middle Ages the need for color and warmth in the drafty, damp stone castles created a tremendous industry in woolen tapestries throughout the continent. The major centers were at Arras (14th and 15th c.), Brussels (15th and 16th c.), Middelburg, Delft and Paris (16th and 17th c.).

In the improved buildings of the Renaissance, tapestries were no longer necessary for comfort, but were desired for decoration. As the craze for copying oil paintings made more and more exacting demands, the process became so time-consuming that it took years to complete one design. There was no creative satisfaction for the weaver in the mechanics of carrying out someone else's cartoon. The client was dissatisfied with both cost and delay.

9TH C. ALTARPIECE from OSLO, NORWAY. *Many early medieval tapestries are long and narrow. Heavy tapestries are drawn across doorways and windows at night. In England French tapestries woven at ARRAS are so renowned that the name arras becomes synonymous with tapestry.*

Tapestries were gradually replaced by more easily procurable, more economical effects. Heavy paper printed with designs, stenciled patterns, draped or stretched fabrics, and even the very paintings the weavers tried so hard to imitate were used as decorative substitutes. By the middle of the seventeenth century the flourishing international business had dwindled to a highly specialized stagnant art. The most active factories were the Gobelin and Beauvais, which of necessity were supported by the French Crown. Private enterprise at Aubusson and the government-sponsored Savonnerie works since the eighteenth century have been producing tapestry-woven carpets of considerable merit.

Currently, an encouraging and courageous renaissance of the tapestry industry is being attempted in France. Perhaps to relieve the starkness of the International Style, wall hangings may again function as they did many centuries ago.

15TH C. FRANCO-FLEMISH GOTHIC tapestry. *Fascinating documentation of contemporary costumes. Simple border IDENTIFYING FEATURE of early designs.*

SAVAGE tapestry from Switzerland. *Subject based on lengendary inhabitants of alpine forests.*

# · MEDIEVAL LITERATURE ·

20TH Century "WHITE COCK"
Tapestry designed by Jean Lurçat

The world of Romanesque man was peopled with spirits and demons and brightened by visions. Dragons and unicorns ran in his forests and the air resounded with the voices of sprites and of angels. His body was attacked by filth, hunger and disease, but his soul and his imagination were free. He was often more interested in determining the number of feathers on the tip of an archangel's wing than he was in attending to the daily needs of his family. These were credulous times in which superstition took the place of reason and no tale was too strange for acceptance.

In this illiterate world legends flowered and were circulated by travelers and passed from father to son. Love, chivalry and religion were the favorite subjects and all three were often combined in one long ballad which was sung by wandering troubadours. For centuries history, fable and mystery were blended in these oral rhyming chronicles.

Some poems dealt with such subjects as the Trojan war or the exploits of Alexander the Great. But France produced a national epic in the Chanson de Roland, which told of the romance of Charlemagne's court. The Celtic hero Cuchulain was first adopted by the French and then nationalized into Britain's Gawain of King Arthur's Round Table. Robin Hood, the champion of the common man, was another English hero of the age.

The Latin of religious writings and of the schools and universities was meaningless to all but churchmen and scholars. The people were not interested in foreign languages or erudite subjects but preferred tales of human experience guided or provoked by the intervention of unearthly spirits. At the end of the Middle Ages the folk lore of the period was made available in part by writings in the vernacular languages.

Dates, Titles or Captions are worked into TAPESTRY BORDERS.

Unmarked pieces dated by border.

1. Romanesque – narrow and simple.
2. Gothic – lettered or geometric.
3. Renaissance – resemble picture frame or architectural setting.

A Roman or perhaps Celtic hero who fought the invasion of ANGLES and SAXONS in the 5TH C., was transformed into England's KING ARTHUR, the Christian ruler whose KNIGHTS embodied medieval chivalry.

TAPESTRIES as well as being FUNCTIONAL and DECORATIVE serve as substitute for written words.

The subjects treated:

RELIGION and MORALS
IMPORTANT PERSONAGES
LEGENDS and MYTHS
CURRENT HAPPENINGS
VERDURES (floral designs)
HERALDRY

"Millefleur" (thousand flowers) popular background.

(Also see page 168)

18TH C. Gothic Tapestry
One of a matched set.
Subject: DON QUIXOTE

# ·MEDIEVAL EDUCATION·

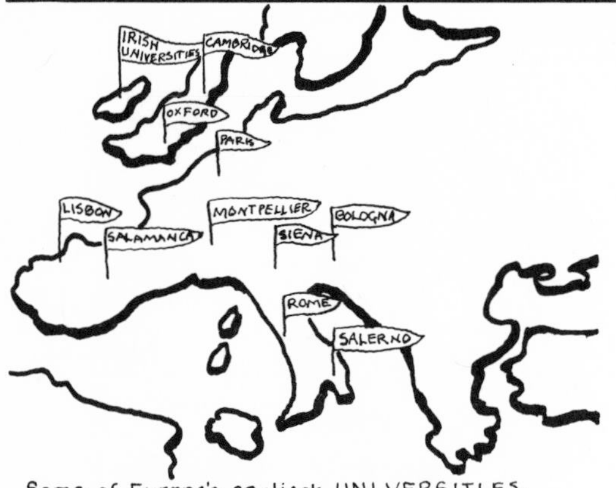
IRISH UNIVERSITIES
CAMBRIDGE
OXFORD
PARIS
LISBON
SALAMANCA
MONTPELLIER
SIENA
BOLOGNA
ROME
SALERNO

Some of Europe's earliest UNIVERSITIES. Graduates of those functioning under a papal charter are qualified to teach anywhere in the world.

From the sixth to the twelfth century the only scholastic institutions in Europe were those sponsored by the Church. Unlike the schools of ancient times where teachers like Socrates encouraged men to develop an intellectual curiosity about all things, the cathedral schools imparted only such information as was necessary to the priesthood, and monastic schools only that which furthered the aims of monasticism.

There were schools for knighthood, but they too were highly specialized. A knight was taught to fight gallantly, and any additional knowledge was considered superfluous.

A professor carries a MACE. Symbol of authority.

Professors and students are classed as CLERKS and are subject to trial only in ecclesiastical courts.

The robes worn by medieval scholars are to be seen today in academic graduations and processions.

But the human mind is difficult to channel or control. Out of the lack of educational opportunity there sprang spontaneous gatherings in pubs or hostels where draughts were downed and thoughts exchanged. Members of the clergy wandered in and contributed ideas culled from Greek and Roman texts, which, because of the lack of contemporary volumes, were preserved on the shelves of church libraries.

From these casual discussion groups the medieval university slowly evolved. It was not until the end of the fourteenth century that organization was brought to the Latin-speaking teachers and students who were meeting in various cities all over the continent. It then became necessary for the studium and the instructors to be licensed by civil or ecclesiastical authority. The seven liberal arts—grammar, rhetoric, logic, arithmetic, geometry, astronomy and music—were taught, as were canon (church) law and Roman (civil) law, theology and so-called medicine.

Although the Moslems, basing their studies on Oriental findings, were making strides in mathematics, medicine, chemistry and other forms of scientific study, European progress was hindered by superstition and lack of experienced teachers. The astronomer was busy casting horoscopes and the alchemist was preoccupied with finding the formula for changing base metal into gold. It was definitely not an age of scientific advancement in the West.

An alchemist in his laboratory tries for gold.

In 1453 the conquest of Constantinople by the Turkish Mohammad sends Greek scholars into Western Europe. They join the staffs of the universities and prepare the way for the RENAISSANCE, the revival of learning.

The eastern continent is dominated by the Turks and other Oriental invaders (see page 58) for many centuries.

*(Renaissance portrait)*

MOHAMMAD II
Organizer of the OTTOMAN system.

# ·ATTRIBUTES IN ART·

While the universities served serious scholars, the masses were educated through the arts.

In an effort to standardize the recognized educational value of artistic expression, the ninth-century Latin translation of the works of Dionysius the Areopagite was eagerly seized by the Church. In his Celestial Hierarchy the entire Kingdom of Heaven was described. A book on Mystic Theology supplied a code of symbolism. That these in recent years have proven to be writings of a fifth-century Dionysius, instead of the revelations of the deceased St. Paul to his friend and convert the first Bishop of Athens, does not minimize the part they played in the philosophy behind the art and literature of the Romanesque period, the Gothic age, and even the Renaissance.

The Apocryphal Gospels of NICODEMUS tell of VERONICA, who wiped the brow of Jesus on the road to Calvary. Her VEIL or HANDKERCHIEF retained His likeness and is her attribute in art.

Building on the framework supplied in these books, and adding to devices already accepted, a good part of the sculpture and painting from the ninth to the sixteenth centuries was planned so that no man, woman or child could fail to recognize the ideas, stories and people presented in the works of art. The system of symbols and attributes is here presented under Christian Symbolism, and the Celestial Hierarchy (page 88). The attribute of a saint usually symbolizes his real or legendary martyrdom. In some cases it may represent an accomplishment such as a book authored by the individual. Or it may suggest the form of the saint's patronage.

It is disappointing that the system is not foolproof. Patron saints of a community were seldom given attributes, because they were automatically recognized. But many pictures have been removed from their original surroundings and the identity of the saints lost. Ignorance of the code caused some medieval priests and artists to collaborate on independent interpretations. The system did not provide for legends respected only in certain areas or for those not sanctioned by the Church. The increasing freedom of the Renaissance mind encouraged painters to break with convention and rigid ecclesiastical authority, and gradually the custom was abandoned. But with all the exceptions there are many examples well worth examination.

In medieval art KING DAVID is numbered among the Prophets. Events of his life are portrayed in Renaissance paintings. A HARP is his personal attribute and symbol of the Book of Psalms.

ST. BLAISE, an Armenian Bishop, was also a physician. His aid is invoked against sore throats. He is a patron saint of wild animals. An IRON COMB is his attribute as he was tortured with one and cast into a lake. His wounds were miraculously healed and he walked upon the water preaching to the populace.

# · CULT of the VIRGIN ·

To understand the exalted position that Mary gradually assumed in Christian theology, it is necessary to examine the religions which were replaced by Christianity.

A fundamental instinct of primitive religions the world over is a fearful worship of the forces of nature. The mother earth with her cycle of awakening, blossoming, bearing and dying has always been gentle and generous and, therefore, the most beloved and least feared power of the universe. Goddesses personifying her purity (virginity) and fertility (motherhood) have long been revered. Common to many versions of heathen religions is the combination of the two attributes in a virgin mother (of the son of a god).

This basic idea was transferred to Christianity during the second century, when the most desirable qualities of womankind were bestowed upon the main female character of the Christian story. Pagan converts endowed the Virgin Mary with the admirable virtues of their former goddesses. Minor honors they conferred upon a growing society of saints.

The contention that the doctrine of the Trinity (325) made Mary not only the Mother of the Son of God, but the Mother of God himself, was upheld by the Orthodox Church (Ephesus, 431). Invocation of her aid was endorsed.

After this, images of her multiplied in such number that the Eastern Church condemned them as idols and sought to destroy them. But the violence of Leo the Image-breaker and his successors was so offensive that the reaction was one of fanatic loyalty to the Blessed Virgin. For the first time miraculous pictures and relics came into use.

During the age of chivalry the popularity of the Virgin grew until she became not only the influential mediator between man and God and the reigning Queen of Heaven, but in the hearts of the people she was the ever-present bountiful and benign heroine of the Middle Ages. The Church encouraged the devotion, and the titles accorded her are numerous and varied. She was the sublime inspiration of prayers, legends, ballads, poems and dramas, as well as the spiritual model for statues and paintings.

The Protestant Reformation of the sixteenth century divested Mary of all honors save that of being the Virgin Mother of Our Lord Jesus Christ.

The disputed dogma of her Immaculate Conception became the triumphant theme of the Catholic Counter Reformation. This raised her to supernatural glories by pronouncing her predestined sinlessness, her perpetual virginity and her eternal sanctification. The Rosary in its present form was adopted as a devotion in her name.

Today, though all but banished from the Protestant sects, the Virgin still is highly honored in the Catholic Church, and she and her images continue to comfort those who seek her kindly patronage.

(Fouquet)

*The Madonna as* •QUEEN of HEAVEN• *modeled by Agnes Sorel, mistress of Louis XI of France. Type of portrait madonna which is strenuously attacked by Savonarola.* *(see page 115)*

(Botticelli)

*Convincing combination of spiritual and human qualities portrayed as Virgin writes:* •MY SOUL DOTH MAGNIFY THE LORD• *Angel behind Madonna is LORENZO de Medici as a boy. Portraits are often to be found in pageantry of decorative scenes.*

HOLY FAMILY *including family of the Virgin* *(Mantegna)*

← *Subjects for PROMULGATION of the FAITH.* *(also see page 121)* →

# ·The VIRGIN in ART·

Oriental
·ANNUNCIATION·
Every country or continent gives the VIRGIN its particular RACIAL CHARACTERISTICS
*
·VIRGIN and CHILD ENTHRONED·
Devotional subject as dictated by ecclesiastical authority.
①
Unorthodox
·HOLY FAMILY·
belonging not to the CELESTIAL REALM but to EARTH is Michelangelo's own interpretation
*
The seven sorrows of the Virgin Mary symbolized by SWORDS.
(see page 87)
Allegorical subject.
·OUR LADY of SORROWS·
*
②
·PASTORAL MADONNA
Decorative Subject
(Raphael)
* *
The long-popular DOGMA of the ·ASSUMPTION· was made an Article of Faith in 1950.
(Titian 16th c.)
③
The disputed dogma of the IMMACULATE CONCEPTION is a favorite 17th c. theme.
* *
In 13th 14th and 15th c. Assumptions and Coronations the entire CELESTIAL HIERARCHY appears in MAJESTIC PANOPLY.
By comparison, later presentations are unpretentious.
Floral crown striking contrast to medieval royal crown (Murillo 17th c.)
SERIES of pictures from the LIFE of the VIRGIN, often composed from "GOLDEN LEGEND" (Voragine 15TH c.) or the SCRIPTURES.
PROTESTANTS consider all but the Biblical subjects are LEGENDARY or APOCRYPHAL.
·The ADORATION of the MAGI·
·CORONATION of the VIRGIN·
In the Marian Year of 1954 Mary is proclaimed Queen of Heaven and Earth.
(Murillo 17th c.)

# · JESUS in ART ·

JOSEPH
NICODEMUS
HORTUS
NICODEMUS · 2 · JOSEPH
②
①
③


For other representations
see EARLY CHRISTIAN (page 52)
CHRISTIAN SYMBOLISM (page 86)
CELESTIAL HIERARCHY
(page 88)

CHRIST
the LAMB of GOD,
one of the earliest forms
of representation
by SYMBOL.

CHRIST IN GLORY
giving the sign of
benediction
DECORATIVE SUBJECT.
*Romanesque Fresco*

CHRIST of
the RESURRECTION.
During the Renaissance
devotional pictures
are not as popular as
incidents from His life.

*Romanesque Storied Capital*
· FLIGHT into EGYPT ·

The imaginary GRIFFIN
appears in medieval decoration
as symbolic of the
TWO NATURES of CHRIST.
(EAGLES' WINGS - Heavenly, STRENGTH of LION - Earthly.)

Until the second
COUNCIL of NICAEA
in 787 when the
VENERATION of IMAGES
is defined,
there are few
DEVOTIONAL IMAGES
of JESUS Himself
but many
of the VIRGIN and SAINTS.

Forerunner of the Crucifix,
the FIVE RED JEWELS
symbolize
the wounds received
on the cross.

JOSEPH of ARIMATHAEA
a wealthy Jewish
disciple
asked Pilate for
the body of Jesus,
which
he placed in a tomb.

According to one legend
he later founded
the first Christian Church
in Britain.

According to the
GOSPEL of ST. JOHN
a man named
NICODEMUS
assisted Joseph
with the
interment.

During the ninth century
the theme of the CRUCIFIXION is introduced
In early presentations
Jesus is resigned to the cruelty of
His torture.

*(12th c. Fresco in Byzantine style.)*

*(10th c. Manuscript)*

The POST-RENAISSANCE PERIOD
brings an
insipid sentimentality
to OFFICIAL DEVOTIONAL ART
which persists even today.

The suffering of Christ
becomes a personal indignity
rather than
an unselfish sacrifice for His fellowmen.

The life of Jesus Christ is very naturally one of the most repeated subjects in Christian art. It is often presented in a succession of events as revealed in the scriptures, or individual incidents may be featured.

In addition to the many scenes in which He appears with the Virgin Mother, there are also the experiences which took place during His ministry. In these we have the introduction of other biblical characters, and in Renaissance pictures many contemporaries of the artists are to be found in the crowds.

The redeemed sinner Mary Magdalene is often in attendance. She is symbolic of repentant frailty, and is identified by her LONG HAIR, a JAR or a SKULL. Her sister Martha represents female discretion and good housekeeping, and her attribute is a LADLE or KEYS. Their brother Lazarus, whom Jesus raised from the dead, in the celestial hierarchy is shown as BISHOP of MARSEILLES.

Joseph of Arimathea and Nicodemus are present at the descent from the cross as those who removed the nails from His body.

There are several Marys who may be present while the sorrowing Mother holds the dead body of her Son. But facts are scarce and legend has confused the identities of the women. In addition to Mary Magdalene, there are Mary of Bethany, Mary Salome, Mary Cleophas and Mary the mother of James and John, and only the Magdalene has a recognizable attribute. The others vary in number at the discretion of the painter.

Joseph, the husband of the Virgin, appears in scenes from Jesus' childhood but died before the ministry. Therefore he is not included in the later events, nor is he featured in the celestial hierarchy.

The crucifixion, if Christ alone is portrayed, is symbolic of our salvation through His sacrifice. When accompanied by the Virgin and the beloved St. John, the theme is devotional. When the scene is enlivened by soldiers and other characters, it is the record of an historical happening.

The late medieval and early Renaissance schools of painting treat the events with dignity and reserve, and appropriate emphasis on the figure of Christ. The classic Renaissance, while not entirely orthodox in its approach, is seldom irreverent. But baroque artists were so eager to show their technical ability that the solemnity of the theme is often forgotten. Jesus is sometimes all but lost in the violence of the portrayals.

The early medieval church had symbols for the two natures of Christ —the human and the divine—and perhaps they are best suggested by that method. For the most unfortunate aspect of the presentation of Jesus in later realistic schools of art is the inability of any artist to grasp either nature in an adult characterization. The interpretation too often substitutes physical weakness for spiritual strength and results in an unconvincing flaccid young man who in no way brings to mind the vital leader who with forceful conviction propounded a doctrine of brotherly love and brought about a moral reformation.

*Three interesting interpretations of the same theme.*
° PIETA = Pity °
*Mary, John the Evangelist and Mary Magdalene mourn the dead Christ.*

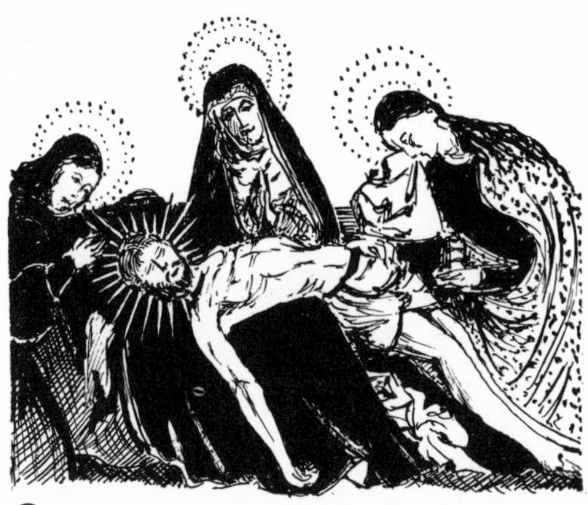

① French primitive against gold background.

② The Renaissance ideal of beauty is seldom sacrificed to the portrayal of human suffering (*Moretto da Brescia*)

③ The dignity and pathos of the scene are overshadowed by the artist's interest in foreshortening. (*Mantegna*)

## ·BYZANTINE EXTERIORS·

(For interiors and details see page 58).

*IDENTIFYING FEATURES:*
HUGE DOMES
SEEMING DISUNITY and CRUDENESS of EXTERIORS.

MINARETS added after Turkish conquest.

ST. Sophia, Constantinople (Now a Moslem Mosque)

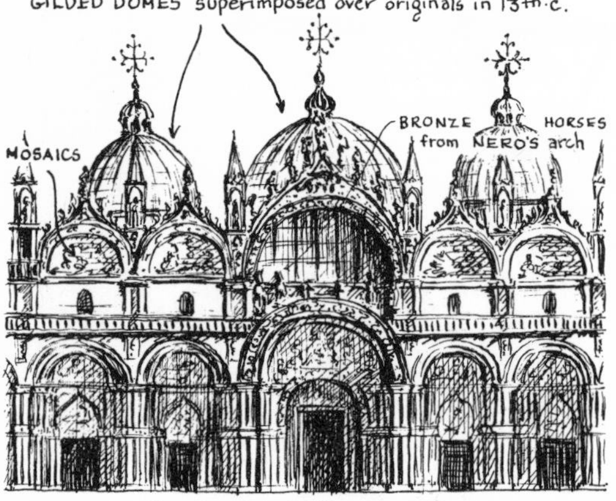
GILDED DOMES superimposed over originals in 13th c.
MOSAICS
BRONZE HORSES from NERO'S arch

St. Mark's in Venice

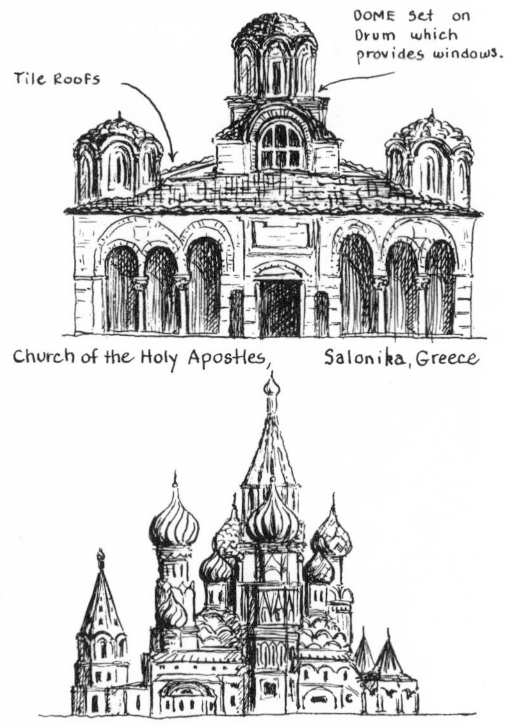
Tile Roofs
DOME set on Drum which provides windows.

Church of the Holy Apostles, Salonika, Greece

St. Basil's Cathedral - The Kremlin, Moscow
The onion-shaped domes found in Eastern Europe are borrowed from Persia and India.

## ·DOMESTIC ARCHITECTURE·

The RURAL COTTAGE
varies little from the Gothic Age
to the
Industrial Revolution
(12th to 19th centuries)

Built by hand of LOCAL MATERIALS,
basic plan is simple.
Details differ in each community.

Local GEOLOGY determines materials used:

WALLS - STONE, BRICK or TIMBER FRAME with fill of CLAY and WATTLE, BRICK or LATH and PLASTER.

Pitched ROOF covered with THATCH, TILE, STONE or SLATE.

FLOORS - Ground floor CLAY, STONE or BRICK. Upper floor, BOARD.

WINDOWS - Small because glass is expensive.

FIREPLACE used for COOKING, HEATING and ILLUMINATION.

CANDLES and OIL LAMPS luxuries of rich.

SANITATION - Water from spring or well.

· · · · · ·

As the Gothic Age wanes Italy's new style is reflected in the · MODEST CITY DWELLINGS · of the growing bourgeoisie (middle class).

In 15th and 16th c. England the HALF-TIMBER HOUSE developes from FUNCTIONAL FRAME to DECORATIVE BEAMING.
Renaissance Details creep in.
Decorative Gable

England France Low Countries Germany

CHRISTIAN
SYMBOLISM
IN ART

Symbolism in colors:

WHITE = Innocence, purity. Light. Gladness. (Worn by Mary prior to Annunciation and in scenes of the Immaculate Conception. Christ in Transfiguration.)

RED = Divine love. Hate. Martyrdom. Power. (Cardinals' robes).

RED and WHITE = Love and wisdom.

RED and BLUE = Heavenly love and heavenly truth. (Worn by Christ and Mary.)

BLUE = Constancy and fidelity. (Mantle of the Madonna. Christ during His ministry. Tunic of St. John.)

GREEN = Hope. Victory. Triumph of life over death. Immortality.

YELLOW. Clear yellow = Faith. Goodness. (Peter: yellow and blue.) Revealed truth. (Worn by Joseph.)
Dirty yellow = Deceit. Treason. Degradation. (Judas. Heretics. Sign of the plague.)
Gold = Divinity. (Background for sacred scenes.)

VIOLET (purple) = Passion, suffering. (Worn by Mary after Crucifixion.) Penance. (Mary Magdalene)

BROWN = Spiritual death and degradation. Renunciation of the world. (Habit of Franciscan and Capuchin orders.)

GRAY = Mourning. Humility. (Worn by some Benedictines.)

BLACK = Pagan death symbol continues in Christian usage. Wickedness.

BLACK and WHITE = Purity of life. Humiliation. (Worn by Dominican and Carmelite orders.)

# · SYMBOLS, ATTRIBUTES and EMBLEMS ·

Symbolism is the practice of expressing the intangible or spiritual by means of visible representations. The Christian Church relied upon signs and symbols for hundreds of years.

The coat of arms of ENGLAND'S KING (Early Medieval). The lion has long been considered the SYMBOL of SOVEREIGNTY. On a shield it becomes an identifying EMBLEM

In the Early Church the original purpose of symbols was to conceal. In the medieval church symbols, attributes and emblems were used to aid religious instruction. Many of these signs are no longer recognized, and without explanation or a key they have become charming but meaningless decoration.

The WINGED LION when it appears unaccompanied by a saint is the EMBLEM of MARK the Evangelist.

Symbolism was essential to the illiterate society of the Middle Ages. It was fraught not only with spiritual meaning but with superstition and mysticism as well. It was conscientiously worked into architecture, sculpture, painting, tapestries, mosaics and stained glass. It was carried over into the Renaissance but was gradually lost as first the pagan past and then the quest for learning captured men's imagination.

Today some of the language is still used in the Catholic and the Anglican Episcopal churches. But as the Reformation demanded a simplification of ritual and direct personal communication with God, symbolism has been given a small part in most Protestant worship.

MANUSCRIPT

The WINGED LION with the saint is the identifying ATTRIBUTE of MARK the Evangelist.

In medieval and Renaissance art the following signs are to be found:

A SYMBOL is a design or object which represents an idea.
Ex. LION = Power, sovereignty

An ATTRIBUTE is an object which accompanies a figure for purposes of identification.
Ex. WINGED LION = St. Mark

An EMBLEM is the attribute representing a person in absentia.

BASE of MARBLE CANDELABRUM

In ecclesiastical ARCHITECTURAL DETAIL the lion is symbolic of CHRIST, the lord of life.

According to folklore, lion cubs are born dead but come to life in three days when breathed upon by their sire. The parallel to the RESURRECTION is obvious.

COLUMN on PULPIT

ST. JEROME in the wilderness is accompanied by the ATTRIBUTE of his old age – the GRATEFUL LION from whose paw he removed a thorn. For the same JEROME as Church Father, see Celestial Hierarchy.

ST. MARY of Egypt, ST. EUPHEMIA, ST. ONUPHRIUS and sometimes ST. PAUL the Hermit have the LION as an ATTRIBUTE.

RENAISSANCE PAINTING

# ·CHRISTIAN SYMBOLISM·

A FISH is the earliest Known Christian SYMBOL.

Letters in Greek word for fish = ΙΧΘΥΣ same as first letters in words meaning: Jesus Christ God's Son Saviour.

The Sacred PAGAN DOLPHIN was most often used, as it offered *concealment.*

Used for *IDENTIFICATION* and as a SYMBOL for ·*CHRISTIANITY*·

A FISH is an ATTRIBUTE of the Apostle Peter.

1 LAMB = *the Redeemer.*
2 SHEEP = *Christians.*
12 SHEEP = *Apostles.*


·*CHRIST THE REDEEMER*·
Hebrew Sacrificial animal most popular representation until 6 th century.

About the 10th century the FISH was abandoned in favor of THE CROSS.
The universal symbol for Christianity then took the form of the criminal's cross on which Christ was crucified.

Other types of crosses carry reverent significance.

Elaborate and ornamental variations are carried in religious processions.

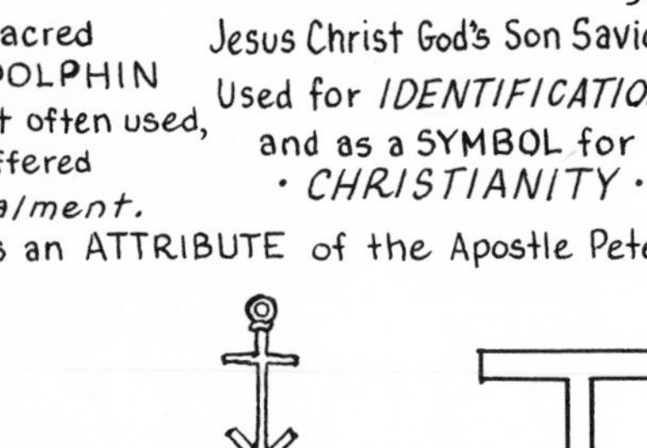

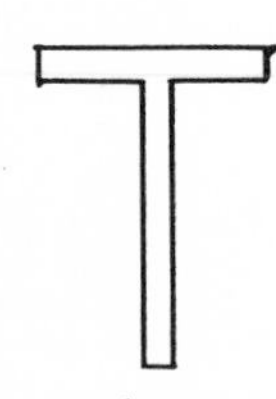

Anchor — Monogram — St. Anthony's

ANCHOR = *Salvation, Hope.*
CONCEALED CROSSES

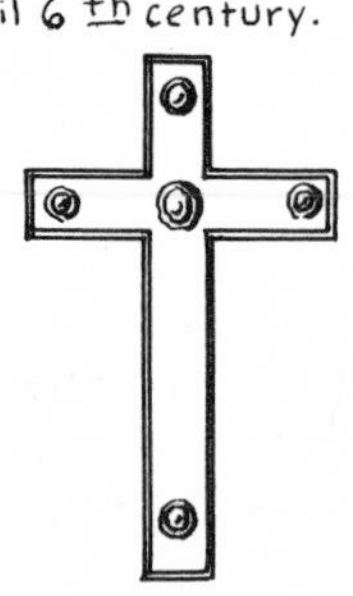

Forerunner of crucifix
FIVE RED JEWELS
Symbolic of *WOUNDS of CHRIST.*

St. Andrew's

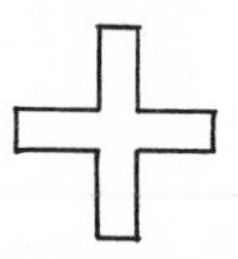

Greek

Maltese

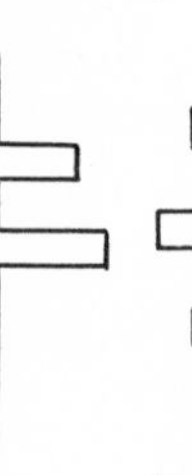

Patriarchal Archiepiscopal — Papal (trinity) — Celtic (see circle) — Calvary


FAITH
HOPE
CHARITY


·LATIN CROSSES·

Ancient victory symbol takes on new meaning.
PALM becomes symbol of Christian martyrdom.

PELICAN with own blood feeding young = *REDEMPTION.*

·HALO· GLORY ·OR· NIMBUS·

Pagan emblem of *DIVINITY*
Greek-Christian attribute of *POWER.*
Latin-Christian symbol of *BEATITUDE.*

Statues of Greek Gods and Roman Emperors are adorned with GOLDEN RADII. Similiar symbol avoided by Christians until after fall of Western Rome.

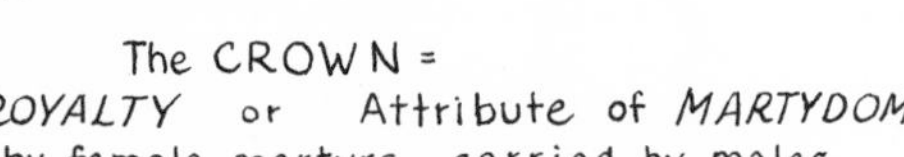

The CROWN =
Symbol of *ROYALTY* or Attribute of *MARTYDOM*
Worn by female martyrs, carried by males.

GLOBE = *Power*
*Attribute of God the Father.*
*Emblem of Christ's sovereignty.*
*Symbol of imperial power of King.*

The CRUCIFIXION = *REDEMPTION*
through sacrifice of Jesus.
Subject appears in art about 6th. Century.

GOLD DISK
12th. - 15th. c.

PLATE
Earliest form
5th. - 12th. c.

GOLDEN FILLET
15th. - 17th. c.

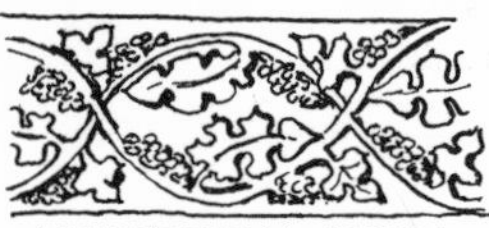

ARCHITECTURAL DETAIL

GRAPES and VINE = *Wine of EUCHARIST.*
WHEAT or CORN = *BREAD*
BREAD BASKET = *Body of CHRIST*

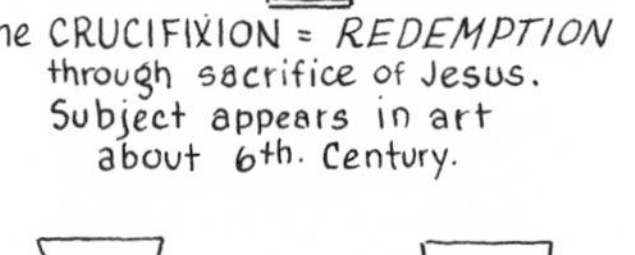

CHALICE = EUCHARIST (Last Supper)
WINE = BLOOD
WAFER = BODY

HOLY ORDERS

SQUARE
Designates *LIVING PERSON* such as donor.

with CROSS = *one of Trinity.*

FLAMING HEART = *Sacred Love.*
Attribute - St. Theresa
Sometimes St. Augustine

APPLE = *Redemption through Fall of Man.*

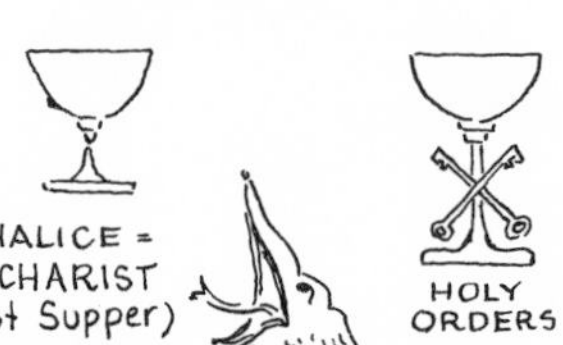

AUREOLE
Radiations often encircle entire figures of TRINITY or VIRGIN.

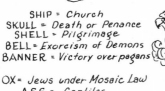

SHIP = *Church*
SKULL = *Death or Penance*
SHELL = *Pilgrimage*
BELL = *Exorcism of Demons*
BANNER = *Victory over pagans*

OX = *Jews under Mosaic Law*
ASS = *Gentiles*
STAG = *Christians*

PEACOCK and POMEGRANATE = *Immortality and Resurrection.*

LILY = *Purity and Chastity.*

The DRAGON and SERPENT = *SIN*

HEXANGLE =
Allegorical figures such as VIRTUES.

The MANDOLA or *almond shaped* aureole surrounding CHRIST or the VIRGIN is often described today as WOMB-SHAPED

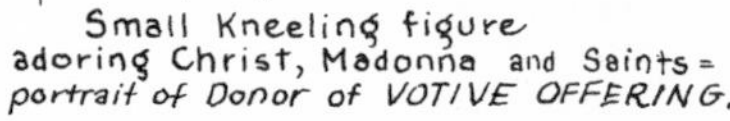

Small Kneeling figure adoring Christ, Madonna and Saints = *portrait of Donor of VOTIVE OFFERING.*

Symbolism to be found in numbers:

ONE = Unity
TWO = The two natures of Christ, human and divine
THREE = The Trinity
FOUR = The four Evangelists, often symbolized by four rivers
FIVE = The wounds of Christ
SIX = Creation (God created man on the sixth day.) Also symbolizes divine power. Six candles on the altar represent constant round of prayer.

SEVEN = The mystic number

The Seven Sacraments—Seven candles on altar
Baptism, Confirmation, Communion, Penance, Marriage, Extreme Unction, Holy Orders

The Gifts of the Holy Ghost:
Wisdom, Understanding, Counsel, Fortitude, Knowledge, Piety and Fear of the Lord

The Seven Deadly Sins:
Pride, Covetousness, Lust, Anger, Gluttony, Envy and Sloth

The Seven Virtues:
The Three Theological Virtues:
Faith, Hope and Charity
The Four Cardinal Virtues:
Temperance, Prudence, Fortitude, Justice

The Gifts, Sins and Virtues in art are personified by female figures.

Seven Joys of the Virgin Mary:
Annunciation, Visitation, Adoration of the Magi, Presentation in the Temple, Christ found by His Mother, Assumption and Coronation

Seven Sorrows of the Virgin Mary:
The Prophecy of Simeon, Flight into Egypt, Christ lost by His Mother, Betrayal of Christ, Crucifixion, Deposition from the Cross, Ascension of Christ

EIGHT = The Resurrection (Christ rose from the grave eight days after He entered Jerusalem.)
NINE = The nine choirs of angels surrounding God
TEN = The Ten Commandments
TWELVE = The Apostles
THIRTEEN = Faithlessness and betrayal (Judas, the betrayer, the thirteen at Last Supper.)
FOURTEEN = The Stations of the Cross (Scenes on the Road to Calvary.)
FIFTEEN = Mysteries of the Rosary (Events in the lives of Mary and Jesus.)
TWENTY-FOUR = Elders of the Apocalypse
FORTY = Period of trial or probation. Moses on Mt. Sinai. The Flood. Christ in the Wilderness. Lent
ONE HUNDRED = Plenitude. Full, complete
ONE THOUSAND = Eternity. When the world did not come to an end during the first generation of Christians, they predicted it would in 1000 A.D.

In the days of hand lettering, many abbreviations are used. Alphabets and spelling are inconstant, so that variations occur.

IHS · IHC · IHΣ
are the first three letters in Ihsus meaning Jesus in Greek.

XP · ☧ · ☧

from XPIΣTOΣ or Christ in Greek

IX = Gk. initials of Jesus Christ.

monogram

Monogram combined with eternal circle was used on Roman standards after reign of Constantine.

INRI

First letters of Latin words meaning "Jesus of Nazareth, King of the Jews."

A ω

"I am Alpha and Omega, the beginning and the ending, saith the Lord". Used as an attribute for the Son of God.

The first letter of Theos, Greek for God. An attribute for St. Anthony. (See Cross and Celestial Hierarchy.)

· CIRCLES and SQUARES ·

ETERNITY. HUMANITY.

OR CLASPED HANDS = MARRIAGE.

Representations of the TRINITY.

TRIPLE CANDLESTICK

The THREE PERSONS of the TRINITY

Also see Celestial Hierarchy

TRIANGLE

sometimes with initials or monogram

TREFOILS
Gothic Cusping
Unity and Infinity

Since 16TH century embroidered on CATHOLIC BISHOPS' VESTMENTS.

# ·THE CELESTIAL HIERARCHY·

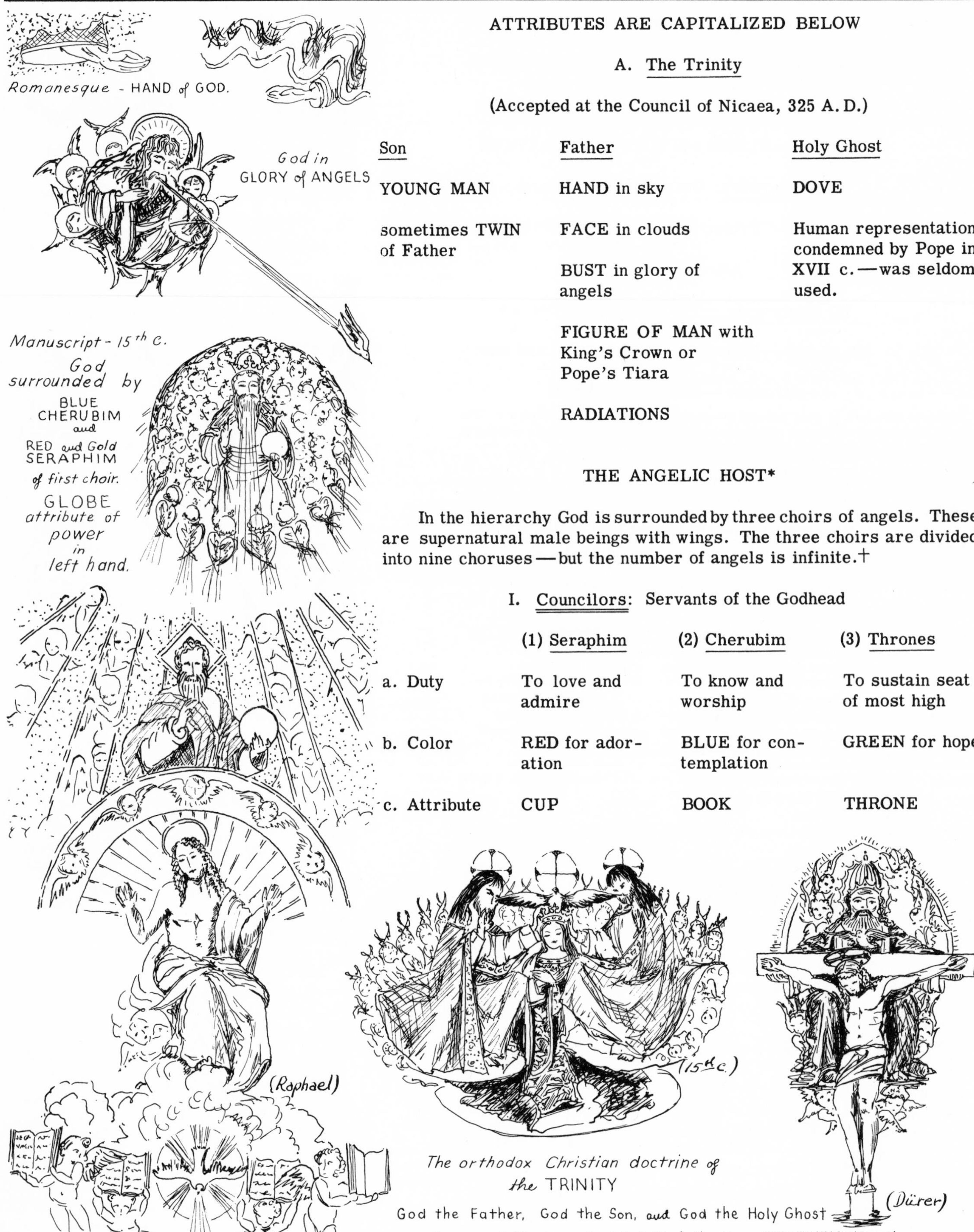

Romanesque - HAND of GOD.
God in GLORY of ANGELS
Manuscript - 15th c.
God surrounded by BLUE CHERUBIM and RED and Gold SERAPHIM of first choir.
GLOBE attribute of power in left hand.
(Raphael)
(15th c.)
(Dürer)


The orthodox Christian doctrine of the TRINITY

God the Father, God the Son, and God the Holy Ghost causes Jews and Moslems to label Christianity a POLYTHEISTIC religion.

ATTRIBUTES ARE CAPITALIZED BELOW

A. The Trinity

(Accepted at the Council of Nicaea, 325 A. D.)

| Son | Father | Holy Ghost |
|---|---|---|
| YOUNG MAN | HAND in sky | DOVE |
| sometimes TWIN of Father | FACE in clouds | Human representation condemned by Pope in XVII c.—was seldom used. |
| | BUST in glory of angels | |
| | FIGURE OF MAN with King's Crown or Pope's Tiara | |
| | RADIATIONS | |

THE ANGELIC HOST*

In the hierarchy God is surrounded by three choirs of angels. These are supernatural male beings with wings. The three choirs are divided into nine choruses—but the number of angels is infinite.†

I. Councilors: Servants of the Godhead

| | (1) Seraphim | (2) Cherubim | (3) Thrones |
|---|---|---|---|
| a. Duty | To love and admire | To know and worship | To sustain seat of most high |
| b. Color | RED for adoration | BLUE for contemplation | GREEN for hope |
| c. Attribute | CUP | BOOK | THRONE |

# ·THE CELESTIAL HIERARCHY·

THE ANGELIC HOST (continued)

II. Governors: Regents of the Stars and Elements

(4) Dominations (5) Virtues (6) Powers

Attribute — GLOBE and SCEPTER with CROSS

III. Ministers: Guardians of the Earth

(7) Principalities — Protectors of great monarchies on earth

Attribute — LILY

(8) Archangels — The seven listed below‡

(9) Angels — Messengers between God and man

Attribute — DEACON'S WAND

*Angels (bearers of good tidings) are popular in both art and literature. The idea of supernatural winged creatures was borrowed from Assyria and Egypt by the Hebrews and then fitted into the Christian pattern.

†Restriction of space often leads to abbreviation of the choirs, and mingling of the colors and attributes. Sometimes three angels with multicolored wings will represent the entire multitude.

As angels are the choristers of Heaven, they are often supplied with musical instruments.

| ‡Archangel saints | Duty | Attribute |
|---|---|---|
| Michael | Patron saint of church militant | SWORD and SCALES |
| Gabriel | Guardian of the Virgin Mary | LILY |
| Raphael | Chief of Guardian angels | PILGRIM'S STAFF |
| Uriel | Regent of the sun | SCROLL or BOOK |
| Chamuel | (wrestled with Jacob) | CUP and STAFF |
| Jophiel | Guardian of Tree of Knowledge (drove Adam and Eve from Garden) | FLAMING SWORD |
| Zadhiel | (stayed hand of Abraham when about to sacrifice his son) | SACRIFICIAL KNIFE |

They appear as warriors with sword, shield and trumpet when grouped together.

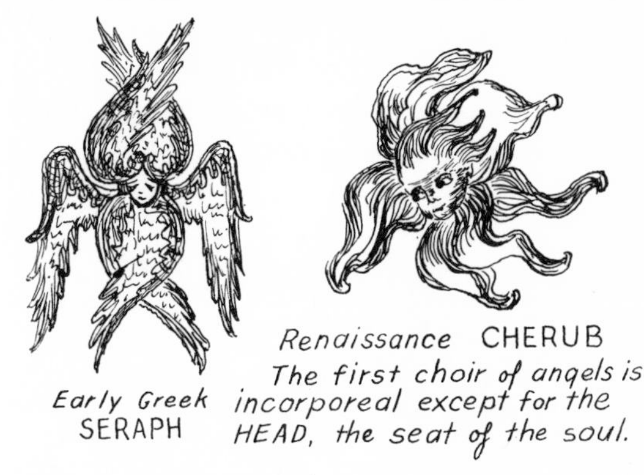
Early Greek
SERAPH
Renaissance CHERUB
The first choir of angels is incorporeal except for the HEAD, the seat of the soul.

Greek
ANGEL
11th c.
Renaissance ANGEL,
CLASSICALLY ATTIRED.
Fashionable
headgear
15th c.
Gothic ANGELS
of the north
wear
ELABORATE COSTUMES
ANGELS of
the Baroque style
are
in motion
and lack
the dignity and
repose of
earlier schools.
LILY
symbol of
purity.
Therefore
symbol of
Virgin Mary.
Attribute of the
ARCHANGEL GABRIEL

The ARCHANGEL MICHAEL also ANGEL of DEATH Attribute: SCALES

The Archangels are first mentioned in the Old Testament and in addition to being Christian SAINTS are revered by Jews and Moslems.

← ARCHANGEL RAPHAEL·

...

As guardian of the VIRGIN MARY the ARCHANGEL GABRIEL appears frequently. The variations in Annunciation scenes are fascinating

# ·THE CELESTIAL HIERARCHY·

B. The Virgin Mary

CROWNED QUEEN OF HEAVEN
(sits to right of Jesus)

·MARY and JESUS·

·The VIRGIN· ·JESUS· ·St. JOHN·

C. John the Baptist

Cousin of Jesus
FUR SHEPHERD'S ROBE
and STAFF with CROSS
(sits on Jesus' left)

·JOHN the Baptist·

D. The Four Evangelists
Witnesses and recorders

| Matthew | Mark | Luke | John |
|---|---|---|---|
| WINGED ANGEL | WINGED LION | WINGED OX | WINGED EAGLE |

·MATTHEW and MARK·

·CHRIST with Emblems of the APOSTLES·

·LUKE and JOHN·

E. The Patriarchs*

The wise leaders of the Old Testament. The selection varies: Abraham, Isaac, Jacob and his twelve sons, Noah, Enoch, Ezra, etc.

F. The Prophets*

Selected from among the many in the Old Testament who were gifted with prophecy: Moses, Aaron, Gideon, Daniel, Isaiah, Ezekiel, David, etc.
SCROLL of PROPHECY

Sibyls—Female prophets from apocryphal writings are sometimes included. Examples: Tiburtina and Cumean Sibyls.

TABLETS with Ten Commandments

·MOSES·
Attribute of HORNS comes from mistranslation of Hebrew text.

A Prophet

An Elder

A Prophet

SCROLL

·DAVID·
Attribute: CROWN or HARP (see page 77).

*On occasion these are replaced by—but often included in—the nameless "Twenty-four Elders of the Apocalypse." (Apocalypse = Book of Revelations of St. John the Divine.)
MUSICAL INSTRUMENTS

# ·THE CELESTIAL HIERARCHY·

## G. The Twelve Apostles

These men were chosen by Jesus from among His disciples to go forth and spread His teachings. According to legend all but John died as martyrs. All are Christian saints.

| | | | |
|---|---|---|---|
| Peter | KEYS to heaven and hell or FISH | Converter of Jews. Founder of Church. | Crucified head down 67 A.D. |
| Andrew | TRANSVERSE CROSS | Brother of Peter | Crucified on transverse cross |
| James Major | PILGRIM'S STAFF | Cousin of Jesus | Beheaded 44 A.D. |
| John | CHALICE with SERPENT, BLUE ROBE | The "Beloved" Disciple, also Evangelist | Escaped from boiling oil |
| Thomas | BUILDER'S RULE | "Doubting" Thomas | Speared |
| *James Minor | CLUB | | Clubbed to death |
| Philip | CROSS on STAFF | | Crucified |
| Bartholomew | KNIFE | | Skinned alive and crucified |
| Matthew | PURSE | Tax gatherer — also Evangelist | Killed with halberd 60 A.D. |
| Simon | SAW | | Crucified 74 A.D. |
| *Jude (Thaddeus) | HALBERD | | Crucified 72 A.D. |
| Judas Iscariot | DIRTY YELLOW ROBE | Shown accepting the thirty pieces of silver or at Last Supper | Hanged self after betrayal |
| *Matthias | LANCE | Chosen in place of Judas | Stoned and beheaded |
| Paul | SWORD | Self-appointed after seeing vision of Christ on road to Damascus. Converter of Gentiles. Author of several New Testament books. | Beheaded with sword 67 A.D. |

**Barnabas** Self-appointed companion of Paul and later of Mark. Author of the apocryphal "Epistle of Barnabas." He is often shown as an apostle and referred to as a prophet. Legendary martyrdom at Salamis.

*Often replaced by Paul, Luke and Mark. Great liberties are taken with the selection and order of the apostles, and because of the many conflicting tales of their deaths the attributes are not constant.

*CHARACTERIZATIONS differ with Age and Artist.*

ATTRIBUTES *presented with infinite* VARIETY.

St. Paul

St. Peter

PURSE of St. Matthew

KNIFE of St. Bartholomew

St. John

1
2
3
4

1. STAFF of St. James Major
2. HALBERD of St. Jude
3. LANCE of St. Matthias
4. CLUB of St. James Minor

St. Thomas St. Philip St. Andrew

Composite impressions of the Church Fathers.

ST. Jerome with CHURCH.

St. Ambrose with SCOURGE.

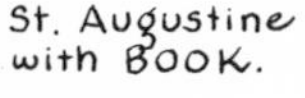

St. Augustine with BOOK.

St. Gregory with DOVE.

Typical GREEK Father.

### H. The Church Fathers

Represent the Church Militant (Church on Earth) as the recognized teachers and interpreters of the creed.

The Roman Catholic Church:

| | | |
|---|---|---|
| St. Jerome (342–420) | CARDINAL with CHURCH in HAND or OLD MAN with BOOK and LION | Translator of "Vulgate" Bible—Greek to Latin. Introduced monastic life in Italy. |
| St. Ambrose (340–397) | BISHOP with MITRE and CROSIER carrying SCOURGE (penance he demanded of others) or BEEHIVE (organization within church) | Bishop of Milan |
| St. Augustine (354–430) | BISHOP with BOOKS sometimes FLAMING HEART and ARROW | Bishop of Hippo Author of Confessions and City of God. |
| St. Gregory (540–604) | TIARA of POPE, CROSIER with PATRIARCHAL CROSS. DOVE on SHOULDER | "Pope Gregory the Great." Instituted celibacy of clergy. Made Purgatory an article of faith. |

The Greek Orthodox Church (Byzantine):

Because of the strong feeling in the Eastern Church against the worship of idols, these men are not represented in sculpture. They most often appear in painting grouped together as saints rather than as mitred bishops. As is usual in the East, the use of names makes attributes unnecessary.

St. John Chrysostom (344–407) "of the Golden Mouth."

St. Basil the Great (328–380) founded monasticism in the East.

St. Athanasius (298–373) opposed Arian heresies.

St. Gregory Nazianzen (329–390)—Christian poet.

St. Cyril of Alexandria (Patriarch of Alexandria from 412–444).

### I. Bishops

Bishops of the Early Church who are honored as propagators of the Faith. Examples:

Sylvester of Rome — Ignatius of Antioch

BEARD, SACERDOTAL ROBE, MITRE and CROSIER

# ·THE CELESTIAL HIERARCHY·

· ST. SEBASTIAN · (Perugino)

· ST. NICHOLAS · (Botticelli)

## J. Martyrs

Individuals who rather than renounce their faith cheerfully went to their deaths. It was considered an honorable and enviable death, and the early Christian martyrs are revered as saints. There are martyrs of both sexes, but the females are listed under the Virgins.

There are numberless saints of both the Eastern and Western churches whose life stories are strange minglings of Christian legend and pagan myth. A few of those well known outside their own communities include:

| | | |
|---|---|---|
| St. Stephen | The first martyr — stoned to death | DEACON'S ROBE, PALM, TWO STONES |
| St. George | Patron of knighthood | SWORD and DRAGON |
| St. Nicholas | "St. Nick," children's favorite | BISHOP — THREE BALLS |
| St. Laurence | Gave church money to poor | TREASURES of CHURCH (MONEYBAG), DEACON'S ROBE, GRIDIRON |
| St. Sebastian | Patron against plague and pestilence | ARROWS |
| St. Cosmo and St. Damian | Patrons of medicine | DRESSED ALIKE, BOX and KNIFE |
| St. Christopher | Patron saint of travelers | PILGRIM'S STAFF, and CHILD on BACK |

ST. STEPHEN · (Carpaccio)

· ST. CHRISTOPHER · Carrying the CHRIST CHILD. (Bouts)

· ST. LAURENCE with his GRIDIRON · (Grünewald)

· ST. COSMO and ST. DAMIAN · Patrons of the Medici family. They appear on Florentine coins. (Lorenzetti)

· ST. GEORGE and the DRAGON · Patron saint of England. (Raphael)

# ·THE CELESTIAL HIERARCHY·

ANTHONY ABBOT and PAUL the HERMIT (Grünewald)

## K. Hermits

Men who, like the holy men of the East, renounced worldly pleasures for the purification of their souls. The most celebrated are Anthony, the founder of the Cenobites (hermits living on the outskirts of villages), and Paul the Hermit, an Anchorite or solitary hermit.

St. Anthony — "Temptations" popular subject.
MONK'S HABIT, BEARD, BELL, CRUTCH and PIG

St. Paul the Hermit — GARMENT OF LEAVES

## L. Virgins

The early martyrs and other young women who dedicated their maidenhood to Christ. All carry the palm of martyrdom. Catherine and Ursula wear royal crowns, the others the martyrs' crown or the crown of the bride of Christ. There are four who are considered special patronesses of the faithful in both East and West.

| | St. Catherine | St. Barbara | St. Ursula | St. Margaret |
|---|---|---|---|---|
| Allegorical Virtues: | Intellect. Contemplative life | Fortitude. Active life | Piety | Purity |
| Attribute: | WHEEL or BOOK or SWORD | TOWER or FORT or FEATHER or SACRAMENTAL CUP | ARROW or BANNER with CROSS or DOVE | DRAGON or CROSS or DAISY or PEARLS |
| Patroness: | of schools and colleges | against violent death. "Christian Pallas Athene" | of young girls | of women in childbirth |

ST. CATHERINE with WHEEL and BOOK ST. MARGARET with CROSS and DRAGON
Both wear martyr's crown. (Gothic Sculpture)

SANCTA·VRSVLA·VIRGO

ST. URSULA with RED and WHITE Christian BANNER (Memling)

CHALICE with HOST (consecrated wafer used in Eucharist) (communion)

Two interpretations of ST. BARBARA ·German print· ·Palma Vecchio·

(Memling) ·ST URSULA· protecting her virgin companions from the barbarians. The legend of her life and martydom appears in series of SCULPTURES, STAINED GLASS and PAINTINGS.

A favorite 16TH c. theme. An allegory signifying the SPIRITUAL UNION between CHRIST and the REDEEMED SOUL.
·The MYSTIC MARRIAGE of ST. CATHERINE· (Cranach)

# · THE CELESTIAL HIERARCHY ·

Virgin Patronesses of the Latin Church:

| | St. Cecilia | St. Agnes | St. Agatha | St. Lucia |
|---|---|---|---|---|
| Attribute: | MUSICAL INSTRUMENT or CALDRON | LAMB | SHEARS or PINCHERS, BREASTS on TRAY | LAMP (wisdom) EYES on PLATTER |
| Patroness: | of musicians | of maidens | against fire and female diseases | against diseases of the eyes |

Virgin Saints of the Greek Church
do not appear in art as often as do the Latin virgins:

Thecla (considered first female martyr), WILD BEASTS

Dorothea, ROSES and ATTENDING ANGEL

Justina, UNICORN

Euphemia, LION

M. Monks, Nuns and Confessors
complete the hierarchy.

Only a sampling of saints is presented in the outline above. For more complete listings and tales of the martyrs' lives, a reference is given in the appendix.

The Early Christian martyrs all lived during the time of pagan domination of the Roman Empire.
· ST. CECILIA ·
(Van Leyden)
· ST. AGNES ·
(Schongauer)
Lucy tore out her EYES and sent them to an admirer, who then became a Christian convert.
· ST. LUCIA ·
(Carotto)
· ST. AGATHA ·
Agatha's BREASTS were cut off at the command of a rejected suitor.
An angel supplied the BASKET of FLOWERS which was delivered to the mocking Theophilus after her beheading.
· ST. DOROTHEA of CAPPADOCIA ·
(Cranach)
· ST. JUSTINA of ANTIOCH · converted her suitor CYPRIAN to a life of chastity and piety. They were both martyred by Diocletian and both are Christian Saints.
Although a miracle saved Thecla from the LIONS and she lived to be ninety she is venerated as a Martyr.
The LIONS refused to devour the Greek Saint Euphemia the Great and the executioner killed her with a SWORD.
· ST. JUSTINA ·
(Moretto)
· ST. THECLA ·
(Costa)
· ST. EUPHEMIA ·
(Mantegna)

•PIETA•  Michelangelo•

# THE RENAISSANCE MOVEMENT

## THE RENAISSANCE MOVEMENT

*Style of Architecture — **Style of Furniture

| Italy | France | England | America |
|---|---|---|---|
| **1400—The Fifteenth Century—1500** New style of architecture and painting flourishes in Italy. Printing invented in Germany. | | | |
| ***EARLY RENAISSANCE (Florence) | | (Gothic Prevails) | |
| **1500—The Sixteenth Century—1600** The acme of Italian production in art and architecture. Religious revolt and reform starts in Germany. Age of Exploration. | | | |
| ***HIGH OR CLASSIC RENAISSANCE (Rome) 1500–1550 | Francis I (Father of French Renaissance) | Tudor (Transitional)<br><br>***ELIZABETHEAN | Exploration |
| **1600—The Seventeenth Century—1700** Spain and the Counter Reformation vainly try to re-establish the temporal power of the church. Age of Scientific Awakening. Age of Colonization. The state becomes all-powerful. France and England adapt Renaissance architecture to regional and national requirements. | | | |
| The Decline | Henri IV<br>Louis XIII | **JACOBEAN | Colonization. |
| ***THE BAROQUE (Venice) | **LOUIS XIV *(Interior architecture) | **RESTORATION | Dutch and English styles copied in East. |
| | Beginning of French influence | **WILLIAM and MARY | Spanish in West. |

# 1400-THE RENAISSANCE MOVEMENT-1700

A new age now known as the Renaissance brought the Middle Ages to a close. An enthusiasm for life started the trend which resulted in the death of the international Church. Its greatest achievement was the emancipation of the minds of men.

The unavoidable reaction against medievalism and the discipline of the Church manifested itself first in Italy and then in Germany. Spiritual stagnation and political dissatisfaction made these two countries receptive to new ideas.

The Holy Roman Empire for centuries included between its borders the lands of modern Germany and Italy. It was comprised of over two hundred units — city-states and principalities. There were many hostile factions. The emperor theoretically was chosen by election from among the minority rulers but actually was often selected and controlled by the pope. (See Church and State.) There was no stated capital, no regular army, and no common coinage or language. In short, there was no natural reason for unification. Yet the first European nation was kept together by fear of the growing strength of its French neighbor and by the iron will of its creator — the Church.

The fall of Constantinople in 1454 sent many Christian refugees to Italy. These Greeks brought with them the ancient philosophy of the dignity of man. Interest was stimulated in the ancient classic cultures. In cities secular universities were formed. Soon the ideals of humanism were examined and adopted in all countries. The age of acceptance gave way to the age of inquiry, discovery and invention.

A great concentration of wealth started action in Italy. Italian bankers had financed much of the new continental trade and commerce which had been stimulated by the crusades, and they were now in a position to dictate.

The course that humanism followed in Italy was a rebirth (renaissance) of culture, and its greatest products were artistic. Literature, architecture, painting, sculpture and the minor arts were Italy's brilliant contribution to the new movement. The rulers of the separate city-states served as patrons of the arts and set a precedent that was followed as the enthusiasm spread to other countries. Competitions were fostered, and the yield was abundant and rewarding. Italian works of art inspired the entire continent.

Superb craftsmanship is displayed in the MINOR ARTS

Carved mirror frame

Pendant of gold, precious stones and Baroque pearls.

Beakers and Goblets carved from semiprecious stones and strange substances such as narwhal horn (considered a safeguard against poison) and bezoar (a remedy for disease) are set in gold with precious stones.

Rospigliosi Cup

attributed to the hand of Italy's foremost goldsmith, Benvenuto Cellini

# ·ITALIAN RENAISSANCE ARCHITECTURE·

Artists vary their
SUBJECT MATTER and MEDIUM.

MADONNA and CHILD with GOD the FATHER
GOD the HOLY GHOST and SERAPHIMS
Ceramic plaque Andrea della Robbia

·LORENZO the MAGNIFICENT·
by Andrea del Verrocchio
Portrait sculpture in wood
is usually tinted.

The artistic forms of the Renaissance movement were inspired by an interest in the civilizations of ancient Greece and Rome. In Italy the people became so enamored of the Roman buildings they had desecrated for centuries that they attempted to revive the ancient style of architecture. In so doing they inadvertently created a new style by using classic motives in new combinations to fill new requirements.

The period divides into three stages: (1) the Early Renaissance, (2) the High or Classic Renaissance and (3) the Baroque. The same divisions are applicable to the painting and sculpture.

As compared to the vertical Gothic style, Renaissance architecture except for its domed churches is predominantly horizontal. The most typical examples are palaces, villas, public buildings and monuments. With this period we also have the beginning of civic planning. Architects were trained and buildings were designed in their entirety before construction commenced. The resulting balance and symmetry between the whole and its parts is most pleasing. For the first time in the history of architecture the domestic dwelling was given foremost consideration —with beauty, comfort and convenience in mind.

During the Middle Ages architecture had been primarily concerned with solutions to structural problems. During the High Renaissance, with the problems of construction fully understood, architecture became a study of the beauty of design and detail. The classic orders, classic moldings, classic ornament, and scenes depicting classical mythology, were combined with Christian subjects to enhance buildings which combined simple post and lintel construction, semicircular arches and complicated domes, and ancient and medieval systems of vaulting. Architects learned to handle the combinations so successfully that formulae were set up for students to follow. This facilitated the spread of the style to other countries, but also caused a monotony which led to its decline.

In one small cast bronze panel
on the East doors
of the Baptistry in
Florence
the Sculptor
GHIBERTI
tells the entire Christian story
of the CREATION.

There are nine other
Biblical scenes.
So skillful
is the workmanship that
Michaelangelo
declared them
worthy of adorning
the
GATES of PARADISE.

# ·ITALIAN RENAISSANCE PAINTING·

So extravagant have been the praises of Italian Renaissance painting that it is supposed by many that all products of the time are undisputed masterpieces. Such, of course, is not the case. They are of varying quality.

The main purpose of Renaissance painting and sculpture was to create beauty. Although primarily a decorative expression, Renaissance art usually tells a story or portrays a likeness. Unlike his medieval grandfather, the Renaissance artist strove for personal recognition which brought honor and monetary reward.

Ingenuity was called upon as the same subjects (often religious) were commissioned over and over again. Competing artists stopped at nothing that would give effective variety. Women of the court or of the streets often modeled for the Virgin—a practice which would not have been tolerated a few years before.

Studios were set up for instruction, and students from all countries came to study line, form, light, shade, color and techniques. During the High Renaissance the figures were placed against intricate architectural backgrounds made possible by the newly acquired knowledge of mechanical perspective. These replaced the landscapes of the early school and the gold backgrounds of the medieval primitives.

While there was much experimentation and visible improvement in painting, there was little change in the well-trained sculptors' stone technique. Both figures and decoration became very classic and some can almost be mistaken for Greek work. The ancient art of casting in metal was revived and the bronze doors, fountains and figures introduce an interesting variation against the dignified stone architecture.

This was an age of exceptionally versatile men. Michelangelo was architect, sculptor and painter; Leonardo da Vinci was both painter and scientist; Benvenuto Cellini, goldsmith, sculptor and author. Vital interest and curiosity about the world around them enlivened imagination and encouraged experimentation in a variety of techniques. The inspiration of the age was not faith but life.

· FAITH ·
An allegorical subject in marble bas-relief.
by the relatively unknown MINO da FIESOLE.

Pagan Gods and Goddesses are brought to life by artists of the Renaissance.

Cast bronze ·VENUS· by Sansovino

No architectural detail is too unimportant for outstanding craftsmen to design and execute.

STONE BALUSTRADE by Donatello.

# ·ARTISTS of the ITALIAN RENAISSANCE·

Portraits provide fascinating social history and documentation of costume.

①
PORTRAIT of a LADY
(Pisanello)


Early portraits are usually in profile.

Gozzoli includes some of his patrons from the powerful de'Medici family among the retinue of the "Journey of the Magi."

OPUS BENOTI


·GOZZOLI· ·FRA FILIPPO LIPPI·

Artists work their own likenesses into their compositions.

(13th and 14th centuries)
Pre-Renaissance Painters

Cimabue — Duccio — Giotto — Simone Martini

1400—Quattrocento—1500
15th Century—Early Renaissance—School of Preparation
The de'Medici family of Florence sponsors the new movement.

**Painters**

(Florence)
Angelico, Fra
Botticelli
Castagno, Andrea del
Cosimo, Piero di
Gaddi
Ghirlandaio
Gozzoli
Lippi, Fra Fillippo
Masaccio
Orcagna
Uccello
Veneziano
Verrocchio

(Central Italy)
Fabriano, Gentile da
Francesca, Piero della
Lorenzetti
Pinturicchio
Sassetta
Signorelli

(North Italy)
Pisanello

(Venice)
The Bellini
The Vivarini

**Sculptors**

Brunelleschi
Donatello
Ghiberti
Quercia, Jacopo della
The Robbia, della
Verrocchio

**Architects**

Alberti
Bramante
Brunelleschi
Cronaca
Lombardo
Michelozzo

1500—Cinquecento—1600
16th Century—Classic Renaissance—School of Perfection
Rome is the center of inspiration with the houses of Borgia and d'Este as patrons. The Republic of Venice shows great talent.

**Painters**

(Florence)
Bronzino
Credi, Lorenzo di
Lippi, Filippino
Michelangelo
Pontormo
Sarto, Andrea del
Vinci, Leonardo da

(Venice)
Bassano
Carpaccio
Crivelli
Giorgione
Lotto
Palma Vecchio
Piombo
Tintoretto
Titian
Veronese

(Central Italy)
Perugino
Raphael

(North Italy)
Boltraffio
Caravaggio
Correggio
Dossi
Luini
Mantegna
Moretto da Brescia
Moroni
Roberti
Sodoma
Solario
Viti

**Sculptors**

Bologna, Giovanni da
Cellini
Michelangelo
Sansovino

**Architects**

Palladio
Peruzzi
Raphael
Sangallo
Sanmicheli
Sansovino
Michelangelo
*Vignola

*(Book on architecture influenced French style)

# · ARTISTS of the BAROQUE STYLE ·

1600 — Seicento — 1700

17th Century — The Baroque — The School of Decadence

The Borghese, Barberini, Aldobrandini households, and the Jesuits, supply financial support for building and decorating. Venice is very active.

## Painters

**16th c. forerunners**
- Correggio
- Mantegna
- Tintoretto
- Veronese

**17th c. Decorators**
- Colonna
- Mantovano
- Mitelli
- Pagni
- Pozzo
- Romano

**Mannerists**
- The Caracci
- Domenichino
- Reni
- Rosa
- Salvi

## Sculptors

- Algardi
- Bernini

## Architects

- Algardi
- Bernini
- Borromini
- Galilei
- Longhena
- Maderna

Important followers of the Baroque Style in other countries:

Rubens and Van Dyck (Flemish)    Hals (Dutch)
El Greco — Velasquez — Murillo — Zurbarán (Spanish)
Charles Lebrun (French)

Eighteenth-century Italians influenced by style:

Tiepolo — Ricci — Piazetta — Magnasco

② High Renaissance Style

• LUCRECE de PUCCI by Bronzino •

③

• LAVINIA with FRUIT by Titian •
One of several portraits of the artist's daughter.

By the end of the 16th century artists are no longer satisfied with the formality of posed portraiture. They prefer to show emotion or action.

• RAPE of the DAUGHTERS of LEUCIPPUS • by Rubens
Flemish master of the Baroque Style.

For Baroque sculpture and decoration see page 106.

# ·THE EARLY ITALIAN RENAISSANCE·

THREE FAVORITE RENAISSANCE THEMES: Pagan, Religious and Biographical.

·The Birth of Venus· BOTTICELLI

·Flight into Egypt· FRA ANGELICO
A charmingly naïve conception of a desert.

·Bartolommeo Colleoni· VERROCCHIO

Sculptors need no preparation.
They immediately work in the classic style.

ROMAN RUINS inspire NEW ARCHITECTURAL TREATMENT.

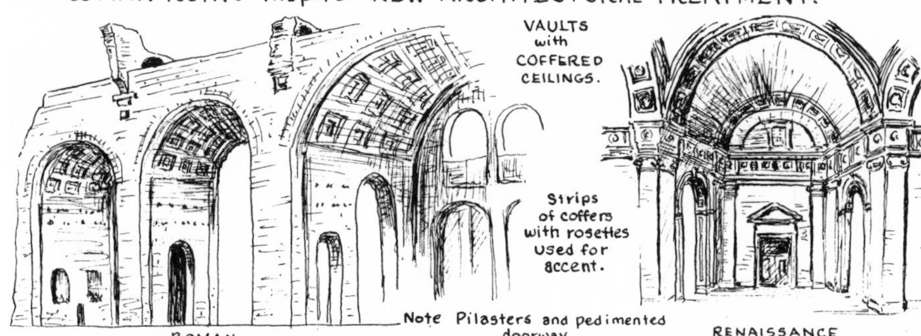
VAULTS with COFFERED CEILINGS.
Strips of coffers with rosettes used for accent.
ROMAN
Note Pilasters and pedimented doorway.
RENAISSANCE

Heavy architectural cornice.

Transitional windows divided by classic column.

Return to Round or COMPASS ARCH now known as FLORENTINE ARCH

Small barred windows for protection.

·Exterior - PALAZZO RICCARDI·

LARGE PALAZZOS (palaces) take up full city block. CORTILES (courtyards) provide protected outdoor living.

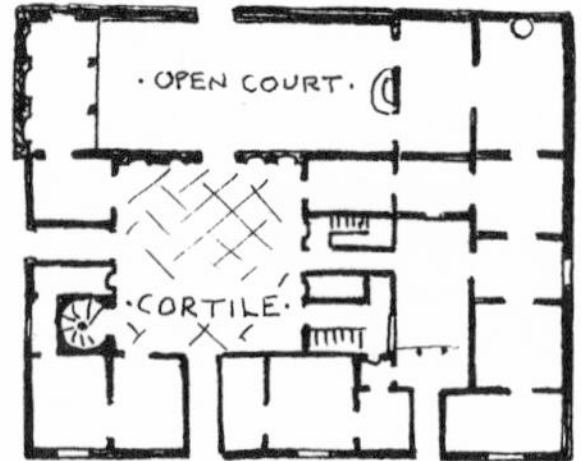
·OPEN COURT·
·CORTILE·

·FLOOR PLAN·

EXTERIORS: STONE Above: { 1st. story - rough or RUSTICATED; 2nd. story - chambered. 3rd. flat blocks.

A GARDEN FACADE with SUNKEN CORTILE.

INTERIORS:

Large Rooms High ceilings
Heavy ceiling BEAMS
often stenciled in JEWEL COLORS.

DOORS, WINDOWS and NICHES
have simple TRIM.

HOODED FIREPLACE, RAISED HEARTH

WALLS: Rough PLASTER Floor: TILE, MARBLE or BRICK

FURNITURE: Carved WALNUT, fruit wood (olive)
CUSHIONS: VELVET, DAMASK, TOOLED LEATHER.

SAVONAROLA CHAIR

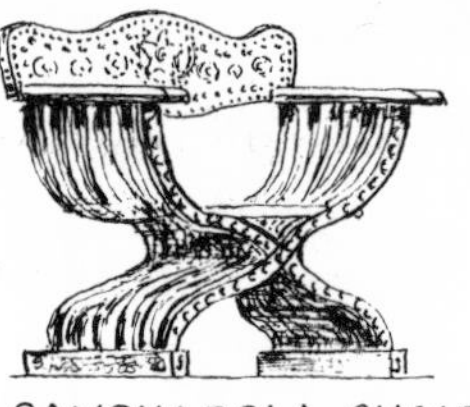

SQUABELLA

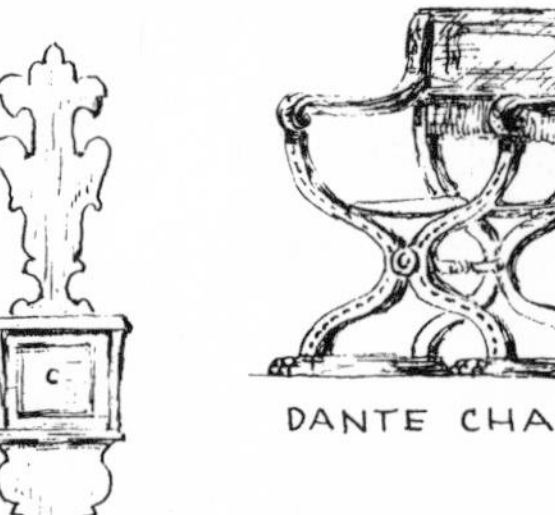

DANTE CHAIR

DRAW LEAF

REFECTORY TABLE

# · THE HIGH ITALIAN RENAISSANCE ·

EXTERIORS: STONE or STUCCO

Balustrade

Corner of building outlined with PILASTERS or RUSTICATION.

SQUARE-TOPPED WINDOWS: PEDIMENTED with hood or triangle.

GRAND CORTILE
LOGGIA


· FLOOR PLAN ·

Central ENTRANCE always ACCENTED with rustication, balcony or portico.

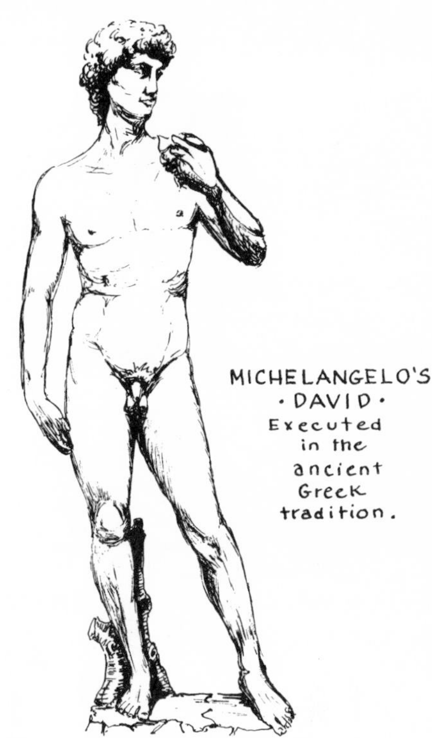

MICHELANGELO'S · DAVID · Executed in the ancient Greek tradition.

FORMAL GARDENS with Fountains and Statuary architectural rather than biological.

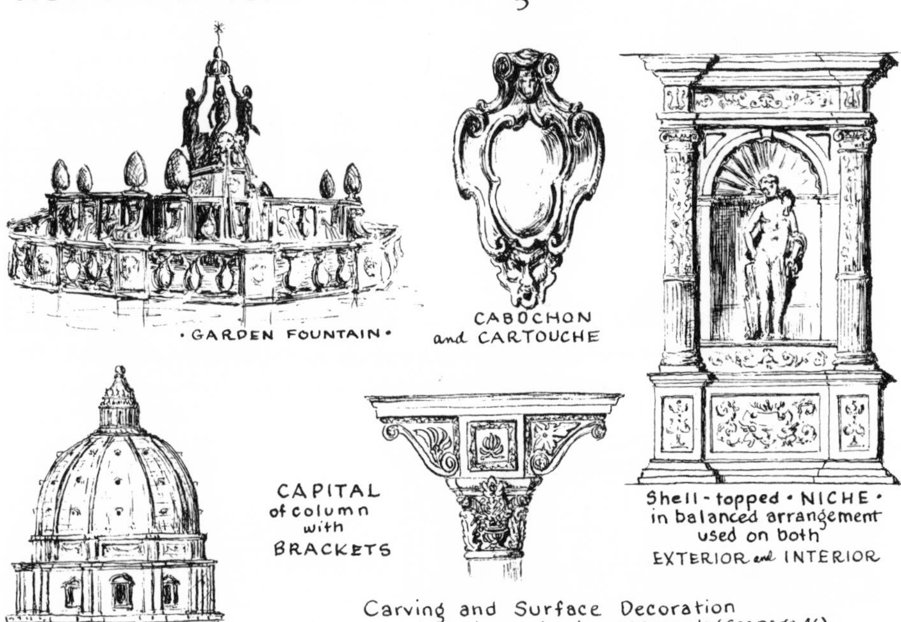

· GARDEN FOUNTAIN ·

CABOCHON and CARTOUCHE

Shell-topped · NICHE · in balanced arrangement used on both EXTERIOR and INTERIOR

CAPITAL of column with BRACKETS

DOME, important feature

Carving and Surface Decoration based on classic ornament (See page 46)

St. Stephen Preaching (Carpaccio) Colorful historic panel.

INTERIORS: CEILINGS - elaborate. Low CHIMNEY PIECES, DOORWAYS, etc. WALLS - often decorated with FRESCOED perspectives. Richly oramented with CARVING in free applications of classic ornament.

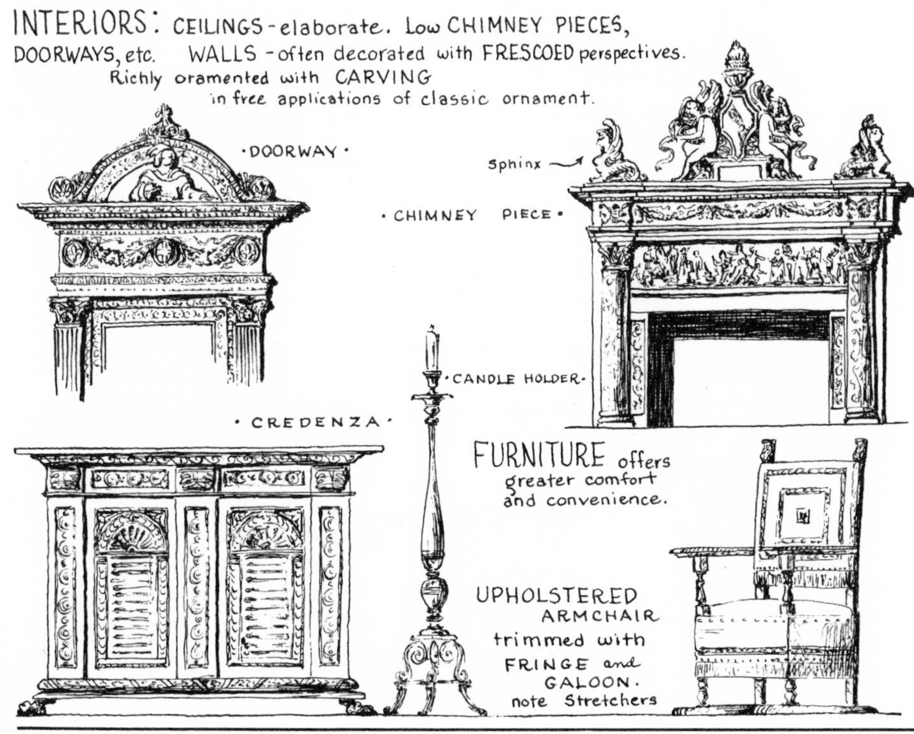

· DOORWAY ·

Sphinx

· CHIMNEY PIECE ·

· CANDLE HOLDER ·

· CREDENZA ·

FURNITURE offers greater comfort and convenience.

UPHOLSTERED ARMCHAIR trimmed with FRINGE and GALOON. note Stretchers

Aurora (Dawn) by Guido Reni
Characterizes the insipid decline which precedes the Baroque.

# ·THE BAROQUE STYLE·

TROMPE L'OEIL
The delight of Italy's decorators.

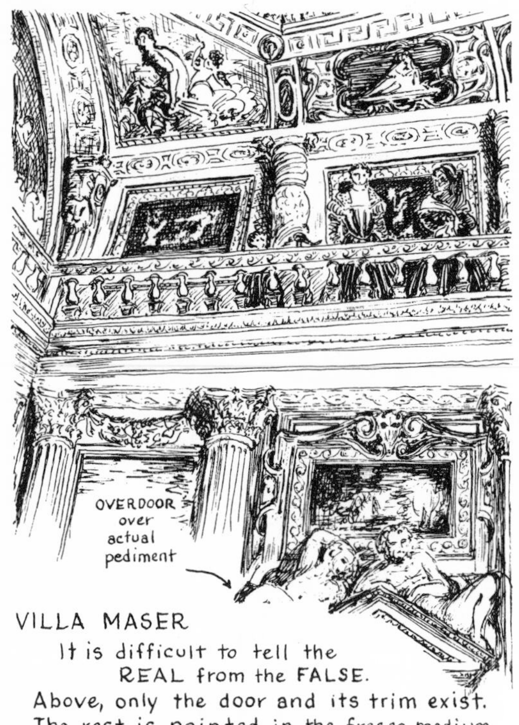
OVERDOOR
over
actual
pediment

VILLA MASER
It is difficult to tell the
REAL from the FALSE.
Above, only the door and its trim exist.
The rest is painted in the fresco medium.

The Baroque is not a stated period but a style which started in Rome and is, according to many experts, better represented in other countries. In Italy the style overlaps both ends of the seventeenth century, during which it enjoyed its greatest popularity. It was born out of the confidence of the Counter Reformation (see page 121), and is to be found in Jesuit churches throughout the continent. It was accepted in joyous revolt against the tiresome standardization of classic forms. Its name derives from the French word meaning bizarre or fantastic. As a style of architecture, it is most often described as: opulent, unorthodox and overdecorated. The painting and sculpture are called: emotional, restless and vulgar. And yet there is an exuberance about the style which fascinates rather than repels.

In Italy some of the most amusing work in painting was completed before the end of the sixteenth century. The florid ceiling decorations and the architectural trompe l'oeil (fool the eye) of the fresco painter are so well carried out that it is hard to discover where the architect left off.

There is a noticeable decline in seventeenth-century Italian canvases. They are for the most part the work of tiresome mannerists. But in Spain, artists revel in religious ecstasy, while in Flanders they show a decided lust for life. In Italy Tiepolo picks up the flamboyant style again in the eighteenth century.

The buildings produced in the various countries of Europe and the Spanish colonies, while characterized by overelaboration of carving and applied decoration, the use of sham materials and trompe l'oeil, and a complete disregard for architectural propriety, are seldom uninteresting. The painting may be unrestrained, but it is an unmistakably violent response to the severity of Protestant decrees.

The architectural style is to be found not only in the churches of the Catholic countries but also in the palatial villas and houses of the ruling class. During the nineteenth-century revivals, it was used for many public buildings. Today stage designers often call upon it for inspiration.

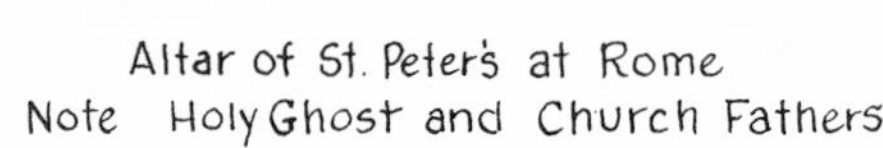

Altar of St. Peter's at Rome
Note Holy Ghost and Church Fathers.

Again and again artists use the human form.
In life-sized and over-life-sized figures they dominate the compositions. Some, like the pair below, are doomed eternally to uncomfortable positions. Others tread the cloudy skys. Often the violence of the action or the dramatic folds of draperies detract from the unity of the work.

·Gilded TABLE·

# · THE BAROQUE STYLE ·

CEILING with framed picture carried by gay cherubs.

Damask-covered walls. Upholstered HEADBOARD, the forerunner of the Hollywood bed.

## · BAROQUE EXTERIORS ·

The final stage of the Renaissance.

The Fountain of Trevi, Rome. Baroque figures against a classic background.

The mania for painted decoration extends even to furniture.

A Boulle clock (bronze with inlays of tortoise shell)

The Louis XIV style is the French counterpart of the Baroque.

GILDED
MIRROR
FRAME

Until the 18th century mirrors are small but considered more valuable than the elaborate frames which surround them.

SHAM FRONT
for
nonexistent
third story.

Baroque facade on a German church.

St. Theresa in Ecstacy

Bernini

Note resemblance to Hellenistic Greek sculpture.

SPANISH BAROQUE in the NEW WORLD

Over-life-size carvings finished in polychrome decorate interiors.

# ·THE RENAISSANCE IN OTHER COUNTRIES·

Spanish doorway with gate of wrought iron. Minute carving called PLATERESQUE (like silversmiths).

While Italy was creating great art, the other European countries were concentrating on learning. When the Renaissance reached the north, it first took the guise of religious and political and social improvement. (See Reformation, page 118, Civil Rights, page 125.)

For years it had been the practice of scholars to take minor religious orders to avail themselves of the only existing schools and libraries. These avid students spent their lives seeking knowledge. Humanism, the progress of self-development in the human race, gave these men new direction. Printed books revealed new realms of thought. The voyages of Columbus and the other explorers opened whole new worlds. Physiology, natural history, astronomy and other natural sciences, classical philosophy and literature, were eagerly investigated. A new-old philosophy, the printing press and the compass slowly eradicated spiritual tyranny as thoroughly as gunpowder wiped out the remnants of feudal practices.

• A Dutch Gable • • • A Flemish Gable •

The classic ideal of beauty which infused the Italians was not of immediate concern in the north, where more practical interests in trade, commerce, finance and government concerned them. But gradually the renown of the Italian artists became so widespread that students from all over Europe traveled to Italy to examine their works.

The Netherlands was the first northern country to excel in painting. The Van Eyck brothers replaced egg tempera with oil pigment. Soon all painters adopted the new medium for detailed work. Fresco, however, continued to be a major decorative expression, particularly in Italy.

CAPITAL of column from Switzerland
German Renaissance CARTOUCHE from Bavaria.

By the seventeenth century, Renaissance architecture was to be found in all European countries. In the early stages the national taste and characteristics predominated. The Spanish Renaissance is distinguished by its wrought iron and tile; the Low Countries by their continued interest in the decorative gable; and Germany by its variety but lack of refinement.

In the eighteenth century the entire continent perfected a High Renaissance style. It takes careful study to distinguish the work of the different peoples. Recent nineteenth- and twentieth-century buildings designed in a Classic Renaissance style closely resemble structures of the actual period. Therefore, the public buildings of Italy, France, England, Spain, Germany, the Low Countries, and even eastern Europe and the Americas give the great cities of Western civilization a marked similarity in appearance.

The Baroque was gaily amusing in all countries except England (and the United States), where it did not make its appearance until the nineteenth-century historic period revival (pages 154, 162, 168).

# ·PRINTING·

The Renaissance gave man the inspiration to throw off the yoke of medievalism. Printing gave him the weapon.

It was not until the invention of movable type that books could be produced in number. Only then did literature have the opportunity to play a part in the lives of average men. The printing press facilitated the circulation of an ideal and accelerated a cause.

It was not difficult to see that written words and the ideas they might convey would have an immediate effect upon men's minds. From the point of view of those who held the power, it was undesirable that mankind be stimulated to thought. It is simpler to lead the ignorant through fear than to guide the enlightened through wisdom. Church and State therefore both tried to control publications. When that was unsuccessful they burned the books and imprisoned the authors. They managed to impede progress but not to destroy ideas.

After an incessant struggle against established tyranny, man first won freedom from both spiritual and political bondage in 1648 with the formation of the United Provinces (Holland). That was only the beginning of the fight for liberty.

JOHANNES GUTENBERG in 1450 set up a printing shop and published the first editions of the Bible reproduced from movable type.

· The RESURRECTION · from Caxton's *GOLDEN LEGEND*, 1483. Caxton was England's first printer.

The art of printing was a late development in the West. The early methods were primitive and improved little until the machine age. In the last hundred years advancement has been rapid. Printing is one field in which progress is easily discernible.

| | | | |
|---|---|---|---|
| 900 | Block printing | | Chinese method |
| 1450 | Movable type | Gutenberg | German |
| 1837 | Photography | Daguerre | French |
| 1846 | Rotary press | Hoe | American |
| 1880 | Linotype | Mergenthaler | American |

There is now a vast selection of type faces, and lettering, if sensitively chosen and artistically arranged, can suggest much through style alone.

1620 - The Blaew Printing Press
The first important improvement since Gutenberg's time.
Hand presses are still used for handbills and posters.

At first CAPITAL LETTERS were painted by hand. Later they were printed from engraved plates.

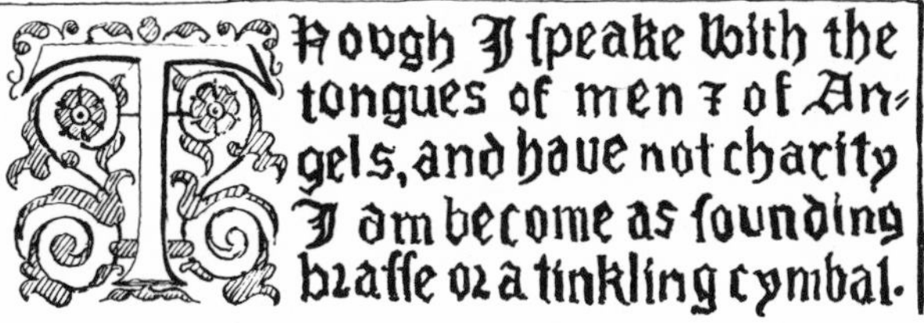

Though I speake with the tongues of men ⁊ of Angels, and haue not charity I am become as sounding brasse or a tinkling cymbal.

The interest aroused by the many printed versions of the Bible is listed as a contributing factor to the Protestant Reformation.
(see page 119)

# · THE GRAPHIC ARTS ·

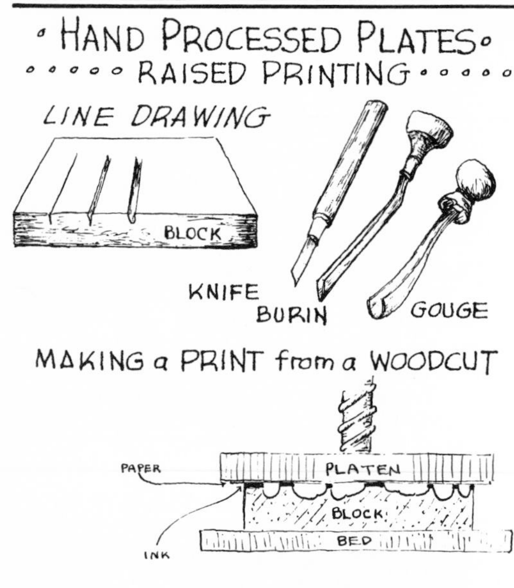

HAND PROCESSED PLATES
RAISED PRINTING
LINE DRAWING
BLOCK
KNIFE
BURIN
GOUGE
MAKING a PRINT from a WOODCUT
PAPER
PLATEN
BLOCK
BED
INK


INTAGLIO PRINTING
· LINE DRAWING ·

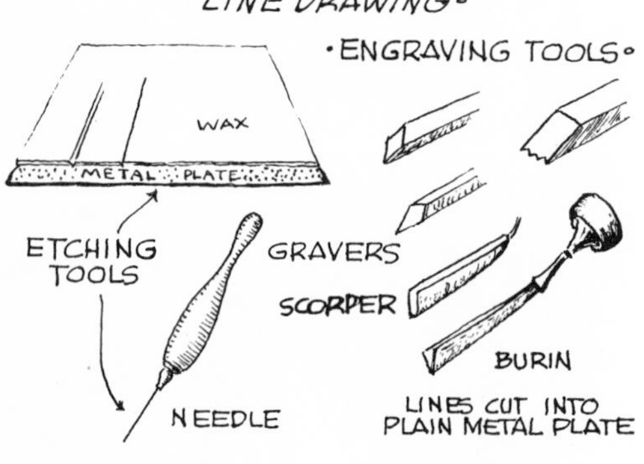

· ENGRAVING TOOLS ·
WAX
METAL PLATE
ETCHING TOOLS
GRAVERS
SCORPER
BURIN
NEEDLE
LINES CUT INTO PLAIN METAL PLATE
PRINTING an ETCHING


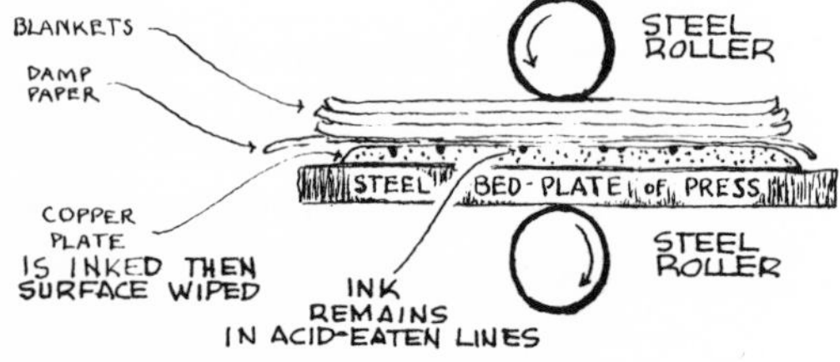

BLANKETS
DAMP PAPER
STEEL ROLLER
COPPER PLATE IS INKED THEN SURFACE WIPED
STEEL BED-PLATE of PRESS
STEEL ROLLER
INK REMAINS IN ACID-EATEN LINES


SURFACE PRINTING
IN TONE and COLOR

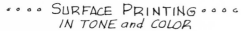

GREASE PENCIL
WATER
STONE
KNIFE
INK


The grease repels the water but attracts the ink. Only inked surface prints.

· HAND PRINTING a LITHOGRAPH ·

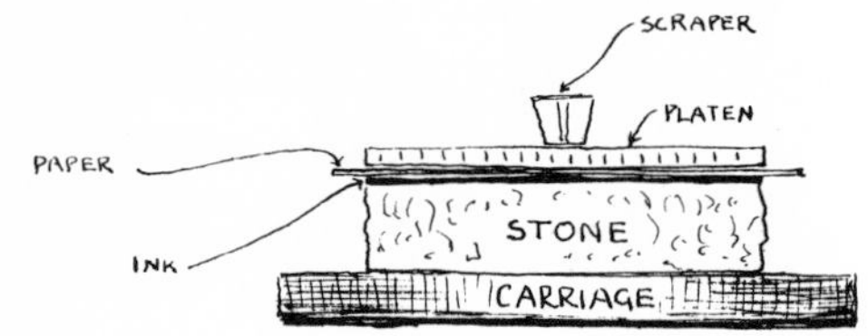

SCRAPER
PLATEN
PAPER
STONE
INK
CARRIAGE


When books were printed in quantity, it next became necessary to devise ways of producing the illustrations in number.

The first duplications were made from hand-carved wood blocks. To the various processes which were not slow to follow, the age of science has added power machinery, photography and the resulting photo-mechanical methods now employed by the printer. These may be used to make reproductions of any type of painting, drawing or hand-processed print. The machine-made reproductions reflect the character of the original work, and unlimited and inexpensive copies in either black and white or color can be run off.

The hand processes described on the chart will supply only a limited quantity of reproductions. Unlike the modern mechanical means, they may be used by the artist to present original ideas. The prints are highly honored and are now considered too valuable for mass illustration except when reproduced through one of the photo-mechanical processes.

Photography itself is a relatively inexpensive, exciting, flexible and artistic medium. It is acceptable for either original creative expression or mechanical reproduction. It is therefore used by amateur and commercial artists as well as by the printer. So arresting have photographs become that today in many publications they have all but supplanted the text.

There are three basic types of printing used for both lettering and illustration:

(1) RELIEF (figure raised above background)

(2) INTAGLIO (figure cut into background)

(3) PLANOGRAPHIC or SURFACE (figure and background level)

## THE HAND PROCESSES

### (1) RELIEF PRINTING

| Process | Tools | Plate | Characteristics |
|---|---|---|---|
| *Woodcut<br>*Linoleum<br>(Good substitute for amateur) | knife<br>gouge | wood block<br>linoleum | Bold design — coarse lines — solid areas often show grain. |
| *Wood engraving | burin | end grain of wood | A refinement of the cut. Black lines on white — or more precise and intricate white lines on black. |

# · THE GRAPHIC ARTS ·

## (2) INTAGLIO PRINTING

| | | | |
|---|---|---|---|
| *Metal engraving | burin | metal plate | Little variation in thickness of lines. |
| Drypoint | needle | metal plate | "Burr" (rough edge) on first few prints. Thin line. |
| Etching (German "to eat") | needle and acid | waxed metal plate | Possible to vary blackness of lines by variation in applications of acid. |
| Stipple | needle and acid | waxed metal plate | Tones and outlines achieved with dots, not lines. |
| Soft ground etching | point and acid | paper over metal plate | Grain of paper detectable in line drawing. |
| | 18th century methods now seldom used. | | |
| Aquatint | needle and acid | resin-covered metal plate | Almost invisible dots from resin. Shading possible. |
| Mezzotint | scraper and rocker | design rubbed into copper plate | Colors and black. Velvety finish. Zigzag grain. |

*Print may be made on paper or fabric.

## (3) SURFACE PRINTING

| | | |
|---|---|---|
| Lithography | wax crayon on soft stone or greasy ink and knife | Looks like crayon drawing. |

Commercial lithographers use a metal plate and power machinery.

Prints from these processes are made in one hue against a background—usually but not necessarily black on white. When more than one color is desired a plate must be made for each change.

## (4) THE SILK SCREEN PROCESS

A new stencil process which can be prepared by hand and powered by hand or machine has come into use. It may be used for original designs or for reproductions of clearly delineated color-compositions. As it may be processed on either paper or fabric, many wallpapers and chintzes are now decorated in this manner.

### TONE SHADING

gradations of dark and light achieved, not by line, but by middle tone of gray.

Makes possible REPRODUCTIONS of wash drawings and watercolors

MEZZOTINTS, AQUATINTS and SOFT GROUND ETCHINGS have almost entirely been replaced by photo mechanical methods.

SCRAPER for MEZZOTINT
ROCKER for MEZZOTINT

### ◦ LINE DRAWINGS ◦

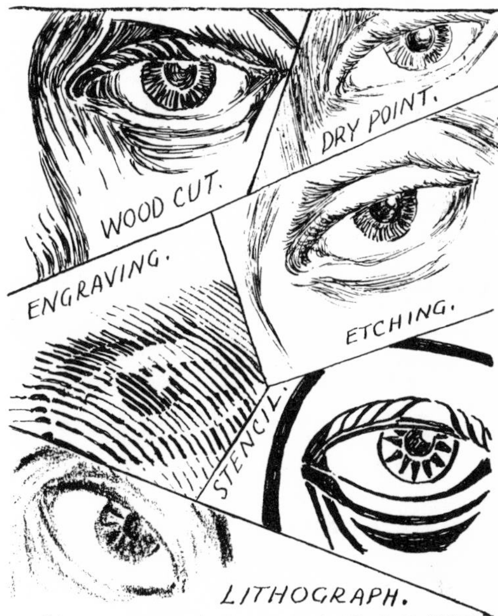
DRY POINT.
WOOD CUT.
ENGRAVING.
ETCHING.
STENCIL.
LITHOGRAPH.

### ◦ THE STENCIL PROCESS ◦

◦ ◦ ◦ the HAND STENCIL ◦ ◦ ◦

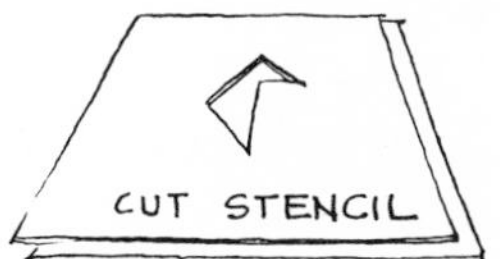
CUT STENCIL

PAINT

BLUNT BRUSH

### ◦ ◦ THE SILK SCREEN STENCIL ◦ ◦

A separate stencil is required for each color. Over-printing effective

All but colored area is painted over with filler.

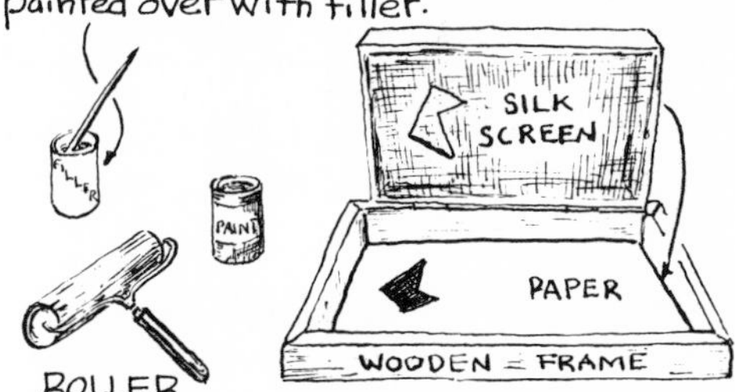
SILK SCREEN
PAINT
PAPER
WOODEN FRAME
ROLLER

# · CHURCH AND STATE ·

The theory of the DIVINE RIGHT of KINGS is of ancient origin.

During the 17th Century it is exercised by the ABSOLUTE MONARCHS

The King and Queen of Germany sponsored by St. Peter and St. Paul are crowned by Christ. Below, the major and minor states of the Holy Roman Empire beg Henry to become their emperor.

A German King during the period of bitter conflict between Empire and Papacy.

The history of the medieval Church is part of the legacy of every person born or living today within the boundaries of the Western world.

It was not through theology that the medieval Church won the unique position it was to enjoy for seven hundred years (800 – 1500). That came about through its gradual organization of the continent.

It is as a governing force in opposition to the state that the Church played one of its major roles.

In the years which followed the end of Western Rome, matters of doctrine were decided by the Early Christian bishops. The meetings took place in various cities of the Eastern Empire, and the Western bishops returned to their territories, where the decisions were disseminated by missionaries.

In the sixth century St. Benedict founded the Benedictine monasteries. They spread through the West and united the people through conversion to the faith.

By the ninth century the entire population of Western Europe was born into the church. The church therefore controlled thousands in what it considered an international state. It expected support from compulsory taxation, in return for which it performed many services in addition to its religious functions. It kept records of births, marriages and deaths. It provided courts which attempted to promote order through the enforcement of Roman (civil) and canon (Church) law. It also maintained such schools and hospitals as existed. In towns and villages it was not only the moral guide but the social center of the common people.

The leadership of the Bishop of Rome was gradually assumed and often contested. Rivalry between the bishops of the old Roman capital and the new capital at Constantinople caused friction in the Early Church councils, where all participants were supposed to meet on equal terms. The councils were called by the emperor, but the rival bishops vied for the right to preside. Apparently it was not until the time of the outstanding Gregory the Great (590 – 604) that precedence was given the Roman bishop, and the title of Pope bestowed upon him. Until then the early bishops were selected by popular acclaim and all called pope, or father.

In 800, Pope Leo III crowned the Frankish King Charlemagne, Holy Roman Emperor. The new empire was created in an effort to join, stabilize and pacify a group of barbaric nations. There was no way of telling that the equality and co-operation between Emperor and Pope which existed during the early Carolingian dynasty would not last.

# · CHURCH AND STATE ·

The feudal practice of lay investiture (see Abuses) slowly gave the state great influence within the Church. For almost two hundred years State and Church opposed and belittled each other as each fought for supremacy.

The ancient cities of the eastern Mediterranean and northern Africa were lost in the rapid Moslem conquests of the seventh century. The bitterness between Rome and Constantinople flared over the iconoclastic issue in the eighth century, and in 1054 further differences caused Constantinople to form her own Church. The Pope was deprived of followers, territories and revenue. Not since its beginning had the Church been so troubled.

At the Lateran Council in 1059, Hildebrand (later Pope Gregory VII) freed the Church from the state by transferring the election of the Pope to the College of Cardinals. The Pope was declared responsible to God for serf and king alike.

From that moment the independence of the Pope started to burgeon. The Golden Age of the Church had begun. Innocent III (1198 – 1216) made himself master of Europe. Through the application of interdict and excommunication he brought one king after another under his control. From that time until the beginning of the fourteenth century papal supremacy was not seriously questioned.

The hundred years of the Babylonian Captivity (papal seat removed to Avignon, 1305 – 1377) and the Great Schism (as many as three popes ruled at once, 1377 – 1417) broke the continental power of the papacy. The schism was mended at the Council of Constance (1414 – 18) with the election of Pope Martin V, but the responsibility of all major decisions was voted to the Ecumenical (general) Council. There was an attempt to condemn the divesting of papal power, but it was too late to strengthen an office which had so demeaned itself.

A succession of Renaissance popes further degraded the pontificate, corruption weakened it. The Spanish Inquisition became the religious dictator and denounced the growing heresies.

The refusal of the Pope to listen to the pleas of conscientious Catholics ended in the Protestant Reformation, which attracted almost all of northern Europe, leaving only the Latin countries and central Europe faithful to Rome.

The Council of Trent (1545 – 1563), which effected valuable church reforms, restored dignity to the papal office. The Society of Jesus (Jesuits) attempted even more. It was in vain. Civil government had strengthened during the years of Roman weakness, and the day of the absolute monarchy had arrived. It lasted about two hundred years (1600 – 1800).

◦ ENGLAND VERSUS THE CHURCH ◦

In 1170 Thomas 'a Becket is murdered in Canterbury Cathedral for resisting the growing power of the King.

POPE INNOCENT III
1198~1215

During the reign of John (1199~1216) the Pope places England under an interdict. The King is forced to submit and to hold his kingdom as a fief of Rome.

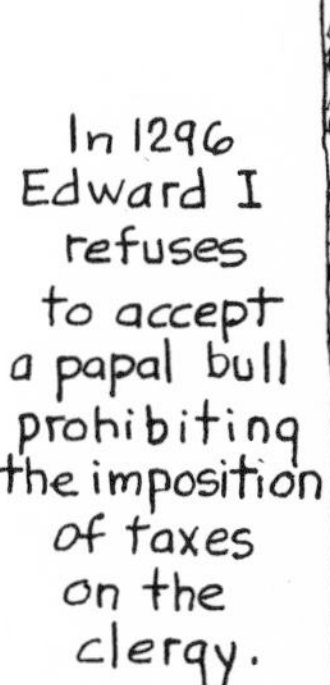

In 1296 Edward I refuses to accept a papal bull prohibiting the imposition of taxes on the clergy.

## • ABSOLUTE MONARCHS •

HENRY VIII (1509-1547) denies the authority of the Pope and becomes head of the CHURCH of ENGLAND

In France LOUIS XIV (1643-1715), a devout Catholic, sets a pattern for the Absolute Monarch.

The ambitious MARIA THERESA, Queen of Hungary (1740-1780) and Archduchess of Austria, tries to enlarge her territory.

FREDERICK the GREAT of Prussia (1740-1786) tries to unite the GERMAN princes and form an empire.

In Russia CATHERINE the GREAT (1762-1796) joins Austria and Prussia in destroying the independence of Poland.

The imperialistic and selfish appetites of 17th and 18th c. rulers keep Europe in turmoil and bankruptcy.

By the end of the eighteenth century the concept of freedom inflamed the world and neither force of words nor force of violence was going to smother it. Now the supremacy of the State was challenged. Inspired by the philosophers and upheld by the will of the people, the revolutionary spirit attacked any authority which restricted individual thought.

The French Revolution destroyed the monarchy and heaped humiliations upon the church. Napoleon made his child-heir King of Rome. The Papal States were restored after Napoleon's defeat, but lost again under Italian unification in 1870. In the Vatican Council of that year the Pope renounced all temporal power. But the claim of Papal Infallibility on matters pertaining to faith and morals was proclaimed after some dissension by the council.

All through the nineteenth century the remaining European monarchies were adding to the colonial possessions from which they derived tremendous revenue. But they were losing control of the governments at home. The war for democracy (1914–1918) lessened the political importance of the remaining kingdoms of Europe and did much to erase the class distinctions which had divided society since the feudal age.

In 1929 the Pope was made sovereign of the newly formed State of Vatican City. This includes the Vatican Palace and Museum, St. Peter's Cathedral and other buildings in Rome which are necessary to the administration of the Holy See. Under the Treaty of Conciliation the Pope is pledged to perpetual neutrality in political disputes. Although the population of the city-state barely exceeds one thousand, over forty nations send diplomatic representatives to the man who today is the spiritual ruler of more than 450,000,000 people.

Religious toleration as practiced in the United States is not universal. Nor is our zealously guarded complete separation of church and state. But many countries have worked out satisfactory systems of state religions wherein the church is not encouraged to participate in civic affairs and the government does not interfere in spiritual matters.

The Communists, feeling that man's devotion to God interferes with his devotion to the state, have tried to convert the world first to communism and then to atheism. While politically they have furthered their ambitions by disrupting government and annexing territory, they have not succeeded in separating man from God.

Writers whose ideas helped to gain RELIGIOUS TOLERATION and CIVIL LIBERTIES

• JOHN LOCKE • Advocator of the NATURAL RIGHTS of MAN

• J. J. Rousseau • Believes in the SOVEREIGNTY of the PEOPLE.

• Voltaire • Satirical critic of the CHURCH and its OPPRESSION

Champions of GOVERNMENT by the CONSENT of the GOVERNED

The theory of STATE CONTROL is introduced to equalize the WEALTH & PRIVILEGES of the INDIVIDUAL

KARL MARX has become the father of both SOCIALISM and COMMUNISM.

# · ABUSES and REFORMS ·

To understand the constant need for reforms in the medieval Church, it is first necessary to understand the conditions which made them advisable.

How the Church gained monocratic control has been explained. As is common under a concentration of power, abuses led to weaknesses in the system. Time and again these were wisely and successfully corrected from within.

The feudal system brought about the practice of lay investitures. The rich Church offices and the accompanying feudal estates were given to appointees of the feudal lords and subsequent temporal rulers, instead of to the choice of the Church. This led to the offense of simony (buying appointments), which in turn led to pluralities (the holding of more than one office). Positions were filled by persons who were willing to pay for them with money or political favor. The men too often were unsuited to the moral obligations involved. This malpractice extended even to the papal seat.

The problem of investiture was largely corrected by Pope Gregory VII, but simony proved more difficult to control.

Excessive Church tithes caused resentment at corruption in high places — especially in some of the monasteries, where the monks had lost sight of the original spiritual aims of the system, and were living in indolent luxury. Their reorganization under the tenth-century Cluny reforms did much to ease this situation. But what completely reconciled the people for many years was the foundation of the mendicant orders of St. Francis (1182 – 1226) and St. Dominic (1170 – 1221). However, the Renaissance brought a return of undesirable practices in the monastic set-up.

Although the clergy for many years had taken vows of celibacy, worldly churchmen had been ignoring them. The desire to hand their rich holdings to their children or other members of their families caused nepotism (the distribution of offices to relatives). There were eleven-year-old cardinals and other equally unsuitable appointments.

Marriage of the clergy was brought to a halt, but simony and nepotism were rampant even after the Middle Ages and Renaissance. Both were contributing factors to the French Revolution (1779), and there was evidence of both among French and Italian nobility in the nineteenth century.

· ORGANIZATION ·

CHURCH COUNCILS
COLLEGE of CARDINALS
REGULAR CLERGY
SECULAR CLERGY
ABBOTS
ARCHBISHOPS
PRIORS
MONKS
NUNS
FRIARS
BISHOPS
PRIESTS
LAY MEMBERS of the CATHOLIC CHURCH


ECUMENICAL COUNCILS, originally called by the Roman Emperor to settle controversial issues, since the Council of Constance, 1414-1418, have been summoned by the Pope.

· SAINT ·
From an authentic portrait of St. Francis of Assisi, showing the Stigmata.

· REFORMERS ·

Wycliffe advocates change in doctrine. Makes first English translation of Bible.

· John Wycliffe · (1320 - 1384)

Erasmus fights corruption within the church.

· Erasmus · (1466 - 1536)

· Savonarola · (1452 - 1498)

This pious zealot tries to reform both Church and State. He is tortured and hanged.

· HERETICS ·

Huss is burned at the stake for discussing Wycliffe's teachings at the University of Prague.

· John Huss · (1373 - 1415)

# ·ABUSES and REFORMS·

The election of Pope Clement VII in 1378 starts the Great Schism.

The Church had never officially sanctioned forgiveness of wrongdoing by payment instead of penance — but for years local priests had accepted votive offerings to beautify church buildings or enrich church coffers in exchange for the remission of sins committed or about to be committed. The sale of indulgences (signed papers guaranteeing the lightening of punishment in purgatory) became a regular source of revenue for high churchmen during the Renaissance.

In the early Middle Ages the Church had gained her position through respect for her teachings, and gratitude for her service to the community. The love of power and wealth so obtained became important to the higher clergy, who were willing to effect any compromises or methods which would enable them to hold their monopoly. Rule through fear was adopted, and reached a peak in the thirteenth century under Innocent III, who ruthlessly employed the spiritual weapons of excommunication and interdict.

Excommunication placed a man outside the benefits of society and condemned his soul to eternal torture. The interdict was imposed on cities, communities and even whole countries when a ruler refused to obey papal commands. It suspended all religious functions, including mass and the sacraments. No confessionals, no marriages, no baptisms, no last rites were administered. The faithful wept in terror as they buried their loved ones without the religious ritual declared necessary to their salvation. King and country soon bowed to the will of the Pope.

A regrettable practice of the Church, which sent people scurrying to the support of the Protestant cause, was the un-Christian brutality used to control any disagreement with the Church's temporal or spiritual decrees.

Having from time to time found violence a more effective weapon than written persuasions or spiritual threats, the Church in the thirteenth century undertook a bloody extermination of the Albigensian heretics. So successful was the enterprise that the Church was encouraged to combat all heresies with force. The crusades were sent abroad and the Inquisition was strengthened at home.

POPE LEO X (1513 - 1521) whose actions precipitate the Protestant Reformation (see page 118)

## ◦ PERSECUTION ◦

Catherine de' Medici who plans the infamous massacre of St. Bartholomew's Eve, 1572. Thousands of Huguenots are murdered in their beds.

## ◦ INQUISITION ◦

Judges.
Priviledged Spectators.
Heretics.

## ◦ TOLERATION ◦

In 1598 Henri IV of France grants religious freedom to the Huguenots in the Edict of Nantes.

# · ABUSES and REFORMS ·

· COUNTER–REFORMS ·

The Holy Office of the Inquisition imprisoned heretics (those accused of disagreement with ecclesiastical opinion) and confiscated their properties. If the suspects were granted a trial, it was apt to be secret, defense was not allowed and confession was most often obtained in the torture chamber. The Church then delivered the guilty to the state for punishment. The prisoners, whether they repented or not, were burned alive at the stake for the eternal salvation of their souls. In this way the Church became richer and rid herself of critics and political enemies, while technically she was not responsible for their agonizing deaths.

The Council of Trent 1545-1563 regulates discipline and formulates the doctrines of the modern Roman Catholic Church.

It also publishes the *Index Librorum Prohibitorum*, a list of writings considered detrimental to faith and morals. Today a current list is prepared by the Holy Office in Rome.

First called for the suppression of heresy by Innocent III, the Inquisition became most active in Spain and the Spanish possessions during the sixteenth and seventeenth centuries. It was used in other countries in a desperate attempt to control the spreading trend of independent thought. It was abolished in France in 1772, and in Spain in 1834.

Another source of dissatisfaction with the organization of the Catholic Church was the charge that the simple philosophy of Jesus of Nazareth was buried under the elaborate theological doctrines and ecclesiastical rituals which had been built around it. It was felt by many that devotion to the Virgin and the invocation of sainted relics was a form of idolatry unworthy of the spiritual concepts on which Christianity originally was founded.

By the beginning of the sixteenth century it became evident that the dominant position of the Church was seriously threatened for the reasons given above. Resentment intensified by the development of intellectual activity and growing pride in the advancement of national interests was making people question, criticize and defy the authority they had so long accepted.

· MARTYR ·

Sir Thomas More (1478-1535) is executed for refusing to recognize Henry VIII as the head of the Church of England.

· DEFENDER ·

Ignatius Loyola (1491-1556) uses his military training to organize the Society of Jesus. It serves as the arm of the Counter Reformation.

The Church burning heretical documents.

# ·THE PROTESTANT REFORMATION·

·WITTENBURG·
Birth place of the Reformation.
To these doors
MARTIN LUTHER
nails his 95 complaints against the administration of the church.

The culmination of the Renaissance movement is to be found in the inevitable revolution against the imprisoning embrace of the all-powerful medieval Church.

The Church in the sixteenth century was still performing great service to humanity, and it was not the intention of anyone to destroy it. Thinking Catholics long had realized that changes should be made in certain practices, but the churchmen who were benefiting by the offenses obviously had no intention of correcting them. Had this adamant stand not been counteracted by the Council of Trent in the following century, the Roman Church might have faded out of existence. As it was, it lost over half its following.

In 1517 money was needed for the completion of St. Peter's Cathedral. Pope Leo X sent out agents to stimulate the sale of indulgences for both the living and the dead. (See Abuses.) It was managed with the brashness of a modern advertising campaign.

This flagrant behavior so incensed Martin Luther, a German monk and theologian, that it started the chain of events which ended in the irreconcilable division of the Christian Church.

Luther's actions were taken in an effort to bring about reforms within the Church. In attacking the corrupt Pope and criticizing methods he was not attempting to weaken the Church but to strengthen it. When the Church refused to be convinced and threatened Luther, he sought the protection of the German princes, and the situation took on political aspects. A new Church was formed under the protection of civil government.

LUTHER'S 16th century translation of the Bible is still the accepted GERMAN VERSION

Luther was only the spark which ignited the combustible spirit of the age. It was the idea of individualism that set off the catastrophic explosion. The restive political factions within the northern part of the Holy Roman Empire fanned the flames. Soon all of Europe was drawn into an intermittent battle which lasted for over a hundred years.

Society was not to benefit by the advantages gained by the reform movement until the end of a cruel period of transition. Few drastic changes in accepted procedure are brought about quickly or without unfortunate mistakes—especially in an age of violence.

IHΣ

Protestant Reformers
FAREL·CALVIN·BEZA·KNOX
John Knox
parts from Calvin and in Scotland founds
the PRESBYTERIAN CHURCH

In Switzerland
John Calvin is the great theological thinker of the age.

In England
Oliver CROMWELL, soldier not theologian, sets up a PURITAN COMMONWEALTH from which many Catholics and some Protestants flee.

# ·THE PROTESTANT REFORMATION·

The Reformation did not give a free choice of religion to every man. From the beginning there were political complications. When the ruler of a state turned Protestant all his subjects were expected to embrace the new belief. Disgruntled Catholics were anxious to do so but faithful ones could not even consider the change. Catholic sovereigns also demanded complete loyalty of all their subjects. This led to tugs of war over souls and territories. Europe was drenched with the blood of martyrs and North America was well supplied with colonists.

All anti-Catholic sentiment did not follow Luther. Some chose the ideas of John Calvin—others the compromise of the Anglican faith. Although the earliest protesters wished to change only the working organization of the Church, later adherents sought to change or modify its theological structure. For many years the strife between Protestant factions was as savage as the fight between Protestants and Catholics.

The urge to persecute became so fanatical that nobody could stop. The hunt swung from heretics to witches, and an estimated quarter of a million women were executed for witchcraft. This includes those at Salem, Massachusetts, in 1692.

In spite of the differences in Protestant beliefs, the originators all agreed upon the danger of a powerful international Church; the denial of the authority of the Pope; the discontinuance of the monastic system; and the rejection of indulgences, some of the sacraments, devotion to the Virgin, and the use of relics. They also agreed upon simpler services in the language of the people, marriage of the clergy, the authority of the Scriptures and an unrestricted study of the Bible. Thus the three oldest branches of the reformed faith and their many more recent offshoots have bonds in common which separate them most definitely from the Church of Rome.

One of the ultimate changes in Christian practice which resulted from the Reformation is a worship of God founded on reverence and faith. The medieval subservience to ecclesiastical decrees sprang from a fearful obligation imposed by the threat of punishment or the promise of reward. This the Protestants abandoned in favor of a belief that the relationship between God and man is a personal one to be worked out by the individual according to the dictates of his conscience.

As freedom of definition is a tenet of the reformed faith, there are as many Protestant sects as there are interpretations of the Word of God.

By the end of the seventeenth century the religious war was over. The strangle hold of the Middle Ages had long been broken and the period of adjustment had passed. England had solved the major problems pertaining to both religious and political liberties but the continent had yet to battle its new oppressor—the State.

NORTH AMERICA
∘ LAND of RELIGIOUS FREEDOM ∘

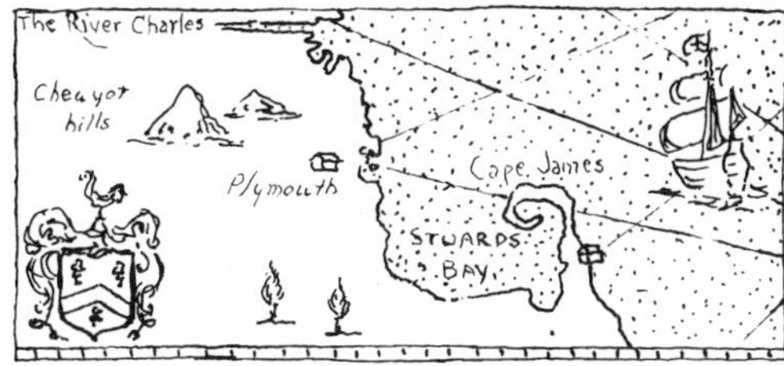
The River Charles
Plymouth
Cape James
STUARDS BAY

The Mayflower brings the PILGRIMS to the new world.

Roger Williams' BAPTIST CHURCH in Salem, Mass., 1633.

In 1680 William Penn and a group of QUAKERS sail from England.

In 1735 John Wesley comes to America to teach the Indians his METHODIST beliefs.

The Apostle of UNITARIANISM William Ellery Channing (1780-1842)

Mary Baker Eddy founds the CHURCH of CHRIST SCIENTIST in 1879.

# ·The AGE of SPANISH DOMINATION·

King of Spain
and the Hapsburg Dominions
and
Emperor CHARLES V 1519-1566
of the
Holy Roman Empire

During the sixteenth and seventeenth century the Iberian peninsula played a major role in world affairs. It was first settled as a province of ancient Rome. The Dark Ages brought an invasion of Visigoths, and the eighth century, the Islamic occupation of the Moors. Spanish Christians succeeded in winning back much of the territory but in the fifteenth century it was divided into the separate kingdoms of Portugal, Aragon, Castile, Leon and Moorish Granada.

The marriage of Ferdinand of Aragon and Isabella of Castile united the two most powerful states. The Moors and Jews were expelled and their confiscated property was used to finance the organization of the country as a united kingdom.

PHILIP of SPAIN
receives the Royal Regalia of England
but only as
the consort of Mary Tudor.

Although Ferdinand and Isabella built a fleet for purposes of exploration, it was Portugal that created the first great colonial empire, with rich holdings in Africa, South America, Asia and the East Indies. She established a trade monopoly in the East and her wealth multiplied. However, her small population was so absorbed in administering the huge commercial enterprise abroad that domestic affairs were neglected. In 1580 her entire empire was annexed by covetous Spain.

In an attempt to bound the expanding acquisitions of Spain and Portugal in 1494, the Pope in grandiose fashion had cut the world in two, giving all new territory west of the Azores to Spain—everything to the east, to Portugal. Under Philip II it became one vast domain and the Spanish king became the nominal ruler of most of the globe.

At home Philip's position was strong. He had inherited the Hapsburg sections of western Europe. He himself added the Italian Duchy of Parma. Although his first marriage helped him to gain Portugal, he was not able to win England during his marriage to Mary Tudor; nor did his third marriage to Elizabeth of Valois yield France. But he ruled what were still the most influential sections of the continent.

For years Spain fought her old enemies the Moslems on African soil. In 1571 she joined Venice in destroying Suleiman's fleet, and temporarily stopped Moslem aggression. But her importance was earned as defender of Catholicism, not as military genius.

While the Council of Trent, which had been called to formulate a plan to combat growing Protestant heresies, deliberated for eighteen years (1545–1563), a Spanish soldier took action.

16th CENTURY
EUROPEAN POSSESSIONS of the SPANISH CROWN.
For New World holdings see EXPLORATION.

DENMARK
THE NETHERLANDS
ENG.
POLAND
THE HOLY ROMAN EMPIRE
FRANCE
SPAIN
PORTUGAL
PAPAL STATES
REP. of VENICE
OTTOMAN MOSLEM EMPIRE (TURKS)

In 1556
CHARLES V
goes into a monastery
and divides the
HAPSBURG DOMINIONS

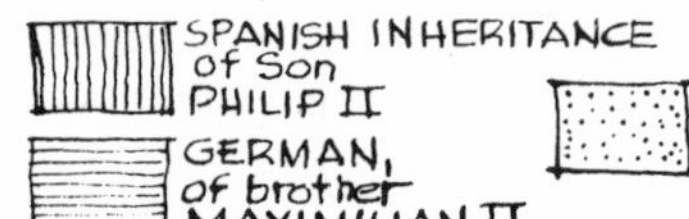
SPANISH INHERITANCE of Son PHILIP II
GERMAN, of brother MAXIMILIAN II
Annexed by PHILIP II

# · The AGE of SPANISH DOMINATION ·

Ignatius Loyola (1491 – 1556) gave up his military career to become a soldier of Christ. He founded the Society of Jesus to suppress Protestantism and to restore the Church and the Pope to their former powerful positions. Under his leadership the uncloistered Jesuits were trained to teach the propagation of Catholic ideals among the laity. They opened schools and missions in all parts of the world. Francis Xavier (1506 – 1552), the "Apostle of the Indies," made many converts as a Jesuit missionary in India and Japan.

The Jesuit system of fighting new ideas by explaining old ones brought many people back into the Church. In defiance of the austere practices of puritanical reformers, the Jesuits glorified the Virgin Mary and her immaculate conception in the most ornate churches ever built. The Society never obtained its goal, but it helped to save the Catholic Church from possible extinction on the continent and was responsible for its introduction in the new world.

The Spanish mystic St. Theresa of Avila (1515 – 1583) was another influential voice of the Counter Reform. And so were the Italian St. Angela Merici (1474 – 1540) as founder of the teaching order of Ursuline Nuns, and the French St. Vincent de Paul (1581 – 1660), the protector of the poor, the sick and the aged, and the originator of the Sisters of Charity.

Because of her accumulation of power and wealth, Spain had few friends and many enemies. Her preoccupation with the collection of gold made her a poor governor of her colonial possessions. Her despotic rule over her crown territories, supported by the savagery of her Inquisition, made all Europe fear and despise her. There were few mourners when her might showed signs of breaking.

In 1588 England won control of the seas by defeating the Spanish Armada. In 1645 after a long, bloody persecution Holland won her freedom from Spain and became the first Protestant democratic state in Europe. France gradually usurped the position of continental leader. Ignoring the papal boundaries, all three countries colonized in North America.

Slowly Spain's huge overseas Empire was whittled away. The Monroe Doctrine (1823) protected the revolts of her South American colonies. The Spanish-American War of 1898 ended her rule in this hemisphere, but she has left the indelible stamp of her culture on Central and South America and on the southwestern section of the United States.

The Counter Reformation introduces new subjects for PROMULGATION of the FAITH. *The Holy Family* including St. Joachim and St. Anne, parents of the Virgin puts emphasis on her lineage and leads to the doctrine of the *Immaculate Conception.* The abstract idea of her eternal sinlessness is popularized by Baroque artists. It is made an Article of Faith in 1854. (For paintings see pages 78 and 79)

### · SPANISH PAINTING ·

15th and 16th century painters reflect taste of their northern dominions.

(1.)

The 17th c. brings Spain her first outstanding artists. The influence of the Italian Renaissance is not difficult to discern.

(2) Pope Innocent X

Velasquez is the first Spaniard to portray truly personal characterizations.

Murillo, religious persuasionist, decorates countless churches with a style which expresses a delicately colored sentimental piety.

*Holy Family with* John the Baptist and his mother Elizabeth. (3)

# · The AGE of EXPLORATION ·

ENGLAND'S *claim on New World* is based on discoveries of JOHN and SEBASTIAN CABOT 1498

AMERIGO VESPUCCI touches the mainland of South America, 1497.

The quest for a water route to the East Indies led to the accidental discovery of a world of uncountable riches—the Americas. Every person in Europe wanted a share of the treasures brought home by the Spanish conquerors. Kings were beleaguered with demands for funds and charters. When royal exchequers would yield no more, companies were formed to raise money by the sale of shares in their enterprises. Areas which did not offer gold had furs and other natural resources to be exchanged for money in home markets. Permanent settlements were founded on foreign shores. Banks were set up at home to handle the profits of the corporations. The entire economic structure of Europe was changed. Social adjustments followed.

FRANCE'S *claim* on voyage of JACQUES CARTIER 1534

Unexplored regions offered opportunity to the adventurous and escape to the persecuted. Many of the eastern colonies of North America were settled by individuals seeking religious freedom.

CHRISTOPHER COLUMBUS is financed by *Ferdinand and Isabella* to find a WATER ROUTE to the Orient. Instead he establishes SPANISH CLAIMS in a New World

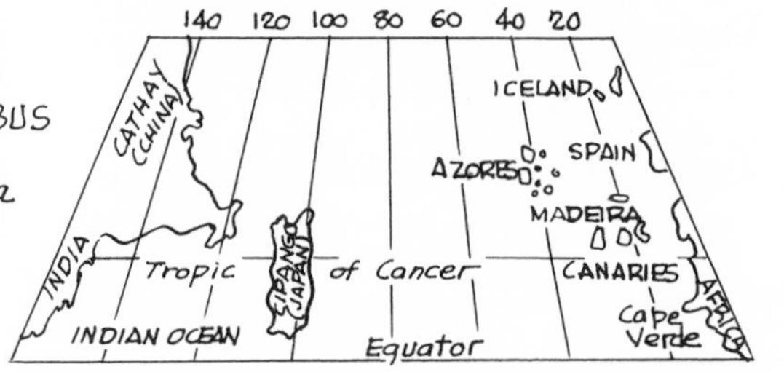

140 120 100 80 60 40 20
CATHAY (CHINA)
ICELAND
SPAIN
AZORES
MADEIRA
INDIA
Tropic of Cancer
ZIPANGU (JAPAN)
CANARIES
INDIAN OCEAN
Equator
Cape Verde
AFRICA

TOSCANELLI'S MAP 1474.
Used by Columbus on his first voyage in 1492.
MEDIEVAL concept of FLAT WORLD

VASCO DA GAMA is the first European to reach INDIA by sea.

PORTUGUESE EXPLORERS found a world empire.

MAGELLAN The first trip AROUND the WORLD. 1520

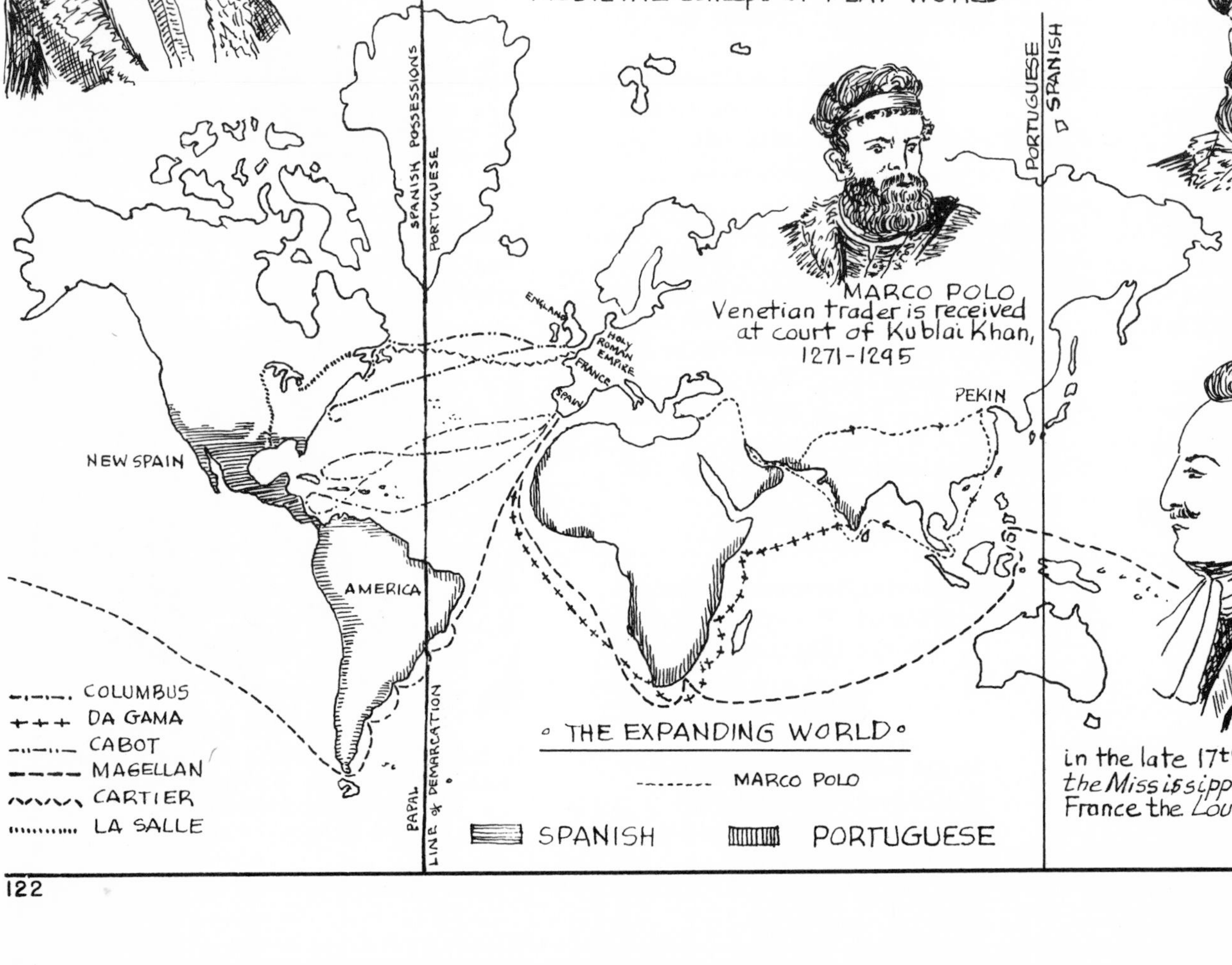

MARCO POLO Venetian trader is received at court of Kublai Khan, 1271-1295

LA SALLE in the late 17th century explores *the Mississippi River* and gives France the *Louisiana Territory*.

SPANISH POSSESSIONS
PORTUGUESE
PORTUGUESE
SPANISH
ENGLAND
HOLY ROMAN EMPIRE
FRANCE
SPAIN
PEKIN
NEW SPAIN
AMERICA
PAPAL LINE of DEMARCATION

COLUMBUS
DA GAMA
CABOT
MAGELLAN
CARTIER
LA SALLE

° THE EXPANDING WORLD °

MARCO POLO

SPANISH PORTUGUESE

# · 16th CENTURY CULTURE ·

## HISTORICAL EVENTS

Classic Renaissance in Italy (page 105)

Age of Exploration

Spanish Domination
Charles V

End of Medievalism

Protestant Reformation begins 1517

Tudors on English throne 1485–1603
Henry VII
Henry VIII
Edward VI
Mary I

Church of England and closing of monasteries under Henry VIII 1534–1536

Counter Reformation
Council of Trent 1545–1563

Religious wars in France 1562–1598

St. Bartholomew's Eve Massacre 1572
Catherine de' Medici

Gregorian Calendar 1582

Elizabeth in England
Philip II in Spain
Spanish Armada 1588

## PROTESTANT LEADERS

Wycliffe (England)

Huss (German)
Luther (German)
Melanchthon (German)

Calvin (Swiss)
Zwingli (Swiss)

Knox (Scottish)

## LITERATURE

### England

Bacon
Donne
Jonson
Lyly
Marlowe
More
Shakespeare
Sidney
Spenser
Wyatt

### France

Montaigne
Rabelais

### Spain

Cervantes
Loyola

### Italy

Ariosto
Castiglione
Cellini
Machiavelli
Tasso

## PAINTING and SCULPTURE

The Early Renaissance in:

### The Netherlands

Bosch (surrealist)
Breughel the Elder (genre)
Gerard David
Leyden
Massys

### Germany

Cranach the Elder
Dürer
Grünewald
Holbein the Younger
The Graphic Arts
Introduction of still-life subjects

### France

Clouet (sculptors)
Jean Goujon
Pilon

### Spain

Morales

### England

No school of art until 18th c.
Hans Holbein (German) court painter for Tudors

Classic Renaissance in Italy (page 105)

## ARCHITECTS

Experimental Renaissance Style:
Lescot—Mansart, F.—Orme (France)
Thorpe (England)

## MUSIC

Social music—madrigals
Scales and octave adopted
Golden Age of Church music
Palestrina (Italy)

## PAINTING IN THE NETHERLANDS

(1) JAN VAN EYCK (died 1441)
The 16th c. sees the decline of Gothic painting and experimentations in Italy's Renaissance style.
During the 17th c. artistic originality is born out of political and religious revolt.

(2) VERMEER (1632-1675)
even in his portraits suggests the sparkling, neat interiors so proudly displayed in the GENRE easel paintings of the Dutch School.

(3) JORDAENS (1595-1678)
In the GENRE painting of the Flemish school the huge canvases depict the verve and vulgarity of the common man.

# · The RENAISSANCE in FRANCE ·

FRANCIS I (1515-1547)
Votive picture on Limoges enamel by L. Limousin

The medieval feudal system divided lands and inhabitants into fiefs which were given to individual nobles. The owners had the right to handle them as they would any personal possession. This practice had worked particular hardship in France, where the feudal dukes and the English kings, through marriage settlements and inheritance, owned and controlled more property than did the King of France.

It was not until the reign of Louis XI (1461 – 1483) that the consolidation of modern France began. His son, Charles VIII (1483 – 1498), attempted to include the Kingdom of Naples in the realm. For a hundred years Italy was the jigsawed battleground of the ambitious French and the grasping Spanish. The French were finally defeated under Francis I.

During the 15th century, Renaissance details had crept into France to ornament medieval and Gothic buildings. When Francis I was a prisoner of war in Italy, he became interested in the new school of art and architecture. He is called the Father of the French Renaissance because upon his release he commissioned Leonardo da Vinci, Cellini, Vignola and other Italian craftsmen to return with him. A school was set up at Fontainebleau, where Renaissance ideals and techniques were taught.

French Renaissance marriage chest
A maximum of decoration and a minimum of function.

Architecture followed Italian Renaissance details and ideas, but soon took on French regional and national characteristics, with great charm, variety and pleasing proportions. The chateaux in the valley of the Loire are fascinating examples of this experimental period.

France conscientiously experimented with all forms of art for almost a hundred years before she worked out a satisfactory style. It was during the reign of Louis XIV that she was given the direction often so necessary to assure production from even the most able craftsmen.

Louis wished to use his absolute powers to make France the foremost country in Europe. Mazarin as Minister of State, and Colbert as Minister of Finance, were responsible for making his desire a reality. So successful were the actions of the three men that for the next hundred and fifty years every country on the continent tried to imitate anything that originated in France.

Encouragement and financial aid were given in all fields of art. The French Academy, the National School of Fine Arts and the Paris Conservatory of Music were founded. The royal support offered the Savonnerie and Gobelins tapestry works, the Sèvres pottery factory and other producers of the decorative arts, gave the French court unrivaled magnificence. This practice was continued through the eighteenth century and by Napoleon in the nineteenth.

Louis XIV architecture was extravagant and of monumental size. Based upon the Italian Baroque, the exteriors are, however, more classical and even the interiors are not so unorthodox. The scale, balance and careful detail for which French architecture is noted first appeared during this period.

French Renaissance Chimney Piece

# · The STYLE of LOUIS XIV ·

INTERIORS: High ceiling decorated with historical or mythological scenes. DEEP CORNICE. MODILLIONS, CAPITALS, TROPHY PANELS in BRONZE D'ORE.

WALLS: Large panels and pilasters of wood or marble.

FURNITURE: Age of Gilded Oak.

Italian influence under Mazarin
Spanish influence from marriage with the Infanta Maria Theresa

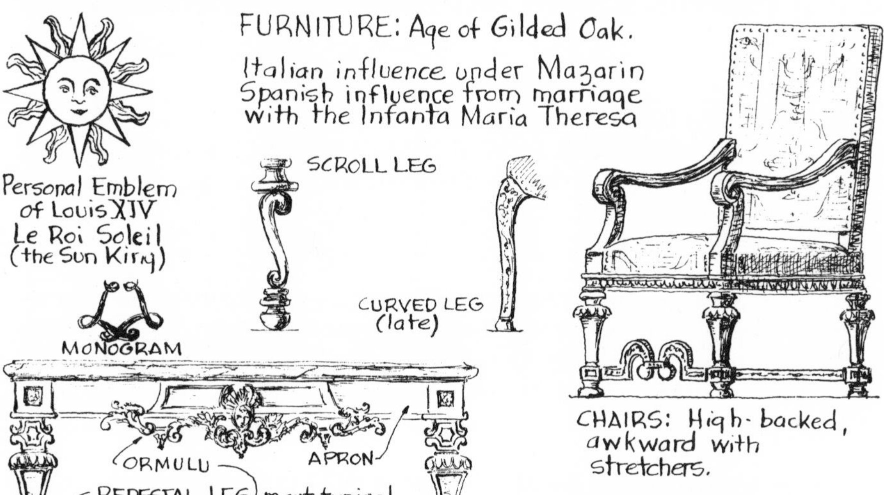
SCROLL LEG
CURVED LEG (late)
MONOGRAM
ORMULU
APRON
PEDESTAL LEG most typical

Personal Emblem of Louis XIV
Le Roi Soleil
(the Sun King)

CHAIRS: High-backed, awkward with stretchers.

TABLE: Marble top
Bronze d'oré ormulu applied to apron and stretcher.

Anne of Austria
Queen of France and Regent for her five-year-old son Louis XIV shown here (at left) with his brother Philippe.

CARDINAL MAZARIN

The Italian minister is not always popular with the people and once is exiled. The devoted royal family recall him and documents show that he becomes the secret husband of the Queen Mother. He devotes his life to strengthening the monarchy and upon his death the position of Louis XIV is secure.

## · THE TRANSITIONAL REGENCY STYLE ·

A period during which the pompous formality of the court of Louis XIV is broken by the informality of the Regency. Reduction in size of rooms and furniture.

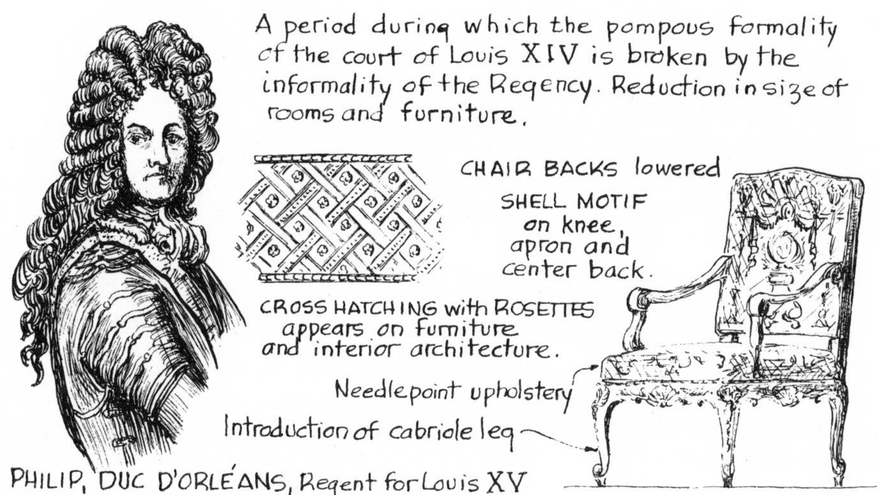
CHAIR BACKS lowered
SHELL MOTIF on knee, apron and center back.
CROSS HATCHING with ROSETTES appears on furniture and interior architecture.
Needlepoint upholstery
Introduction of cabriole leg

PHILIP, DUC D'ORLÉANS, Regent for Louis XV

Jean Baptiste Colbert (1619-1683)
His financial, maritime and Colonial policies fill the treasury and support the extravagances of the court.

# ARCHITECTURE of the FRENCH RENAISSANCE

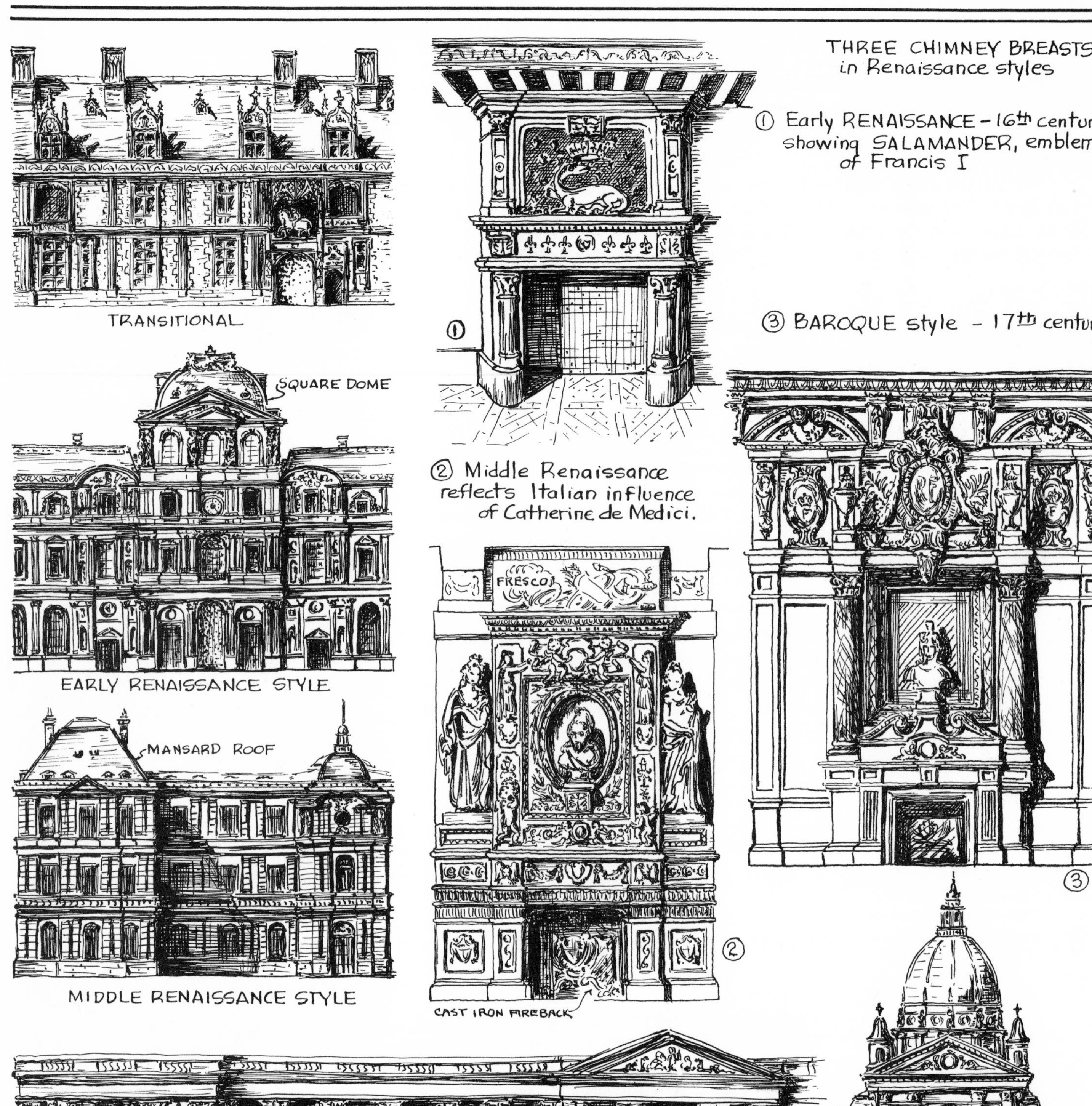
THREE CHIMNEY BREASTS
in Renaissance styles
① Early RENAISSANCE – 16th century
showing SALAMANDER, emblem
of Francis I
TRANSITIONAL
①
③ BAROQUE style – 17th century
SQUARE DOME
② Middle Renaissance
reflects Italian influence
of Catherine de Medici.
FRESCO
EARLY RENAISSANCE STYLE
MANSARD ROOF
③
②
MIDDLE RENAISSANCE STYLE
CAST IRON FIREBACK

CLASSIC RENAISSANCE STYLE

BAROQUE

Examination shows that in architecture as in everything else change is gradual, not abrupt. Ideas are seldom as spontaneous as they appear to be and the lasting changes which they bring are born of evolution rather than revolution.

# ·CIVIL LIBERTIES·

England richly deserves the title of Mother of Civil Liberties because she was the first modern nation concerned with the human rights assured by representative government.

The English forced the Norman conqueror to call the GREAT COUNCIL to carry on the tradition of representation in government established by the 10th c. WITAN

WILLIAM I (1066-1087)

From the early Middle Ages through the seventeenth century unintimidated Englishmen repeatedly demanded consideration and justice from Church and state alike. English history is the story of their successful struggle. It is a testimony for the dignity of man.

Under the feudal system in Europe the serf was given no legal rights. But in England during the twelfth century the principles of common law (custom and usage in addition to written law) were introduced for the benefit of all citizens.

The pro-papal tendencies of HENRY III (1216-1272) were responsible for the founding of the Houses of Parliament by his brother-in-law, Simon de Montfort

In 1215 when royal power was abused by King John, he was forced by the barons to sign the Great Charter (Magna Carta) which placed the king under the law, not above it. This was the first signed contract between a ruler and his subjects. In an age of great inequality it guaranteed every man a trial by a jury of his peers.

The first national system of representative government, the two-chambered English Parliament composed of the House of Lords and House of Commons, is an outgrowth of the Great Council called by the nobles under Simon de Montfort. To this meeting were summoned representatives of every social class and every county.

England was the first country openly to defy papal authority, Edward I refused to pay taxes to Rome. He then instigated one of England's most notable reforms by placing taxation under parliamentary control.

The seal of SIMON DE MONTFORT Father of the parliamentary system.

There are many instances of conflict between king and Parliament, occasioned most often by disagreement over the money raised by taxation.

Although the Tudor rulers (1485–1603) dominated the assembly and ruled as despots, they proved able monarchs who seldom overtaxed their subjects. The local lands and riches, confiscated by Henry VIII from the Catholic Church, were considered royal domain. These were used at Henry's discretion. His daughter Elizabeth was generously financed by her privateers, who preyed upon gold-laden Spanish vessels returning from the New World.

The Tudors' seventeenth-century Stuart successors, imbued with the theory of divine right, attempted to continue the pattern of absolutism. Selling lands and charters to colonizers and trade companies in America gave them a small revenue but did not support their extravagances. They levied taxes on the people of England, who loudly demanded that Parliament limit the king's authority on monetary and judiciary affairs. In 1628 Charles I gave up those privileges by signing the Petition of Right. In 1640 drastic measures by the Long Parliament deprived the Crown of more power.

Coronation of EDWARD I (1272-1307) son of Henry III

Plots to replace Protestant Elizabeth with Catholic Mary lead to Mary's execution

MARY STUART
Queen of Scotland

Her son James I (1603-1625) starts the Stuart line of English kings.

During the seventeenth century, England was not free from religious persecution, as the exodus of both Protestant and Catholic colonists to America testifies. The establishment of the Church of England by Henry VIII was followed by more than one unsuccessful plot to restore Catholicism as the national faith. The high-church ritual which William Laud, Archbishop of Canterbury, tried to impose upon the people was one of the causes of the civil war known as the Puritan Rebellion. The King's Cavaliers lost to Cromwell's Roundheads; Charles I was beheaded and Cromwell became Lord Protector of England.

The monarchy was restored after ten years of military rule and puritanical reform. But when unfair arrests continued among religious and political opponents, justice against imprisonment on such charges was insured by the Habeas Corpus Act of 1679.

His insistence upon a fixed liturgy and his support of the divine right of Charles II ends in civil war.

WILLIAM LAUD
Archbishop of Canterbury

In 1688 when James II attempted to fill a majority of government positions with Roman Catholics, he was deposed.

In what is known as the Glorious Revolution, the Protestant daughter of James II, by his first wife, was invited to occupy the English throne as co-regent with her husband Prince William of Orange (Holland).

Gives the king's power to the cabinet.

ROBERT WALPOLE (1676-1745)
England's first prime minister.

At the same time (1689) the Bill of Rights was passed. This denied the theory of divine right by restating the traditional limitations of royal power. It declared the Anglican Church the official national church which every English sovereign must join and support. The Act of Toleration gave religious freedom to all Protestants (except Unitarians). Although complete religious liberty in England was not enjoyed until the nineteenth century, except for Holland, England was more tolerant than any other European country.

During the early eighteenth century, the present Cabinet System of government developed out of the two strong seventeenth-century political parties: the Tories (Conservatives) representing the landed nobility, and the Whigs (Liberals) representing the middle class.

One of the founding fathers of American liberty.

THOMAS JEFFERSON,
author of the U.S. Declaration of Independence

The cabinet is made up of ministers from the party winning the majority of parliamentary seats in a popular election. The Prime Minister is the leader of the majority party. He is also the head of the government. Since the establishment of this system, the British sovereign has reigned but has not ruled the Empire.

A step toward personal liberty which is followed by the U.S. in 1863 in Lincoln's Emancipation Proclamation

CZAR ALEXANDER II of RUSSIA (1855-1881)
Frees the serfs in 1861.

When shortsighted action by George III (1760–1820) and his ministers caused the American colonies to protest taxation without representation, the first active revolution (1775–1783) against royal tyranny began. The colonists, imbued with their English love of freedom, declared their independence (1776) and established a government which guaranteed: life, liberty, the pursuit of happiness, and government by the consent of the governed.

# ·The RENAISSANCE in ENGLAND·

In England the sixteenth century effected the transition between the Middle Ages and the Renaissance. England's self-improvement did not follow an artistic trend. Instead she busied herself with government, exploration and colonization. Until the middle seventeenth century the Renaissance movement had only a superficial effect upon architecture, none upon painting. But her literature and drama were magnificent declarations of the new philosophy of humanism, and the reign of Elizabeth Tudor is known as England's Golden Age.

ELIZABETH I
While England has no organized school of art, her primitive artists supply many interesting portraits.

Freed from the domination of the church by Henry VIII, England was the first northern country to concentrate on the development of secular architecture. The result was a minor domesticated Gothic style which supplied only a few household furnishings. Henry's wanton devastation of the monasteries was a great architectural loss.

Under Elizabeth, England prospered and became a great sea power. In her gratitude, Elizabeth was generous, and made fitting rewards. This began a tradition which made people eager to serve the Crown. The system not only won the loyalty of British subjects, but it paid dividends in the growth and stability of the country.

The nobility built great country estates with enormous formal gardens. The ancient Roman art of topiary was revived; and house and garden were blended into one impressive, harmonious scheme.

·The TOPIARY. Levens Hall, Westmorland·
Topiary is the highly skilled art of growing and trimming evergreens in fanciful shapes.
The practice is not unknown today.

The houses were outfitted with a limited assortment of heavy oak furniture in proper scale with the tremendous, ornate rooms. The pieces were well suited to their intended background; but because of their large proportions and the roughness of the oak, they do not combine well with the more delicate styles which followed in the late seventeenth and eighteenth centuries and with which they are sometimes placed.

The Tudors were succeeded by the Stuarts. England was searching for a satisfactory architectural expression. The domestic exteriors varied in design according to the whims and tastes of architect and client. They were always of Renaissance inspiration and should be so classified. Today we admire them for their ingenious variety and gigantic size.

Under the influence of Inigo Jones, who was especially interested in the works of the classic Italian architect Palladio, buildings and windows became smaller, more refined and more classic —but less suited to the English climate than the large bay-windowed Elizabethan house. His work, however, was interrupted by civil war, and many of his designs were never carried out. During the ten years (1649–60) of Cromwellian rule there was a minimum of building.

· KNOLE in Kent ·
is representative of the enormous houses erected by the nobility of the Elizabethan and Jacobean periods.
The park extends for miles.
The house itself is built around seven court yards, covers over five areas of ground and has over two hundred rooms.
It was started about 1570 and was probably designed by John Thorpe.

# ·The RENAISSANCE in ENGLAND·

The TRANSITIONAL TUDOR STYLE (a form of domesticated Gothic) comes between the medieval Gothic and the type of early Renaissance architecture and furniture known as Elizabethan

(1485) The Tudor Monarchs: (1558)

HENRY VII (1485) EDWARD VI (1547)
HENRY VIII (1509) MARY I (1553)

The HALF TIMBER or STONE HOUSES feature GABLED ROOFS.

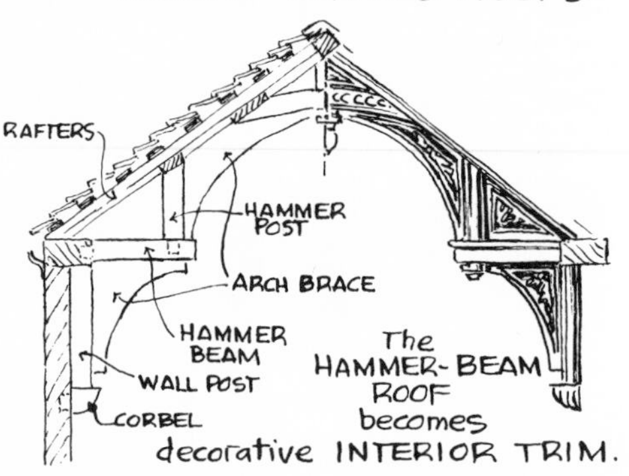

RAFTERS
HAMMER POST
ARCH BRACE
HAMMER BEAM
WALL POST
CORBEL
The HAMMER-BEAM ROOF becomes
decorative INTERIOR TRIM.


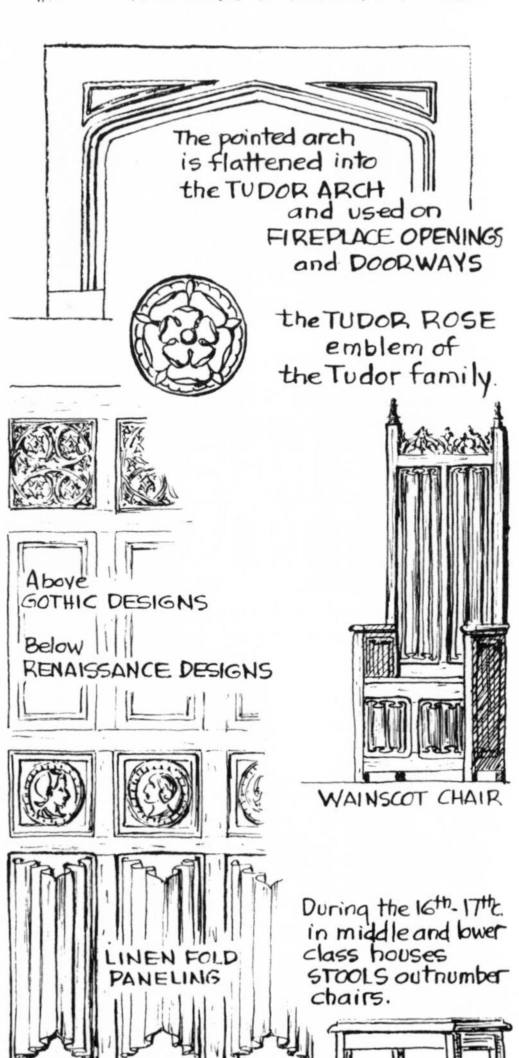

The pointed arch is flattened into the TUDOR ARCH and used on FIREPLACE OPENINGS and DOORWAYS
the TUDOR ROSE emblem of the Tudor family.
Above GOTHIC DESIGNS
Below RENAISSANCE DESIGNS
WAINSCOT CHAIR
LINEN FOLD PANELING
During the 16th-17th c. in middle and lower class houses STOOLS outnumber chairs.
WAINSCOT PANELLING


England was not to produce her best furniture for another hundred years, but Jacobean oak pieces of the middle seventeenth century were taken to the American colonies, where copies and adaptations were made in native woods.

As Tudor, Elizabethan and Jacobean furniture is all made of coarse oak, it is often combined. Early and Middle Renaissance continental designs are in the same scale, but the refinement of detail and the polish of the original finish does not make a happy combination. However, suitable refinishing will bring the pieces into harmony.

The Great Fire of London in 1666 erased all traces of medievalism. Architecture became lighter in scale and more classic in detail. The furniture was more graceful and more comfortably proportioned. Oak was abandoned in favor of softer woods (walnut in particular).

Sir Christopher Wren was commissioned by Charles II to redesign and rebuild St. Paul's Cathedral and fifty-three city churches after the destruction caused by the fire. These were the first buildings designed for Protestant worship, and they were copied and adapted throughout England and America.

Trade with the colonies and the Orient was giving England a wealthy middle class, and the demand for small yet comfortable houses was filled by Wren and other architects of the period.

The exteriors reveal that Renaissance proportions and details were at last mastered. The correctness and the restraint of the designs form an interesting contrast to the experimental picturesque quality of architecture of the Jacobean period.

The interior architecture reflects the release from the puritanical Commonwealth. Large panels, pedimented doorways and elaborate chimney pieces ornamented with carved swags of fruits and flowers are characteristic decoration. It makes a charming background for the contemporary Restoration and William and Mary furniture styles. Later Queen Anne and Chippendale pieces also look well against it.

Both architecture and furniture of this period seem familiar to us, because they were automatically part of the culture of all British dependents. English and American furniture of the four styles mentioned above may be mixed without hesitation.

## · THE ELIZABETHEAN STYLE ·

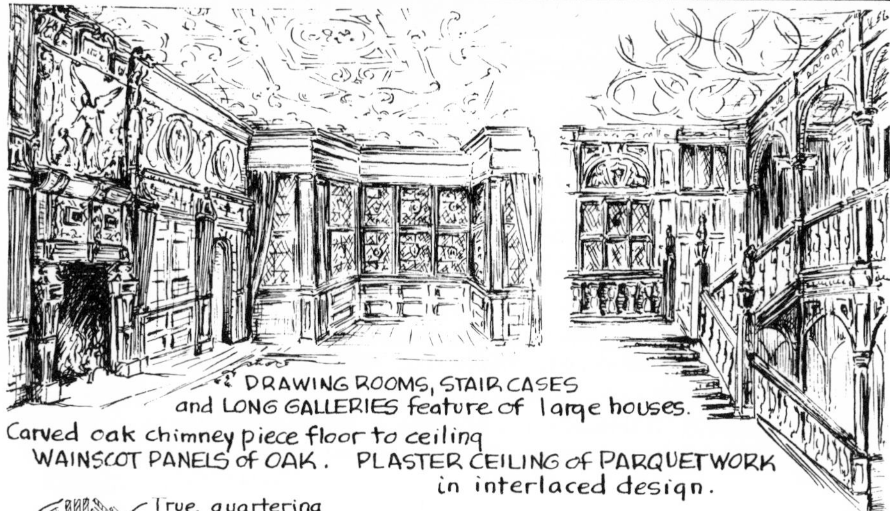

DRAWING ROOMS, STAIR CASES and LONG GALLERIES feature of large houses.

Carved oak chimney piece floor to ceiling
WAINSCOT PANELS of OAK. PLASTER CEILING of PARQUETWORK in interlaced design.

True quartering
Methods of QUARTERING OAK
prefered process eliminates warping

FURNITURE: Quartered OAK decorated with carving and PARQUETRY (inlay in solid wood)

IDENTIFYING FEATURE: Bulbous leg with CUP and COVER

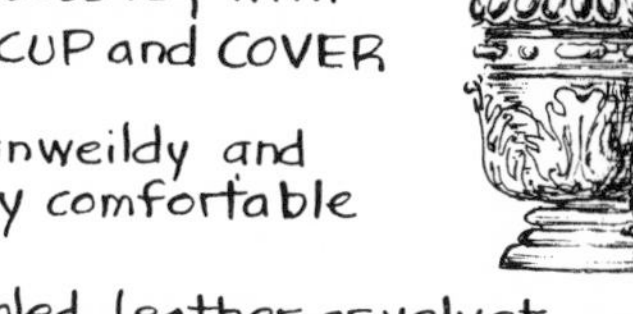

Peasants sleep on straw cots
Nobles have large built-in 4-POSTER BEDS with straw mattresses no springs

Pieces unweildy and not very comfortable

Tooled leather or velvet upholstery

COURT CUPBOARD · WAINSCOT CHAIR · REFECTORY TABLE · FARTHINGDALE CHAIR

## EXTERIOR ARCHITECTURE of the ENGLISH RENAISSANCE ...

### · TYPES of ROOFS ·

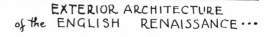

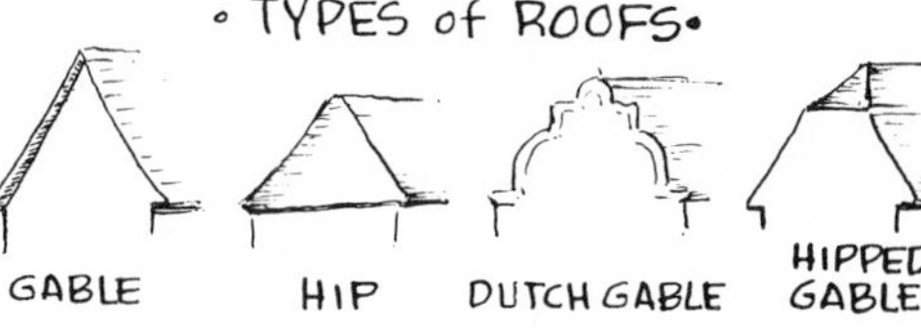
GABLE
HIP
DUTCH GABLE
HIPPED GABLE

### · THE 16th CENTURY ·

CARVED CHIMNEYS
ORIEL WINDOW
BAY WINDOW

RED BRICK with STONE TRIM or STONE for NOBILITY.

Transition between early and classic Renaissance.

## · THE JACOBEAN STYLE ·

CLASSIC MOTIFS used
Proportions still not fully understood.
WALLS: Oak paneled. Plain plaster ceiling. Mitred molding over mantle.
Furniture style found in Colonial America.
FURNITURE: OAK DECORATION (most common forms): SPLIT SPINDLE and MITRED MOULDINGS used on PANELING for WALLS and FURNITURE

The STUART LINE
JAMES I (1603-1625)

MITRED MOLDING

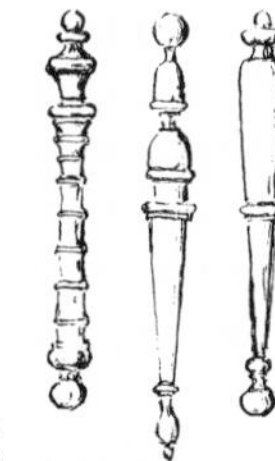

LATHE-TURNED SPINDLES are split and used as APPLIED DECORATION

Many European pieces of the period are similar.

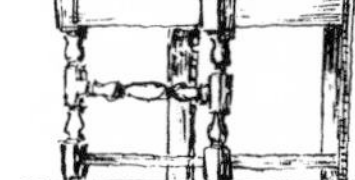

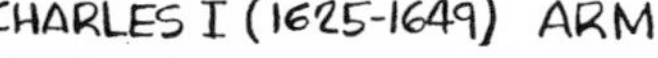

CHARLES I (1625-1649) ARM CHAIR SIDE CHAIR

### · THE 17th CENTURY ·

The short-lived Italian classic style introduced in England by Inigo Jones.

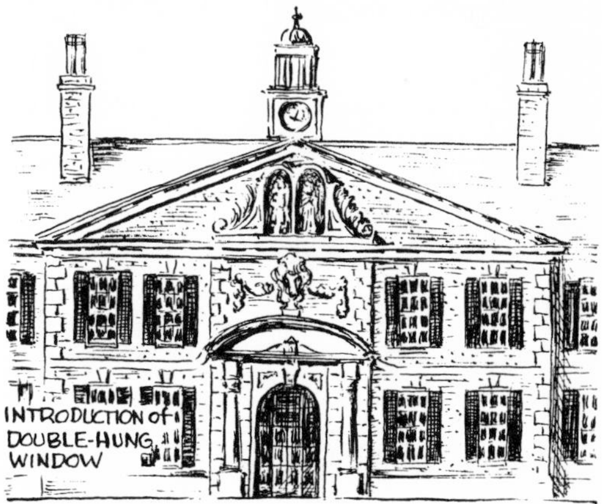
INTRODUCTION of DOUBLE-HUNG WINDOW

Sir Christopher Wren nationalizes the Italian style through the use of native materials.

# ·17th CENTURY CULTURE·

· 17th C. INDIVIDUALISTS ·

SPAIN'S EL GRECO is more popular today than he was in the 17th c. His fluid style has impressionist tendencies and the soulful agony of his gaunt figures foreshadows expressionism. (pages 182, 183)

REMBRANDT takes the dramatic but mechanical *chiaroscuro* (light and shade) technique of the 16th c. CARAVAGGIO and endows it with a supernatural quality.

POUSSIN working within the emotional framework of the Baroque School cultivates a return to classic figures.

## PAINTERS and SCULPTORS

Subject matter: religious, mythological, fashionable portraiture or simple daily life (genre)

### Spain

Period of greatest contribution

| | |
|---|---|
| El Greco (Often called first impressionist) | Murillo |
| | Ribera |
| | Velasquez |
| | Zurbarán |

### Flemish School

| (Portraits) | (Genre Painting) |
|---|---|
| Jordaens | Jordaens |
| Rubens | The Teniers |
| Van Dyck (court painter to Charles I of England) | Synders (animals and still life) |

### Holland-Dutch School

(Portraits)

Frans Hals · Maes · Rembrandt

| (Landscapes) | (Genre Painting) |
|---|---|
| Cuyp | Dou |
| Hobbema | Hooch |
| Potter | Maes |
| Ruisdael | Metsu |
| Goyen | Steen |
| | Terborch |
| | Vermeer |

### France

| | |
|---|---|
| Champaigne (Flemish) | Largillière |
| Le Brun (court painter to Louis XIV) | Lesueur |
| | Mignard |
| | Rigaud |

The brothers LeNain (genre)

(Landscapes)

Poussin · Lorrain

(Sculpture)

Puget · Girardon

### England

Sir Peter Lely · Sir Anthony Van Dyck

(Both Flemish portrait artists)

## HISTORICAL EVENTS

Gradual wane of Spanish domination

Success of Netherlands revolt against Spain 1567 – 1609

Protestant Holland (Dutch)

Catholic Flanders (Flemish)

Stuarts on English throne
James I
Charles I (beheaded)

Cromwells in England 1649 – 1659

Restoration of English monarchy Charles II

Great Plague 1665

1666 Great Fire of London

James II (abdicated)

Louis XIII
Richelieu

Louis XIV
Mazarin
Colbert

Age of Colonization in America

Jamestown 1607

Plymouth 1620

Huguenot emigration from France 1685

Witch hunts

William and Mary in England

### Italy

Baroque Period

(See page 106)

# ·17th CENTURY CULTURE·

## LITERATURE

The philosophy of the age is most influential in the development of thought and action in the following century.

| France | Britain | Germany | Italy |
|---|---|---|---|
| Bayle | Browne | Leibnitz | Campanella |
| Descartes | Bunyan | | |
| Gassendi | Hobbes | | |
| Pascal | Locke | **Holland** | |
| | Milton | Spinoza | |

Prose, poetry and drama make interesting contributions.

| France | | Britain | |
|---|---|---|---|
| Boileau | Molière | Shakespearean productions | (poets) |
| Corneille | Sévigné (letters) | Beaumont and Fletcher | Carew |
| La Fontaine | | Theatres closed 1642–1660 | Herrick |
| | | | Lovelace |
| | | | Milton |
| | | | Suckling |
| | | | Dryden |
| | | Boyle | |
| | | Congreve | |
| | | Dryden | Pepys (diary) |
| | | Wycherley | |

## MUSIC

(1600—The Baroque Period—1750)

Italy introduces the opera.
Harpsichord, precursor of piano, invented.

## ARCHITECTS

| France | England | Italy |
|---|---|---|
| (Early Renaissance) | (Classic Renaissance) | (Baroque) |
| Le Mercier | Gibbs | Algardi |
| Mansart, F. | Jones | Bernini |
| (Classic Renaissance) | Vanbrugh | Borromini |
| Mansart, J. H. | Webb | Longhena |
| Perrault | Wren | Maderna |

·17th Century WRITERS·

Scientists follow his philosophy of INDUCTIVE REASONING, based on facts as opposed to DEDUCTION, founded on "reasonable assumptions".

· Father of Modern Science. ·
FRANCIS BACON (1561-1626)

Accepts only WORD of GOD (the Bible) as the RULE of FAITH

· Blind Puritan Poet-Philosopher ·
JOHN MILTON (1608-1674)

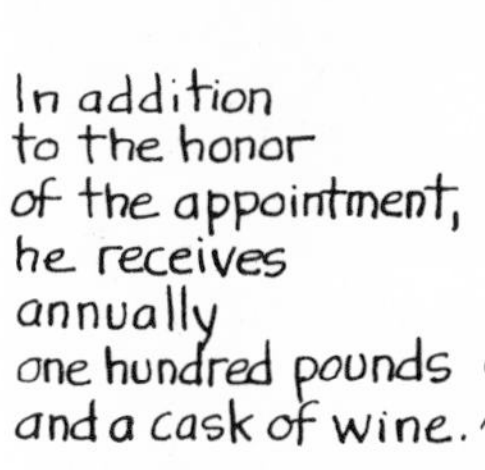

In addition to the honor of the appointment, he receives annually one hundred pounds and a cask of wine.

· England's first Poet-Laureate ·
JOHN DRYDEN (1631-1700)

Today her commentary is an important source of information.

· Accomplished letter writer ·
MARQUISE de SEVIGNE (1626-1696)

# ·17th CENTURY ENGLAND·

SHELDONIAN THEATRE 1669.

Closed on moral grounds by the Puritans, the theatre reopens with the Restoration and bawdy behavior is witnessed on the stage and in the audience.

INTERIORS:
Introduction of LARGE WOODEN PANEL

Rooms symmetrically balanced

CHIMNEY PIECE DOORS and WINDOWS selected for accents in intricate wood CARVING

PLASTER CEILING often decorated with elaborate ornament

Wood carving by ·GRINLING GIBBONS·

In 1689 William III and Mary II are crowned as joint sovereigns

# ·THE RESTORATION STYLE·

· CHARLES II (1660-1685) · JAMES II (1685-1689)·

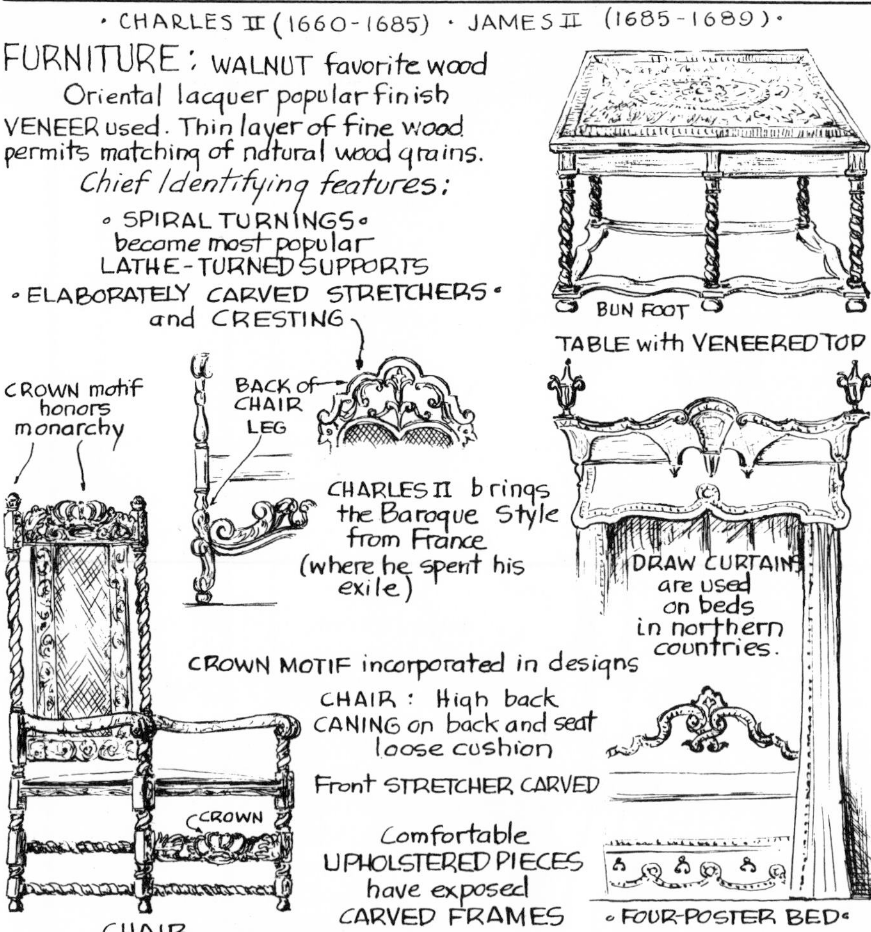

FURNITURE: WALNUT favorite wood
Oriental lacquer popular finish
VENEER used. Thin layer of fine wood permits matching of natural wood grains.

*Chief Identifying features:*

- SPIRAL TURNINGS· become most popular LATHE-TURNED SUPPORTS
- ELABORATELY CARVED STRETCHERS· and CRESTING


BUN FOOT
TABLE with VENEERED TOP
CROWN motif honors monarchy
BACK of CHAIR
LEG
CHAIR
CROWN
·FOUR-POSTER BED·
DRAW CURTAINS are used on beds in northern countries.


CHARLES II brings the Baroque Style from France (where he spent his exile)

CROWN MOTIF incorporated in designs

CHAIR: High back CANING on back and seat loose cushion

Front STRETCHER CARVED

Comfortable UPHOLSTERED PIECES have exposed CARVED FRAMES

# ·THE WILLIAM AND MARY STYLE·

(REIGN - 1689 - 1702)

FURNITURE: Many features borrowed from other countries.

WALNUT featured.

*Identifying features:*

VENEERING makes possible the use of decorative natural WOOD GRAINS (crotch, burl, oyster, etc.)

MARQUETRY becomes very intricate.

JAPANNING (Inferior domestic imitation of Oriental lacquer) used.


INVERTED CUP on leg.
TEAR-DROP handle
SPANISH FOOT
BUN FOOT
FLEMISH SCROLL for legs and stretchers
·CHAIR·
HIGH BOY or CHEST on CHEST
LOWBOY


Decorated drawer with MARQUETRY DESIGN in realistically tinted woods

Marquetry is an inlay of wood veneers.

In the earlier method called INTARSIA the inlay is made in a solid wood ground

CABINET PIECES MOST typical furniture.

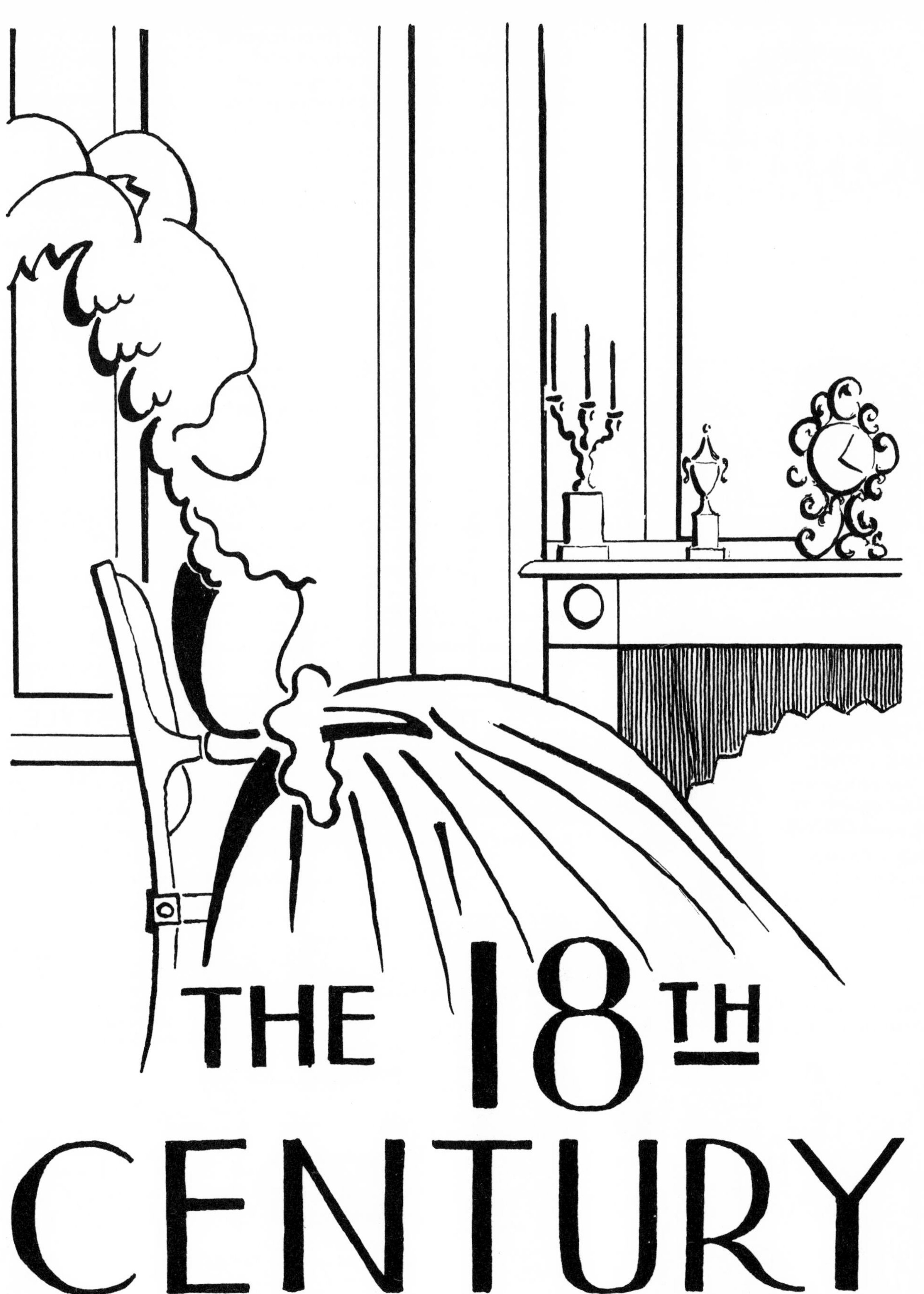

# THE 18TH CENTURY

## 1700—THE EIGHTEENTH CENTURY—1800

*Style of Architecture

**Style of Furniture

Age of Intellectual Activity.
The peak of European culture under the leadership of France.
England's American Colonies revolt.
Demands for political freedom destroy absolute monarchy in France.
*Exterior Architecture classified as High or Classic Renaissance.

| Italy | France | England | America |
|---|---|---|---|
| | Régence (Transitional) | **QUEEN ANNE | |
| | | *GEORGIAN | Mid-Colonial |
| The Rococo | **LOUIS XV *(Interior Architecture) | Int. Architecture | |
| (Venice) | | **CHIPPENDALE | |
| | **LOUIS XVI *(Interior Architecture) | **HEPPLEWHITE | Georgian Colonial (Copies of English styles of exterior and interior architecture and furniture) |
| | | **ADAM *(Interior Architecture) | |
| | Directoire (Transitional) | | |
| | First Republic | **SHERATON | |

• OVERDOOR •
Style of Louis XV

# ·THE AGE OF FRENCH INFLUENCE·

There are many instances in history of aggressive conquerors inflicting their way of life upon the conquered. But the position of France in the eighteenth century is unique. Having established boundaries for her own protection, she sat back to enjoy a peaceful interlude. Suddenly she was besieged by visitors who begged to be taught every phase of her culture. Her government, army, architecture, furniture, accessories, painting, sculpture, literature, fashions, manners, and most of all her colorful courts at Paris and Versailles, were assiduously copied. French became the international language of scholarship and diplomacy. Even the self-sufficient British Isles kept a watchful eye on French styles.

It is not surprising that the century is renowned for the introduction of truly gracious living. For the first time appropriate equipment was designed to meet all household and personal needs. The outstanding artistic contributions are not the works of painting or sculpture but the architecture, furniture and accessories designed to add beauty and comfort to the lives of the few who could afford to purchase them.

The experimental scientists of the seventeenth century (the Century of Genius) turned the new era over to the philosophers. The Age of Reason and Enlightenment enthusiastically collected information which would enable man to answer all questions through the process of reason. The dictionary and encyclopedia were compiled. In a time of social and economic inequality, man was awarded (in theory) complete equality.

In 1776 a situation arose which gave France the opportunity to uphold the philosophy of the rights of man—and at the same time to strike at her cocky English neighbor. She actively assisted in the revolt of England's American colonies.

Within a few years, the people of France were insisting upon their rights and demanding the end of the monarchy. The Revolution (1789) beheaded the king and queen but replaced them with dictatorship, anarchy, terror and corruption.

The Corsican Napoleon Bonaparte brought order out of the internal chaos in France, but as emperor he embroiled the country in an endless war for continental supremacy.

During the ten years of Napoleon's reign (1804–1814) (see map, page 155), he so dominated the continent that France ceased to be the most admired country in Europe and became the most feared. Since his defeat, France has never resolved her political difficulties nor regained her position of leadership.

The eyes of the world are upon FRANCE:

Russia with admiration.

PETER the GREAT (1682-1725) employs a French architect to lay out the new capital city of St. Petersburg.

America for support.

BENJAMIN FRANKLIN (1706-1790) as an American diplomat in France secures military and financial aid for the American Revolution.

England with apprehension.

HORATIO NELSON (1758-1805) after defeating the French on the Nile (1798) destroys the fleet with which Napoleon intends to invade England. (Trafalgar 1805)

# ·ARCHITECTURE of the HIGH RENAISSANCE·

French painting seldom expresses great depth of feeling but it is usually decoratively pleasing.

① CLAUDE LORRAIN (1600-1682) uses landscapes as a background for Biblical themes.

② NATTIER (1685-1776) portrays lovely pink and white ladies of the court.

③ The style of LOUIS DAVID (1748-1825) is as flexible as his politics. The Classic Revival (Empire) becomes his most prolific period.

The HIGH RENAISSANCE becomes the first PUBLIC and DOMESTIC INTERNATIONAL STYLE.

Regardless of country, Renaissance architecture is recognized by the REPETITIOUS USE of classic forms and ornament. STONE is the most usual building material.

A- CUPOLA
B- DOME
C- PORTICO
D- PEDIMENT
E- BALUSTRADE
F- COLONNADE
G- PALLADIAN WINDOW
H- CLASSIC COLUMN
I- DORMER WINDOW
J- RUSTICATION
K- CLASSIC STATUES
L- FLAT ROOF
M- KEYSTONE
N- URN


·ELEVATION showing TYPICAL FEATURES·

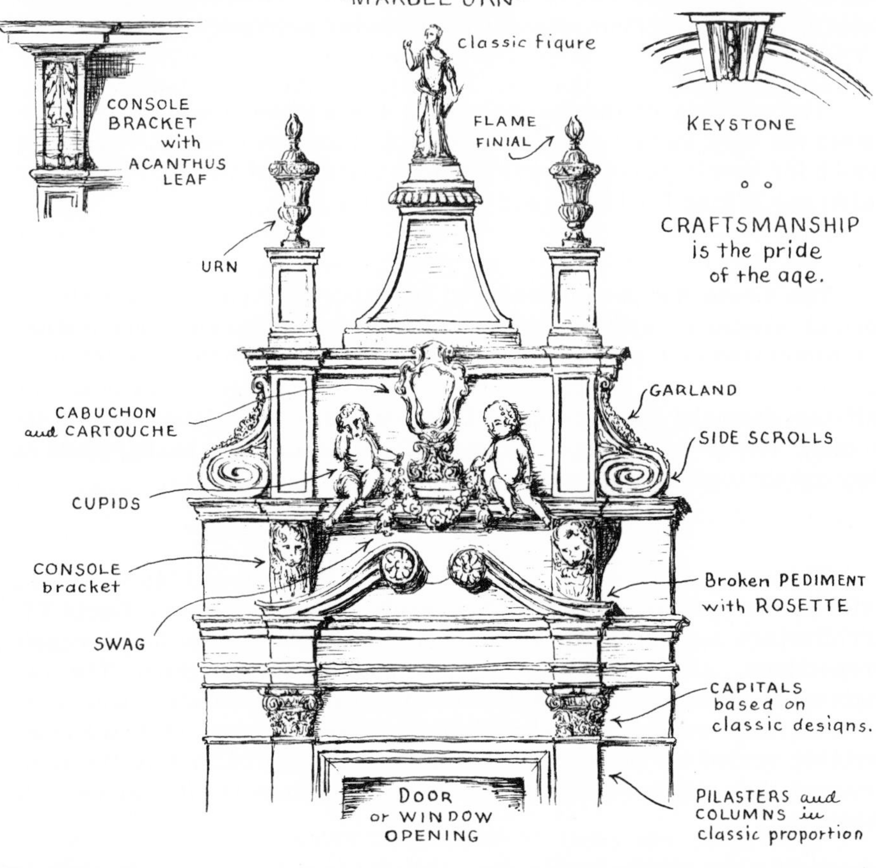

·DORMER WINDOW·
·MARBLE URN·
·DORMER WINDOW·
CONSOLE BRACKET with ACANTHUS LEAF
classic figure
FLAME FINIAL
KEYSTONE
URN
CRAFTSMANSHIP is the pride of the age.
CABUCHON and CARTOUCHE
GARLAND
SIDE SCROLLS
CUPIDS
CONSOLE bracket
Broken PEDIMENT with ROSETTE
SWAG
CAPITALS based on classic designs.
DOOR or WINDOW OPENING
PILASTERS and COLUMNS in classic proportion


·VARIATIONS of these ornamental DETAILS appear again and again in DIFFERENT COMBINATIONS·

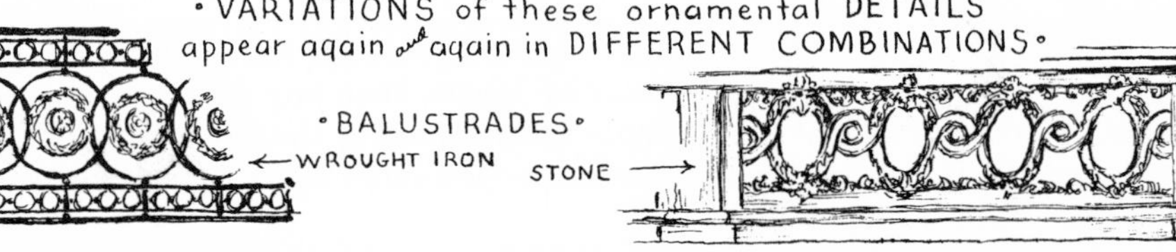

·BALUSTRADES·
WROUGHT IRON
STONE

# ·THE 18th CENTURY IN FRANCE·

In France the scale of living introduced by Louis XIV set expensive standards which his heirs found increasingly difficult to maintain. Emigration from heavy taxation and religious persecution had all but eliminated the middle class.

MADAME DE POMPADOUR (1721-1764) Excavations at ancient Pompeii are financed at her suggestion.

A privileged five per cent of the population lived in the security of wealth and power, while the majority were little better off than they had been during the unenlightened Middle Ages. The extravagances of the nobility and the higher clergy impoverished the state, while it provided a few with luxury and comforts never before experienced. In some cases the indulgences and obscenities of the opulent Romans were equalled if not exceeded.

The hotels and chateaux produced and furnished for this minority will probably never be surpassed in beauty of formal balanced design. Based upon Italian architecture of the High Renaissance the French style, on the whole, has more variety, greater refinement of proportion, and an even finer quality of construction and finish. The exterior architecture is classified as Classic Renaissance.

The interior architecture and furniture fall into two major period styles — Louis XV and Louis XVI. Accessories such as lamps, porcelain, table silver and other now-standard household equipment were introduced.

MARIE ANTOINETTE (1774-1793) wife of Louis XVI. As queen her whims influence the arts.

The regency of the Duc d'Orléans was a transitional interlude between the very formal court of le Roi Soleil and the court of Versailles, which for twenty years was guided by the tastes of Mme. de Pompadour, mistress of king Louis XV, and patron of the arts.

The Louis XV period produced an elaborate style of relatively informal elegance with complete disregard for classical inspiration. Characterized by freehand curves, the detail and ornament were intricate and fussy. It was an effeminate style using pastel colors in satins, taffetas, damasks and brocades. The men dressed as elaborately as the women. Never have people so perfectly matched their backgrounds as they did throughout the eighteenth century in France.

On July 14, 1789, the French Revolution begins with the storming of the prison Bastille, symbol of absolutism.

The excavation of the ancient ruins at Pompeii in 1748 inspired a return to formal classicism with severely classic ornament. Louis XVI architecture and furniture are pleasing compositions with impeccable proportions, and beautifully scaled and executed detail. The two eighteenth-century French styles have always been used interchangeably, because they were both designed for the same society. They are comfortably scaled to human measurement. For approximately the same reasons, late eighteenth-century English furniture is often mixed with them.

The small cities of the provinces copied every period style, although the Louis XV style enjoyed popularity longer than any other. In native woods by local craftsmen, in simple adaptations of the prevailing court taste, provincial boiserie and furniture are often more appealing than elaborate Parisian specimens.

# ·The STYLE of LOUIS XV·

Great-grandson of Louis XIV

• LOUIS XV • King of France 1715-1774

Style characterized by almost complete absence of straight lines.

The FREEHAND CURVE is used wherever possible.

At height of period (epoque) BISYMMETRIC BALANCE changes to ASYMMETRIC BALANCE.

COVE

Interior boiserie showing ROUNDED CORNER and COVE forming transition between wall and ceiling

• • •

Balanced BOISERIE (panelling) DOOR and WINDOW OPENINGS balance each other. FAKE and SECRET DOORS used to maintain balance.

FALSE DOORS

CHIMNEY piece with trumeau balanced by CONSOLE TABLE with trumeau

FLOOR PLAN bisymmetrically balanced.

Favorite motifs in architecture and furniture:

•ROCOCO SHELLS and SCROLLS•

CAEN STONE widely used in France.
Period DETAIL applied to EXTERIORS.
•Window with iron balcony•

## FURNITURE:

Carved frames-gilded or painted. Made in matched sets.

IDENTIFYING FEATURE-
Delicate CABRIOLE LEG with SCROLL FOOT.

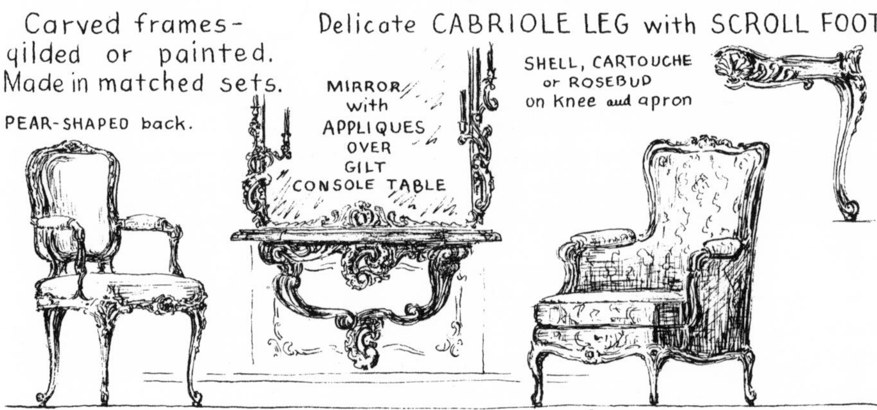

PEAR-SHAPED back.
MIRROR with APPLIQUES OVER GILT CONSOLE TABLE
SHELL, CARTOUCHE or ROSEBUD on knee and apron


ARMCHAIR (FAUTEUIL) sometimes CANED • BERGÉRE upholstered in brocade.

•FURNITURE proportioned for COMFORT•

## ACCESSORIES:

Designed and scaled to conform with style.

ARCHITECTURAL DETAILS depart from classic forms.

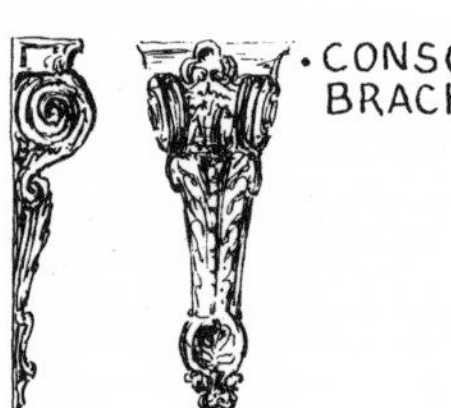

•CONSOLE BRACKETS•

CHANDELIER with PEAR-SHAPED NATURAL ROCK-CRYSTALS.

## COLORS:

Pastel shades and gray.

FABRICS:

Satin, taffeta, damask, brocade, fine needle work.

•KEYSTONE•

BOISERIE with TRUMEAU over MANTLE

In other countries the style is termed Rococo.

•Two Italian designs•

•GIRANDOLE•

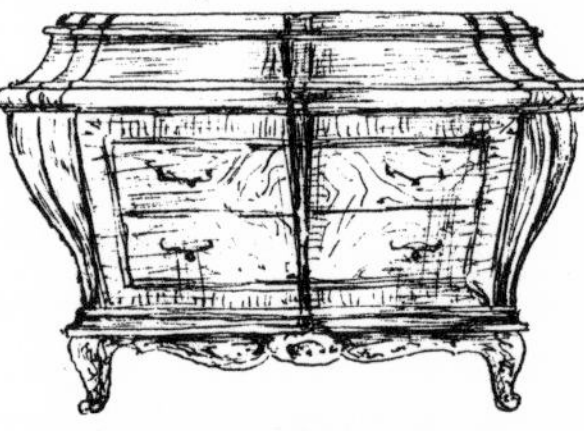

• BOMBE CHEST•

# ·The STYLE of LOUIS XVI·

COLORS and PROPORTIONS same as LOUIS XV
ARCHITECTURAL DETAILS
RETURN to CLASSIC MOTIFS and
COMPASS CURVES.

NICHE

OVAL favorite shape for rooms, windows, tabletops and chair-backs.
FLOOR PLANS – Symmetrically balanced.

LOUIS XVI (1774-1792)
Grandson of Louis XV.
Beheaded in 1793 · His son Louis XVII disappears or is killed · His two brothers are restored to the throne as:
LOUIS XVIII (1814-1824) · CHARLES X (1824-1830)
Charles is deposed.

FURNITURE: Chief identifying features:

Typical DECORATION:

GUILLOCHE · SQUARE URN ·
STICK and RIBBON · BOWKNOT ·
CUT CORNERS with ROSETTES ·
TROPHY PANELS Like Louis XV often garden implements or musical instruments.
CLASSIC FRIEZE · CASKET · GARLANDS · ACANTHUS LEAF · HUSK ·

Characteristic LEG
ROUND, TAPERED and FLUTED, it springs from square ROSETTE

·ARMCHAIR·

·CONSOLE TABLE carved and gilded·

SIDE CHAIR with painted frame

DOORWAY with OVERDOOR IN BAS-RELIEF

Typical ARABESQUE used in panels and fabric design.

MAHOGANY COMMODE with applied ornament of BRONZE D'ORÉ ORMULU

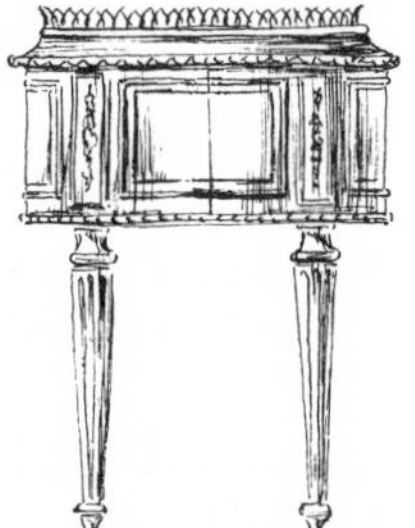

OVAL TABLE with BRASS GALLERY

Architectural ORNAMENT picked out in GOLD LEAF

· Andirons · Clock and vases · Candelabra ·

Upholstered end of DAYBED.

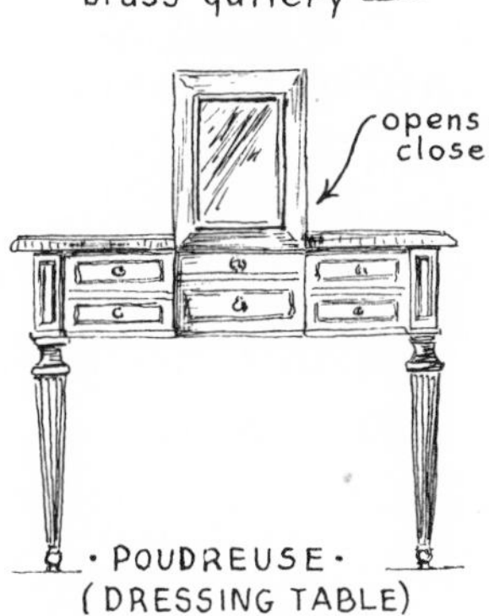
opens and closes

· POUDREUSE ·
(DRESSING TABLE)

Flat-topped secretary has marble top with brass gallery

(Late)
· SECRETARY ·

# ·18th CENTURY CULTURE·

## ·LITERARY FIGURES·

At a crucial moment Paine's writings flame the spark of American liberty and the ties with England are burned.

THOMAS PAINE
(1737 - 1809)

Smith's defense of FREE TRADE influences the policy of the growing British Empire.

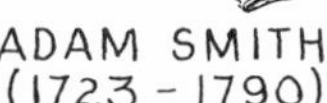

ADAM SMITH
(1723 - 1790)

Fielding brings reality to plot and characters in a new literary form — the NOVEL.

HENRY FIELDING
(1707 - 1754)

EDWARD GIBBON
(1737-1794)

Gibbon's writings reconstruct the crumbling empire of ancient Rome.

IMMANUEL KANT (1724-1804) introduces the theory that morality is controlled by a CATEGORICAL IMPERATIVE.

## PHILOSOPHERS

Seventeenth- and eighteenth-century writers did much to bring about political, economic and social reforms.

| France | Britain |
|---|---|
| Condillac | Bentham |
| Helvetius | Berkeley |
| Montesquieu | Hume |
| J. J. Rousseau | Malthus |
| Voltaire | Smith |

**Germany**

| | |
|---|---|
| Hegel | Kant |
| Fichte | Mendelssohn |

**U. S. A.**

Paine

## POETS, ESSAYISTS, NOVELISTS, DRAMATISTS

**Britain**

Addison and Steele

| | |
|---|---|
| Boswell | Johnson (dictionary) |
| Burke | Pope |
| Burns | Richardson |
| Cowper | Sheridan |
| Defoe | Smollett |
| Fielding | Sterne |
| Gray | Swift |
| Gibbon | Walpole |
| Goldsmith | |

| France | Germany |
|---|---|
| Beaumarchais | Goethe |
| Boileau | Klopstock |
| Diderot (encyclopedia) | Lessing |
| J. B. Rousseau | Wieland |
| Voltaire | |

## HISTORICAL EVENTS

Age of French hegemony

The Absolute Monarchs

Louis XV ) France
Louis XVI )

Maria Theresa (Austria)

Frederick the Great (Prussia)

Romanovs in Russia:
Peter the Great
Catherine the Great

Bourbons in Spain (beginning with grandson of Louis XIV)

House of Hanover in England
George I, II and III

France and England at war.
British acquire Gibraltar, Canada and India, start colonial empire.

Industrial Revolution starts in England 1765

Battles for Independence

American Revolution: Declaration of Independence 1776.
French Revolution 1789
Irish Rebellion 1798

# ·18th CENTURY CULTURE·

## PAINTING and SCULPTURE

Flattering portraiture was the favorite subject for oil painting; sentimental or satirical scenes of daily life were presented through the graphic arts.

### France

| (Painters) | (Sculptors) |
|---|---|
| Boucher | Bouchardon |
| Fragonard | Clodion |
| Lancret | Coustou |
| Lebrun | Coysevox |
| Nattier | Legros |
| Watteau | Pigalle |

(Genre)

Chardin   Greuze

(Landscapes)

Robert   Vernet

### Italy

Caneletto
Crespi
Guardi
Longhi
Magnasco
Piazetta
Ricci
Rotari

### England

(Portraits)
Gainsborough
Hogarth
Hoppner
Laurence
Raeburn
Reynolds
Romney

(Landscapes)
Constable
Crome
Turner
Wilson

(Graphic Arts)

Hogarth (Eng.)   Piranesi (It.)
Rowlandson (Eng.)

### Spain

Goya

### Colonial America

Peale, C.W.   Savage   Stuart
Copley   Smibert   Trumbull

## ARCHITECTURE

(Classic Renaissance Style)

### France

Chalgrin   Soufflot
Gabriel   Vignon
LeNotre (gardens)

### England (Georgian)

Adam Bros.   Kent
Chambers   The Woods

**Germany:**   von Erlach   von Hildebrandt   Neumann

## MUSIC

(1600—The Baroque Period—1750)

Germany perfects the fugue.
J.S. Bach   Handel

(1750—The Classical Period—1820)

The sonata is introduced.
Domenico Scarlatti (Italy)
(harpsichord virtuoso)
K.P.E. Bach (Germany)
Gluck (Germany, opera)

The symphony makes an appearance.
Beethoven   Haydn
Cherubini   Mozart
Stradivari
(violin-maker)

### ·SOCIAL PRACTICES·

·THE FRENCH SALON·
Intelligent conversation is the entertainment at a salon, where fashion, philosophy, science and the arts meet.
These informal gatherings do much to promote the inquiring spirit of the age.

·VAUXHALL GARDENS·
A permanent carnival provides music, amusements and refreshments to fashionable London.

THE COFFEE HOUSE
is the English counterpart of the French salon, the mental clearing house of the intelligentsia. Women are excluded.

• • •

The education of women is sadly neglected until the revolt of the modern woman in the mid-nineteenth century. The U.S.A. is the first country to give women the vote (1919).

# ·THE 18th CENTURY IN ENGLAND·

·The LAST of the STUARTS·

QUEEN ANNE (1702-1714), second daughter of James II. She outlives her husband and children.

·THE HOUSE of HANOVER·

The German Elector, great grandson of James I, is given the throne. The stolid Hanoverians and their dull courts leave fashion-setting to the nobility.

GEORGE I (1714-1727) never learns to speak English.

Enamel and jewelled pendant of ST. GEORGE and the DRAGON, Patron Saint of England is emblem of the Garter.

GEORGE II (1727-1760) England gains Canada and India during his reign.

GEORGE III (1760-1820) · England looses America but gains the Christmas tree, which is brought from Germany by Queen Charlotte.

During the late years of George III, his eldest son as Prince of Wales and Regent is social leader.

During this period English life, strengthened and balanced by its successful middle class, produced its best examples of civic and domestic architecture. Classified as High or Classic Renaissance, all English architecture of the eighteenth century is more familiarly known as Georgian. The term is often used as a convenience to describe some of the equally well-designed buildings of the late seventeenth century.

Based on parallel demands and identical principles, the English version of Classic Renaissance exterior public architecture is hauntingly similar to the fifteenth-century Italian, and the contemporary French. But in domestic architecture indoors and out, the same bisymmetric balance and proportion, the same classic moldings and designs—when combined by English artisans—are unmistakably different from their continental counterparts. Our Colonial Georgian closely resembles the English style from which it was copied.

Eighteenth-century England produced a great deal of charming and beautiful furniture. First came the likable style of Queen Anne. Then the hand of her German successors shows up in the adaptations of the following period, which England candidly refers to as the Forty Years of Bad Taste (1710–1750).

During the last half of the eighteenth century, three now-famous cabinetmakers had establishments in London. They were Thomas Chippendale, George Hepplewhite and Thomas Sheraton. All three were used by the firm of Adam Brothers to carry out its furniture designs. The three men doubtless had other employers in common. Therefore, it is not surprising that they had a definite influence on each other, and that there should be certain repetitions and similarities in their work. But through the years the characteristics which separate and distinguish the furniture as the work of three different workshops have been analyzed into what are known today as the styles of Chippendale, Hepplewhite and Sheraton. Publications of their work were widely subscribed to by contemporary cabinetmakers outside of London and in America. They copied and combined the designs originated in London, so that the "styles" refer to the products of a large school of followers as well as to the work of the men themselves. It is only when a piece is signed or a bill of sale has been preserved that we can be sure of the origin.

With the removal of the tariff in 1747 mahogany became the most popular wood for furniture. However, the provinces and colonies continued to use the wood they had at hand.

# · THE FURNITURE STYLE OF QUEEN ANNE ·

CHARACTERISTICS: Stretchers are no longer a necessity but are not entirely discontinued. Pediments decorative feature of large cabinet pieces. Hoop outline used on many pieces.

FINISHES: WALNUT in burl grain favorite wood. Marquetry, laquer also used.

BRASSES: (handles and locks) SPREAD EAGLE

CUSHION MOLDING replaced by DOUBLE PEDIMENT.

CHIEF IDENTIFYING FEATURE: CABRIOLE LEG unornamented or with CONVEX SHELL on Knee. Ends in DUCK FOOT.

American pieces:
· MAHOGANY and FRUIT woods ·
(refined and exaggerated curves)
Concave shell.

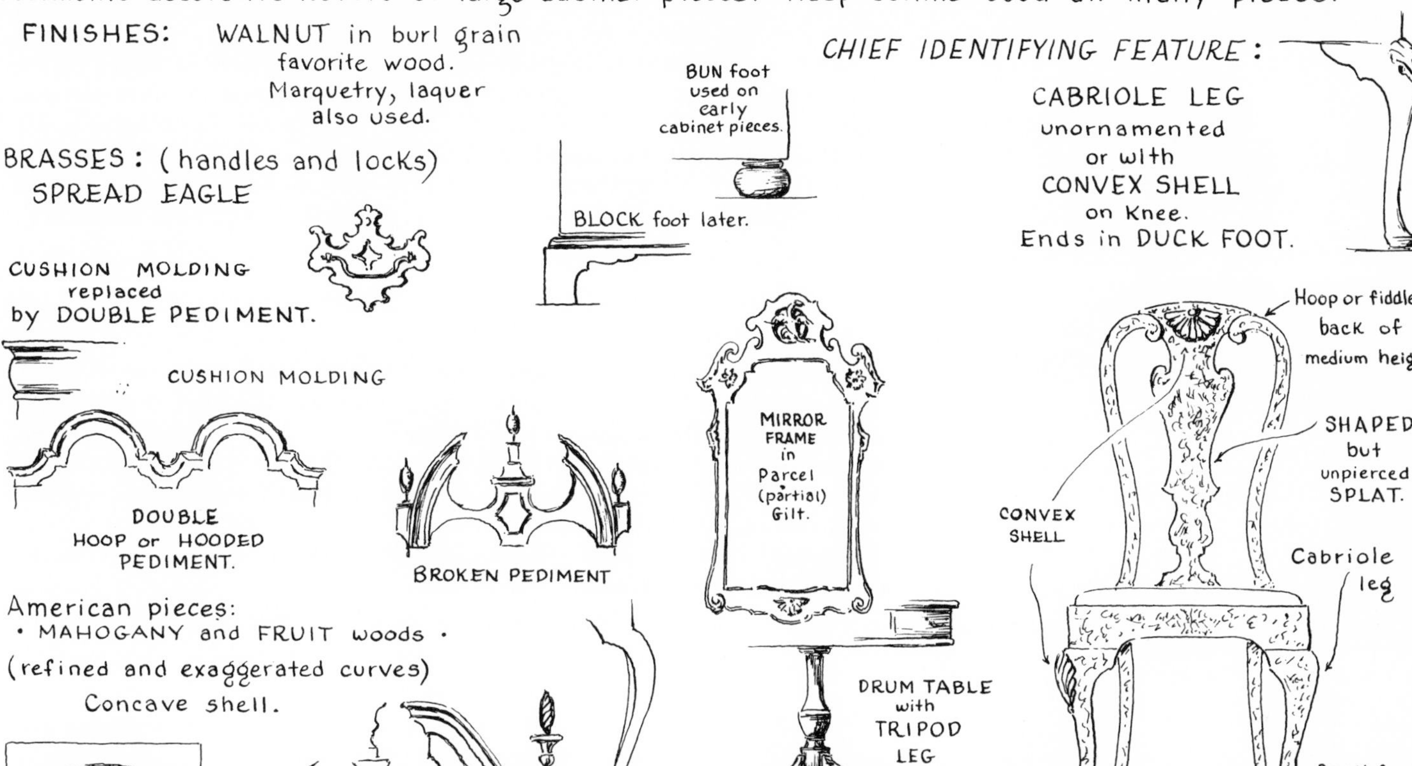

BUN foot used on early cabinet pieces.
BLOCK foot later.
CUSHION MOLDING
DOUBLE HOOP or HOODED PEDIMENT.
BROKEN PEDIMENT
MIRROR FRAME in Parcel (partial) Gilt.
Hoop or fiddle back of medium height
SHAPED but unpierced SPLAT.
CONVEX SHELL
Cabriole leg
DRUM TABLE with TRIPOD LEG
SWAN-NECK PEDIMENT
Duck foot
· TYPICAL CHAIR ·


# · THE EARLY GEORGIAN STYLES 1710-1750 ·

· THE FIVE EARLY GEORGIAN STYLES: I-V ·

**I · DECORATED QUEEN ANNE ·**
Plain walnut now decorated with parcel gilt. Varied motifs in place of shell. Solid splat now pierced. Duck foot now CLAW and BALL or DONKEY'S FOOT.

**II · The LION YEARS ·**
Often in mahogany. Knee, apron, arm ends decorated with FIERCE HEAD. SHAGGY, HAIRY FOOT on cabriole leg.

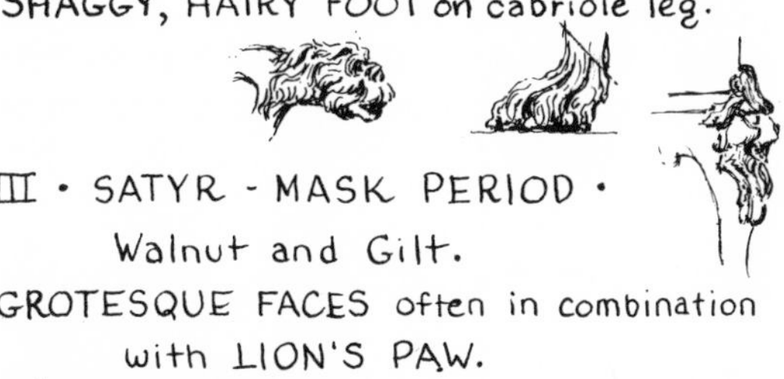

**III · SATYR - MASK PERIOD ·**
Walnut and Gilt.
GROTESQUE FACES often in combination with LION'S PAW.

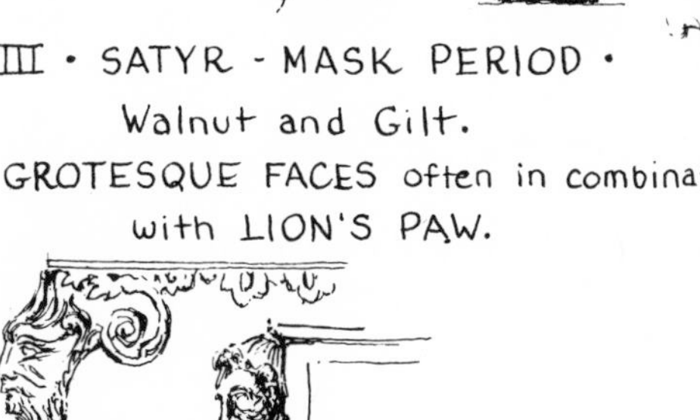

Back lowered

Typical ornate Chair Keeps Queen Anne form with decoration added in: gilt, parcel gilt, laquer (red and gold, black and gold). marquetry, carving, piercing. Heavy German taste influences designs.
Decoration and ornament added in 5 specified places:
(1) top rail, (2) splat, (3) apron, (4) Knee of cabriole leg, and (5) foot.

**IV · CABOCHON and LEAF DESIGN on KNEE ·**
Not to be confused with later Chippendale pieces.
MAHOGANY

**V · ARCHITECTS' FURNITURE ·**
Gilded pieces for houses of their design. Many built-in features (consoles, mirrors, bookcases, etc.) Cabinet pieces most acceptable. Upholstered furniture burdened by ornate frames.

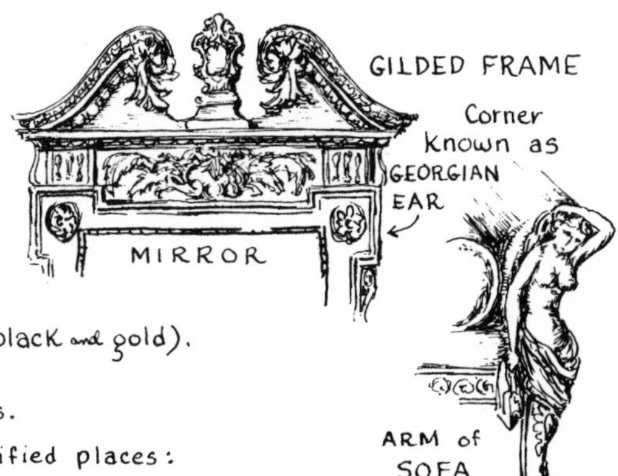

GILDED FRAME
Corner known as GEORGIAN EAR
MIRROR
ARM of SOFA

# · The STYLE called GEORGIAN ·

## · EXTERIORS ·

Typical Classic Renaissance Style.

Prior Park, Mansion and Palladian Bridge. "Natural" park actually carefully landscaped.

## INTERIORS:

Large painted panels bisymetrically balanced. French influence evident in arrangement.

· PANEL ·
· STYLE · (space between panels)
· FIELD · (inside)
· MOULD ·
· DADO ·
Ⓐ
Ⓑ
Ⓒ
Early
Middle
Late
Ⓐ Dado cap or chair rail
Ⓑ Apron panel
Ⓒ Baseboard

· THREE CHIMNEYPIECES ·

White stone QUOINS strengthen corners.

England's wealthy middle class enjoys the comfort of modest, dignified houses of red brick with white stone trim, slate roof.

## · LATER GEORGIAN FURNITURE ·

Many pieces of furniture made during the eighteenth century are so architectural in design that it is more satisfactory to classify them as products of the period than as the work of any particular cabinetmaker. The term Georgian is sufficient identification for such furniture.

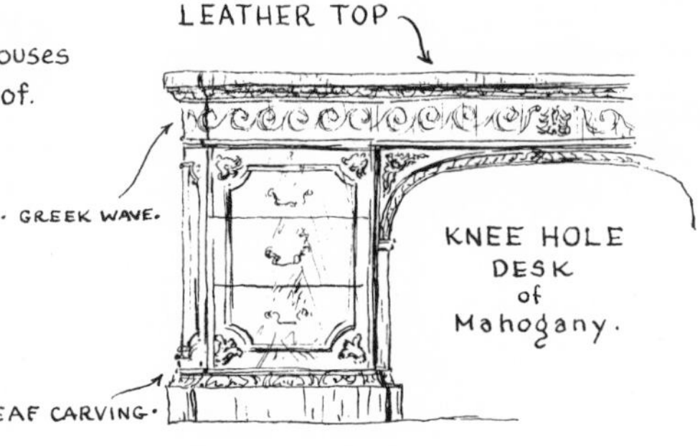
LEATHER TOP
· GREEK WAVE ·
· LEAF CARVING ·

KNEE HOLE DESK of Mahogany.

Note: Carved classic motifs.

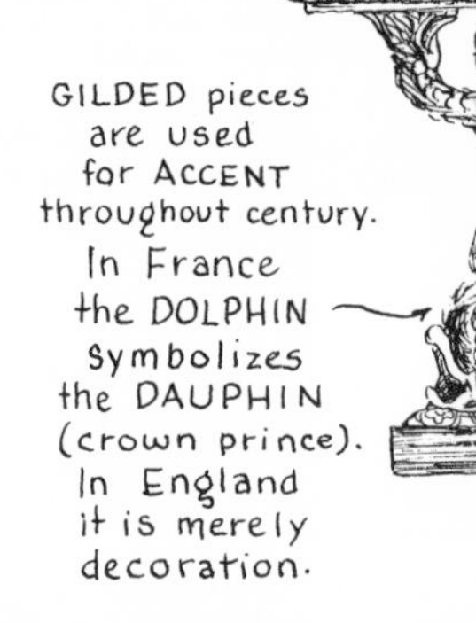

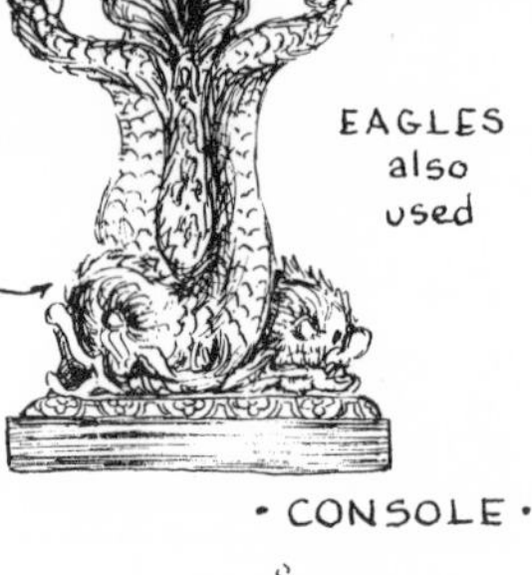
MARBLE TOP
EAGLES also used

GILDED pieces are used for ACCENT throughout century. In France the DOLPHIN symbolizes the DAUPHIN (crown prince). In England it is merely decoration.

· CONSOLE ·

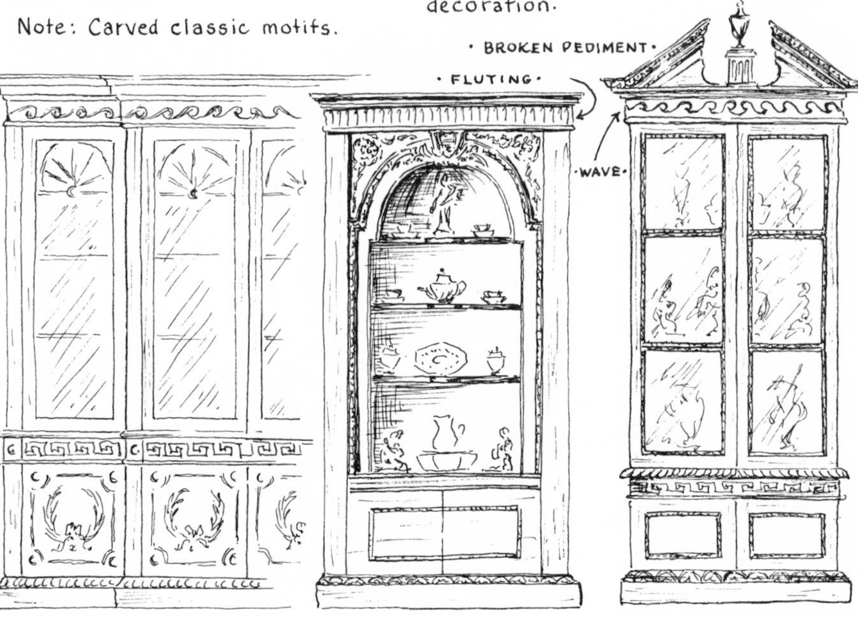
· BROKEN PEDIMENT ·
· FLUTING ·
· WAVE ·

Section of · BREAKFRONT BOOKCASE · · CORNER CUPBOARD · · CABINET ·

Pieces originally in PAINTED PINE. Have since been stripped.

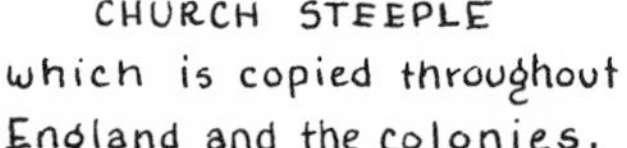

CHURCH STEEPLE which is copied throughout England and the colonies.

# · The STYLE called CHIPPENDALE ·

The English cabinetmaker popularizes a type of chair already in existence.
Today it bears his name. Least delicate style of the late Georgian period, it is a pleasing combination of CURVES and STRAIGHT LINES.

Other Chippendale designs are influenced by many sources, FRENCH and CHINESE principle ones.

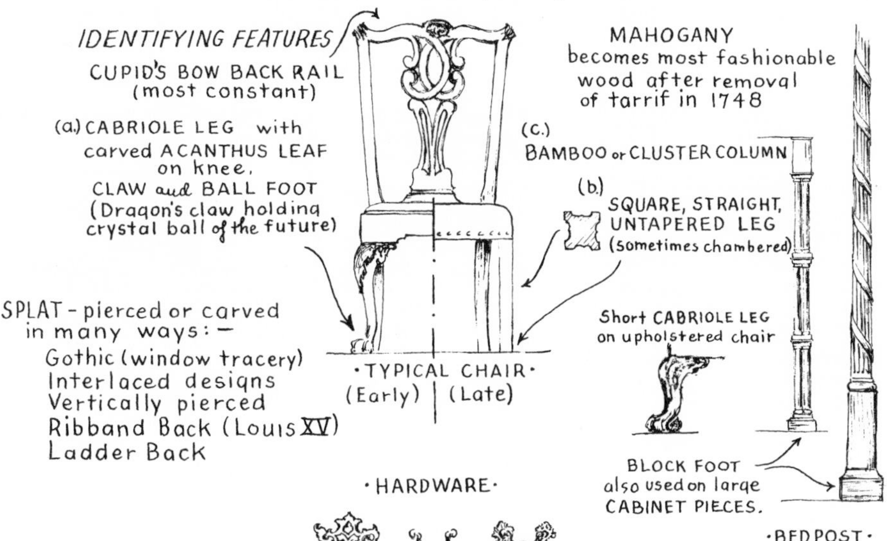
IDENTIFYING FEATURES
CUPID'S BOW BACK RAIL (most constant)
(a.) CABRIOLE LEG with carved ACANTHUS LEAF on knee.
CLAW and BALL FOOT (Dragon's claw holding crystal ball of the future)
SPLAT - pierced or carved in many ways: —
Gothic (window tracery)
Interlaced designs
Vertically pierced
Ribband Back (Louis XV)
Ladder Back
· TYPICAL CHAIR ·
(Early) | (Late)
MAHOGANY becomes most fashionable wood after removal of tarrif in 1748
(c.) BAMBOO or CLUSTER COLUMN
(b.) SQUARE, STRAIGHT, UNTAPERED LEG (sometimes chambered)
Short CABRIOLE LEG on upholstered chair
BLOCK FOOT also used on large CABINET PIECES.
· HARDWARE ·
· BED POST ·

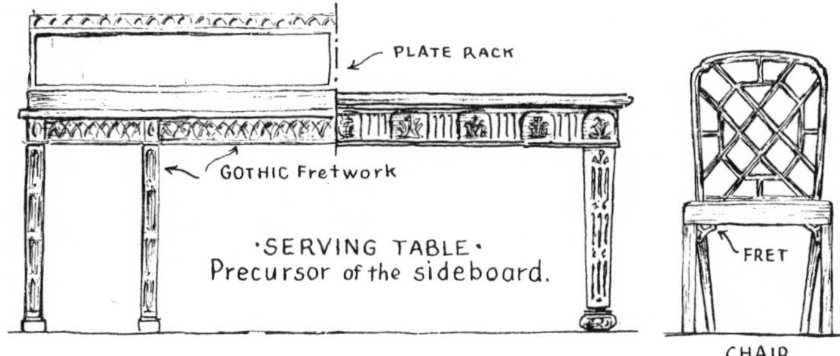
PLATE RACK
GOTHIC Fretwork
FRET

· SERVING TABLE ·
Precursor of the sideboard.

CHAIR in the FRENCH TASTE

CHAIR in the CHINESE MANNER

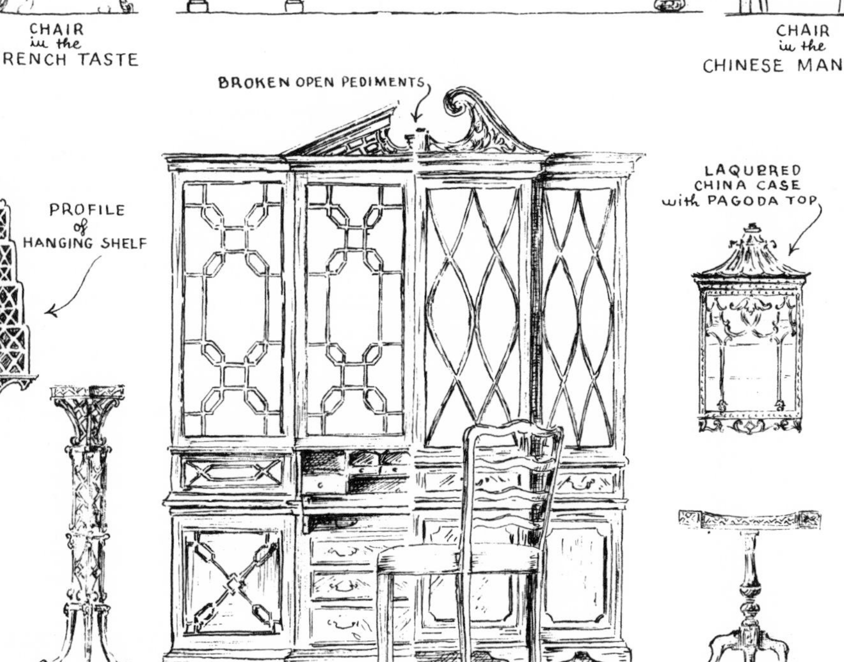
BROKEN OPEN PEDIMENTS
PROFILE of HANGING SHELF
LAQUERED CHINA CASE with PAGODA TOP

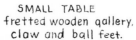

Fretwork
· CANDLE STAND ·

· BREAKFRONT DESK · · BOOKCASE ·
· LADDER BACK CHAIR ·

SMALL TABLE
fretted wooden gallery, claw and ball feet.

· MID-CENTURY INTERIORS ·

For a brief period there is much carved or applied plaster ornament.
It is sometimes described as ENGLISH ROCOCO
or because it forms a background for the furniture of Thomas Chippendale it is also referred to as · CHIPPENDALE ·

An English room in the "French Taste"
Note Fireplace without a mantle or shelf.

Room designed around imported Chinese wallpaper.

The elaborate gilt mirrors of the period, for the most part neither designed nor executed by Chippendale, bear his name.

# ·The STYLE called HEPPLEWHITE·

## ·DEVELOPEMENT of the MIRROR·

Polished metal is used as a reflecting surface until the invention of mirrors. Metaling the back of glass is done on small pieces during the Middle Ages. In the 16th century Venice makes a commercial enterprise of mirror-making. In the 17th century England sets up her own factories.

·16th CENTURY·

Table mirror
Frame embroidered in straw.

·17th CENTURY·

Mirror for table or wall.
Veneered walnut frame.
Brass cresting removable.

EARLY 18th CENTURY

Larger frame with bevel-jointed mirror in 10 sections.

EARLY 19th CENTURY·

Convex mirrors become popular in America.

Larger built-in mirrors become an architectural feature during and after the 18th century.

· · ·

Also see mirrors on pages:
48, 99, 106, 140, 141, 145, 146, 147, 149, 150, 151, 157, 166, 169, 170, 174.

A well-designed usable design which shows the influence of the contemporary English designers and the prevailing French styles.

Louis XVI (oval back) | Louis XV (cabriole leg)
Chippendale (camel back) | Adam (cabinet pieces)

Concave contours (Serpentine front also used by Sheraton.)

*Chief Identifying features:*
of MOST ORIGINAL DESIGN:

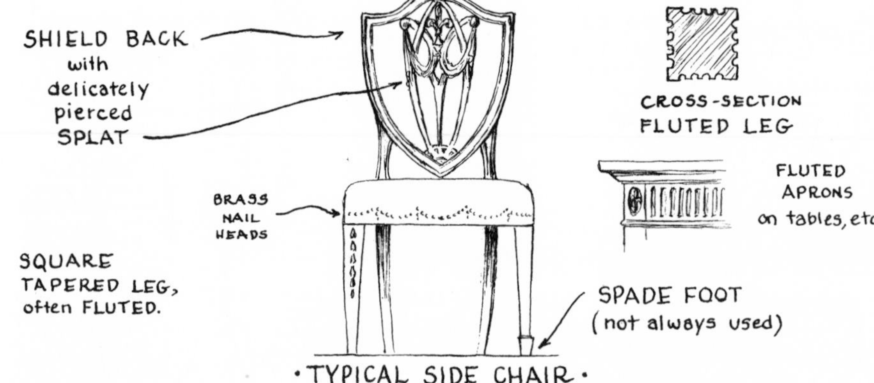
SHIELD BACK
with delicately pierced SPLAT
BRASS NAIL HEADS
SQUARE TAPERED LEG, often FLUTED.
SPADE FOOT (not always used)
CROSS-SECTION FLUTED LEG
FLUTED APRONS on tables, etc.

·TYPICAL SIDE CHAIR·

**FINISHES:**
Mahogany with satinwood inlays.
Satinwood with painted designs: floral swags, etc. (Louis XV).

UPHOLSTERED PIECES
classified by exposed portion of frame.

**FAVORITE MOTIFS:**
inlaid, painted or carved

- OVAL PATERA
- HUSK or HONEY SUCKLE CHAIN or SWAG
- ANTHEMION design in MARQUETRY
- PRINCE of WALES FEATHERS
- ·Narrow MARQUETRY BANDS·
- STALKS of WHEAT

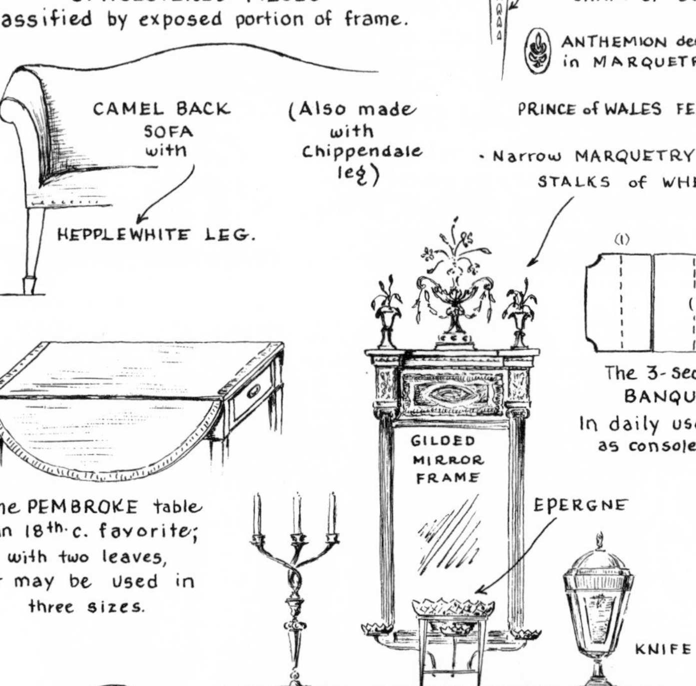
CAMEL BACK SOFA with
HEPPLEWHITE LEG.
(Also made with Chippendale leg)
(1) (2) (3)
(PLAN)
GILDED MIRROR FRAME
EPERGNE
KNIFE BOX

The 3-sectioned drop-leaf BANQUET TABLE
In daily use ends serve as consoles or serving table.

The PEMBROKE table an 18th c. favorite; with two leaves, it may be used in three sizes.

OVAL BRASS HANDLES

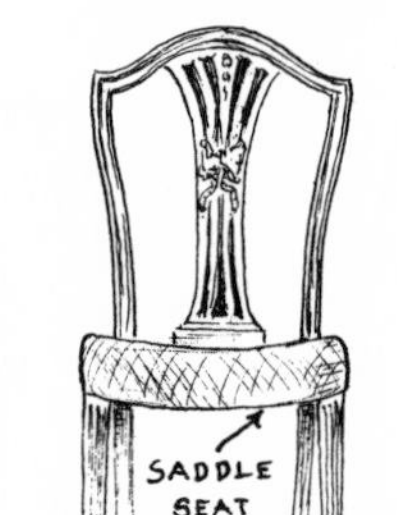
SADDLE SEAT

·CAMEL BACK CHAIR· ·SIDEBOARD· ·INTERLACED HEART BACK·

# ·The STYLE called SHERATON·

The most delicately proportioned of all eighteenth century styles. Light in scale. Graceful combinations of straight lines and curves.

*Chief identifying features:*

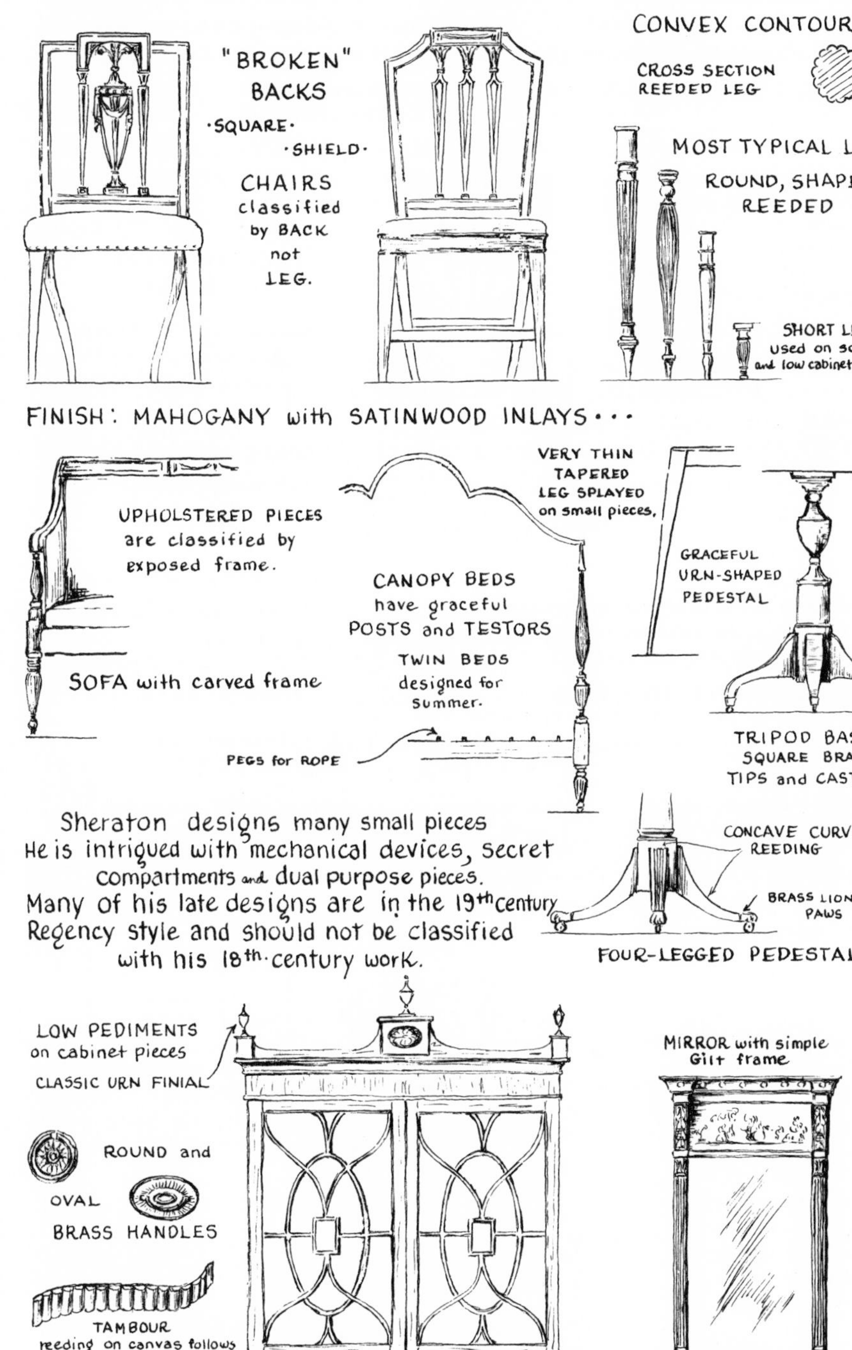

"BROKEN" BACKS
·SQUARE·
·SHIELD·
CHAIRS classified by BACK not LEG.
CONVEX CONTOURS
CROSS SECTION REEDED LEG
MOST TYPICAL LEG: ROUND, SHAPED, REEDED
SHORT LEG used on sofas and low cabinet pieces.
FINISH: MAHOGANY with SATINWOOD INLAYS···
UPHOLSTERED PIECES are classified by exposed frame.
SOFA with carved frame
CANOPY BEDS have graceful POSTS and TESTORS
TWIN BEDS designed for summer.
PEGS for ROPE
VERY THIN TAPERED LEG SPLAYED on small pieces.
GRACEFUL URN-SHAPED PEDESTAL
TRIPOD BASES SQUARE BRASS TIPS and CASTORS
CONCAVE CURVE with REEDING
BRASS LION'S PAWS
FOUR-LEGGED PEDESTAL


Sheraton designs many small pieces
He is intrigued with mechanical devices, secret compartments and dual purpose pieces.
Many of his late designs are in the 19th century Regency style and should not be classified with his 18th century work.


LOW PEDIMENTS on cabinet pieces
CLASSIC URN FINIAL
ROUND and OVAL BRASS HANDLES
TAMBOUR reeding on canvas follows tracks.
MIRROR with simple Gilt frame
SEWING TABLE with TAMBOUR FRONT
SPLAY - BASED SECRETARY
BENCH for reveal of WINDOW


## ·LIGHTING FIXTURES·

Until the introduction of OIL and GAS in the 19th century CANDLES are the source of illumination.
From single sticks to huge chandeliers the fixtures are decorative.

· CANDLE STICKS ·
BRASS
SILVER
PORCELAIN
CUT CRYSTAL
GLAZED POTTERY
· WALL SCONCES ·
GILDED WOOD
· CHANDELIERS ·
BRONZE
CUT CRYSTAL
·Early · 18th century · Late ·

# ·The STYLE called ADAM·

ROBERT ADAM (1728 - 1792)

The architecture of Robert Adam is a neo-classic style greatly influenced by his studies in Italy and by the court of Louis XVI. The architectural firm of the Adam Brothers was the leader of the classic trend in England. Headed by Robert, an enthusiastic designer, and an ingenious businessman, it was one of the most enterprising and unusual firms of any age. In addition to building the house, the firm supplied furniture, rugs (often copying the ornamental ceiling design) and all the accessories (lighting fixtures, grates, urns, and the silverware). Porcelain plaques which were the work of Adam's friend Josiah Wedgwood appeared on ceilings and furniture. Many accessories were of Wedgwood. The rooms echoed the Wedgwood colors—blue, soft green, etc., with classic motifs in white.

A patent for a composition material enabled Adam to embellish surfaces with a profusion of pseudo-carving. So much is used that many of his ceilings and fireplaces are likened to confectioners' work. Another patent enabled him to copy French marble in a cheap composition of marble dust. It is these substitutions which cheapen Adam's designs, but as a style of interior architecture there is both charm and elegance in its classical adaptations.

WEDGWOOD URN of JASPERWARE.
Greek shapes in raised designs are made in unglazed china
Background colors: blue, soft green, raspberry, chamois and black.

The furniture is of eclectic inspiration and combines French and Italian elements with the work of contemporary English cabinetmakers. It reflects little of Robert Adam's versatility as a designer.

Both the Louis XVI and Adam styles resulted from the enthusiasm over Pompeii, as did a large part of the classic revival. Yet it is not difficult to distinguish the eighteenth-century elegance and elaboration from the sharp directness of the nineteenth-century Classic Revival.

Chimney piece with built-in GRATE of cast iron.
Note interesting contrast in black and white marble.
Urn and candlesticks are wedgwood.

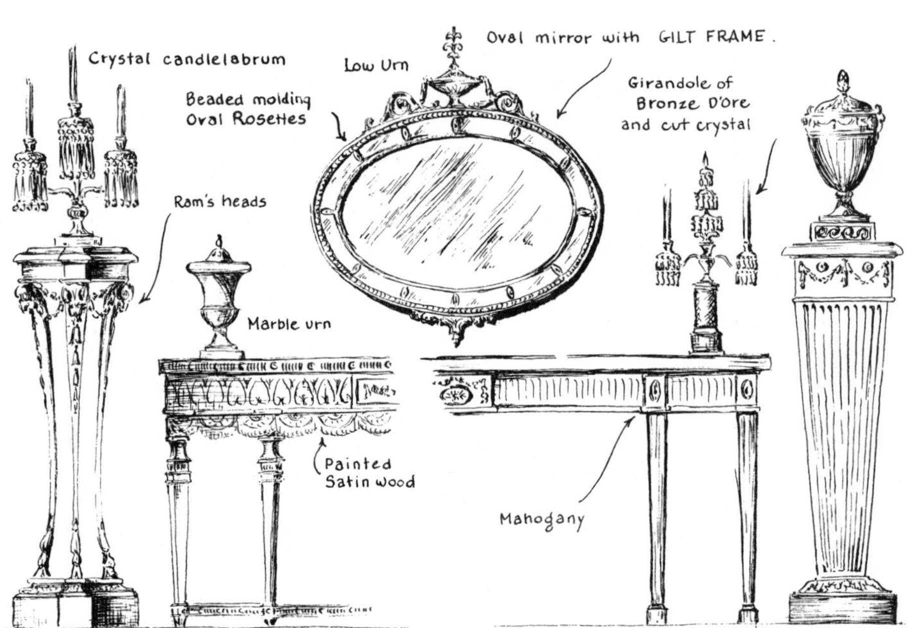
Crystal candelabrum
Low Urn
Oval mirror with GILT FRAME.
Beaded molding
Oval Rosettes
Girandole of Bronze D'ore and cut crystal
Ram's heads
Marble urn
Painted Satin wood
Mahogany

Candlestand • Console • • • Serving Table flanked by knife boxes on pedestals.

# ·The STYLE called ADAM·

EXTERIORS: Stone or Brick with WHITE TRIM with the usual GEORGIAN Proportions.

In the United States of America many details which predate ADAM are known as Adam-type.

*ex.* FAN-SHAPED OVERDOORS, OVAL WINDOWS *etc.*

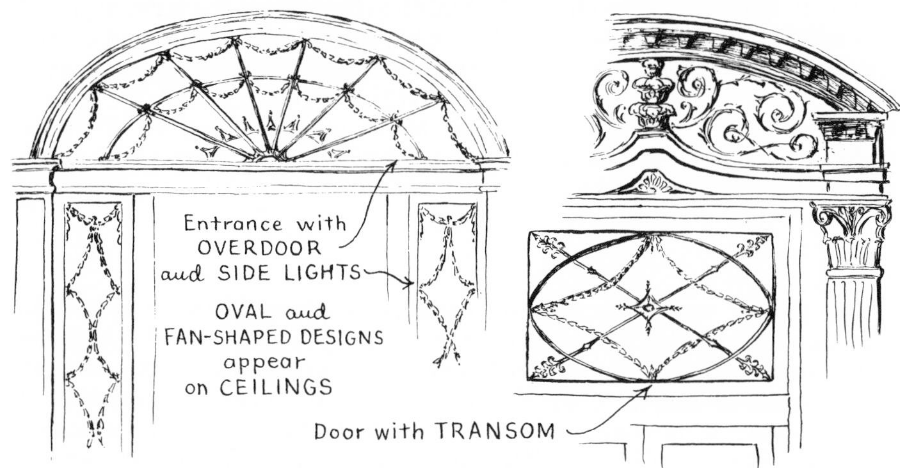
Entrance with
OVERDOOR
and SIDE LIGHTS
OVAL and
FAN-SHAPED DESIGNS
appear
on CEILINGS
Door with TRANSOM

INTERIORS: Elaborate with classical decoration in panels. Details in white plaster and COMPO-CARVING against softly tinted walls and ceilings also gold against white.

CORNICE with
ANTIFIX FRIEZE
·BUILT-IN PICTURE FRAME·
FAN MOTIF
·PIER GLASS·
PALLADIAN WINDOW
GILDED
BEADED FRAME
FAVORITE MOTIFS:
OVAL SHAPE
LOW URN
RINCEAU
ANTIFIX
GRIFFIN
PATERA
HUSK SWAG

Sunken panels with ARABESQUE in COMPO-CARVING

° ° °

ROOMS are balanced bisymmetrically as is all high renaissance architecture.

NICHES and FRIEZES (in bas-relief) feature classic statues.

RAM'S HEADS

DRAPERY SWAG

## FURNITURE:

Semicircular or fan-shaped CONSOLES and COMMODES.

Shield, Oval or Fan-shaped chair-backs.

Many borrowed forms, particularly in LEGS.

Turnings and block feet are added to Hepplewhite and Sheraton styles.

SQUARE,
FLUTED.
ROUND,
CARVED.

FINISHES:

Gilt, Mahogany and Satinwood with painted decoration.

° ° ° ° ° °

Contemporary Louis XVI influence.

Ancient Greek influence.

CANING
NOT SO
DELICATE AS
HEPPLEWHITE

·SIDE CHAIRS·

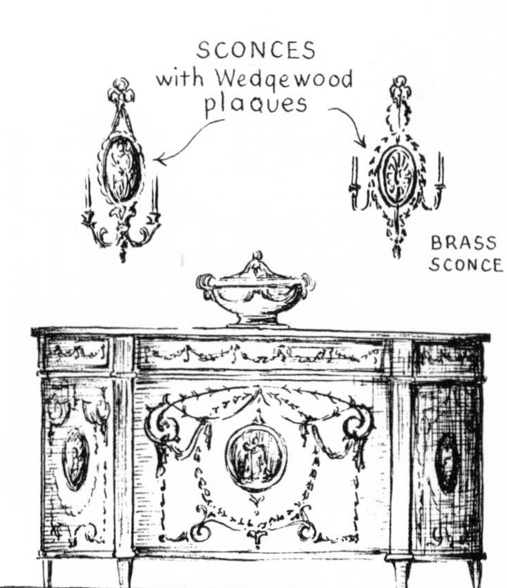
SCONCES
with Wedgewood
plaques
BRASS
SCONCE

COMMODE of PAINTED SATINWOOD

# ·18th CENTURY ACCESSORIES·

The marked contrast between rich and poor in appearance and deportment is clearly shown by artists of the period.

Life sized portrait of a lady by Reynolds (1723-1792)
Pictures of this kind are part of the decorative scheme in the great houses.

With social conscience Hogarth (1679-1764) reveals conditions in the slums.
He also satirizes the rich in a series of prints such as the "Rake's Progress" and "Marriage à la Mode"

The term MINIATURE which now refers to any object on a small scale derives from the Latin "minium" the red lead which outlined the small paintings in medieval manuscripts.

The small paintings of the Renaissance are often in oil or enamel on copper but during the 18TH century WATERCOLOR on IVORY is used for portraiture.

·ACTUAL SIZE·

REFINEMENTS of the AGE –

The most utilitarian objects are designed and executed with taste and care.
Note: accessories on pages-140, 141, 146, 147, 148, 149, 150, 151.

The Oriental HANDLELESS tea cup.

Silver and China service is designed for the new imported beverages TEA and COFFEE.

FORKS and TABLE KNIVES are introduced c.1500. They are used by the nobility in the 1600'S and come into fairly general use in the 1700'S
The spoon is of ancient origin.

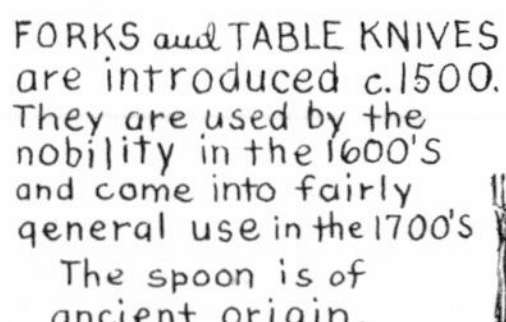

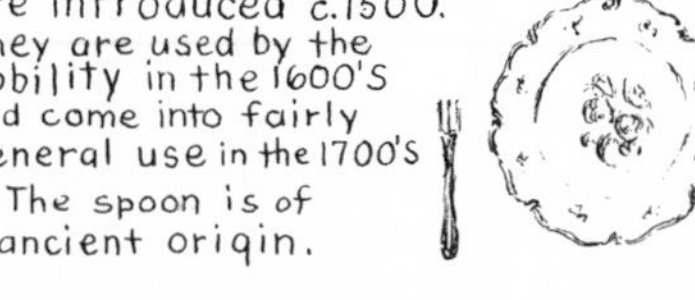

After perfecting the method of making oriental porcelain (China) it is no longer necessary to import the ware.
Sets of plates and figurines are made in European factories (see page 44).

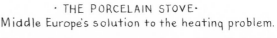

·CLOCK·
(LOUIS XV)

·ANDIRON·

·BOUILLOTTE LAMP·

·COMPOTE·

·BAROMETER·
(LOUIS XVI)

· THE PORCELAIN STOVE·
Middle Europe's solution to the heating problem.

Rococo Style (Louis XV)

(Classic Style) (Louis XVI)

STOVES
are almost of ceiling height.

ACCESSORIES
are designed to conform with every style of architecture and furniture.

The GRATE
is designed to hold coal in the regular woodburning fireplace.
In recent years it has been converted to radiant gas heating and non-heat giving electric coals.

SCIENCE
THE
INDUSTRIAL
REVOLUTION
Music
FICTION
POLITICAL
AND
SOCIAL
REVOLT

# THE 19TH CENTURY

## 1800—THE NINETEENTH CENTURY—1900

*Style of Architecture | | | **Style of Furniture

England revolutionizes entire world.
Every phase of culture effected by scientific invention.
Ascendency of the intellectual arts.

| | France | England | America |
|---|---|---|---|
| | *1804–1850 THE GREAT CLASSIC REVIVAL | | |
| Italian Empire<br>German<br>Beidemeier | **EMPIRE<br>Napoleon | **ENGLISH REGENCY<br>George III–IV | **AMERICAN EMPIRE<br>(Duncan Phyfe) |
| | *1850–1900 THE HISTORIC PERIOD REVIVALS | | |
| | Louis Philippe<br>Second Republic<br>Second Empire<br>(Napoleon III)<br>Third Republic | **VICTORIAN<br>(Awful Eighties)<br>(Gay Nineties)<br>Edward VII<br>(1901–1910) | |

An American-born Protestant sect.
In 1830 Joseph Smith of N.Y. State
founds the CHURCH of the LATTER-DAY SAINTS
based on the BOOK of MORMON as revealed by the Angel Moroni.

# ·THE GREAT CLASSIC REVIVAL·

In France the decadent and extravagant hereditary aristocracy was wiped out with the monarchy in the Revolution (1779). A succession of representative forms of government were soon replaced by the Empire of Napoleon. The Little Corporal presented loyal citizens with confiscated estates and suitable titles. The court was functioning again with a new cast of characters when Napoleon set forth to conquer Europe.

NAPOLEON IER EMPEREUR

The EMPEROR NAPOLEON I
Pride of France and Terror of Europe, places family and friends on every throne he can make available. (See below)

Sudden determination to erase all traces of the immediate past caused designers to lift an entire culture from the remote past. The movement was more of a rebirth than the Italian Renaissance. Classic forms were diligently copied in architecture, furniture, accessories and clothing. The style spread to all countries.

In France, where Napoleon emulated Caesar, the revival was Roman. Triumphal arches and commemorative columns were erected in honor of Napoleonic victories. His Egyptian campaign added obelisks and sphinxes. England and America were inspired by Greek sources.

The PRINCESS BORGHESE
Pauline, sister of Napoleon, as VENUS by Canova

The neo-classic style is easily recognized because no matter to what use the buildings were to be put most of them looked like pedimented pagan temples. But while the theme is unvaried, the national characteristics of the work of the different countries lend variety. It is a period of dignified but superficial charm. It is lamentable from a functional point of view and unoriginal from an artistic one. But to the eye it is not unpleasing. Excellent examples are to be found in the major cities of Europe and the eastern and southern United States. The style followed the pioneers through the Ohio Valley. Thomas Jefferson used it for the University of Virginia and his beloved Monticello. The Capitol Building, the White House and the Washington Monument in the nation's capital are representative of the era.

The Classic Revival is the last of the handcraft periods. The workmanship, finish, and detail on the furniture and accessories is in most cases a delight to examine. The furniture, lamps, andirons and decorative accessories are often used with late eighteenth-century things, and it is not unusual to find them in sophisticated urban houses and apartments of today.

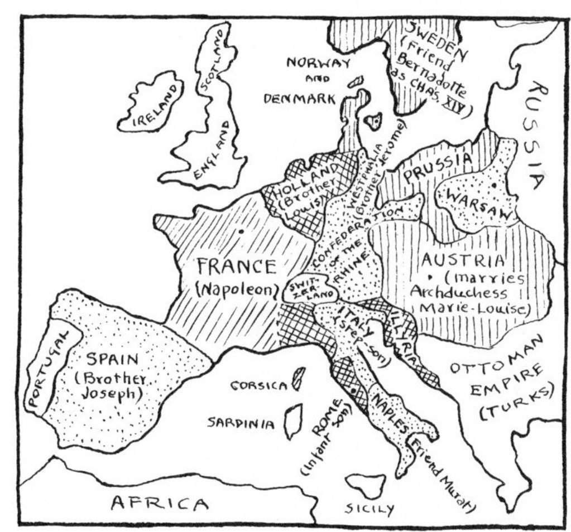
SWEDEN (Friend Bernadotte as CHAS XIV)
NORWAY AND DENMARK
RUSSIA
SCOTLAND
IRELAND
ENGLAND
PRUSSIA
WARSAW
FRANCE (Napoleon)
AUSTRIA • (marries Archduchess Marie-Louise)
SPAIN (Brother Joseph)
PORTUGAL
CORSICA
SARDINIA
OTTOMAN EMPIRE (TURKS)
AFRICA
SICILY

· EUROPE under NAPOLEON ·

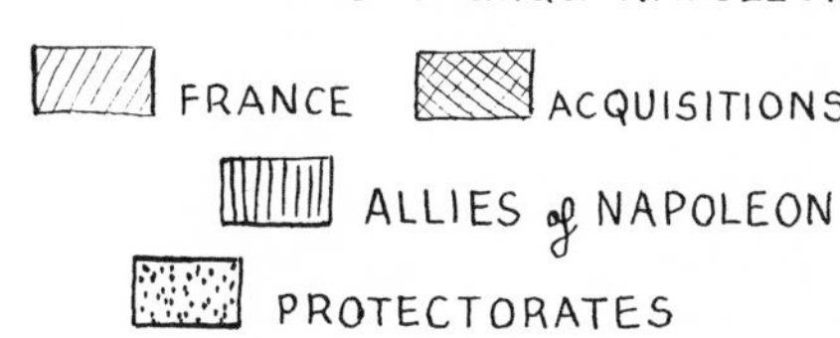
FRANCE
ACQUISITIONS
ALLIES of NAPOLEON
PROTECTORATES

The entire West thought in terms of classical treatment. Even George Washington was so imbued with the trend that he consented more than once to pose in classic regalia. However absurd the classic ideal may appear when fitted to men two thousand years later, the work of the artists and the sculptors of the period comes very close to technical perfection, although it is too often lacking in depth of feeling.

The preoccupation with ancient patterns did not cease with the termination of the French Empire but continued until about 1840, when it was replaced by an enthusiasm for medieval romanticism.

# ·ARCHITECTURE of the CLASSIC REVIVAL·

·PUBLIC BUILDINGS·

·LA MADELEINE in PARIS·
Not a Roman temple but a Christian church.

·AN EARLY 19TH c. ENGLISH TOWN·
The Grecian town hall. The Roman commemorative column, and the Egyptian library bring all the ancient influences to the one square.

·PARLIAMENT, VIENNA·
Adaptations of the style persist in public architecture today.

·DOMESTIC ARCHITECTURE·

In England Regency architects plan block-terraces. The balanced exteriors add to the dignity of the community.

Gracious detached houses offer dignity and comfort.

The age brings opulence to Napoleon's France, imagination to the England of George IV and America's Southern States.

·AN INTERIOR of 1823· showing costumes and window treatment.

CHARACTERISTIC WALL TREATMENTS: Striped, medallioned or scenic papers. Draped and swagged fabrics. Panels painted in Pompeian style.
POPULAR COLORS: Empire GREEN · Pompeian RED · Mellow GOLD·

·PASTRY SHOP·
Nothing is too unimportant to be treated in the classic manner. CARYATIDS appear on architecture, furniture and accessories.

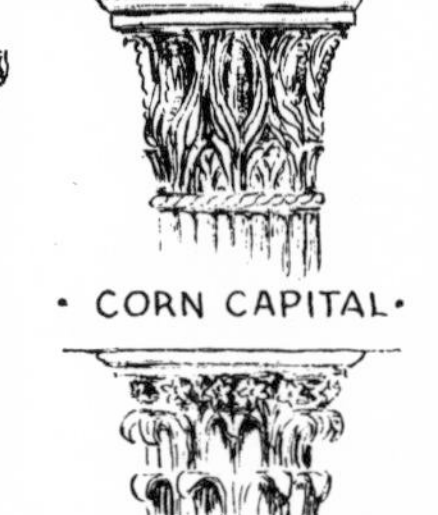

·CORN CAPITAL·

·TOBACCO CAPITAL·
Two paying crops are interpreted in the CLASSIC tradition.

Benjamin Latrobe for the U.S. Capitol, Washington.

# ·FURNITURE of the CLASSIC REVIVAL·

The same BASIC DESIGNS of both OUTLINE and ORNAMENT are used in all countries.
GREEK, ROMAN and EGYPTIAN motifs appear on all surfaces.
Because of the similarity in design and scale the work of the different countries is easily combined.

The ACCESSORIES are noteworthy.

FAVORITE MOTIFS which are used as decoration on architecture, furniture (carving and ormulu), wallpaper and fabric:-

MEDALLION · SPHINX · LANCE · LION'S HEAD · VICTOR'S LAUREL WREATH
CORNUCOPIA · GRIFFONS · LYRE · ANTEFIX · WINGED VICTORY · · · ·

TYPICAL WOODS and FINISHES :-

French: Mahogany, Amboyna. English: Rosewood, Black and gold laquer.
American: Crotch mahogany. German: Satinwood with Ebony inlays.

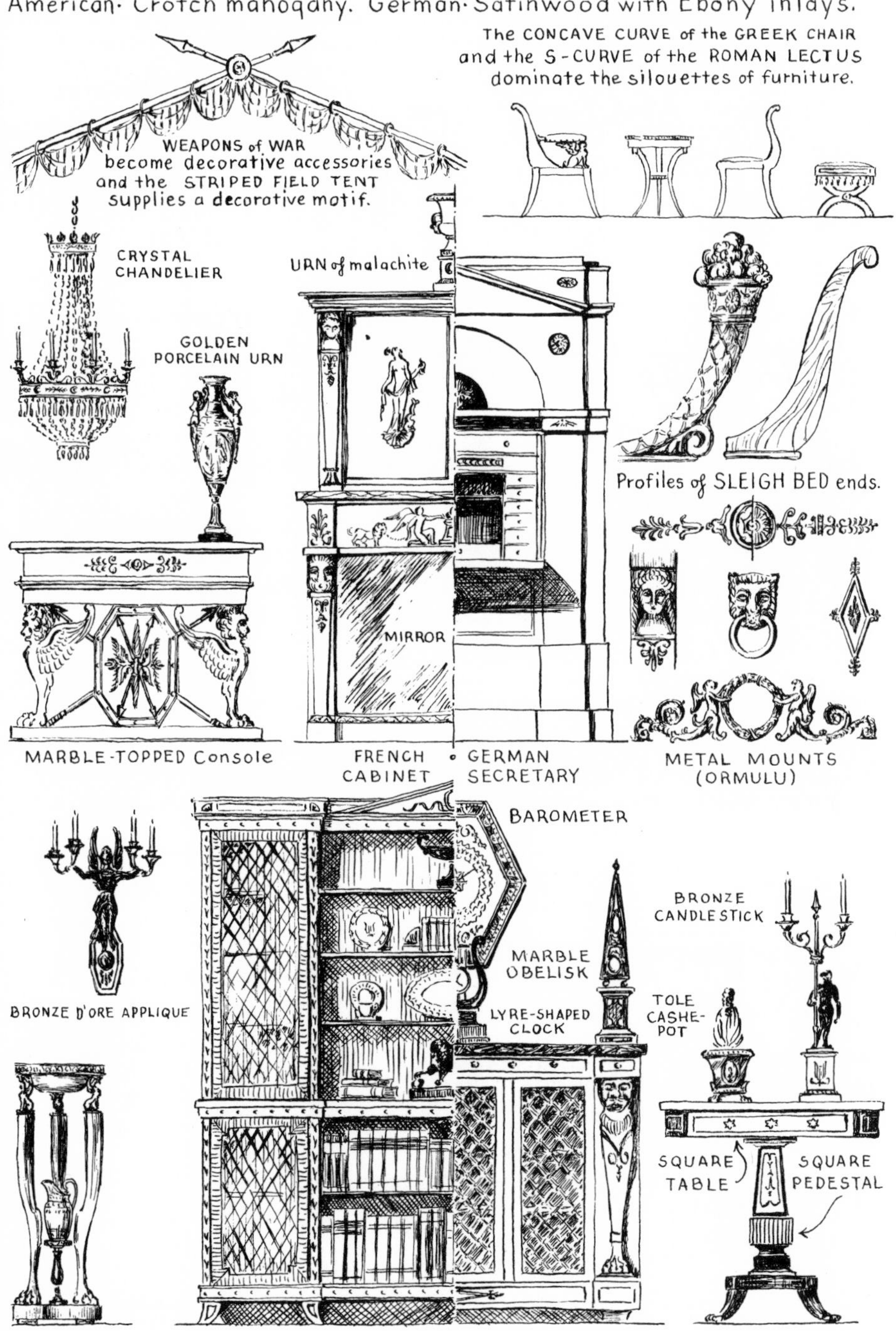
The CONCAVE CURVE of the GREEK CHAIR and the S-CURVE of the ROMAN LECTUS dominate the silouettes of furniture.
WEAPONS of WAR become decorative accessories and the STRIPED FIELD TENT supplies a decorative motif.
CRYSTAL CHANDELIER
GOLDEN PORCELAIN URN
URN of malachite
MIRROR
Profiles of SLEIGH BED ends.
MARBLE-TOPPED Console
FRENCH CABINET
GERMAN SECRETARY
METAL MOUNTS (ORMULU)
BAROMETER
BRONZE CANDLESTICK
MARBLE OBELISK
LYRE-SHAPED CLOCK
TOLE CASHE-POT
BRONZE D'ORE APPLIQUE
SQUARE TABLE
SQUARE PEDESTAL
·WASH STAND·
· BOOKCASES · with heavy wire GRILL.
·SQUARE TABLE·

Four SOFAS of the period showing some essential differences in the furniture of the four countries:

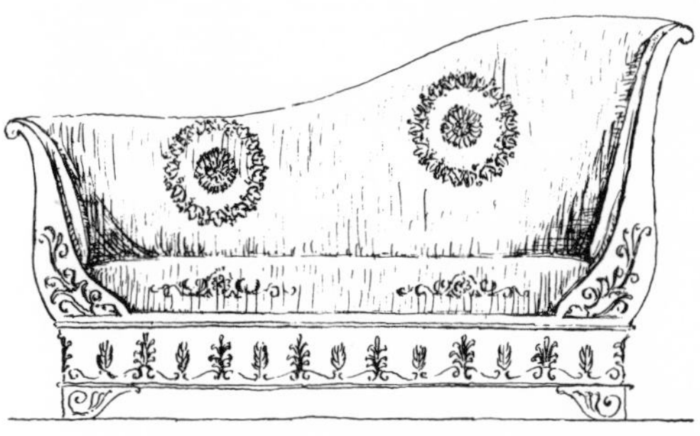

· FRENCH EMPIRE ·
The frame of this meridienne is decorated with the lightweight rather tinny ORMULU used so lavishly. The upholstery is damask.

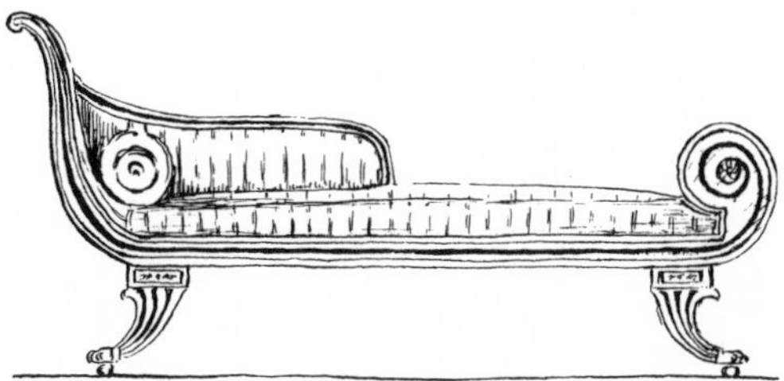

· ENGLISH REGENCY ·
The most characteristic ornament in English pieces is done in INLAYED BRASS - a process superior in quality to the French Ormulu.

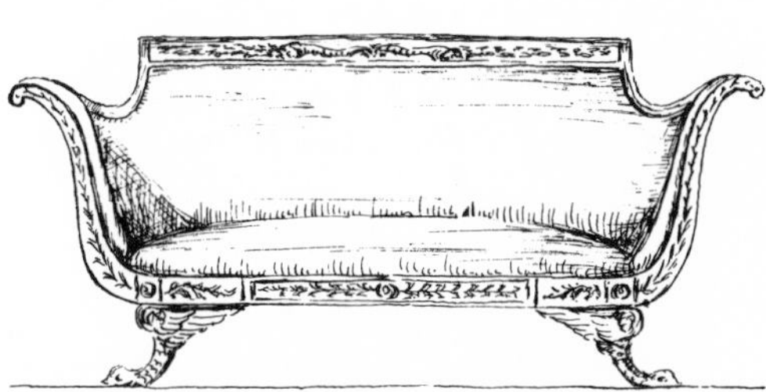

· AMERICAN EMPIRE ·
The favorite ornament is CARVING. (Samuel McIntire)

GOLDEN SATINWOOD + EBONY

· GERMAN BIEDERMEIER ·
The natural beauty of the wood is emphasized.

# ·19th CENTURY · CHRONOLOGY·

·SPIRIT of the CLASSIC REVIVAL·

The British poet is so obsessed with the idea of freedom for Greece that he goes to fight the Turks.

George Noel Gordon
·LORD BYRON
(1788-1824)

·BRITISH WOMEN WIN A PLACE IN THE LITERARY PROFESSION·

With gentle satire Jane Austen describes society in a rural England which is oblivious to the Napoleonic threat.

·JANE AUSTEN·
(1775 - 1817)

·THE BRONTË SISTERS·
Anne, Emily and Charlotte as painted by their brother Branwell. Isolated on the moors, they write of imaginary people.

·RUSSIA SPEAKS·

She makes valuable contributions during the brief period between the end of feudalism and the beginning of communism.
(1861-1917)

Tolstoy describes ART not as the production of pleasing objects but a MEANS of UNION among men

·LEO TOLSTOY·
(1828-1910)

## LITERATURE

Literature is the most influential artistic expression of the century.

### Classicism

#### Britain

| | |
|---|---|
| Byron | Austen |
| Coleridge | The Brontës |
| Keats | |
| Shelley | De Quincey |
| Wordsworth | Lamb |

(Mysticism)
Forerunner of Pre-Raphaelites,
poet, engraver and mystic
William Blake

#### France — Chateaubriand

#### United States

Seldom has the pen been used to better advantage than by our founding fathers.

| | | |
|---|---|---|
| Franklin | Jefferson | Madison |
| Jay | Hamilton | Washington |

The critical review and the monthly magazine replace the pamphlet.

The novelist becomes a major contributor to social commentary and reform. All writers respond to classic, romantic and realistic inspiration.

### Realism

| France | Russia |
|---|---|
| Balzac | Chekhov |
| Baudelaire (poet) | Dostoievsky |
| Dumas | Gogol |
| Flaubert | Pushkin |
| France | Tolstoy |
| Gautier | Turgenev |
| Hugo | |
| de Maupassant | **Norway** |
| Stendhal | |
| Zola | Ibsen |

## HISTORICAL EVENTS

1803 Louisiana Purchase
Napoleonic Conquests 1804–1814.
French Empire

War of 1812 between United States and Britain
1814 British burn Washington, D. C.

1815 Napoleon's 100 Days
Battle of Waterloo
Louis XVIII on throne

1823 Monroe Doctrine

Spread of Industrial Revolution
Scientific inventions

1832 Bloodless Revolution in England
Reform Bill

1830 Revolution in France
Louis Philippe on throne 1830–1848

Victoria reigns in England 1837–1902

Foreign concessions in China

Louis Napoleon, French President 1848

1849 Gold Rush: Opening of western frontiers in U. S. A.

Second Empire: Louis Napoleon and Eugénie 1852–1870

Russo-Turkish Crimean War 1853–1855.
Florence Nightingale

# ·19th CENTURY · LITERATURE ·

## HISTORICAL EVENTS

Victoria
Empress of India
Gladstone
Disraeli

1860 Kingdom of Italy proclaimed: Garibaldi
American Civil War 1861–1865

Franco-Prussian War 1870–1871: Bismarck
German Empire formed

French Republic

European partition of Africa

Paris World Fair 1889
Eiffel Tower
First automobile (Benz)

The Gay Nineties
Edward, Prince of Wales

1894 Chino-Japanese War

1898 Spanish-American War

1899 Boer War: British and Dutch in South Africa

1900 Boxer Rebellion in China

Suez and Panama Canals

1904 Russo-Japanese War

Unrest in the Balkans

1914–1918 World War I

## LITERATURE

### Britain

#### Romanticism

The Brownings
Bulwer-Lytton
Fitzgerald
Kingsley
Macaulay
Morris
The Rossettis
Scott
Stevenson
Swinburne
Tennyson
Thackeray

#### Realism

Conrad
Dickens
Eliot
Hardy
Meredith
Trollope

Arnold
Carlyle
Kipling
Ruskin

#### Science

Darwin
T. H. Huxley
Newton

#### Drama (late)

Barrie
Du Maurier
Dunsany
Pinero
Shaw
Wilde

#### Mystery

Collins
Doyle

#### Psychological Fiction

Henry James

### United States

#### Poetry

Bryant
Dickinson
Field
Holmes
Longfellow
Lowell
Riley
Whitman
Whittier

#### Fiction

Cooper
Hawthorne
Irving
London
Poe
Melville
Twain

#### Essays

Emerson — Thoreau

## PHILOSOPHY

Schopenhauer (Ger.) Nietzsche (Ger.)
John Stuart Mill (Br.)
Herbert Spencer (Br.)
William James (U.S.) Karl Marx (Ger.)

·THE ROMANTIC ERA·

His historical novels recreate the colorful pageantry of history. He wrote 298 books.

·ALEXANDRE DUMAS· (1802-1870)

Creator of the immortal Kim and documentor of Victoria's Empire in India.

·RUDYARD KIPLING· (1865-1936)

Victoria's Poet Laureate makes the Knights of the Round Table come to life.

·ALFRED, LORD TENNYSON· (1809-1892)

·WALT WHITMAN· (1819-1892)
Unconventional American poet, inspiration of the "moderns".

# ·19th CENTURY · PAINTING and SCULPTURE·

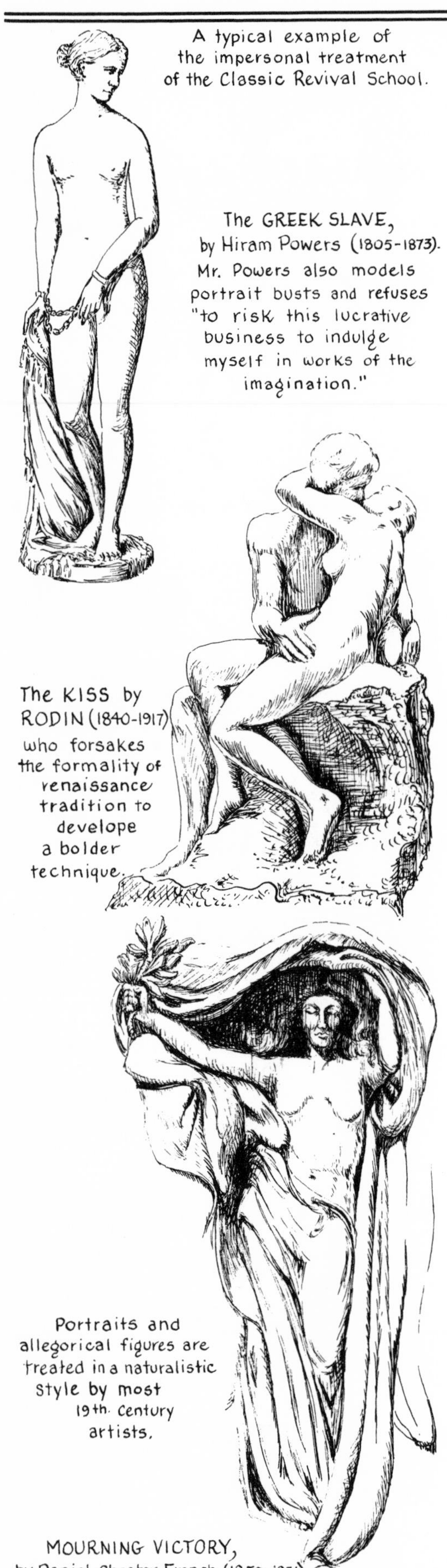

A typical example of the impersonal treatment of the Classic Revival School.

The GREEK SLAVE, by Hiram Powers (1805-1873). Mr. Powers also models portrait busts and refuses "to risk this lucrative business to indulge myself in works of the imagination."

The KISS by RODIN (1840-1917) who forsakes the formality of renaissance tradition to develope a bolder technique.

Portraits and allegorical figures are treated in a naturalistic style by most 19th century artists.

MOURNING VICTORY, by Daniel Chester French (1850-1931).

## PAINTING AND SCULPTURE

### Classicism

The Classic Revival was inspired by the political ideals of the Roman Republic as admired by the French Revolutionists. The writings of the German Winckelmann were largely responsible for the widespread imitation of classic art forms.

The artists, most of whom studied in Rome, were skillful technicians but not gifted interpreters.

#### France

| (Painters) | (Sculptors) |
|---|---|
| David | Bosio |
| Gros | Canova |
| Guérin | Chaudet |
| Ingres | Houdon |
| Prud'hon | Lemot |
| Vien | Pradier |

#### Denmark

Thorwaldsen

#### Spain

Goya

#### Britain

18th-century painters work through Regency.

(Sculptors)

| | |
|---|---|
| Bacon | Flaxman |
| Banks | Nollekens |
| Chantry | Westmacott |

Three painters who broke with classic subject matter and Renaissance technique:

Bonington Constable Turner

#### United States

In Colonial times and during the Federal period, of necessity, most artists were educated abroad. Portraits and American history were most called-for subjects.

| (Painters) | | (Sculptors) | |
|---|---|---|---|
| Gray | Peale | Ball | Greenough |
| Healy | Sully | Brown | Powers |
| Huntington | Trumbull | Crawford | Reinhart |
| Jarvis | Vanderlyn | Frazee | Story |

### Realism in Sculpture

The least tradition-bound man is the forceful French Auguste Rodin. A few of his gifted but less original contemporaries are listed below. Some of them worked into the 20th century but because their work is realistic they are classified with 19th-century artists instead of the Moderns.

#### France

| | |
|---|---|
| Barye (animals) | Dubois |
| Carpeaux | Fremier |
| Chapu | Jouffroy |
| Dalou | Mercie |
| David D'Angers | Saint-Marceau |

#### Britain

| | |
|---|---|
| Bates | Gilbert |
| Brock | Stevens |
| Drury | Swan |
| Frampton | Thornycroft |
| Ford | Toft |

#### United States

| | | | |
|---|---|---|---|
| Adams | The Borglums | MacMonnies | Taft |
| Barnard | Dallin | MacNeil | Ward |
| Bitter | French | Saint-Gaudens | Warner |

# ·19th CENTURY · PAINTING and SCULPTURE·

## PAINTING

### Romanticism

A large majority of artists throughout the century painted in what was termed the Grand Manner (Renaissance style). But their inspiration was romantic and overpowered by sentimentality. Military campaigns, foreign possessions in the growing colonial empires, historical events of past and present, and simple genre subjects, with few exceptions, were given the identical superficial, pictorial treatment.

**France**

Delacroix, Delaroche, Decamp, Detaille, Dupré, Flandrin, Gericault, Gerome, Gleyre, Meissonier, Neuville, Vernet

**USA**

Leutze

**Germany**

Winterhalter (portraits)

**Britain**

Alma-Tadema, Etty, Maclise

(Genre and Animals)

**Britain**

Frith, Morland, Landseer, Mulready, Leslie, Webster, Wilkie

**France**

Bonheur, Jacque, Breton, Marcke, Cottet, Simon

**Denmark**

Block, Zorn

### Realism

By the middle of the century the academic principles of classic revival art had been made even more shallow and stylized by its imitators. Romanticism had introduced a flamboyancy which was equally lacking in honesty. Three separate reform movements started.

In France:
**The Barbizon School (of poetic landscape)**

Corot, Millet, Daubigny, Rousseau, Diaz, Troyon

**Dutch followers:**

Israels, Mauve

**Realists**

Bonnat (Spanish)
Boudin (French)
Courbet (French)
Stevens (Belgian)
Thoma (German)

**Originality in the United States:**

Artists who developed interesting individual styles within the framework of realism

Chase (in 1896 founded school now Parson's School of Design)
Eakins (realism)
Homer (seascapes)
La Farge (stained glass)
Ryder (mysticism)
Sargent (portraits)
Whistler (Impressionism)

In England:
**The Pre-Raphaelite Brotherhood**

(spiritual mysticism)

Hunt, Millais, Rossetti

**Followers:**

Brown, Hughes, Burne-Jones, Sandys, Collinson, Watts

**American Follower:**

Davies

**Arts and Crafts:**

Crane, Morris

In the United States:
**The Hudson River School**

(grandeurs of nature)

Bierstadt, Doughty, Church, Durand, Cole, Kensett, Moran

**Precursor:**

Inman

**Follower:**

Inness

**Genre painters:**

Bingham, Mount

**Indian Life:**

Catlin, Johnson

**Still Life:**

Harnett

**Originality in France:**

Daumier (cartoons)
Doré (illustrations)
Monticelli (oils)
Puvis de Chavannes (murals)
Rodin (sculpture)

· PAINTING ·

Sentimentalism pervades all approaches.

· CLASSICISM ·
The Abduction of Psyche, by Prud'hon (1758-1823)

· ROMANTICISM ·
The children of Edward IV, by Delaroche (1797-1856) These boys are reputed to have been killed so that their uncle might become Richard III of England in 1483.

· REALISM ·
The Angelus, by Millet (1814-1875)

# ·19th CENTURY · ARCHITECTURE·

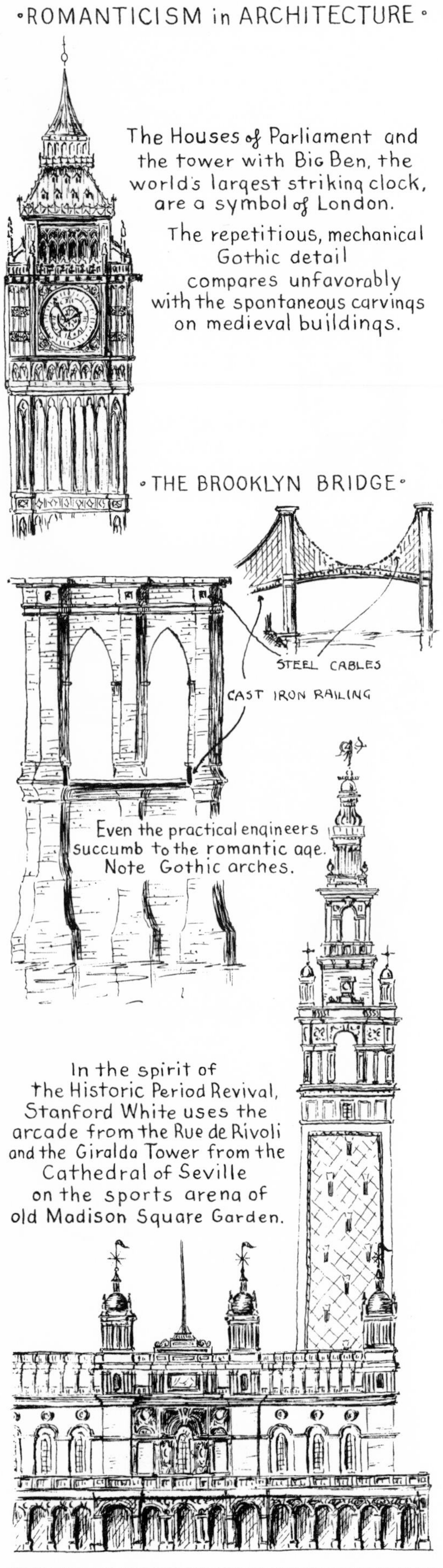

·ROMANTICISM in ARCHITECTURE·
The Houses of Parliament and the tower with Big Ben, the world's largest striking clock, are a symbol of London.
The repetitious, mechanical Gothic detail compares unfavorably with the spontaneous carvings on medieval buildings.
·THE BROOKLYN BRIDGE·
STEEL CABLES
CAST IRON RAILING
Even the practical engineers succumb to the romantic age. Note Gothic arches.
In the spirit of the Historic Period Revival, Stanford White uses the arcade from the Rue de Rivoli and the Giralda Tower from the Cathedral of Seville on the sports arena of old Madison Square Garden.


## AMERICAN ART

### 1820 — Primitive American Artists — 1870

The few trained artists in this country could not keep up with the ever-increasing demands of the expanding nation. Nor could the modest citizens of the new republic afford to commission them. Therefore, unknown and unskilled hands were put to work. The resulting utilitarian and aesthetic products are fascinating combinations of cultural styles from many sources brought together in the new world. Documentations of these primitive crafts are to be found in the Index of American Design. An interesting collection of the primitive paintings recently has been given to the National Gallery in Washington.

## ARCHITECTURE

### Architects of the Classic Revival:

| France (Empire) | England (Regency) | | United States (Federal) |
|---|---|---|---|
| Chalgrin | Burton | Nash | |
| Percier and Fontaine | Cockerell | Smirke | Bulfinch |
| | Hope (interiors) | Soane | Jefferson |
| Poyet | | Wilkins | Lafever |
| Vignon | | | Latrobe |

Italy — Canina

### Architects of the Historic Period Revivals:

The romantic school includes adaptations of all styles so far described.

The Gothic revival is inspired by the taste of Horace Walpole, the novels of Sir Walter Scott, the writings of John Ruskin, and the restorations of the French architect Viollet le Duc.

| France | England | | United States |
|---|---|---|---|
| (Baroque) | (Gothic) | | |
| Garnier | Barry | Repton | Upjohn (Gothic) |
| Girault | Bentley | Scott | |
| Labrouste | Butterfield | Shaw | (Classic Renaissance) |
| Perret | Pugin | Wyatt | McKim, Mead and White |

British Influences:

Pugin Morris Ruskin
Eastlake — Hints on Household Tastes

United States (Romanesque):

Richardson
Root

The great realists in the architectural field are the architect-engineers who use new materials in new forms to serve new purposes.

| France | England | United States |
|---|---|---|
| Eiffel | Paxton | Roebling |
| Eiffel Tower | Crystal Palace | Brooklyn Bridge |
| (iron) | (iron and glass) | (steel) |

With the industrialization of England comes a need for Town Planning: Buckington Howard Owen Salt

# ·19th CENTURY · MUSIC ·

<u>MUSIC</u>

1820—The Romantic Period—1900

<u>Composers</u>

The transition between the classic and romantic schools:

Beethoven

Romanticism in German instrumental music:

| | |
|---|---|
| Brahms | Schumann |
| Liszt | Strauss |
| Mendelssohn | Wagner |
| Schubert | Weber |

Russia leads a nationalistic trend:

| | | |
|---|---|---|
| Balakirev | Cui | Moussorgsky |
| Borodin | Glinka | Rimsky-Korsakov |

<u>Norway</u>: Grieg <u>Poland</u>: Chopin
<u>Germany</u>: Wagner
<u>Bohemia</u>: Dvorak; Smetana
<u>United States</u>: Foster (folk songs) MacDowell

Other Russian contributions:
Modernism: Tchaikovsky
Romanticism: Rachmaninoff

Grand opera replaces the eighteenth-century opéra comique, and wins world acclaim.

| Italy | Germany | France |
|---|---|---|
| Bellini | Beethoven | Bizet |
| Donizetti | Meyerbeer | Gounod |
| Puccini | Spohr | Offenbach |
| Mascagni | Strauss | Massenet |
| Rossini | Wagner | |
| Verdi | Weber | |

<u>England</u>—The operettas of Gilbert and Sullivan.

<u>Opera Singers</u>

The rich New World adopts European opera, and to sing at the Metropolitan Opera House in New York becomes the goal of every operatic star.

| | |
|---|---|
| Emma Eames | Caruso |
| Geraldine Farrar | Edouard de Reszke |
| Melba | Jean de Reszke |
| Sembrich | Scotti |

Music is the powerful emotional outlet of the age.

· COMPOSERS ·

LUDWIG VAN BEETHOVEN
(1770-1827)
His sonatas and symphonies thrill the world.

ROBERT SCHUMANN
(1810-1856)
Pianist and composer of lyric melodies.

GUISEPPE VERDI
(1813-1901)
His opera "Aida", an Egyptian tale, is part of the celebration for the opening of the Suez Canal.

JOHANN STRAUSS, JR.
(1855-1899)
The world swings to the music of the Waltz King.

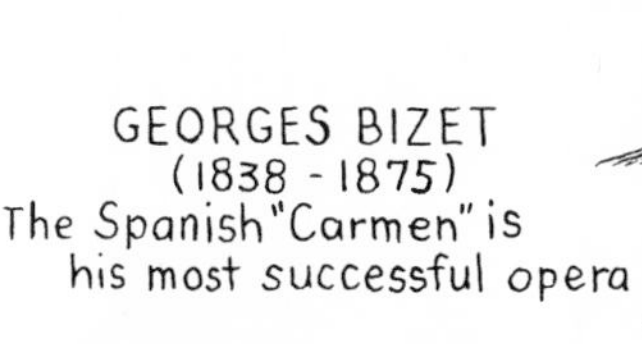

GEORGES BIZET
(1838-1875)
The Spanish "Carmen" is his most successful opera

NIKOLAI RIMSKY-KORSAKOV
(1844-1908)
Father of modern composition.

# · SCIENTIFIC DISCOVERIES ·

· AMERICAN INVENTORS ·

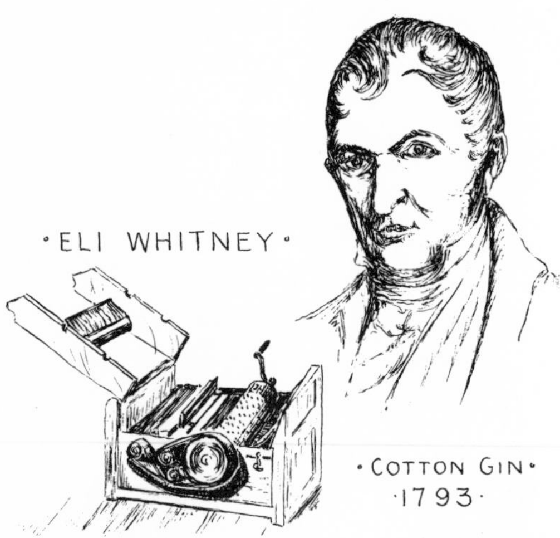
· ELI WHITNEY ·
· COTTON GIN ·
·1793·

· ROBERT FULTON ·
STEAMBOAT
·1807·
CYRUS Mc CORMICK
·REAPER·
·1831·

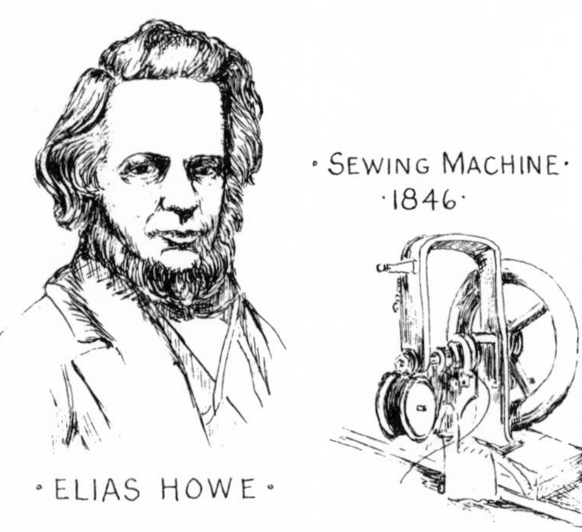
· SEWING MACHINE ·
·1846·
· ELIAS HOWE ·

The part played by machines in modern civilization has yet to be fully tested.

In the last two hundred years, the devices below, together with many others, have completely changed the path and pace of civilization.

A few of the eighteenth-century inventions which started the revolution in industry:

| | | | |
|---|---|---|---|
| 1705 | Steam pump | Newcomen | English |
| 1733 | Flying shuttle | Kay | English |
| 1769 | Steam engine | Watt | Scottish |
| 1784 | Automatic loom | Cartwright | English |
| 1793 | Cotton gin | Whitney | American |

Some of the inventions which brought about changes in transportation:

| | | | |
|---|---|---|---|
| 1800 | Macadam roads | MacAdam | Scottish |
| 1807 | Steamboat | Fulton | American |
| 1825 | Steam locomotive | Stephenson | English |
| 1885 | Automobile | Benz | German |
| 1903 | Airplane with engine | Wright Brothers | American |

The communication of ideas and the reporting of factual information which for so long was left to the artist and the writer now reaches everyone through:

| | | | |
|---|---|---|---|
| 1876 | Telephone | Bell | American |
| 1893 | Motion picture machine | Edison | American |
| 1896 | Wireless telegraph | Marconi | Italian |
| 1907 | Radio | DeForest | American |
| 1922 | Radar | Taylor and Young | American |
| 1926 | Television | Baird | Scottish |

A handful of materials and weapons enables us to exterminate our fellow men with great efficiency. Some of these can be used for progress rather than destruction:

| | | | |
|---|---|---|---|
| 1242 | Gunpowder | Roger Bacon | English |
| 1865 | Repeating rifle | Winchester | American |
| 1846 | Nitroglycerin | Sobrero | Italian |
| 1876 | Dynamite | Nobel | Swedish |
| 1919 | Atom-smashing theory | Rutherford | English |
| | | Mietzsch, etc. | German |
| 1952 | Hydrogen bomb | U. S. Government | |

Discoveries which have eased pain, exterminated disease or prolonged life:

| | | | |
|---|---|---|---|
| 1628 | Circulation of blood | Harvey | English |
| 1798 | Vaccination | Jenner | English |
| 1847 | Chloroform | Simpson | Scottish |
| 1867 | Antiseptic system | Lister | English |
| 1885 | Pasteurization, and inoculation for rabies | Pasteur | French |
| 1895 | X-ray | Roentgen | German |

# ·THE VICTORIAN ERA·

During the last quarter of the eighteenth century new inventions in the textile industry started the industrial revolution in England. After the turn of the century it spread to the continent of Europe and the United States. Brought about by successful scientific experimentation which produced many new types of machinery, it completely changed man's way of life. It affected it economically, politically, and socially. The developments it brought about in commerce, transportation, communication, illumination, agriculture, and the methods of warfare have necessitated a great number of adjustments within a short time. This revolution is still in effect and has encompassed the entire civilized world.

The end of the Napoleonic wars gave the countries of Europe an urge for national unity. After Napoleon's defeat there were skirmishes all over the continent for the establishment of independent states. By the middle of the century nationalism was the motivating force behind European politics. It was responsible for the unification of both Italy and Germany in 1870 and played a large part in both the world wars to come.

But across the channel stability and prosperity were enjoyed. Equality was bestowed upon all religions; complete freedom was given to the press. Overnight England was transformed from an agricultural country into an industrial one. The demand for new markets for the output of the prolific machines turned nationalism into colonial imperialism. Her farflung empire was the envy of all Europe.

Land was claimed in every part of the globe. Africa was parceled out. All the major European nations became colonial empires, but none could compare with Great Britain. As the foremost world power, she became the international pacesetter.

Late nineteenth-century domestic architecture, furniture and accessories were victims of the mechanical era. Because of concentration on the quantity the machines were capable of putting forth, with little or no attention to either design or quality, originality and aesthetics reached a new low. This unfortunate disregard for artistic integrity affected the production of the visual arts, and today the popular output of the period is viewed with amusement.

However, the intellectual arts of music and literature are dynamic expressions of an age of activity. European musical compositions remain unsurpassed, and the British novel inadvertently became one of Britain's most convincing forms of propaganda.

The Congress of Vienna (1814-15) restores the states taken over by Napoleon.

PRINCE METTERNICH (1773-1859) Austrian foreign minister dominates continental politics until the rise of Napoleon III.

QUEEN VICTORIA rules the British Empire for 63 eventful years (1839-1902) The PRINCE CONSORT runs the royal household and his taste affects all domestic establishments even after his death in 1861

In France during the Second Empire of NAPOLEON III (nephew of the first Napoleon) the EMPRESS EUGÉNIE makes Paris the center of women's fashions – a position she is allowed to maintain today.

# · The DECLINE of the CRAFTSMAN ·

The work of the craftsman was to hold a place in society until the introduction of the machine, but by the end of the sixteenth century the craftsman himself no longer enjoyed the respected position he had earned during the Gothic Age and Renaissance. An appreciation for the growing lyrical media of literature, drama and music had robbed him of his important role of teacher and chronicler. The popular Late Renaissance interpretation of the writings of Aristotle decreed the ''necessary'' arts (medicine and productive crafts) inferior to the ''fine'' arts. To Aristotle the so-called fine arts were those that brought pleasure, and included stone sculpture, music and literature. To these the Renaissance added its beloved painting. Thus the prestige of the craftsman was wiped out.

The processes themselves had to be adjusted to the changing times as some techniques were outmoded or abused while new ones were devised to fill growing needs. Increased demand accelerated output and even before the machine took over there were few instances in which one man saw a design through to completion.

The workshop of William Morris (London, 1862) (see Pre-Raphaelite Brotherhood) was the product of the romantic Victorian-Gothic revival. It led indirectly to the formation of societies which fought against the Royal Academy's exclusive selection of oil paintings and demanded instead national recognition for all forms of expression. The demands were just and deserved their success. It is only regrettable that they started a preoccupation with medieval subjects and techniques at a time when fertile creative minds should have been concentrating on original designs to be handled by the machines which were destined to change the cultural patterns of the entire world.

The middle 19th c. brings a revolt against formalized classicism.

° ° °

In 1851 the dream of the Prince Consort comes true. The International Exhibition of Arts and Industry opens in the fabulous new Crystal Palace.

· MIRROR FRAME ·

CAST IRON is used indiscriminately indoors and out.

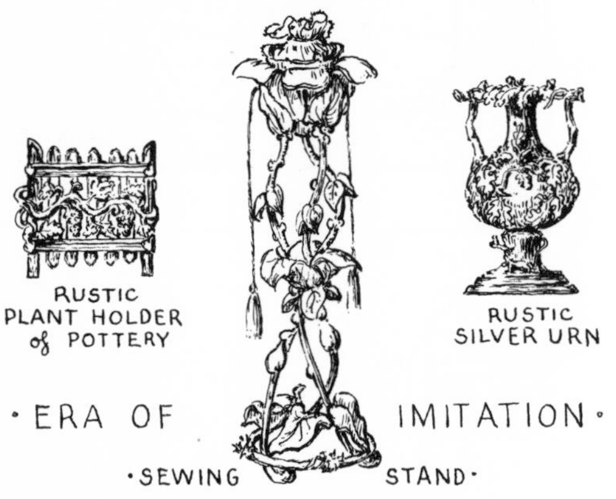

RUSTIC PLANT HOLDER of POTTERY

RUSTIC SILVER URN

· ERA OF IMITATION ·

· SEWING STAND ·

The romantic impulse overcomes simplicity and common sense. The unguided manufacturer dazzles an enthusiastic public with a fascinating assortment.

In 1868 in an effort to bring integrity into contemporary compositions CHARLES EASTLAKE recommends the Gothic past. Without attempting to understand his basic principles manufactures turn out a line of merchandize that contradicts rather than supports his contentions.

Quality of WORKMANSHIP also suffers. Machine carving is glued in place.

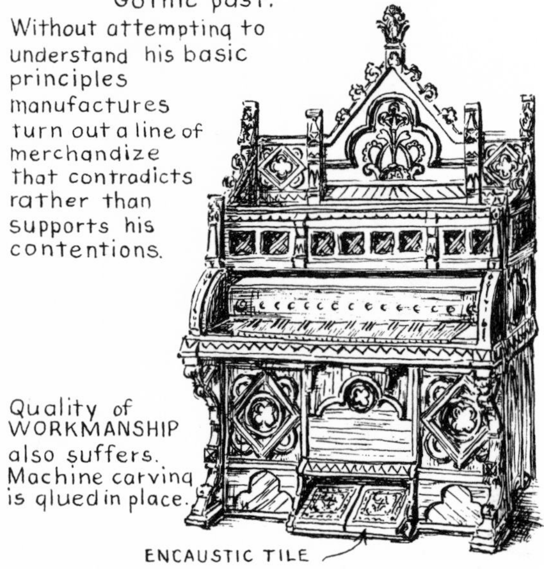
ENCAUSTIC TILE

· "EASTLAKE" ORGAN 1876 ·

WILLIAM MORRIS tries to stabilize eclectic public taste by stressing medieval hand crafts through the ARTS and CRAFTS movement.

TAPESTRY DESIGN by MORRIS from his poem "The Orchard"

# · The DECLINE of the CRAFTSMAN ·

While the arts and crafts movement created a diversion which delayed well-designed mechanical production for over half a century, it gave us an appreciation of interesting techniques which had fallen into disuse. Today the high cost of labor precludes the wholesale manufacture of articles by any but the fastest methods. But the various forms of handwork are not excluded from the living rooms, basements and garages of those who have leisure. Old techniques can be used to express new ideas and so be revitalized.

The rule of Morris: "Have nothing in your house that you do not know to be useful or believe to be beautiful", is a worthy one. The changing standard of beauty betrays it.

In 1862 the Morris firm executes a series of stained glass windows showing the legend of · TRISTRAM and ISOLDE · designed by Burne-Jones.

The day of the professional craftsman has passed but the work of his hand lives on—to be studied, not imitated, by his admirers. Regardless of age, the pieces most worthy of examination are those in which ingenuity has overcome the restrictions of the assignment through sensitive grasping of the subject and through appreciative handling of the chosen medium. A true craftsman takes that quality which sets his medium apart from any other and by emphasizing it, becomes its master. Through understanding, a limitation may become a force—through camouflage, it becomes an acknowledged weakness.

Thus to hide the stitches on a tapestry or to ignore the lead divisions of a stained glass window is to disregard the most interesting and unique feature of the work. To stand in front of a tapestry, a mosaic or a piece of stained glass and in wonder and amazement exclaim: "It looks just like a painting!" is to admire a painstaking accomplishment which appears to be the refinement of a process but which is actually a betrayal of the principles of a technique. This misguided admiration has brought discredit to more than one worthy form of artistic expression.

When the product of one process is made to look like the product of another, one method has lost its identity, and one if not both processes stand to lose their value.

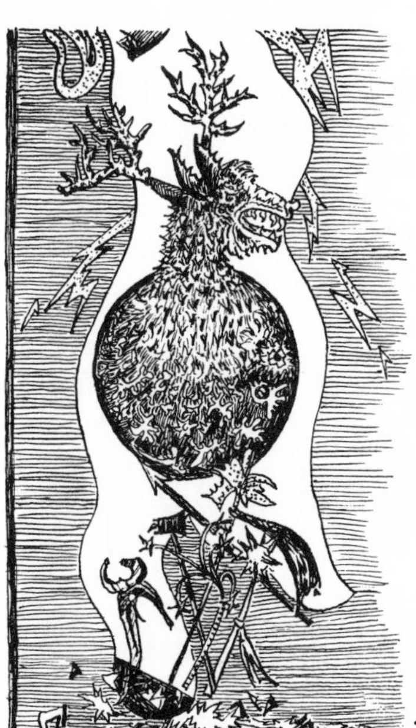

20th c. TAPESTRY DESIGN ·NAZI WARFARE· by Jean Lurçat.

ENAMELED NECKLACE in the medieval tradition of the 19th c. movement is not appropriate for costumes of the era.

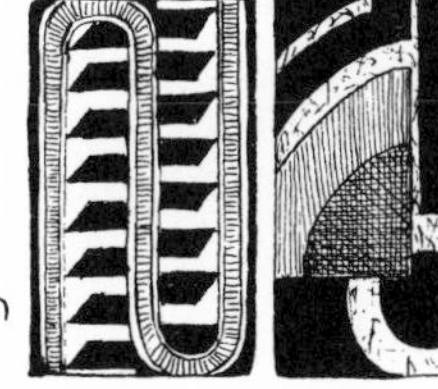

ENAMELED CIGARETTE CASES. An ancient technique is used to decorate utilitarian objects of the era.

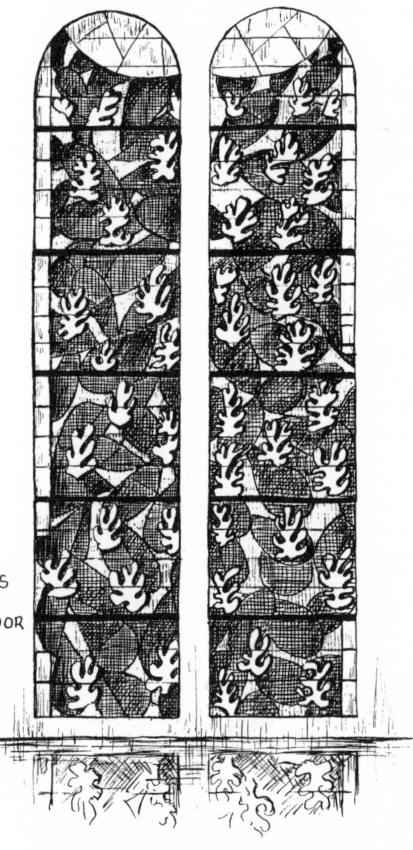
BRILLANT COLORS of the STAINED GLASS reflect on MARBLE FLOOR

In 1952 Henri Matisse uses the medieval technique in a fresh unconventional style.

# ·HISTORIC PERIOD REVIVALS·

· The PICTURESQUE IDEA ·
(Also see page 162)

The industries born of the age of invention made fortunes for their owners. This new moneyed class had little discrimination. In attempting to establish itself as the social and intellectual as well as the financial equal of the established aristocracy, it either bought houses and possessions from the original owners or had them copied. Through ignorance and misunderstanding these copies were not accurate reproductions but distortions or combinations of more than one style. Thus we have a series of so-called revivals, in which the various characteristics of the different periods were romantically mingled, abused and distorted almost beyond recognition. These include the medieval styles, especially Gothic and a combination of Byzantine-Romanesque; all forms of Renaissance architecture, with a little Moorish and Turkish thrown in for variety.

The Royal Pavilion at Brighton, playground of George IV and William IV, reflects the eclectic tastes of an expanding empire with its tent-shaped roofs, Indian domes, and its Chinese galleries.

Where one period style is adhered to as in The OPERA HOUSE, Paris (Baroque Style), the result is a building which might be mistaken for a structure of a former age.

The Church of Sacré Coeur Atop Montmartre in Paris, completed in 1919, for years is described as "eclectic modern" Instead it is a product of the romantic revivals.

The Gothic Revival design for St. PANCRAS RAIL ROAD STATION, London, reflects nothing of the new industry which it serves.

New York's two great stations also reflect the past. The Grand Central is Baroque Revival and the interior of the Pennsylvania is taken from the Baths of Caracalla in ancient Rome.

The Academy of Fine Arts in Philadelphia is a conglomeration of medieval styles.

A period of adaptation is the transition between the romantic 19th century styles and functional architecture of the 20th c. Period decoration is applied to funtional plans.

The LINCOLN MEMORIAL, Washington, D.C. adapted from the classic Greek.

# ·HISTORIC PERIOD REVIVALS·

Former ages and earlier centuries produce architecture in variations of ONE SELECTED THEME.
The 19th. century works variations on EVERY KNOWN STYLE and consequently has no characteristic identifying feature.

(OVAL FRAMES for MIRRORS and PICTURES)

INTERIORS:

High ceilings.
Elaborate plaster moldings in Baroque Style.
Wide, ugly machine wood work for sliding doors.
Velours, velvets in bright or muddy colors.
Too many figured surfaces used together.
Red roses on wallpaper and carpet, etc.

HOUSES large and spacious but floor space is not well utilized.

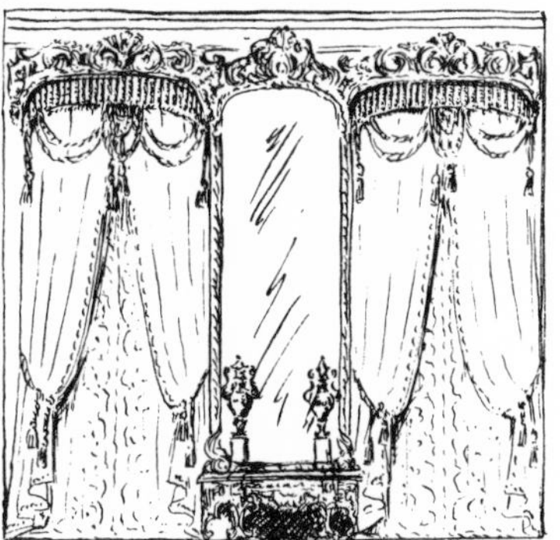

(ALABASTER VASES)

Pierglasses and gilded plaster valances for formal window decoration. Windows - large sheets of plate glass. Early - Hand-carved wood or repoussé metal. Late - Machine carved. Velour draperies over lace curtains with silk cords and tassels.

(PALMS, RUBBER PLANTS ASPIDISTRA + PAMPAS GRASS used as decoration.)

In the 80's and 90's CURIOS from all over the world are collected in the TURKISH COZY CORNER.

· THE ROMANTIC MOVEMENT ·

The GOTHIC CASTLE appears on city streets.

CAST IRON is of great importance in decoration. Even the deer are mold-cast.

By 1900 rows of houses of classic renaissance adaptation in red brick or brownstone are unifying city blocks.

Gothic cottages appear in suburban and rural areas. Gables and verandas are enhanced by jig-sawed "ginger bread." (1840 - 1880)

The enthusiasms of the awful eighties produce some of the most illogical effects ever seen in architecture.

# ·FURNISHINGS of the VICTORIAN AGE·

The designs of the architecture, furniture and accessories show progressive confusion in taste. and deterioration in the quality of the workmanship.

Glass Domes protect Objects.

Oil Lamps

C. 1850

Marble Chimneypiece
Showing small round opening for built-in coal grate.

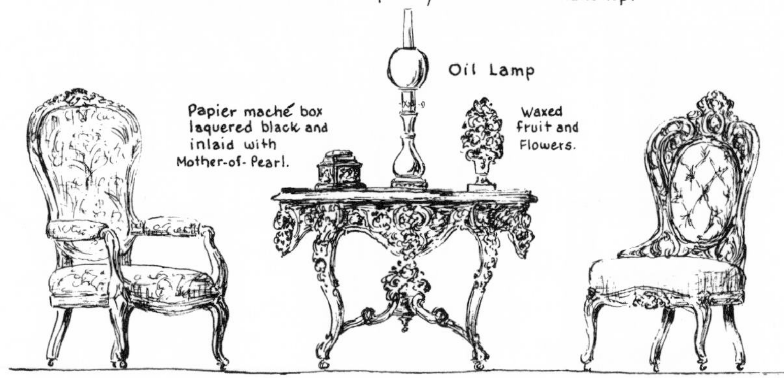

Oil Lamp
Papier maché box laquered black and inlaid with Mother-of-Pearl.
Waxed Fruit and Flowers.


The furniture styles of Louis XIV, XV and XVI are adapted, Influence Victorian designs. Furniture made in matched sets as it was in 18th c. France. WOODS: Rosewood, black walnut.

Early - Pear-shaped back. Hand-finished. (Louis XV) Short cabriole leg - brass castor.

Middle - Belter chair with pierced frame and tufted upholstery.

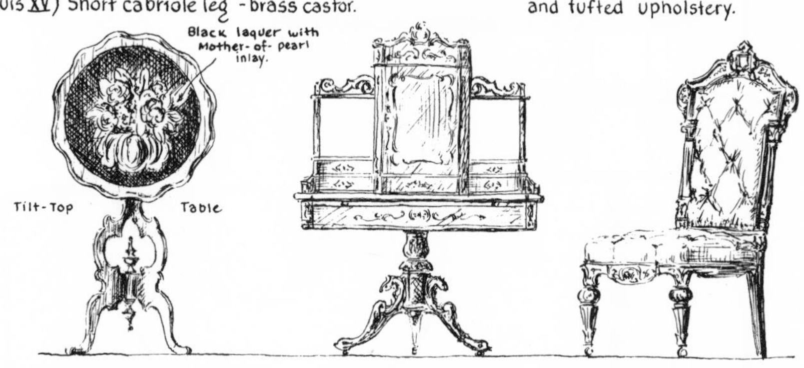

Black laquer with Mother-of-pearl inlay.
Tilt-Top
Table


C.1870. Machine carving incised or applied by glueing in place.

This ladies' desk provides almost everything but writing surface.

Late - Louis XIV chair Machine finish.

Parian Ware - (unglased porcelain resembling marble)
Rodgers Group - genre subjects in plaster.
Milk Glass
Ceramics
C. 1870


The overmantle and whatnot are designed to display the wares of growing industries. Lambrequin lightens the black marble.

Gas Fixtures
C. 1890


Renaissance elegance in machined GOLDEN OAK.

Mirror tilts

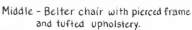

TOLE (painted tin) tray.

Picture made of shells.

The PARLOR-WORK of the ladies supplies some interesting ornaments.

Painting on velvet or glass. (Fruit also decorates plates)

"In Memoriam" embroidered picture.

CUSHION

Animals are popular. Needle point pattern stamped on perforated paper called BERLIN-WORK.

HAIR of the deceased is worked into jewelry and pictures.

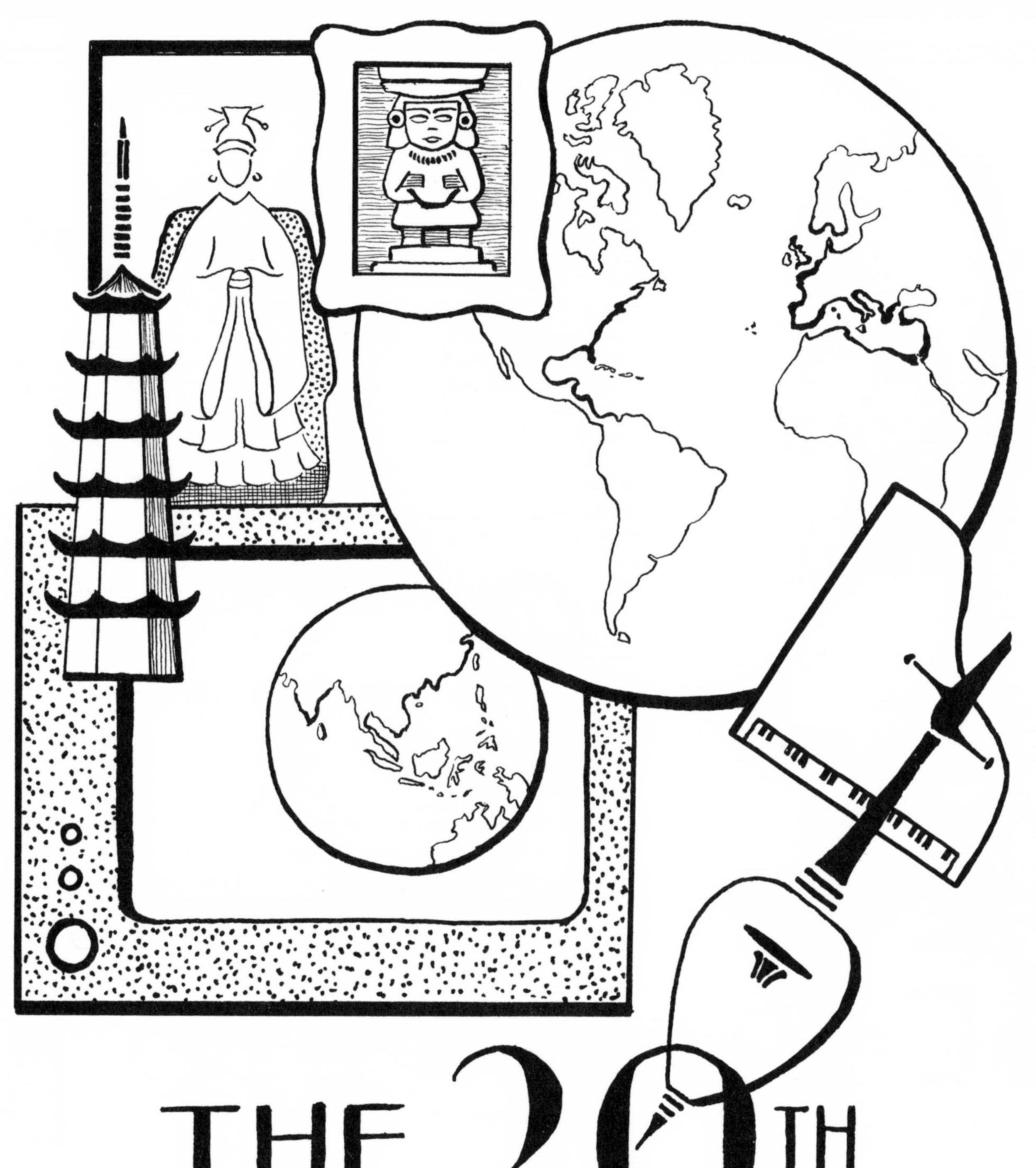

# THE 20TH CENTURY

## 1900—THE TWENTIETH CENTURY—2000

*Style of Architecture

**Style of Furniture

Age of scientific achievement.
International experimentation
and individual expression in the arts.
Western culture exposed to world-wide influences
and responsibilities.

| | |
|---|---|
| 1900 | Art Nouveau an unsuccessful experiment for a twentieth-century style. |
| 1900–1924 | Modification and adaptation of historic styles. |
| 1918–1940 | Europe develops an *INTERNATIONAL STYLE. |
| 1925 | Paris Exposition introduces **MODERNISTIC. |
| 1946– | Postwar era in this country brings acceptance of ***FUNCTIONAL styles which are still in experimental stage. |

• FASCES •

Symbol of ancient Roman civil authority.
Adopted as emblem of
Mussolini's Fascist party.

Often used as architectural ornament.

# THE WORLD TODAY

The First World War (1914–18) was an attempt to replace the European monarchies with democratic forms of government. The second (1940–1946) crushed dictatorship in Europe and imperialism in Japan. Victory in both these wars was made possible by the participation and resources of the United States.

This country in the New World was founded on principles and practices first conceived in Europe. Its power lies not only in its rich land but also in the people who have chosen to develop it. The first settlers came to enjoy a choice of religion and self-government. So successful was their venture that every year more and more Europeans crossed the ocean to become a part of it. One hundred years after the formation of the new republic its population had grown from under five million to over fifty. Immigration averaged half a million a year between 1870 and 1900; a million annually from 1900 to 1914. The applicants became so numerous that it was necessary to control the influx. One hundred and fifty million citizens now live within the North American boundaries of the United States. It is the largest single nation of the West.

Today the demand for freedom has become universal. Economics has made the European nations slow in giving independence to their Asian and African colonies. England is parting with her world empire. Realistic, as always, she recognizes that a territory which has been released becomes a friend, while one which had to fight for its freedom is likely to remain an enemy. However, she considers it expedient to hold on to certain militarily strategic spots.

In many areas of the world today, especially in countries still trying to win their independence from the remnants of nineteenth-century colonialism, a struggle is being waged between two ideologies. One is the Western tradition which supports man as an individual. The other was born of the maladjustments of capital and labor, the two factors necessary to industry. It was evolved by Germans (Marx and Engels) living in Victorian England, and it has been embraced by the Russians of the Soviet Union. It is a concept which denies man his individual rights, and establishes him as co-contributor-benefactee within what may become an omnipotent world state.

° ° °

Human history becomes more and more a race between education and catastrophe.
H.G. Wells (1866-1946)

The hope of the postwar world:
The FOUR FREEDOMS
(1) Speech and expression,
(2) Religion, (3) freedom from want,
and (4) freedom from fear of aggression.
F. D. R.

The United Nations, N.Y.C.

"Grant us grace fearlessly to contend against evil, and to make no peace with oppression; and, that we may reverently use our freedom, help us to employ it in the maintenance of justice among men and nations."
The Book of Common Prayer - Cranmer (1489-1556)

SIR RABINDRANATH TAGORE (1861-1941)
Bengali Poet
Winner of the Nobel Prize for Literature, 1913.

The East can patiently wait until the West, in its mad hurry after the expedient, loses its breath and stops.
The East knows she is immortal - and thus shall wait the East till her time has come.

# ·The ROLE of PAINTERS and DESIGNERS·

· INDUSTRIAL DESIGN ·

WALTER GROPIUS (1883- ) architect, designer and teacher of art in an industrial society.

BAUHAUS

BAUHAUS, Dessau, Germany. A functional building for designers. Closed by Hitler, reopened in 1956.

The AUTOMOBILE is an example of the success of the combined skills of engineer and designer.

A span of fifty years - Early horseless carriage. A modern car.

The mobility of the population made possible by the motor car and the ideas advanced through motion pictures are responsible for rapid unification of cultural patterns in this country.

Mass production tends to standardize taste.

We are beholden to a handful of French painters for leading all creative artists away from the heterogeneous standards of the Victorian era.

In the eighteen-thirties when Louis Jacques Mandé Daguerre snapped the shutter on his camera, he also brought to a close the necessity for one kind of artistic endeavor.

At that moment, a machine relieved the artist of the responsibility of reproducing an exact image. Since the dawn of civilization, the painter had made it one of his dedicated tasks to learn to copy nature as faithfully as he could. It was years before anyone realized that his role had changed, or that a substitute goal was suggested. In all, a century was to pass before the public would recognize a new artistic objective.

The sponsors and acknowledged arbiters of painting, the French Salon, supported Classicism, Romanticism and Realism. But year after year the selections had become so stereotyped that it was hard to distinguish one exhibition from another. Imagination seemed to have died. The work was as colorless as a negative.

The first rebellion against the domination of academic tastes was a gentle one. Inspired by the Dutch masters Hobbema and Ruisdael, the Barbizon School of Poetic Landscape took painting out of the studio into the open air.

In 1874 came open revolt. A group of young men whose work had been turned down repeatedly by the Salon opened their own exhibition. They had something new to show. They had found a solution to the challenge of the machine age.

By presenting the impression of what they saw instead of a facsimile of the subject, they gave art a new starting point. Another innovation was their use of color. In defiance of the experts' dark, colorless tones, they spread bright unmixed pigments on their canvases. It was as if the windows had been opened—sunlight and fresh air poured in.

Official recognition was reluctantly given the Impressionists and they were allowed to exhibit at the Salon. Public acceptance, however, was so slow that they are classified as moderns.

Because the producer of fine arts was given no assigned task, in the middle nineteenth century young painters in this country who were not interested in reproducing its natural beauties went abroad to study. They joined international students in Italy and Germany but more particularly in Paris. There painters, sculptors, writers and musicians showed the uncertainty of their position by breaking one tradition after another. The grudging acknowledgement of Impressionism encouraged other artists to group together and experiment with new approaches and new techniques.

# ·The ROLE of PAINTERS and DESIGNERS·

The Armory Show of 1913 introduced modern art in the United States. The electrifying effect it created was immediately neutralized by the war. After that, activity again centered in Paris. Confusion and disillusion intensified by introspection led to an overdose of individualism. Dreams and neuroses and the restlessness of the era were interpreted in stone, paint, prose, poetry and song. But, while the intimate nature of the woe may escape us, we cannot fail to realize that it is also the turmoil of the times that was given expression.

Among the many isms of so-called modern art there is something which can appeal to everyone. We have respect for mankind but we do not like every individual we meet. Because we do not admire every picture we see, we have no reason to condemn a whole artistic movement.

Modern painters have changed tactile values to texture. They can, through the psychology of color and line, deliver great emotional impact. They have responded to both instinct and intellect, and therefore appeal to both. But the variety, which is one of the great strengths of the school, divides its devotees into so many groups that it weakens the chances for united acclaim.

The artists of the first half of the twentieth century destroyed dependence on the past. They have prepared the way for future generations to communicate their ideas with nimble diversity and uninhibited dexterity. Looking back on this period, scholars are going to be able to tell that the people were not a race regulated entirely by the repetitious and impersonal rhythm of the machines.

The titans of the age, however, are the men who have used its most powerful tools (the machines) to the best advantage.

In this day of science, industry and commerce the important artists are those who serve them. These are the men who learned to control power machinery by designing objects which a machine could effectively produce; who recognized the advantages of mechanical reproduction; and who perceived the beauty of mechanical precision and accepted it as an art as expressive of our age as the crafts were of earlier times.

The first school of industrial design was the German Bauhaus headed by Walter Gropius. It did not open until 1920.

In a few short years the world was flooded with a variety of merchandise which commercial artists have sold through compelling advertising and irresistible packaging.

A few years ago the Detroit Institute of Arts sponsored an exhibition of ordinary household equipment based on the union of function and beauty of line and form. It proved that utilitarian objects are no longer the mediocre output of mere machines but the product of some of the most creative minds of the century.

• INDUSTRIAL DESIGN •
The demands of the housewife and the collaboration between science and industry have encouraged the designer to put the past behind him.
Materials and designs are experimental. –with FUNCTION as a basic starting point. Regardless of price, the majority of products on the market today are well designed.
· HARDWARE ·
Coffee Pot
COOKING at the TABLE
Electric Toaster
enameled iron
pottery
· STOVE-TO-TABLE WARE ·
Electric Fan
Air Conditioner
The last one-half of the 20th century may well be known as the Age of Elegant Informality.

# ·20th CENTURY ARCHITECTURE·

FORERUNNERS of the DESIGNS of TODAY

In a world of "vanity, display and carnal taste" an obscure 19th c. American religious sect transposes its "purity" into furniture design.

Based upon utility, motivation and results parallel the functional movement of today.

·SHAKER SWIVEL CHAIR·

suggests simple design to a world which rejects it in favor of the cozy corner on page 169.

The AUSTRIAN WERKBUND EXPOSITION

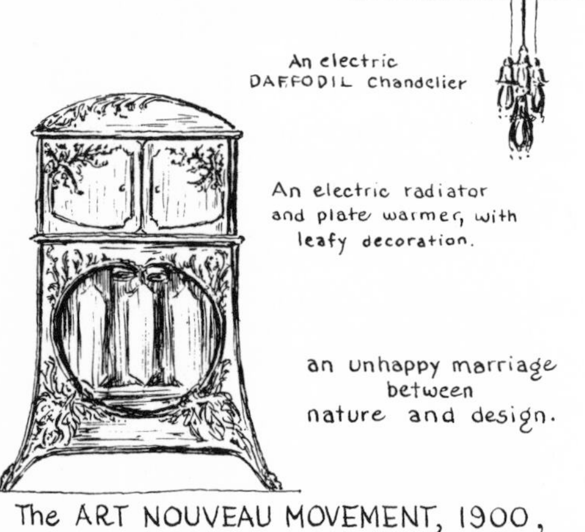
An electric DAFFODIL chandelier
An electric radiator and plate warmer, with leafy decoration.
an unhappy marriage between nature and design.

The ART NOUVEAU MOVEMENT, 1900,

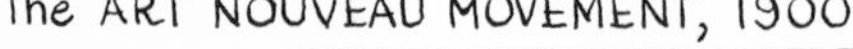

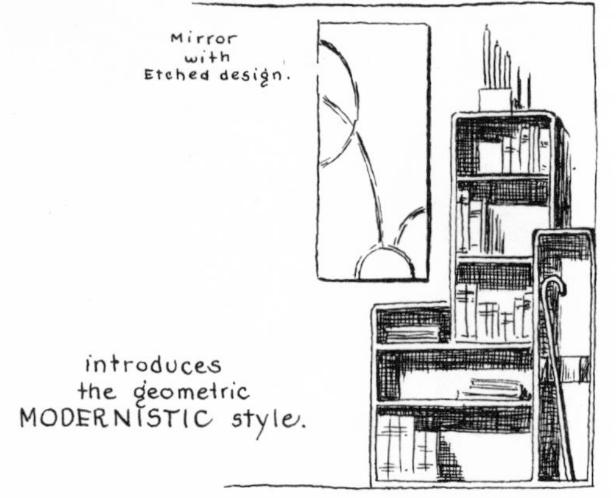
Mirror with Etched design.
introduces the geometric MODERNISTIC style.

·EXPOSITION d'ART et DECORATION, 1925·

The Chicago World's Fair of 1893 turned the public from its meaningless wanderings in the romantic past and resulted in a demand for nothing but Classic Renaissance styles.

Stunted by architectural repetitions, reproductions and adaptations, even the invention and introduction of structural steel toward the end of the nineteenth century had failed to excite or stimulate the minds of the architectural profession. Most architects were delighted at the stabilization of taste and happily arranged the same ornamental features on all buildings whether short or tall.

Only one man had the imagination and vision to foresee the changes which the new building material was to make possible, and he was virtually ignored. Born in Chicago in 1856, Louis Sullivan has only recently been appreciated and his slogan, "Form follows function," has become the basic law of progressive twentieth-century designers. For years we were hampered by narrow minds and false ideals and we have just started to recognize the unlimited possibilities which lie before us.

The twentieth century opened inauspiciously. In Paris the Exposition Universelle introduced Art Nouveau. It was an attempt to base designs upon natural forms, but it had not been consistently developed. The public soon lost interest.

It was at an exposition in Paris, in 1925, that a new style at last won international acclaim. The "modernistic" designs were outmoded almost before the exhibition closed. But architects and designers were at last convinced that the twentieth century was obligated to use its new materials in new designs. However, the persistent public continued to venerate the past.

Resistance to change and continued admiration for period styles continued to retard progress in domestic architecture and furniture design. Between the two wars architects and manufacturers were forced to concentrate on reproductions and adaptations of eighteenth-century styles. For upholstery, brocades and damasks originated for fashionable court life were reproduced in dirt-resistant colors at popular prices. Living rooms all over America were decorated with a formality which was completely unsuited to the American way of life.

The new architectural conception of mass, texture and color was both advanced and retarded by economics. A simplification of style was necessitated by soaring costs. It was soon reflected in public buildings, but conservative bankers refused to finance unconventional housing. Compromises were effected until after World War II, when public demand finally endorsed functional domestic architecture. At the middle of the century we stood where we might have been at the beginning had Louis Sullivan's lone voice not been silenced.

# ·20th CENTURY ARCHITECTURE·

Maidless postwar years bring demand for functional living.
SIMPLICITY, INFORMALITY and PRACTICALITY
are stressed without sacrifice of style.

Spacious and dramatic effects made possible through the daring but honest use of structional materials.

Houses designed to take advantage of natural settings.

MASS and PROPORTION enriched by TEXTURE and COLOR.

The Age of the Skyscraper city comes and goes.
It solves one problem by increasing office space but adds to traffic congestion and housing difficulties.
The trend of the Atomic Age is toward decentralization in suburban areas.

Compare this house built by Louis Sullivan in 1889 with its more popular contemporary on page 167.

A fluid floor plan including outside terraces is designed in 1909 by Frank Lloyd Wright.

Louis Sullivan in the Wainwright Building, St. Louis (1891), makes no attempt to conceal the structural frame.

Cantilever construction at high tide allows the living room of the house to hang over the water.

Large picture windows and windowwalls are intended to blend indoors and outdoors.

The first skyscrapers are functional but are decorated in a period style. The Woolworth Building in N.Y.C., (1911-1913) for years the world's tallest, is bedecked with Gothic ornamentation, most of which is lost 60 stories above the city.

WHITNEY MUSEUM OF AMERICAN ART

Air conditioning (climate control) eliminates NEED for windows. Desirable in art galleries, etc., where wall space is used.

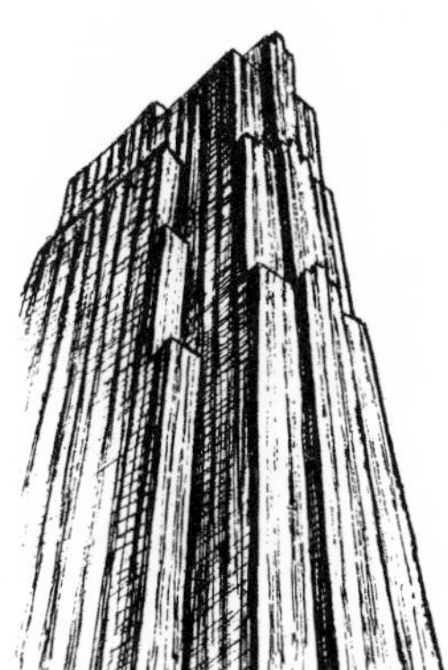

R.C.A. Building N.Y.C. is a dramatic unadorned skyscraper.

# ·20th CENTURY FURNITURE·

### · 20th CENTURY INTERIORS ·

Elimination of costly architectural detail.
Outside materials carried indoors.
(NATURAL outdoor BEAUTY blended with interior)
Informal (assymetric) balance
for informal life
in a house divided into
AREAS rather than ROOMS.

LIVING ROOM

GARDEN
of town house
is planned
as a room.

It is actually a
continuation of
the living room.

BRICK TERRACE,
GRAVELLED GROUND,
and RAISED BEDS planted
with evergreens
simplify gardening
and supply year-round vista.

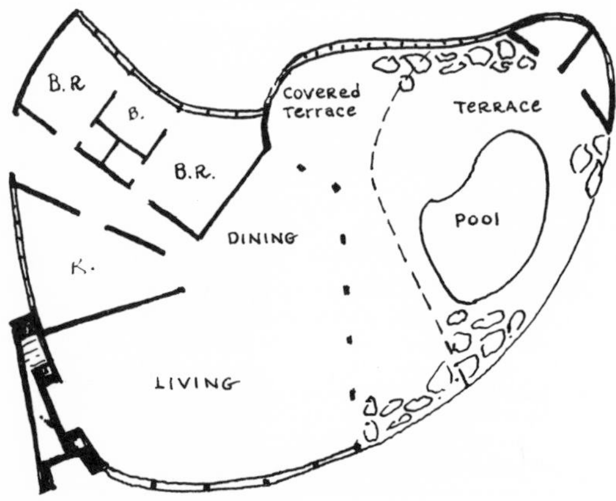
B.R.
B.
B.R.
Covered Terrace
TERRACE
Pool
DINING
K.
LIVING

MOUNTAIN VILLA
built into natural contour of hillside.
Houses are planned
to simplify process of living.

The family-room kitchen which resembles the Colonial New England kitchen is a development of the servant-less household.

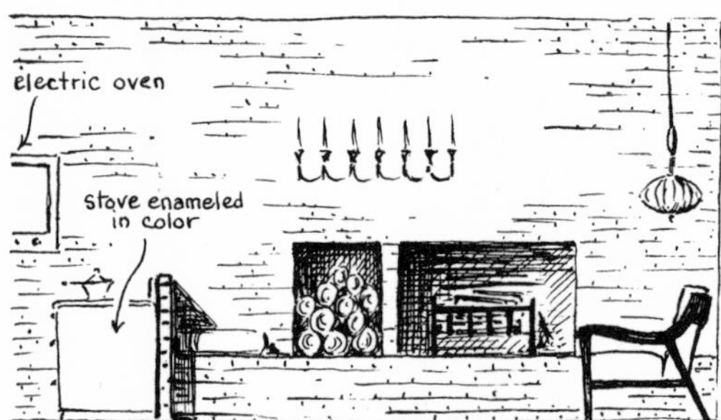
electric oven
stove enameled in color

An anachronism of the age is the cleavage to the fireplace and candleholder. These are kept for decorative and psychological reasons.

FURNITURE: FORMS, MATERIALS and CONSTRUCTION original and unorthodox.
BLOND and DARK WOOD in solid or veneered pieces.
FRAMES of CHROME, BRASS, WROUGHT IRON, ALUMINUM as well as wood.
TOPS of PLASTIC, GLASS, MIRROR. ORNAMENT in MARQUETRY and MOSAIC.
Many pieces will combine with traditional furnishings.

An amoeba-shaped table by NOGUCHI
Chair of LAMINATED WOOD by CHARLES EAMES.
Chair with iron legs and shell seat of MOLDED PLASTIC.
ANCIENT ETRUSCAN BRONZE

FOAM RUBBER changes the construction of comfortable upholstered pieces.
SIMPLICITY OF LINE is stressed.
COLOR and TEXTURE add interest.

MODULAR FURNITURE
facilitates the chore of
the frequent mover or
the chronic rearranger.

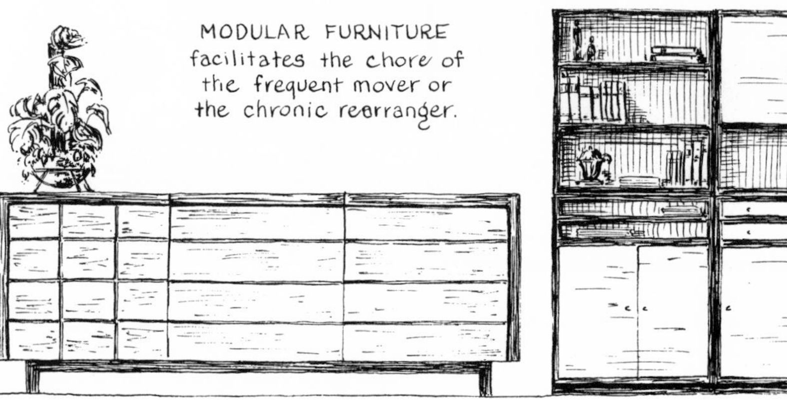

Pieces are arranged on separate bases.

Storage, major problem of
today's constricted quarters.
Carefully planned storage typical
of furniture and housing.

Shelves for china
shallow drawers for silver and place mats.
small table
wicker
grills
STORAGE
wicker chair wrought iron legs

· Cabinet for one room apartment ·
MULTIPLE-PURPOSE furniture is useful.

stacking chairs
of bent wood.

# ·20th CENTURY ACCESSORIES·

The AGE of INDUSTRY abounds with ACCESSORIES.

STYLE is available in every price range. QUALITY is expensive.

FABRICS:
Copies and adaptations of traditional designs, primitive, geometric, microscopic and imaginative patterns cover plain, textured and transparent fabrics.
Never has there been such variety.
Interesting textures achieved by combining natural and synthetic fibres.

RUGS and WALL PAPERS
designed for period and modern schemes.

In addition to NATURAL fibres such as wool, cotton, linen, silk, hemp, etc.
science has added RAYON, NYLON, DACRON, GLASS, PLASTIC and promises to add more.

Synthetics tend to reduce cost, increase durability and facilitate upkeep.

The unlimited use of COLOR on backgrounds, furniture and decorative and utilitarian objects in BRILLIANT or SUBDUED HUES is a great contribution of the times.

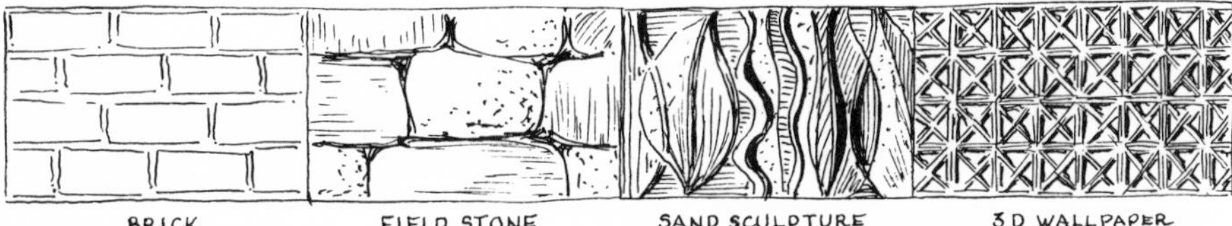
BRICK
FIELD STONE
SAND SCULPTURE
3 D WALLPAPER

Texture of wall construction often minimizes need of added interest.

PLASTER WALLS painted in colors ranging from TINTS to BLACK.

The ancient MOSAIC technique is appearing on walls, furniture and 3-dimensional pictures.

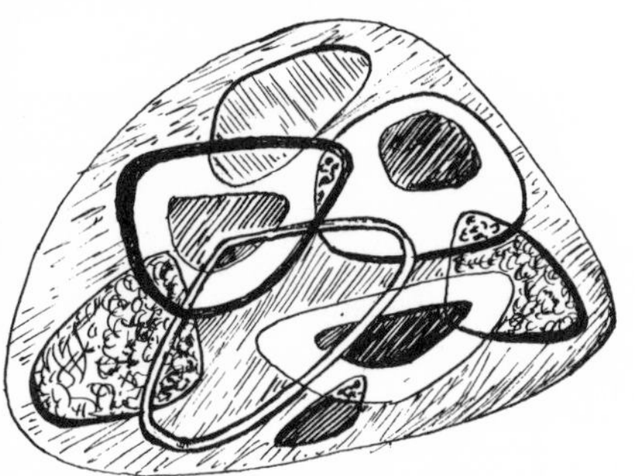

The influence of the microscope is evident on this table top in the traditional MARQUETRY technique.

PLANTS and Chemical-stone Sculpture make large-scale accessories extremely suitable to open-space floor plans.

Two types of 20th c. DECORATION
· ECLECTIC - FUNCTIONAL ·

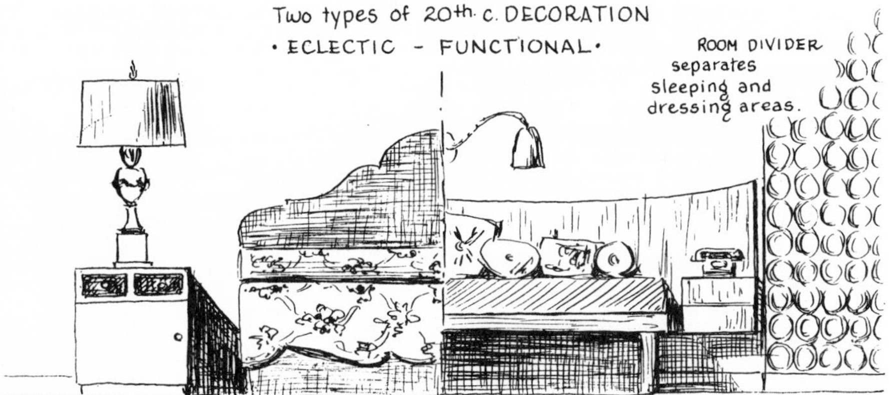
ROOM DIVIDER separates sleeping and dressing areas.

Twin beds against large upholstered HEADBOARD ·· DOUBLE MATTRESS 60"x 80" wide.

· ELECTRIC LIGHTING ·

Built-in concealed indirect lighting gives subtle overall glow.

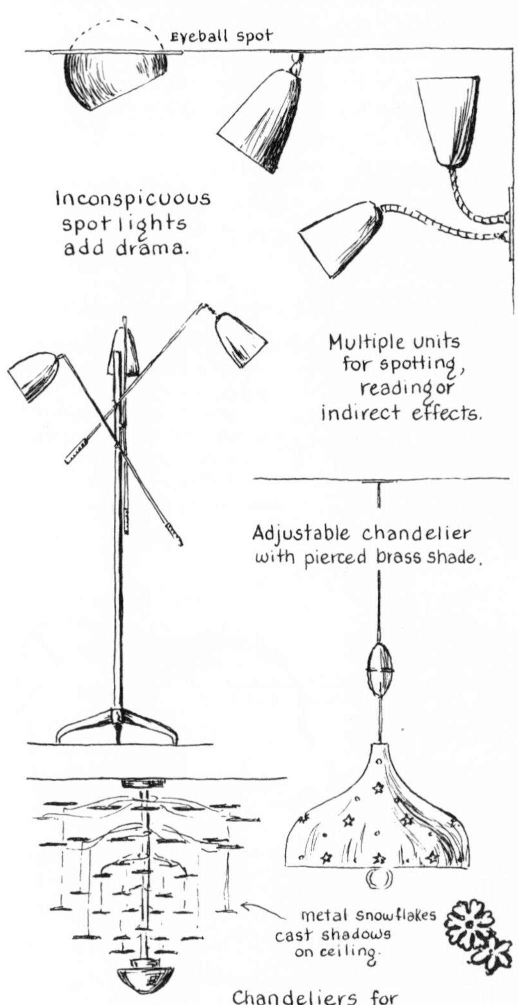
Eyeball spot
Inconspicuous spot lights add drama.
Multiple units for spotting, reading or indirect effects.
Adjustable chandelier with pierced brass shade.
metal snowflakes cast shadows on ceiling.

Chandeliers for decoration and general lighting.

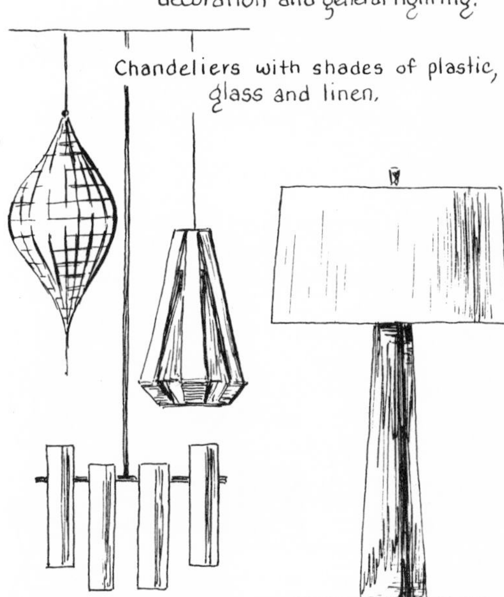
Chandeliers with shades of plastic, glass and linen.

Table Lamps are decorative feature as well as a source of illumination.

# ·20th CENTURY ARCHITECTS·

· THE INTERNATIONAL STYLE ·

The Einstein Tower, Potsdam, (Mendelssohn, 1921) reflects its astronomical function.

Workers' houses in Holland constructed to give good living at a minimum cost are designed by Oud in 1924.

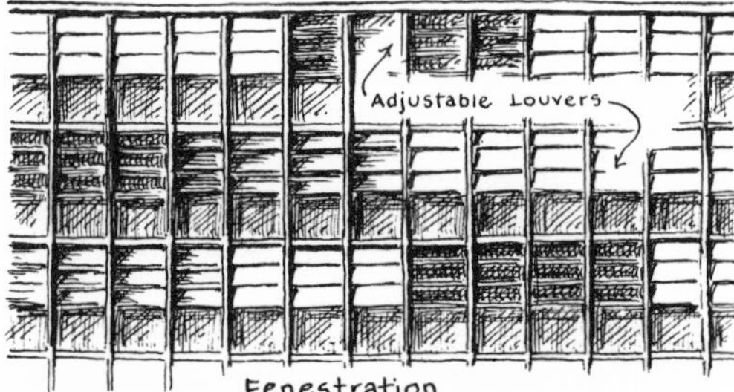
Adjustable Louvers

Fenestration plays a large part in 20th century designs. Tropical architecture provides interesting solutions to the problem of light control. (Ministry of Education, Rio de Janeiro)

Le Corbusier builds a city in India, 1954. Open staircases and pierced walls provide ventilation.

Reinforced Concrete makes effective and inexpensive buildings.

## ARCHITECTS

Far-sighted, progressive men who tried to turn public taste from romance to reality—the nineteenth-century forefathers of a twentieth-century style:

Austria: Loos
Belgium: Van de Velde
Britain: Mackintosh, Voysey
France: Perret (reinforced concrete)
Germany: Olbrich, Endell, Hoffman
Holland: Berlage, Dudok
United States: Sullivan

---

A handful of the popular transitional architects who concealed good planning under exteriors of accepted historic period styling:

England: Lutyens
Sweden: Ostberg
United States: Gilbert (Gothic skyscraper)
Goodhue (eclectic)
Pope (classic)

---

The eclectic-modern school of architecture which combines the classic heritage with the modern principles of function is headed in this country by:

Edward D. Stone

---

Proponents of the functional International Style which between the two world wars is developed to meet the needs of industry and the changes in economy:

Britain: Fry
Finland: Aalto, Saarinen
France: Le Corbusier, Lurcat
Germany: Gropius (Bauhaus)
Mendelsohn, Taut,
Van der Rohe
Holland: Oud
Hungary: Breuer
Sweden: Asplund
United States: Hood, Raymond, Belluschi,
Lescaze, Neutra

## HISTORICAL EVENTS

1914–1918 World War I
1916 Irish Easter Rebellion
1917 Bolshevists in Russia: Lenin

1920–1936 League of Nations

Postwar adjustments and dissatisfactions

1922 Mussolini dictator of Italy

1929 Stock market crash in U.S.

1930–1953 Stalin sole head of Russian government

1931 Spanish Revolution
Social and economic reforms

1933 Rise of Hitler in Germany
1934 Hitler becomes Reichsführer

1934–1936 Italy attacks Ethiopia. Useless appeal to League of Nations discredits the organization.

1936 Civil War in Spain, between Loyalists and rebel Insurgents under Franco. Fascist Italy and Germany send troops to Franco. Russia sends planes to Loyalists. Spain is devastated for alien interests.

1939 Franco victorious dictator

# ·20th CENTURY DESIGNERS·

### HISTORICAL EVENTS

1937 Stalin purges "Old Bolshevists."

1937 Rome-Berlin axis declared.

1938 Hitler takes Austria.
Hitler given Sudetenland.

1939 Hitler takes Czechoslovakia.

1939 World War II

1941 Atlantic Charter:
Four Freedoms—Churchill-Roosevelt.
December 6—Japan attacks Pearl Harbor.
U. S. enters war.

1945 Atomic bombs dropped by U. S. on Japan end war.

1945 Tito, communist dictator of Yugoslavia

1945 United Nations Charter

1946 Nuremberg trial of Nazi war criminals

1947 Marshall Plan aid for European rehabilitation

Gradual disintegration of Britain's overseas empire

1950 Communists encourage active revolts in Far East: Korea, China, Indonesia.

1952 Hydrogen bomb

### ARCHITECTS

A special place is reserved in architecture for:
Frank Lloyd Wright.

His engineering genius and the originality of his organic architecture have turned American designers from the impersonal International Style to a more intimate national expression.

### DESIGNERS IN AMERICA

#### Industry

Men who will design anything from Pullman trains to toothpaste tubes:

Walter Darwin Teague     Raymond Loewy

#### Interiors

Starting with a select and limited clientele, interior designers have alerted and educated the general public to the pleasure of colorful and distinctive backgrounds for daily living.

Elsie de Wolfe (pioneer)
Nancy McCelland (traditionalist)
McMillan, Inc. (restrained eclectics)
William Pahlmann Associates (flamboyant eclectics)
Knoll Associates (functional modernists)

#### Furniture

The designs of these men vary from conservative to unconventional but all are suitable to the life of today.

Charles Eames
Knoll Associates
Paul McCabb
George Nelson
Tommi Partzinger
Jens Risom
Robsjohn-Gibbings
Edward Wormley

· ECLECTIC MODERN ·

A simplification of traditional styles is considered modern (1910 - 1940)

German Embassy, Leningrad, 1912.

Theatre des Champs Elysées, Paris

· 20th CENTURY CHURCHES ·

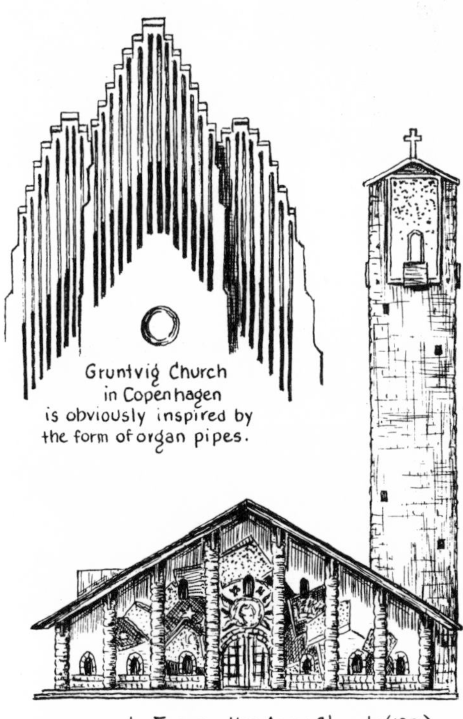

Gruntvig Church in Copenhagen is obviously inspired by the form of organ pipes.

In France the Assy Church (1950) has already started a vigorous renascence in ecclesiastical design.

# ·20th CENTURY PAINTERS·

· IMPRESSIONISM ·
A visual approach.

SEURAT'S technique of "pointillism" demonstrates the Impressionists' theory of light. Influenced by works of Constable and Turner, outlines are softened and color is applied in strokes of varying hues, values and intensities. The eye blends them into forms and accents.

· CHRIST, by REDON ·

Redon is a friend and contemporary of the Impressionists but his style is VISIONARY and expressive rather than visual.

POST- IMPRESSIONISM ·

· Young Woman by VINCENT VAN GOGH ·

## PAINTERS

This outline endeavors to explain the seething trends of the last seventy-five years. The men are too versatile, the styles too fluid, for rigid classification. The divisions suggest but one phase of development from which many individual styles have evolved.

1875—Age of International Experimentation—1950

### The French Impressionists

The refreshing nineteenth-century rebels whose new conception of painting influences all the arts:

| | | |
|---|---|---|
| Bazille | Guillaumin | Renoir |
| Bonnard | Pissaro | Morisot |
| Cassatt | Manet | Seurat |
| Cézanne | Monet | Sisley |
| Degas | | Vuillard |

English followers:

| | |
|---|---|
| Sickert | Ethel Walker |

### The Post-Impressionists

Cézanne, not satisfied with Impressionism, continues experimentation and inspires other individualists to do the same.

| | | |
|---|---|---|
| Gaugin | Segonzac | Toulouse-Lautrec |
| Rédon | Seurat | Utrillo |
| Rousseau, H. | Signac | Van Gogh |

### The Nabis (prophets):

lead us into the present century.

| | | | |
|---|---|---|---|
| Bonnard | Denis | Séruzier | Vuillard |

### Academicianists

Even conservatives cannot help being influenced by the gaiety of the new palette and the change in technique.

Augustus John (England)
Henri Fantin Latour (France)

# ·20th CENTURY PAINTERS·

## Les Fauves

The first twentieth-century group to shock the world with the impact of its use of color is known as the Wild Beasts.

| | | |
|---|---|---|
| Camoin | Puy | Matisse |
| Derain | Manguin | Roualt |
| Dufy | Marquet | Van Dongen |
| Friesz | | Vlaminck |

• 20th CENTURY INNOVATIONS •

Woman with Red Hair - MODIGLIANI (1884-1920)
A revealing caricature in oils.

## Cubists

From Cézanne's angular landscapes evolves cubism—the reduction of objects to geometric planes and forms.

| | |
|---|---|
| Braque | Picasso |
| Delaunay | Villon |
| Gris | Marin (water color) |
| Kupka | |

Like Cézanne, Picasso has many facets. Over a span of years he has tried a variety of styles and media.

The Farmer's Wife, (1923) MIRO
An appealing fantasy in a flat technique.

## Expressionists

Originating in Germany, expressionism is a direct outgrowth of Freud's science of psychology. The artist attempts to express what he feels rather than what he sees.

Religious anguish: Rouault
Poetic nostalgia: Chagall, Pascin
Social cynicism: Modigliani, Soutine
Despair: Munch Fantasy: Miro
Soulful violence: Kokoschka

Collage by BRAQUE
A collage is a composition formed from a collection of materials.

## Futurists

In 1912, in defiance of cleavage to the past, these Italians made a cult of present and future scientific discoveries, chiefly by representing speed and motion:

| | | | |
|---|---|---|---|
| Boccioni | Carrà | Balla | Severini |

Probably the most famous futurist painting is <u>Nude Descending a Staircase</u> by Duchamp, who does not belong to the group.

# · 20th CENTURY ARTISTS ·

· SURREALISM ·

City of Drawers (1936) DALI
The symbolism of Freud.

· ABSTRACTION ·

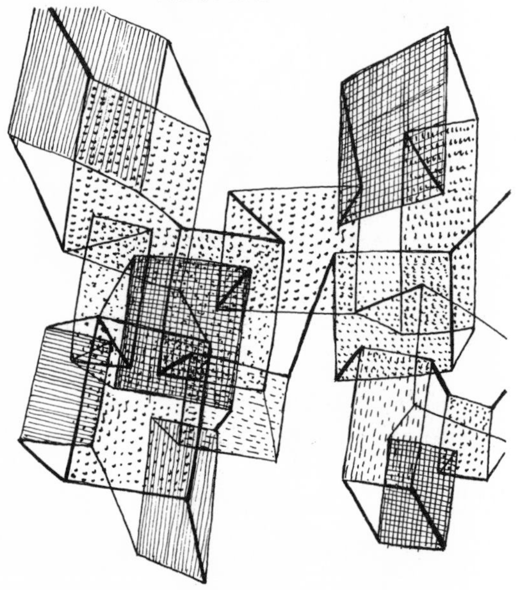

The Floating City KLEE
Imaginative interpretation through suggestive lines or symbols.

· NON-OBJECTIVE COMPOSITION ·

Light Unity KANDINSKY
Texture and color add great interest to this type of work.

## Vorticists

A British movement paralleling the Cubist-Futurists. Wyndham Lewis leads an attempt to reflect the complexities of the machine age.

| Painting: | Sculpture: | Literature: |
|---|---|---|
| Fernand Leger | Jacob Epstein | Ezra Pound |
| Edward Wadsworth | Henri Gaudier-Brzeska | Rebecca West |

## Dadaists

In 1916 disillusion, frustration and defiance of accepted standards find outlets in irrational absurdities under the Dada movement.

Poetry:

Hugo Ball    Huelsenbeck    Tzara

Painting:

Duchamp    Baziotes    Motherwell

Collage: Ernst, Schwitters

Photography: Man Ray, Hans Richter

## Surrealists

Men who escape from reality into the world of macabre or sometimes humorous imagination:

| | | |
|---|---|---|
| Arp | Dali | Miró |
| Burra (water color) | Ernst | Roy |
| Chirico | Klee | Tanguy |
| | Masson | |

## Abstractionists

From cubism and surrealism comes an approach called abstraction. The subject, though labeled, is no longer recognizable in familiar form. This leads to the introduction of nonobjective art.

Manessier

Paul Klee    Stuart Davis

Ben Nicholson

## Nonobjectivists

Based on metaphysics and following mathematical concepts, nonobjective painting and sculpture is an intellectual exercise stimulating to the artist and to a limited, educated following. It expresses the beauty of form, shape, proportion and color not through the representation of objects but through design. The effect of these men upon the arts of industry is important.

| Painting: | | Sculpture: | |
|---|---|---|---|
| Bauer | Mondrian | Calder | Mohaly-Nagy |
| Kandinsky | Pollock | Gabo | Moore |

# ·20th CENTURY SCULPTORS·

FAMILIAR SUBJECTS
presented in uninhibited and original 3-dimensional techniques.

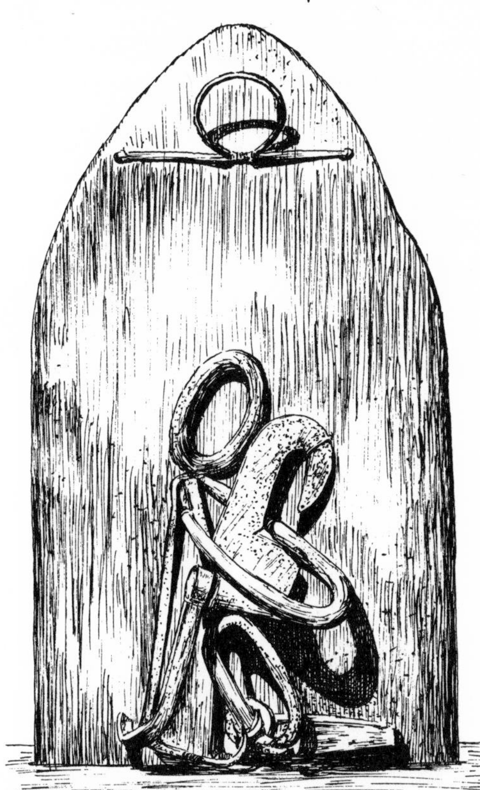

Pieta Michael James
The grandson of philosopher William James creates a religious sculpture from cast-off materials. (Compare with interpretations on pages 81-96)

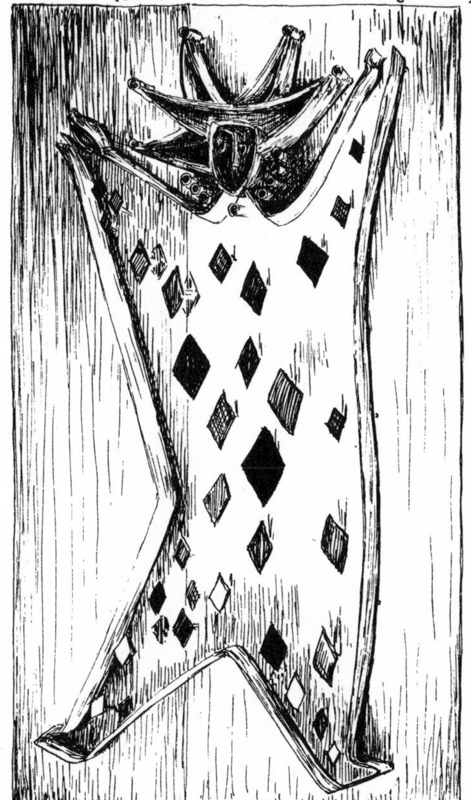

Harlequin Helen Tynell
A gay design in silvery metal and colored enamels.

## Primitive Influences

Interest in the native cultures of the Americas, Africa, the South Seas, etc., is rewarding. Sophisticated artists find there is much to learn from the straightforward primitive approach. Central and South American artists revive the art of fresco with force and national consciousness.

Orozco Portinari Rivera Tamayo

## Realists

The name speaks for itself, but no longer is the demand for an exact photographic likeness. The techniques are varied.

"The Eight" of the Ashcan School:

| | | Followers: | |
|---|---|---|---|
| Davies | Luks | | |
| Glackens | Prendergast | Bellows | Kroll |
| Henri | Shinn | DuBois | Speicher |
| Lawson | Sloan | Hopper | Soyer Bros. |

## Stylizists

Masters of sophisticated simplification.

Georgia O'Keeffe Grant Wood

## Romanticists

Artists who lend enchantment to reality:

| | | | |
|---|---|---|---|
| Benton | Burchfield | Pierce | Sutherland |
| Brackman | Eilshemius | Piper | Tchelitchew |

## SCULPTORS

While borrowing some of the styles mentioned above, the sculptor is still strongly influenced by classic subjects and simplifications of traditional techniques.

| France: | England: | Sweden: | United States: | |
|---|---|---|---|---|
| Bourdelle | Dobson | Milles | Faggi | Laurie |
| Maillol | Gill | | Friedlander | Manship |
| | Stevens | | Zorach | |

Original artists who work in more varied styles:

Archipenko Brancusi Epstein Gaudier-Brzeska Mestrovic
Modigliani Moore Lipchitz Zadkine

Led by the experimental painter, artists in all fields try one approach after another, looking always for new methods and new skills with which to express their moods and interests. There is no reason why every individual cannot enjoy the same flexible satisfaction in the appreciation of their works.

# ·20th CENTURY MUSICIANS·

MUSIC and CUBISM

Pierrot with Clarinet LIPCHITZ

Still Life BRAQUE

The Three Musicians PICASSO

## MUSICIANS

The instrumental music of the present century is eclectic in origin and style. Like the other arts, it has defied convention. Experimentations have been made with tones, scales, chords, harmonies, rhythms, meters, orchestrations and individual instruments.

The scientific inventions of phonograph, sound-film, amplifier, radio and television have taken all kinds of music into every household. The general public is better informed about music and more conscious of it than ever before, but it is not unnatural that the taste of the vast casual audience is not as discriminating as the trained ear of the dedicated music lover of former generations.

The first revolt parallels the Impressionistic movement in painting. It too starts in France, led by the nineteenth century:

Debussy
Roussel Ravel
Eric Satie and "Les Six"

Expressionism appears in German music, under:
Schoenberg

Nationalism and native folk songs form the basis of the works by:
Finland: Jean Sibelius England: Vaughan Williams
Hungary: Bartók and Kodály Jewish elements: Ernest Bloch
South America contributes for the first time. Her folk music has been blended with North American jazz.

Jazz is indigenous to the United States. From native cultures of both North and South America, ragtime and blues have developed into boogie-woogie and the sweet and hot rhythms which constitute popular selections.

Jazz makes its debut in concert hall and opera house sponsored by:

| Roy Harris | George Gershwin | Morton Gould |
|---|---|---|
| Shostakovitch | | Aaron Copland |

### Early Composers

W. C. Handy George M. Cohan Irving Berlin

### Bands

The recordings of big-name bands have made good renditions available to all, and have taken unskilled amateur musicians out of circulation.

Paul Whiteman Benny Goodman Guy Lombardo

# ·20th CENTURY MUSICIANS·

RHYTHM produced by ABSTRACTION

## Opera, Operetta and Musical Comedy

Modern opera with its characteristic dissonance is dynamic. But the facile media of operetta, motion picture and television for which much worthwhile music is being composed are causing opera to fall from popular favor.

United States: Deems Taylor; Gian-Carlo Menotti
Germany: Kurt Weill; Ernst Toch
England: Benjamin Britten

Lilting operetta was the transition between opera and musical comedy.

Victor Herbert     Sigmund Romberg

Revue and musical comedy, outgrowths of music hall and vaudeville, supply song and dance between the two wars. The postwar trend is toward more serious themes.

Irving Berlin     George Gershwin
Jerome Kern     Cole Porter
Rodgers and Hart     Rodgers and Hammerstein

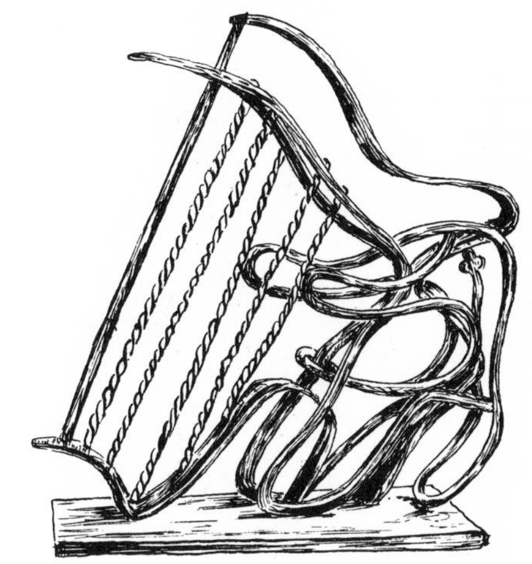

Harp Player (bronze)     LIPCHITZ

## The Dance

The Russian Ballet becomes a neo-classic medium of stylized interpretation.

Stravinsky — composer
Diaghilev — choreographer
Nijinsky, Pavlova — ballet dancer

Individualistic interpretive dancing is introduced by:
Isadora Duncan

Other rhythmic inspirations are devised by:
Ted Shawn     Ruth St. Denis     Martha Graham

Symbolic choreography in musical comedy:
Agnes De Mille

Lobster Trap and Fish Tail     CALDER
Motion supplies extra rythm to a mobile.

Since 1920 a neo-classic trend has been apparent in serious composition. Without compromising the gain of modern orchestration, it is introduced in Russia by:

Stravinsky     Prokofiev

Originality: Shostakovitch

Segment of Number Nine     POLLACK

# ·20th CENTURY AUTHORS·

19th CENTURY NOVELISTS
who strongly influence writers of today.

FYODOR DOSTOEVSKY (1821-1881)
diagrams the minds of his characters.

ÉMILE ZOLA (1841-1902)
Many of our contemporary authors follow the example of the master of STARK REALISM by revealing unpleasant truths.

CHARLES DICKENS (1812-1870)
uses a literary caricature to highlight conditions in need of reform.

## AUTHORS

"Fiction today draws to itself writers who would even yesterday have been poets, dramatists, pamphleteers, historians." Virginia Woolf.

The novel continues to be the important form of literary expression based upon overlapping themes inherited from:

| England | (19th century) | France |
|---|---|---|
| Social: Austen | | Stark realism: Zola |
| Historical: Scott | | Science fiction: Verne |
| Humanitarian: Dickens | | **Russia** |
| Detective: Conan Doyle | | Psychological: Dostoevsky |

### Novelists

Writers in many moods use different techniques to present a variety of subject matter.

H. G. Wells
Arnold Bennett
John Galsworthy
W. H. Hudson
D. H. Lawrence
Aldous Huxley
A. J. Cronin
Somerset Maugham
Joyce Cary
Nevil Shute
Graham Greene
Evelyn Waugh

Maxim Gorby, Romain Rolland, Thomas Mann
Mikhail Sholokhov, Eric Remarque
Franz Kafka, Franz Werfel, Stefan Zweig
Scholem Asch, André Gide

Sigrid Undset, Elizabeth Goudge
Ellen Glasgow, Edith Wharton, Willa Cather
Edna Ferber, Pearl Buck

Booth Tarkington, Theodore Dreiser, Upton Sinclair
F. Scott Fitzgerald, John Dos Passos
Sinclair Lewis, Thomas Wolfe, Louis Bromfield
John Steinbeck, John Hersey
Ernest Hemingway, Thornton Wilder, William Faulkner

### Stream-of-consciousness
or interior monologue

Sigmund Freud's psychoanalysis is largely responsible for what appears to be the most permanent of the experimental literary forms.

James Joyce, Virginia Woolf, Dorothy Richardson
Marcel Proust, Thomas Mann

# · 20th CENTURY AUTHORS ·

## Poetry

Poets follow the experimental trend and produce extremely individualistic styles as they break with tradition.

Amy Lowell
Alfred Noyes
John Masefield
Stephen Vincent Benét
Edna St. Vincent Millay
The Sitwells

Gertrude Stein

Carl Sandburg
Vachel Lindsay
Robert Frost
Edgar Lee Masters
Elinor Wylie
Dylan Thomas

## Humor

Ring Lardner
Damon Runyon
Robert Benchley
Ogden Nash
Dorothy Parker

## The Irish Renaissance

The Abbey Theatre makes Ireland's first contribution since the Book of Kells.

William B. Yeats
Lady Gregory
Sean O'Casey
J. M. Synge
George William Russell (''A. E.'') (poetry)

## Drama

Eugene O'Neill

Lillian Hellman
Maxwell Anderson
T. S. Eliot
Arthur Miller

Tennessee Williams

Noel Coward
Christopher Fry
Robert Sherwood
William Saroyan

## Philosophy

Three men in diversified fields who have influenced contemporary thought:

| Darwin | Marx | Freud |
|---|---|---|
| (1809–1882) | (1818–1883) | (1856–1939) |
| (naturalist) | (economist) | (physician) |

Henri Bergson
Havelock Ellis

Bertrand Russell
Benedetto Croce
George Santayana

A. N. Whitehead (science)
John Dewey (education)

Jules Romains (unanimism)
Jean Paul Sartre (existentialism)

Albert Schweitzer (humanitarianism)
Paul Tillich (liberal Christianity)

· 20th CENTURY INFLUENCES ·

MARCEL PROUST (1871-1922)
Writers in all countries are conscious of the honesty of his introspective documentation of his early life.

ERNEST HEMINGWAY (1898- )
Winner of the Pulitzer Prize in 1954, his dynamic personality is reflected in his work.

ALBERT SCHWEITZER (1875- )
His "Quest of the Historical Jesus" is doing much to liberate Protestant theological teachings.

# · CONCLUSIONS ·

*The only difference between a rut and a grave is their dimensions.*
*Ellen Glasgow (1874-1945)*

An honest approach to our present problems reveals that in this almost servantless era our greatest need is for a house which is simple to operate and maintain. The formal standard which was enjoyed by the aristocracy of Europe two hundred years ago is incongruous in the democratic world of today. Appropriate and practical but tasteful informality is possible through imaginative planning and careful selection.

Frank Lloyd Wright's organic architecture is built to conform with the site and eliminates costly landscaping and professional gardening. Electrical appliances lighten the burden of housekeeping. So do blond woods, nontarnishing metals and dirt-resistant fabrics. Simplified and appropriate architectural forms cut the cost of the house, the furniture of Charles Eames and other realistic designers reduces the cost of furnishing it. But even greater improvements will be possible if the consumer will encourage and support nonconformist ideas.

It is intelligent, however, not to discard or destroy well-designed, well-made, usable furnishings which can be adapted to the present way of life. Many antiques can be used in conjunction with contemporary furniture and modern settings, and it is possible for a traditional house to become the background for new furniture designs.

There are two requirements for the successful combination of products from different ages or from a variety of sources. One: that they come from similar cultural levels (formal and informal — court and country — styles seldom mix). Two: that they be of the same general scale and proportion (heavy and delicate — coarse and intricate — pieces do not combine well).

As every artistic expression is a reflection of the age which produced it, to appreciate an object fully or to make proper use of it, it is first advisable to be familiar with the society which produced it.

If, on the other hand, the problem is not to make use of the old but to design something new, let it be remembered that we do not progress in any field through imitation, because it stifles originality, paralyzes thought and breeds sterility. Progess is to be achieved not by copying someone else's ideas but by developing our own.

EXPERIMENTAL PUBLIC BUILDING
which may benefit
DOMESTIC ARCHITECTURE

CONCRETE ARCHES - Livestock Judging Pavilion, Raleigh, No. Carolina.
Roof is suspended on steel cables and the parabolic arches transmit the weight to the ground.

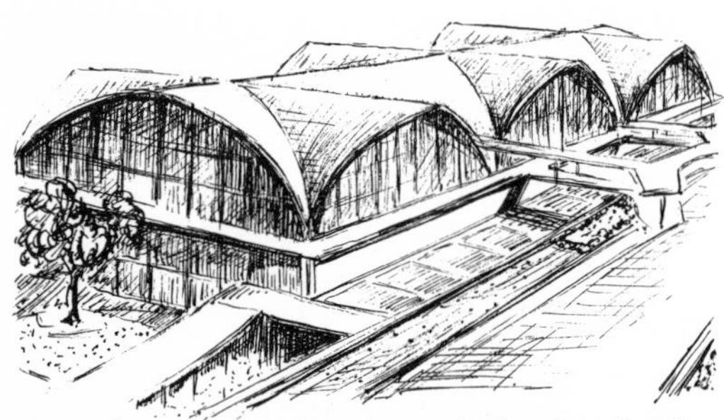

CONCRETE VAULTS - Airport Terminal Building, St. Louis, 1955
Large protected areas uncluttered by internal supports.

PLASTIC DOME - The Milan Trienniole, 1954 offers a suggestion for a summerhouse of cardboard impregnated with plastic.

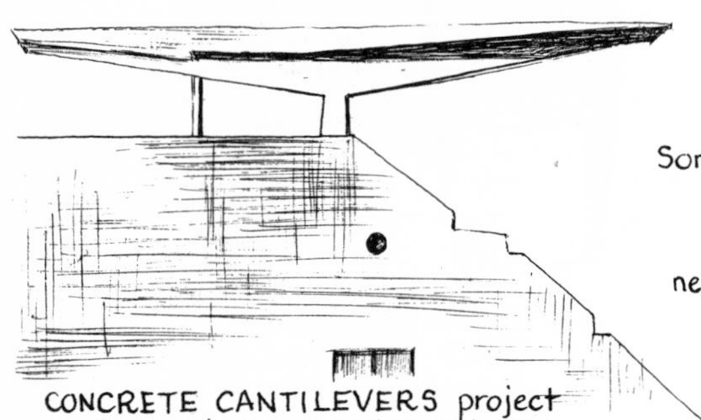

CONCRETE CANTILEVERS project 42 feet, shelter spectators in the Madrid Hippodrome, 1935

Some of the houses on page 175 have incorporated new forms of construction.

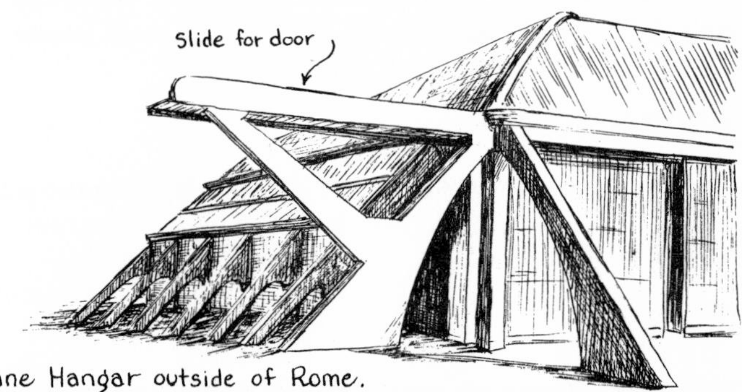
Slide for door

Airplane Hangar outside of Rome.

# · CONCLUSIONS ·

To summarize the main contributing sources of our colorful past, we first have the giants of the ancient world: Mesopotamia, Egypt, Greece and Rome. Then followed the Middle Ages and domination by the Christian Church. The modern European nations were of importance in the following order. For two centuries artistic Italy influenced all countries. For the next hundred and fifty years, the entire globe felt the brutal hand of Spain. Germany invented printing and started the religious rebellion. The Dutch excelled as traders and bankers and for decades Amsterdam was the financial center of the West. French culture enthralled the continent for a century and a half. For a hundred years the seafaring British controlled one-quarter of the land and one-quarter of the people of the earth. In the first half of the twentieth century, German nationalism and a theory of racial supremacy started the wars which devastated Europe and brought the days of her superiority to a close.

The past can continue to serve us if we view it with objective reason rather than with sentimental attachment.

It is a textbook which requires constant re-evaluation and timely revision. Outmoded subjects must be deleted; new ones added. It should be copied only in identical situations; but in many instances adaptation is to be encouraged. Neglected portions should be examined for events and objects which have been overlooked and wisdom which has been set aside.

The past can tell us that change is inevitable, yet it is always resented. A change is not only justified, it is mandatory, when the circumstances which fathered a condition, an object, a technique, no longer exist. Today there is not time to recognize, evaluate, assimilate and adjust to one cataclysmic innovation before it is amended or replaced by another.

But we have a possible means of stimulating, accelerating, and expanding the intellectual processes to enable man to keep up with the rapid changes necessitated by the velocity of scientific advance.

Audio-visual machinery is, today, the educational tool that sculpture was to the Middle Ages, and that printed texts were only a few years ago. The younger generation is forming its ideas from impressions picked up on the motion picture and television screens.

Through further development of this medium, people in all countries, of every mental capacity, from all walks of life, can be reached. It can be made the most eloquent and influential ambassador Western culture has yet known. It might even become its most powerful weapon.

"We can only pay our debt to the past
by putting the future in debt to ourselves."

John Buchan, Lord Tweedsmuir

PAST, PRESENT and FUTURE
are inter-dependent.

Albert Einstein (1879 - 1955)
his formula $E = mc^2$ starts the
ATOMIC AGE
Although Einstein himself now belongs to the past it will be many years before the world assimilates his theories.

A modern fabric
is designed from
a Mesopotamian vase.

The recent discovery of
the DEAD SEA SCROLLS
has already
shed new light on the
origins of Christianity.

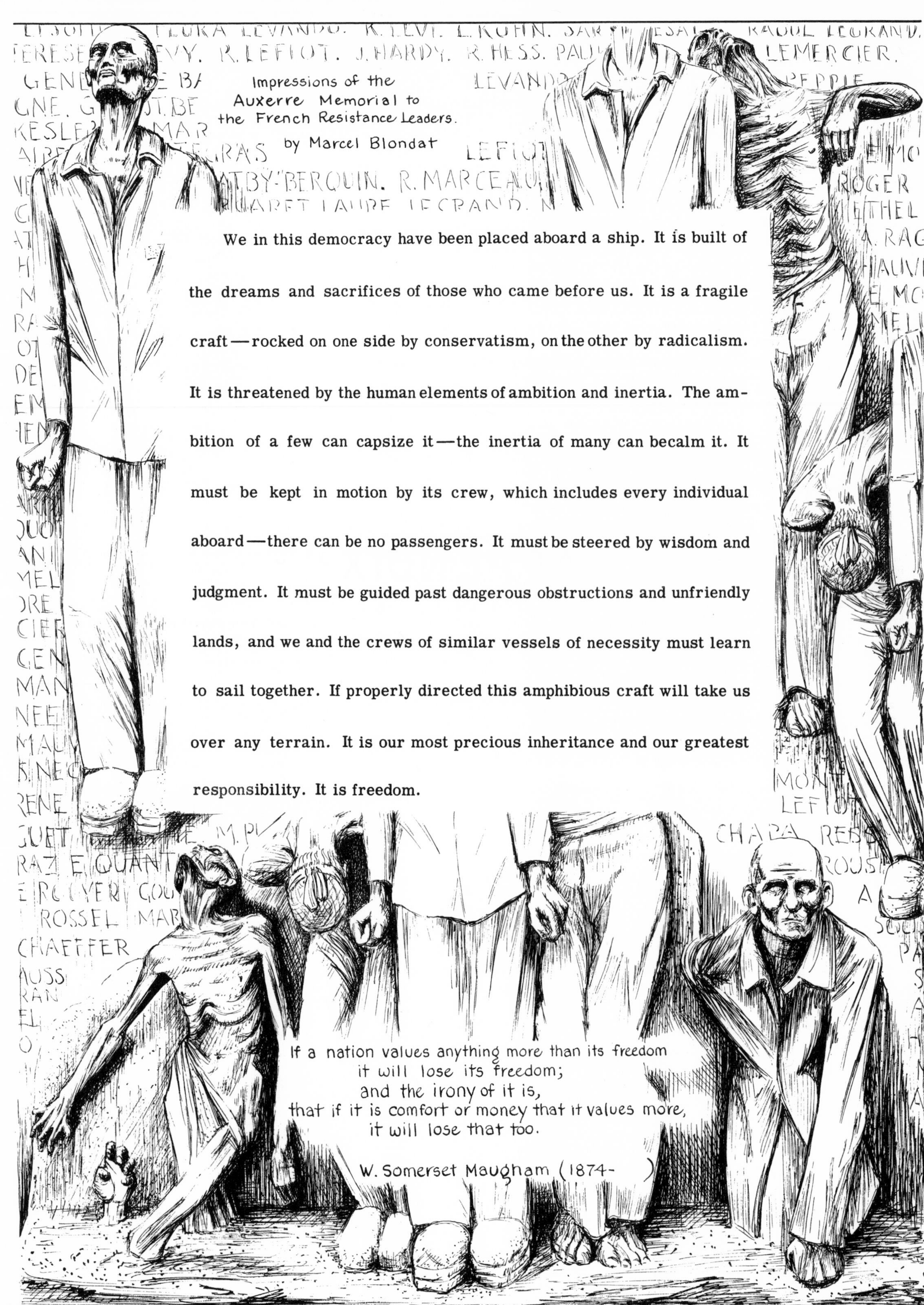
Impressions of the
Auxerre Memorial to
the French Resistance Leaders.
by Marcel Blondat
If a nation values anything more than its freedom
it will lose its freedom;
and the irony of it is,
that if it is comfort or money that it values more,
it will lose that too.
W. Somerset Maugham (1874- )

We in this democracy have been placed aboard a ship. It is built of the dreams and sacrifices of those who came before us. It is a fragile craft—rocked on one side by conservatism, on the other by radicalism. It is threatened by the human elements of ambition and inertia. The ambition of a few can capsize it—the inertia of many can becalm it. It must be kept in motion by its crew, which includes every individual aboard—there can be no passengers. It must be steered by wisdom and judgment. It must be guided past dangerous obstructions and unfriendly lands, and we and the crews of similar vessels of necessity must learn to sail together. If properly directed this amphibious craft will take us over any terrain. It is our most precious inheritance and our greatest responsibility. It is freedom.

# ·APPENDIX·

## THE ILLUSTRATIONS

In an effort to simplify the presentation of the illustrative material I have taken certain liberties. In order to cover the necessary points in the allotted space I have rendered composite features of the architecture and furniture, and have, in other instances, rearranged features or used only a representative portion of a composition. And, I have not counted the jewels in every crown, or the strings on every harp. I have, however, in each sketch given as distinct an impression of the object as the technique will allow.

A. T. B.

## REFERENCE BOOKS

The following reference material is submitted in the belief that an extensive bibliography is of value only to the advanced scholar and that a few carefully chosen sources better serve the interest of the beginning student and the layman for whom this book is intended.


Age of Fable. Bulfinch. (Modern Library)
Greek and Roman mythology on which ancient and much of Renaissance art is based. Also some medieval legends which were popularized during the nineteenth century medieval revival.

Art Today. Faulkner, Ziegfeld, Hill. (Holt)
Technicalities and examples from every phase of the visual arts are submitted in a crystal-clear presentation.

A Brief History of Sculpture. Auerbach. (Studio Publications)
One hundred pages of text and 67 plates give a quick survey of the historical periods and a detailed commentary on individual modern approaches.

The Encyclopedia of Furniture. Aronson. (Crown)
A well-illustrated, alphabetized reference book on furniture including terms, decorative motifs and basic styles.

Encyclopedia of Painting. (Crown)
A fine reference book on individual artists, schools of painting and painting terms from prehistoric times to the present day.

Gods, Graves and Scholars. Ceram. (Knopf)
Archeologists in search of relics of the undocumented ages of antiquity.

Good Reading. Edited by the Committee on College Reading. (Mentor)
An excellent guide. Arranged according to historic periods, it lists literature of the periods and about the periods.

A History of Architecture. Fletcher. (Scribners)
Considered a professional text, but the concise comparative method and the wealth of illustrations make it acceptable to anyone.

The History of the World. Sédillot. (Mentor)
A breezy but reliable account of world history in 240 pages.

Signs and Symbols in Christian Art. Ferguson. (Oxford)
A beautifully arranged and illustrated work which also gives legends from the lives of the saints. Not as sensitive but more clearly presented than the nineteenth-century books of Anna Jameson (Sacred and Legendary Art and Legends of the Madonna).